AUSTRALIAN DISCOVERY

VOLUME TWO—BY LAND

LACHLAN MACQUARIE,
Governor of New South Wales, 1810–21.
From Lieutenant-Colonel Gardyne's copy of the original portrait by
John Opie in the Mitchell Library, Sydney.

AUSTRALIAN DISCOVERY
By Land

EDITED BY

ERNEST SCOTT

PROFESSOR OF HISTORY IN THE
UNIVERSITY OF MELBOURNE

ILLUSTRATED WITH SIXTEEN
CONTEMPORARY PORTRAITS & MAPS

LONDON AND TORONTO
J. M. DENT AND SONS, LTD
NEW YORK: E. P. DUTTON & CO. INC.

Reprinted with the permission of the original publishers

JOHNSON REPRINT CORPORATION   JOHNSON REPRINT COMPANY LIMITED
111 Fifth Avenue, New York, N.Y. 10003   Berkeley Square House, London, W.1

FIRST PUBLISHED . . 1929

Landmarks in Anthropology, a series of reprints in cultural anthropology

General Editor: Weston La Barre

First reprinting, 1966, Johnson Reprint Corporation

PRINTED IN THE UNITED STATES OF AMERICA

INTRODUCTION

"NEW HOLLAND is a very large tract of land. It is not yet determined whether it is an island or a continent, but I am certain that it joins neither to Asia, Africa nor America." William Dampier arrived at that conclusion in 1688, and a century later no more confident opinion could have been expressed. The myth about the existence of a Great Southern Continent stretching from the tropics to the Antarctic Pole had been demolished by Cook, after whose time it was no longer possible for a reasonable man to believe that there was any other very large habitable land-mass in the South Seas than that whose western shores were known to the Dutch as New Holland and whose eastern coasts had been named New South Wales by Cook himself. But it was not yet certain whether New Holland and New South Wales were parts of one undivided territory, or whether there was a strait between them, or whether there were two or three large contiguous islands. Thus Pinkerton, in his *Modern Geography* (1807), stated under the heading "New Holland": "Some suppose that this extensive region, when more thoroughly investigated, will be found to consist of two or three vast islands intersected by narrow seas, an idea which probably arises from the discovery that New Zealand consists of two islands, and that other straits have been found to divide lands in this quarter formerly supposed to be continuous."

Several contemporary writings show that the belief was general that a strait would be found dividing New Holland. James Grant, in his *Narrative of a Voyage of Discovery* (1803), expressed his regret that his orders did not permit him to take his ship, the *Lady Nelson*, northward from Port Jackson in 1801—"we might betimes have ascertained if the Gulf of Carpentaria had any inlet to Bass Straits; and this I trust will not be thought chimerical when it was not known whether other Straits did not exist as well as that dividing New Holland from Van Diemen's Land." The Institute of France, also, in preparing instructions for the voyage of exploration commanded by Nicholas Baudin (1800), directed a search to be made for a strait which it was supposed divided New Holland "into two great and nearly equal islands."

This problem, however, was solved by Flinders during his explorations in the *Investigator*. When he examined Spencer Gulf in March 1802, he found as he worked northward that the shores converged and the water became continually shallower. When he entered the gulf he thought it might be the conjectured strait, which should lead through to the Gulf of Carpentaria. As it tapered to an end, he concluded that "our prospects of a channel or strait cutting off some considerable portion of Terra Australis grew less." After Flinders' voyage the hypothesis of a bifurcated Australia was destroyed.

The situation chosen by Captain Arthur Phillip for the first colony planted by the British in Australia was extraordinarily suitable for the purpose for which it was intended; but the very geographical features which made Sydney a natural gaol at the same time made the country inland from that locality extremely difficult to explore. For about thirty miles from the coast stretched a plain. Then rose, steep and rough to a height of about 1000 feet, a great scarp, "the truncated edge of a sandstone plateau." Officially the first Governor named the northern section of this plateau the Carmarthen Hills, and the southern section the Lansdowne Hills; but the inhabitants found a more expressive name for the whole range. These blue mountains looked as though they ought to have a name signifying their colour as seen from the coast through the bright atmosphere of a Sydney morning; and so the first history of New South Wales, that by David Collins, spoke of them as "commonly known in the colony by the name of Blue Mountains, from the appearance which land so high generally wears."

The first attempts to ascertain the nature of the interior of Australia were necessarily made from Sydney, because there was no other settlement till strategic motives, rather than the necessity of occupying additional territory, occasioned an extension. Governor Phillip himself was the first Australian inland explorer, and his first attempt, through heavily timbered country, did not take him even as far as the foot of the scarp after five days of toilsome travelling. Collins relates that in April 1788:

> "His Excellency, desirous of acquiring a knowledge of the country about the seat of government, and profiting by the coolness of the weather, made during the month several

excursions; in one of which, having observed a range of mountains to the westward, and hoping that a river might be found to take its course in their neighbourhood, he set off with a small party, intending if possible to reach them, taking with him six days' provisions; but he returned without attaining either object of his journey—the mountains or a river. He penetrated about thirty miles inland, through a country most amply clothed with timber, but in general free from underwood. On the fifth day of his excursion he caught, from a rising ground which he named Belle Vue, the only glance of the mountains which he obtained during his journey; and as they then appeared at too great a distance to be reached on one day's allowance of provisions, which was all they had left, he determined to return to Sydney Cove."

Phillip took the lead in later expeditions, in one of which (1789) he discovered the Hawkesbury River; other energetic men strove to reveal the character of the territory, and their efforts led to the finding of the Nepean River (which is the upper Hawkesbury), the Grose, and some outlying ridges of the mountain mass. But all early attempts to get beyond the wall were defeated by the peculiarly broken, precipitous and irregular character of a region where, instead of broad river-valleys winding through the hills, as in ordinary mountain lands, deep gorges seemed to cut across every ridge, and every stream tumbled over a succession of waterfalls. According to a physiographer's technical description, "in place of steep ranges with broad valleys between, there are here rather broad undulating plateaux dissected by narrow deep gorges and bounded by fault-scarps or huge monoclinal folds." The early records contain many illustrations of the difficulties. William Paterson, exploring the River Grose, had to clamber up the rugged flanks of five waterfalls in ten miles. George Bass spent fifteen days trying to find a pass through the mountains. He and his companions equipped themselves with scaling-irons for the feet and hooks for the hands; they had strong ropes by means of which members of the party could be lowered down ravines; they were strong and determined men; but they were completely baffled. A settled conviction grew that, as Collins stated it, "an impassable barrier seemed fixed to the westward." Courageous efforts were made by Ensign Barrallier of the New South Wales Corps and by the botanist George Caley, but both failed, though they were capable and hardy explorers. Governor King in 1806 voiced the conclusion that the mountains were impassable, and that further efforts to master them would be "as chimerical as useless." The Governor reported:

> "As far as respects the extension of agriculture beyond the first range of mountains, that is an idea that must be given up, as the rocks to the west of that range wear the most barren and forbidding aspect which men, animals, birds and vegetation have ever been strangers to; a better proof of which may not be adduced than the remark of one of Cayley's party in returning, who exclaimed, on seeing two solitary crows, that 'they had lost their way.' "

Success was not attained, indeed, till 1813; and then its achievement was not the result of a search for the sake of solving the problem as one of geographical importance, but for the practical reason that it was desired to ascertain whether there was good grazing ground for cattle amongst or beyond the mountains. Gregory Blaxland, the leader of the expedition, was the younger brother of John Blaxland, and the two had come to Australia in 1806 as settlers who had obtained land grants from the Secretary of State on condition that they invested a stipulated amount of capital in the colony. It was expected that, being experienced in agriculture, they would by their example contribute to the improvement of agricultural methods in New South Wales. But they found it profitable to engage in cattle-breeding rather than in the production of wheat and other crops, and they were continually on the look-out for fresh pastures for their herds. Three governors, King, Bligh and Macquarie, found them troublesome people. But it was the Blaxland keenness for the acquisition of land that led at last to the solution of the Blue Mountains problem.

In 1812 a severe drought afflicted the little colony. It was desirable in the public interest to find other lands for cultivation and stock-raising than the cramped area between the sea and the hills; and the Blaxlands particularly were interested in ascertaining the possibilities which might exist beyond the blue ridges. It happened that in 1810 Gregory Blaxland accompanied Governor Macquarie on a boat journey up the Hawkesbury River as far as it was navigable. According to the story afterwards written by Blaxland, the idea came to his mind on this expedition that the way to cross the mountains was not to follow a valley, but to climb to the top of a ridge and track it westward. He was confirmed in this theory on a later expedition, when he took with him three European servants and two natives. He found himself blocked by the sheer walls of rock, as previous explorers had been; but, he said:

"This journey confirmed me in the opinion, that it was practicable to find a passage over the mountains, and I resolved at some future period to attempt it by endeavouring to cross the river, and reach the high land on its northern bank, by the ridge which appeared to run westward, between the Warragomby and the River Grose. I concluded, that if no more difficulties were found in travelling than had been experienced on the other side, we must be able to advance westward towards the interior of the country, and have a fair chance of passing the mountains. On inquiry, I found a person who had been accustomed to hunt the kangaroo on the mountains, in the direction I wished to go, who undertook to take the horses to the top of the first ridge. Soon after I mentioned the circumstance to His Excellency the Governor, who thought it reasonable, and expressed a wish that I should make the attempt. Having made every requisite preparation, I applied to the two gentlemen who accompanied me to join in the expedition, and was fortunate in obtaining their consent. Before we set out, we laid down the plan to be pursued, and the course to be attempted, namely, to ascend the ridge beforementioned, taking the streams of water on the left, which appeared to empty themselves into the Warragomby, as our guide; being careful not to cross any of them, but to go round their sources, so as to be certain of keeping between them and the streams that emptied themselves into the River Grose."

The gentlemen referred to were Lieutenant William Lawson, formerly of the New South Wales Corps, and the youth William Charles Wentworth, who was hereafter to be one of the outstanding figures in Australian public life. Blaxland's *Journal*, reprinted in this volume, tells its own tale of the traverse of the Blue Mountains without any need of amplification. But it is desirable to add that fourteen years after the event a claim was put forward, not by Lawson himself, but on his behalf, and apparently with his knowledge—since he was living in New

South Wales at the time, and did not disavow the use of his name in this manner—that he was the originator of the theory that the Blue Mountains would be found crossable by climbing to the top of the table-land and pursuing the high ridges. It was asserted that Lawson "secured an agreeable companion in Mr. William Wentworth and a persevering assistant in Mr. Gregory Blaxland." (This claim appeared in *The Australian*, March 13, 1827.) But there is no evidence that Lawson propounded such a theory, or that he claimed to have done so immediately after the expedition proved successful; nor did he make any statement over his own name in support of the assertions. Nor did Wentworth ever contest the authorship of the expedition. Blaxland's statement of its genesis is deserving of full credit. As a student in England a few years later Wentworth competed for the Chancellor's medal at Cambridge, the prescribed subject being a poem on "Australasia." There was not much poetic merit in the piece as a whole; but there certainly was truth in the concluding passage wherein Wentworth described the toilsome journey in which he had shared, and its successful issue:

" And as a meteor shoots athwart the night
The boundless champaign burst upon our sight,
Till, nearer seen, the beauteous landscape grew
Op'ning like Canaan on rapt Israel's view."

Blaxland's discovery was the first important step forward in the revelation of inland Australia. No attempt had been made up to this time to penetrate the continent from any other point on the coast. One great chance had been missed. In 1803 Colonel David Collins was sent to occupy Port Phillip, which was discovered in February 1802 by Lieutenant John Murray in the *Lady Nelson*. Grimes, the surveyor who accompanied Murray, made a careful chart of the harbour, as also did Flinders, who entered in the *Investigator* in the following April. Flinders gave an encouraging account of the country surrounding Port Phillip, which, he wrote, "has a pleasing and in many parts a fertile appearance, and the sides of some of the hills and several of the valleys are fit for agricultural purposes; it is in great measure a grassy country, and capable of supporting much cattle, though better calculated for sheep." This was an intelligent observation, which should have incited Collins to explore the country inland when he had established his company in a suitable place. But Collins never had his heart in the task committed to him. "The disadvantages of Port Phillip" were all that he saw. "Every day's experience convinces me that it cannot nor ever will be resorted to by speculative men. . . . When all the disadvantages attending this bay are publicly known, it cannot be supposed that commercial people will be very desirous of visiting Port Phillip." Acting on Collins's extremely fallacious report, Governor King ordered the abandonment of the first Port Phillip settlement, on the ground that it appeared " totally unfit from every point of view to remain at, without subjecting the Crown to the certain expensive prospect of the soil not being equal to raise anything for the support of the settlement." Collins's surveyor did, it is true, enter the lower reaches of the River Yarra, but made no attempt to explore beyond a few yards from the shore, and, taking his cue from the commander, reported that the soil was "neither in quality nor quantity sufficient for cultivation to repay the cares of the husbandman." But it is evident that had the country inland from Port Phillip been explored in 1803, the difficulties which were incidental to exploration over the Blue Mountains from Sydney would not have been encountered, and the key to the great river system of Australia would have been found probably more than twenty years before it was revealed by Sturt.

But through the failure of Collins, the further exploration of Central Australia was fated to be pursued from the eastern side of the continent until settlement was commenced again on the south and on the west. Governor Macquarie was thoroughly sensible of the importance of Blaxland's work, but determined to have his report officially confirmed before signifying that the Government would reward the explorers. He therefore sent Surveyor G. W. Evans in charge of a party to traverse Blaxland's route and examine the country beyond the point reached by him. Evans started in November 1813, reached the terminus of Blaxland's journey, and travelled for three weeks beyond that point. His important discovery was the River Macquarie; and from the summits of the hills he saw stretching towards the horizon "a vast extent of flat country" which "far surpassed in beauty and fertility of soil" any that he had seen elsewhere in New South Wales or Van Diemen's Land. But the Governor miscalculated distances when he judged that the Macquarie was "supposed to empty itself into the ocean on the western side of New South Wales at a distance of from two to three hundred miles from the termination of the tour." Evans's journey, however, enabled a town to be established at Bathurst, the first inland centre in Australia; and the Governor caused a road to be constructed from Sydney to this point. In a further expedition (1815) Evans discovered the Lachlan River, revealing a still further great stretch of valuable territory.

During the next seven years a group of enterprising men, expert in bushcraft and excellent judges of country, filled up gaps on the map between Evans's two rivers and the Murrumbidgee, which was found by Throsby in 1821. Officially the exploratory work was in charge of the surveyor-general of New South Wales, John Oxley, who was appointed to that office in 1811. The first task committed to him was to trace the courses of the two rivers, the Macquarie and the Lachlan, and "ascertain their final termination." But he found that both streams, though broad, deep and swift during part of their course, simply oozed away into impenetrable marshes, which seemed like inland seas. His journeys of 1817–18, when he was accompanied by the eminent botanist Allan Cunningham, were heroic efforts, but resulted in disappointment and delusion. In the watershed of the Macquarie Oxley found "a country of running waters, on every hill a spring and in every valley a rivulet." But the river itself disappeared. On his return journey to Sydney in 1818, Oxley crossed twelve rivers, and guessed that they all drained into a great central lake. He did not suspect the existence of the vast river-system of the Murray and the Darling.

The discoveries made between 1813 and 1820 were not only geographically important; they heralded a new era in the history of Australia. A new province, of incalculable extent as yet, but certainly vast and potentially rich, was opened. A new political situation was created. As long as the settlement at Sydney was confined to the stretch of territory between the mountain-wall and the sea, with its comparatively small agricultural outposts on the Hawkesbury, at Parramatta, and wherever else patches of agricultural or grazing ground could be found, there was no serious obstacle to the continuance of the colony for the purposes for which it was founded. Those purposes might be condemned for moral reasons, or the current theories of criminology might change and new methods be preferred. But the area was suitable for its grim uses, it was sufficient, and there was not much temptation for anyone to suggest that it might be employed for nobler ends. The revelation of the immense interior, however, made all the difference. The Napoleonic wars ended in 1815, and the disruption of commerce occasioned by those wars plunged Great Britain into poverty. People were eager for opportunities to emigrate. The time was ripe for the opening of fresh avenues of trade. These discoveries came opportunely. It was as if a new world had swum into the orbit of the old, and its vacancy called for alleviation.

During the terms of the next four Governors—Brisbane, Darling, Bourke and Gipps—problems of exploration were concurrent with land problems. How were these great areas to be permitted to be occupied? The growth of the Australian wool trade, following the brilliant experiments of John Macarthur in the breeding of merino sheep, made the new lands immediately profitable. There were fortunes in wool. Jason's golden fleece, "the sea-born wonder of all lands," was an irrecoverable treasure of antiquity; and if Jason had been living in the first quarter of the nineteenth century it would have been worth his while to think better of his project—

> " To reach the oak-grove and the Golden Fleece,
> Or, failing, die at least far off from Greece," . . .

and try his luck with merinos in the back country of New South Wales. In vain did the Government endeavour to restrain the owners of flocks from "trespassing" on Crown land beyond the limits prescribed for occupation. The Governors made "squatting" regulations, and they were ignored. The Secretary of State, who, with his officials, never really grasped the magnitude of the problem, made Downing Street regulations, and they also were ignored. Governor Gipps stated the case with picturesque imagery and serious truth when he wrote, "As well attempt to confine an Arab within a circle traced on sand as to confine the graziers or wool-growers of New South Wales within bounds that can possibly be assigned to them." In despair, seeing all their orders disregarded and their regulations laughed to scorn, the Government grasped at the plausibly ingenious theories of Edward Gibbon Wakefield, who wrote his "Letter from Sydney" as the result of an enforced period of reflection in Newgate prison, and who "hocussed" his generation into accepting him as an expert in colonisation, of which, in fact, he was totally destitute of personal experience.

This confusion was the result of the geographical discoveries which have been described, with their natural corollary of throwing open for use immense areas of valuable land. Greater discoveries followed within a few years. Those made by Allan Cunningham directed the attention of the eager sheep-men northwards, to the country which was hereafter to become Queensland. Cunningham was a botanist, trained at Kew

Gardens, who was sent out to New South Wales in 1815 to collect plants for that institution. He was glad to take advantage of the opportunity offered to him, to accompany John Oxley on his journey beyond the Blue Mountains in 1817. During the next four years he applied himself to botanical collecting along the coast, under P. P. King, and his *Journal* (preserved in the South Kensington Natural History Museum) contains abundant evidence of the diligence and delight with which he pursued his investigations. New species of plants, fresh varieties, the beauty of leaf and flower and the majesty of the great trees gave him the joy of the discoverer.

In 1823 Cunningham led an expedition of his own, the chief result of which was the discovery of Pandora's Pass through the eastern end of the Liverpool Range to the northern plains. Still more important was his expedition of 1827 across these plains, over the present Queensland border, into the great stretch of fertile territory which he named the Darling Downs. He recognised at once that he had found "very considerable grazing country," and the squatters, following his tracks in the ensuing years, proved him right. Cunningham's rich services in the cause of exploration and science were never rewarded by the grant of a yard of land, and this at a period when lavish land-grants were being made to persons who benefited from his efforts. Indeed, the authorities were grotesquely unaware of his rare and shining merits. When, after spending four years in England arranging his specimens at Kew, Cunningham returned to New South Wales as Colonial Botanist, he found, to his disgust, that he, one of the most eminent men of science of his age, was expected to grow vegetables for the higher ranks of the Civil service in a patch of ground in the Botanical Gardens. Unwilling to devote himself to what he called "the Government Cabbage Garden," he went on a botanical excursion to New Zealand. "I am now about to enter with all my might on a more legitimate occupation," he wrote. But he was already in failing health; and on his return to Sydney he had to acknowledge that "I have failed in my best endeavours to patch myself up." He died in 1839.

Of all the inland explorers of Australia, Allan Cunningham was the best equipped by knowledge to discern the economic value of the fresh lands brought within the purview of those who were competent to make use of the opportunities thrown open by discovery. He was a man of science of high distinction, a traveller of unconquerable courage and resource. In botanical collections throughout the world the name "Cunningham," after the scientific names of plants, appears on hundreds of the little painted labels which distinguish species and varieties. Sir J. D. Hooker truly said of him that "Cunningham's botanical researches are by far the most continuous and extensive that have ever been performed in Australia, or perhaps in any other country."

The researches so far described related to the region north of the River Murray. The nature of the country south of that stream was as yet unknown. Governor Brisbane, who desired to ascertain its possibilities, proposed to land a party of convicts at or near Wilson's Promontory, provide them with food and equipment, and let them find their way back to Sydney if they could. If they succeeded, they were to have their freedom; if they perished by the way, as they were likely to do, that would be their misfortune. But a better plan was propounded by Hamilton Hume, who had already done some useful exploratory work, and was at this time (1824) in occupation of a property at Lake George. It was that an expedition should start from his home, and make its way south to Westernport. The Governor approved, and suggested that Hume should be associated with William Hilton Hovell, a retired sea-captain, who had had an adventurous life in many parts of the globe. Hume and Hovell set out in October 1824, crossed the Murrumbidgee, and were the first explorers to find the great river which they named the Hume, but which was at a later date renamed the Murray. They came to this river on November 16, crossed it, and soon found themselves in the rugged mountain country of northern Victoria. They crossed three fine rivers on their journey farther south, the Mitta-Mitta, the Ovens and the Goulburn; became entangled in the Plenty Ranges; scrambled to the top of Mount Disappointment in the hope of being able to get a glimpse of the sea, but found their view blocked by the big timber; and at length came out upon fairly level, meadow-like country, through which they toiled wearily to the shores of Corio Bay, a branch of Port Phillip. Both the leaders believed themselves to be at Westernport, and did not discover that they had made a mistake till some years later. In fact, they were one degree out in their calculations. The error of reckoning was Hovell's, but Hume was at the time just as much in the belief that the expedition had reached Westernport as was his colleague.

The mistake had two consequences of importance. First, it induced the Government to send an expedition to occupy Westernport in 1826, in the belief that the surrounding country was as promising as Hume and Hovell had described it to be.

This was withdrawn in 1828, in consequence of the unfavourable reports of the commanding officer, who was convinced that Westernport did not " possess sufficient capabilities for colonisation on a large scale." The second consequence was that the description given by Hume and Hovell of the territory which they had traversed directed attention to its pasturage resources, which was the main incentive to the unauthorised occupation of the Port Phillip country by John Batman and other squatters after 1835.

Hume and Hovell were the first explorers to traverse the present state of Victoria; it was traversed again, farther west, by Major Thomas Mitchell in 1836. Crossing the Murray at the point of its junction with its tributary the Murrumbidgee, Mitchell marched over rich grassy plains which were later to provide pasture for great flocks of sheep. "I felt conscious," he wrote, "of being the harbinger of mighty changes, for our steps would soon be followed by the men and the animals for which it seemed to have been prepared." To his great surprise, when he came upon the sea-coast at Portland, he found men and animals already there; for the Henty brothers had established a whaling station at this favourable spot in 1835. "Australia Felix," the name which Mitchell gave to this land, did not endure; but it was not inapt.

Mitchell's journey connects naturally with that of Hume and Hovell on account of the region which it unveiled, but in chronological sequence it followed a series of explorations which provided a solution to the great river problem of Australia. A considerable number of rivers had been found since Evans came upon the Macquarie and the Lachlan—the Murrumbidgee, Bogan, Castlereagh, Namoi, Gwydir, Barwon, Abercrombie, Dumaresq and Logan amongst them. Had these rivers, or some of them, independent courses to the sea, or did they flow into some great inland lake? The solution of those questions was to be the achievement of one whose name will ever shine brightly in the history of Australian exploration—the intrepid, chivalrous, gentle, patient Charles Sturt. He came to Australia in 1827 as a captain in the 39th regiment with a dislike of the military duty assigned to him—"highly prejudiced against it" was his own phrase. In Sydney he became acquainted with Oxley, Cunningham and Hume, and conversed with them about the expedition in which they had taken part. Oxley was a sick man no longer capable of leadership. Sturt was fascinated by the prospect of taking up the work which these men had been doing. Routine garrison duty gave no scope for his eager intelligence; discovery was entirely to his taste; and he was delighted when the Governor decided to give him an opportunity to take an expedition into the interior "to determine the supposed existence of an inland sea."

The chief result of Sturt's expedition of 1828–9 was the discovery of the Darling, which he named. The season was unfortunately unfavourable for seeing this great river in full flood, and Sturt could not realise that it is the stem-stream into which flow the immense spread of rivers which drain the plains of central Queensland. Drought had, in the year of this enterprise, laid its parching hand upon New South Wales. The interior was baked and blistered with heat. The rivers were dry. All the more surprising was it, therefore, when, after traversing country so desolate and so arid that Sturt's men on finding a little mud in a river-bed were glad to squeeze it through pieces of cloth to get a drop of water to moisten their mouths, they came, on January 18, 1829, to the banks of a river from seventy to eighty yards broad, and gleaming silvery more than forty feet below its banks.

The travellers climbed down the steep banks to the water, but to their intense disappointment found it salt. "The cup of joy was dashed from our hands before we could raise it to our lips," wrote the leader. Sturt, accompanied by Hamilton Hume, followed the river down-stream for forty miles from the camp and found that it continually increased in breadth; but as the water was still salt he could not risk further exploration. He was compelled to retreat from the Darling to his depot on the Macquarie, which river also was reduced to a chain of water-holes by the terrific drought. An examination of the bed of the Castlereagh, also dry, convinced Sturt that it was a tributary of the Darling, and he was assured that the Macquarie flowed into that river in seasons when there was water enough to enable it to do so. There was no doubt, from the great depth of the Darling's banks, that "furious torrents must sometimes rage in it;" but Sturt was unable to form an opinion as to what became of it when, in a season of plentiful rainfall, it received immense contributions of water from the rivers which poured into it. "Its course is involved in mystery," he wrote. "Does it make its way to the south coast, or exhaust itself in feeding a succession of swamps in the centre of the island?"

That problem was to be solved by Sturt's expedition of 1829, when he discovered the Murray. His immediate object on this

b

journey was to trace the course of the Darling; but in case there should again be perplexity through finding the water salt, it was determined to follow the course of the Murrumbidgee, whose waters were known to be sweet, in the belief that this river was connected with the Darling watershed. The theory proved to be correct. Sturt also judged it possible that it would be desirable to travel some distance by water—an extremely fortunate conjecture; he therefore took with him the frame and timbers of a strong whaleboat. His party travelled to the Murrumbidgee through rich and delightful country, and found the river itself foaming and eddying in a strong current. He was convinced that it would be found to form a junction with another river, and that this river would be navigable.

Arriving at this conclusion, Sturt resolved upon a bold course. He hazarded the entire success of his expedition upon it, and probably also the lives of himself and his men; but it was not a reckless expedient. It is easy enough to-day, with the map open before us, to see that Sturt did the perfectly right thing when he resolved to fit together the parts of his boat, take to the water with a selected band of men, and send back his bullock drays and stores. But Sturt had no map of the country. He only knew of the existence of sundry streams, of the source and ultimate course of not one of which was anything at this time ascertained. It was a remarkable feat of imagination on Sturt's part to conclude that these streams reached one great channel by which they flowed to the sea. But that was the idea which now possessed his mind, and he was certain that he had reached the point on the Murrumbidgee where he must put it to the test. "The Murrumbidgee kept up its character," he wrote in a letter, "and is a magnificent stream. I do not know its fate, but I am obliged to abandon my cattle and have taken to the boats. Where I shall wander to God only knows. I have little doubt, however, that I shall ultimately make the coast. Where do the Hume and the Goulburn and the other streams flow to?" What was in his mind is apparent from that question; and the idea in its absolute rightness came to him in a brilliant flash of inspiration.

Sturt's men proceeded to construct the whaleboat, and also built a smaller boat to carry part of the provisions. He chose six men to accompany him, and on the morning of January 7, 1830, the voyage down-stream commenced. On the following day the smaller boat struck a sunken tree and was wrecked, but most of the useful stores were recovered. On January 14th the

Murrumbidgee was found suddenly to take a southerly direction, and the boat shot forward with great velocity. A little later it was "hurried into a great and noble river." Sturt had entered the Murray, as he afterwards named it; though it was the same river as Hume and Hovell had crossed in 1824, which they named the Hume. Eight days later another large river was found, coming from the north. He was convinced that this was the Darling, which he had discovered 300 miles away. "An irresistible conviction impressed me that we were now sailing on that very stream," he wrote. This remarkable expedition finished its work when it reached "the termination of the Murray," where seagulls overhead heralded the first craft that had ever floated on the waters of the great river of Australia.

The discovery of the Murray, like the preceding revelations of the character of inland Australia, had important political consequences. The Wakefieldians in England wished for an opportunity of demonstrating the efficacy of their theory. Previously, the published accounts of that part of the Australian coast which was shortly to pertain to the new province of South Australia had given no reason to hope that fertile lands lay behind the rocky and sandy edge. But Sturt's story suggested great possibilities. "My eye never fell upon a country of more promising aspect or of more favourable position," was his verdict. In 1831 the first project was launched for founding a new colony in the region which Sturt had brought under public notice. Wakefield and his enthusiastic supporters took up the idea; and South Australia came into being in 1836.

The foundation of South Australia led to a series of important expeditions being projected from Adelaide, its capital, westward across the arid country above the Great Australian Bight, and northward into the region of the great lakes, into the centre of the continent, and ultimately through to the extreme north opening upon the tropical Timor Sea. Edward John Eyre—who was later to become famous as Governor of Jamaica—in 1841, accompanied by only one white man, Baxter, and three aboriginals, faced immense difficulties in a waterless waste on an expedition of more than three months between South and Western Australia. Baxter was murdered by two of the blacks, but Eyre struggled on through the hot sand with the third, who remained faithful, till he was rescued by a French whaler in Thistle Cove near Esperance. He had hoped to trace out a track for a road between the southern colony and that by this time established on the Swan River in the west; but that road was never made, though the transcontinental railway, constructed in the twentieth century, runs, through a large part of its course, not very far from Eyre's route.

Charles Sturt, who had resigned his commission in the army and accepted the post of Assistant Commissioner of Crown Lands in South Australia, deduced from the flight of birds an ingenious theory as to the existence of good pasture land in the middle of the continent. His argument was this:

> "Birds observed east of the Darling in the summer of 1828 in about lat. 29° 30′ S. and long. 144 had invariably migrated to the west-north-west. Cockatoos and parrots, known while in the colony to frequent the richest and best-watered valleys of the higher lands, would pass in countless flights to that point of the compass. In South Australia, in lat. 35° and long. 138°, I had also observed that several birds of the same kind annually visited that province from the north. I had seen the *Psittacus Novæ Hollandiæ* and the shell paroquet following the shore-line of St. Vincent's Gulf like flights of starlings in England. The different flights, at intervals of more than a quarter of an hour, all came from the north and followed in one and the same direction. Now, although the casual appearance of a few strange birds should not influence the judgment, yet from the regular migration of the feathered race a reasonable inference may be drawn. Seeing that these two lines if prolonged would meet a little to the northward of the tropic, I formed the following conclusions. First, that the birds migrating on those lines would rest for a time at the point where those lines meet. Secondly, that the country to which they went would resemble that which they had left—that birds which frequented rich valleys or high hills would not settle down in deserts and flat country. Thirdly, that the intervening country, whether owing to deserts or to large sheets of water, was not such as these birds could inhabit. Indeed, such large migrations from different parts to one particular point argued no less strongly the existence of deserts or of sea to a certain distance, than the probable richness of the country to which as to a common goal these migrations tended."

Sturt endeavoured to test this theory on his expedition into the interior in 1844. At the head of a competent party, he followed the course of the Darling to Menindie, 180 miles north of the junction of that river with the Murray, and then struck north-west for the Barrier Range, which was not at that time suspected to contain vast wealth in silver ore. From these hills the party moved north into desert country. The sufferings of men and animals were intense. In January 1845 they were toiling across plains in the blistering summer heat. On January 27 they pitched their tents at a sheltered spot called Rocky Glen, where there was a lagoon and some pasture; but from that depot they were not able to move for six months because they had no hope of finding water anywhere else between their camp and the Darling, more than 200 miles south. "We were locked up in this desolate and heated region," wrote Sturt, "as effectually as if we were ice-bound at the Pole." He saw clearly enough, too, that this enervating detention would paralyse his expedition. Not till the following July, when rain fell, was the party able to move away from Rocky Glen; and then it was forced back by the waterless waste. Ultimately, Sturt, in broken health, had to choose between facing another summer at Rocky Glen and making a rapid dash to the Darling. He chose the latter alternative, himself carried on a bullock-dray because he was too weak to ride; and by easy stages the shattered expedition made its way back to Adelaide, where the gaunt and sun-scorched travellers with their skeleton cattle arrived on January 19, 1846.

This was Sturt's last essay in exploration. He had hoped to reach the centre of the continent, but was baulked by the torrid summer and the waterless waste. But for broken health, however, he would have tried again. "I can only say," he wrote, "that I would not hesitate again to plunge into those dreary regions, that I might be the first to place my foot in the centre of this vast territory, and finally to raise the veil which still shrouds its features, even though, like those of the veiled prophet, they should wither the beholder."

Central Australia nearly turned Sturt's attempt to reveal its secrets into a great tragedy; for two famous expeditions it achieved that end. The first was that of a Prussian man of science, Ludwig Leichhardt. He had come to Australia with letters of introduction to a German mission to aboriginals in Queensland, and his first exploratory work was of a purely scientific character. He hoped to secure an appointment as naturalist on an expedition to be led by Mitchell through the continent to the Gulf of Carpentaria. As Mitchell's plans did not mature, Leichhardt in 1844 raised funds for an expedition of his own, which he conducted to Port Essington in the extreme north. It was the longest journey accomplished through the tropical regions of Australia up to this date. It occupied fifteen months, and the travellers arrived at the coast famished and with scarcely a rag to their backs.

The courage displayed by Leichhardt prompted the people of Sydney to subscribe to fit out a second expedition, and the Legislative Council of New South Wales supplemented the subscription by voting £1000. On this occasion (1846–7) Leichhardt hoped to traverse Australia from east to west, but was driven back to the coast after fighting against drought and heat for five months. Nothing daunted, however, he started again in 1848, planning to march from Moreton Bay to the Swan River. From this journey he never returned, and no authentic trace of him and his party has ever been found. His fate is one of the mysteries of Australian history which there is no hope of clearing up. A. C. Gregory, who led a party in search of Leichhardt, found on the Barcoo River a tree marked with the letter L, and the remains of several camps which may have been Leichhardt's were examined, but none of the traces were satisfactorily connected with his fate. The several expeditions which went in search of him, however, did find good pastoral country; and probably the scouring of the interior in the endeavour to solve the mystery did more to reveal the real nature of central Australia, to distinguish its economically useful tracts from its patches of desert, and to prove that seasonal variations made all the difference to its value, than his own expedition would have done if he had succeeded in his stated object.

The second tragedy of the interior was that of Burke and Wills in 1861. It was the best equipped expedition that ever set forth to explore any part of Australia. In Melbourne, where it originated, there was keen desire to ascertain what good pasture-lands there might be in the centre of the continent. By public subscription and Government subsidy £12,000 was raised, camels were brought from India, a scientific staff was engaged, and all the preparations appeared to be so carefully planned as to ensure success for a journey which, starting from a depot established at Menindie on the Darling, was to terminate at the Gulf of Carpentaria.

But a mistake was made in entrusting the command to Robert O'Hara Burke. He was a police officer of undoubted courage, but he had no knowledge of bushcraft, and his impatient rashness brought calamity to the enterprise and death to himself and to Wills. G. J. Landells, chosen as second in command, quarrelled with Burke before the expedition reached the Darling, and returned to Melbourne with the artist, Ludwig Beckler, who also found Burke's manner unendurable.   W. J. Wills, who had been taken as surveyor, was then appointed by Burke to Landells' position.

Burke, having formed his depot at Menindie, hurried on to Cooper's Creek. Finding grass and water plentiful, he sent back an order to move the depot to Cooper's Creek, and waited six weeks for this order to be executed. But he became impatient, and determined to make a dash for the Gulf of Carpentaria. He took with him three men, Wills, King and Gray, with provisions for three months, borne on six camels. The provisions were nearly exhausted before the sea was reached, and the camels all succumbed to Burke's impetuous speed. Burke and Wills went ahead of their two companions, and reached the estuary of the Flinders River, but did not obtain a glimpse of the sea, nor dared to spend the two extra days that would have been necessary to cut their way through the jungle to the beach.

The return journey was a march to death. Gray died by the way, but Burke, Wills and King managed to get back to Cooper's Creek, though terribly emaciated by their privations and exertions. They had expected to find the depot there; but the man who had been left in charge of it, having waited six weeks longer than he had been ordered to wait and finding his provisions diminishing, departed for Menindie seven hours before Burke and Wills arrived. He left behind a small stock of provisions, which the three eagerly ate. The obvious course was to follow to Menindie as soon as they had rested; but a strain of perversity in Burke brought calamity. He insisted on making for Adelaide, because, he said, there was a cattle station at Mount Hopeless 150 miles away. Wills argued strongly for taking the Menindie route, but could not persuade the leader, and accompanied him on the fatal journey along Cooper's Creek in the direction of Adelaide. Both men perished by the way; King fell in with a native tribe, who succoured him till he was rescued by a relief party under the command of Alfred Howitt.

To the Burke and Wills expedition, however, pertains the credit of being the first to traverse the continent from south to north, though this success was only barely achieved. John McDouall Stuart, starting from Adelaide, attempted the same feat in 1860. His memorable attainment on this journey was the reaching of the centre of the continent (April 22, 1860), where he erected a cairn upon which he placed a pole with the British flag nailed to it. The red sandstone hill which he found near the central point he named Central Mount Sturt, "after my excellent and esteemed commander of the expedition in 1844 and 1845, Captain Sturt"; but the name was afterwards changed to Central Mount Stuart by the Governor of South Australia. Stuart found in the centre of the continent a fine stretch of well-grassed country, but in his advance farther north was defeated by lack of provisions, attacks by aboriginals, and shortage of water.

He made another attempt in 1861, and this time penetrated 100 miles beyond his farthest point in the previous year, but found the hot plains and the thick scrub "as great a barrier as if there had been an inland sea or a wall." But his long experience as an explorer, and his consummate knowledge of bush travelling, were rewarded by complete success when he made his third attempt in 1862. On July 24 of that year his party emerged from their seven months' journey upon the north coast of the continent near Port Darwin. Stuart himself spent every grain of his strength in these three great journeys, which left him a sick and partially blind man; but they were of the utmost value in demonstrating the truth about central Australia—that in favourable seasons much of the country is good grazing land.

The inland journeys of Mitchell, Gregory, Landsborough, Stephen Hart, McKinlay, and Frederick Walker also did much to dispel gloomy ideas of the barrenness of the interior, which the failures of Sturt, Leichhardt and Burke and Wills had engendered, McKinlay demonstrated the possibility of driving sheep across the continent, and all the explorers just named found excellent pastoral lands, from which, in fact, fortunes have been made in later years by enterprising men with knowledge, experience, and sufficient discernment to distinguish between seasons when man and beast cannot live in drought-stricken territory and those when the feeding-grounds are green with nourishing grasses.

Turning next to the south-east corner of the continent, a sharp contrast is presented in the mountain ranges which extend from the Monaro table-land across the New South Wales border into the Victorian Alps and the steep slopes of Gippsland. The pioneer in Gippsland exploration was Angus Macmillan, a Scottish Highlander who came to Australia in 1838, and found employment with a squatter, Lachlan Macalister, who had a sheep-station near Goulburn. These were the squatting days, and Macalister, on the look-out for desirable lands to occupy with his flocks, sent Macmillan to examine the country south of Monaro, then entirely unknown. In a narrative written by himself, Macmillan stated that he heard from aboriginals "that a fine country existed near the sea-coast." In May 1839 he started to look for it, accompanied by one black of the Maneroo tribe, who knew something of the lay of the land. He did not reach the coast on this journey, but found a good site for a cattle-station for his employer, and then returned. He started again early in 1840, when, travelling over "some of the worst description of country I ever saw," he succeeded in breaking through the range leading down to the coast, but did not quite get there. Provisions ran short, "and as some of the party were unwilling to prosecute the journey on short allowance," he retreated with the determination to bring cattle down to the district which he had discovered. This he did in October 1840, when he cleared a road over the mountains and drove 500 head of cattle over it to the Avon River; after which he cleared a track to Port Albert. "When I started to explore the district," Macmillan said, "I had no guide but my pocket compass and a chart of Captain Flinders. We had not even a tent, but used to camp out and make rough gunyas wherever we remained for the night."

Macmillan wanted to call the district which he had thus opened Caledonia Australis, because it reminded him of his native country; a Highlander was naturally struck with the similarity between this region of rough peaks and green valleys through which tumbled cool, sparkling rivers, and the hills and glens of Scotland. But Caledonia Australis was Latin, and long; the name Gippsland, after the Governor of New South Wales at that time, was suggested by a Polish traveller, Count Strzelecki, and endured.

Strzelecki was a geologist, who came to Australia in 1838 to make researches in his own field of science; he was, indeed, one of the first to discover traces of gold in this country. It is owing to him, likewise, that the highest mountain in Australia bears a Polish name, that of the celebrated patriot of his country, Kosciusko. In 1840 the Count set out with a small party to traverse the rough country which Macmillan had already crossed; but he was less skilful than his predecessor, though he was rewarded with the gold medal of the Royal Geographical Society, whilst Macmillan received no official recognition. Strzelecki miscalculated his whereabouts and the distance to the coast. Planning to march through Caledonia Australis to Westernport, he and his companions toiled for twenty-two days over the hills and across the swamps, cutting their way with terrific exertion, reduced to the verge of starvation by the exhaustion of their provisions. They arrived at Westernport in a ragged and famished condition. If they had followed Macmillan's directions, they would have reached the sea with comparatively little difficulty.

The exploration of the western part of Australia makes a chapter of history in itself, because, though that country is connected continuously by land with eastern and southern Australia, the country forming the connection is less like a link than a cleavage. An enormous stretch of territory, much of which is desert and all difficult to traverse, even in favourable seasons, lies between. After the commencement of colonisation in 1829 many journeys into the interior were made from the capital, Perth, with the practical object of finding good land for settlement. The first expedition that attracted much general attention to Western Australia was that of George Grey and Lushington in 1837–8 and again in 1839. The discovery of the Glenelg, Irwin and Gascoyne rivers rewarded Grey's efforts, and brought him under the notice of the authorities in England, with the consequence that he was appointed Governor of South Australia and afterwards of New Zealand and South Africa.

Apart from Grey, the most famous of the explorers of Western Australia were the brothers John and Alexander Forrest and Ernest Giles. The colony on the Swan River had existed for forty years, however, before John Forrest, who was in 1869 a junior officer in the Survey Department, undertook to lead an expedition into the interior, primarily to investigate a story which some natives had told that white men had been murdered on the shores of a great lake to the east of the Hampton Plains. It was thought that traces of Leichhardt might be found by examining the locality. Forrest soon satisfied himself that there was no foundation for the report; but he travelled for 200 miles through territory which he found entirely worthless for pastoral or settlement purposes, but which nevertheless he believed to be richly mineralised. In 1870 Forrest set out again with his brother to travel overland from Perth to Adelaide. He knew that the difficulties would be great, for the route lay over the ground which had brought Eyre to a desperate plight, and nearly to disaster, in 1837. But, being prudent as well as courageous and very strong, Forrest arranged for a schooner with provisions to meet him at Esperance Bay for a first renewal of necessities, and at Eucla for a second supply. These plans succeeded; so that, though Forrest and his party certainly suffered severely from thirst, especially between Esperance and Eucla, they travelled through the waterless territory with the knowledge that there was relief for them at the appointed place.

Adelaide was reached after a journey of five months. The object was not merely geographical discovery. It was desired to ascertain whether there was any good pastoral country inland from the Bight. On this point Forrest's reports were reassuring. He satisfied himself that water could be found in some places by digging, that there were excellent patches of grass land, and that in seasons of liberal rainfall the district was worth using for stock purposes.

A third important journey of Forrest, who again had his brother Alexander with him, was for the purpose of examining the tropical areas of Western Australia which was drained by the Murchison, Gascoyne, Fitzroy and other rivers, flowing into the sea on the north and north-west. Splendid grazing-land was found between the rivers, with abundance of water. But Forrest's determination to return after an examination of the desert country east of these river valleys brought him into difficulties and privations which tried the courage and endurance of his party.

Ernest Giles made three expeditions into the arid lands west of Stuart's transcontinental track—in 1872, 1873 and 1875, on the third of which he travelled overland to Perth and back. By this time there was no longer much occasion to send out exploring expeditions, because the general character of the continent was well known, and there was no lack of enterprising mining prospectors and pastoralists who were continually on the move to find profitable ground.

This book brings together a collection of the original narratives of the men who unveiled the face of Australia. The stories which they wrote are scattered over many volumes, and few people, even among those who are keenly interested in the tale of the discovery of this continent, have the opportunity of gaining access to first-hand records of these memorable achievements. Many of the volumes are rare; few are easy to obtain. Here, however, the reader will find Blaxland's own narrative of the first crossing of the Blue Mountains, and the most important passages describing the discoveries of other men who cut their way through trackless regions and prepared the way for the pastoralist, the miner and the farmer. By these men, in the manner represented herein by themselves, was the continent of Australia made known.

ERNEST SCOTT.

Melbourne,
1929.

LIST OF PRINCIPAL DATES

1813. Blaxland, Lawson and Wentworth find a way across the Blue Mountains.
1815. Evans discovers the Lachlan.
1818. Oxley explores the Macquarie and discovers the Castlereagh.
1821. Throsby finds the Murrumbidgee.
1823. Allan Cunningham finds Pandora's Pass.
1824. Hume and Hovell's expedition to Westernport.
1825. Lockyer explores the Brisbane River.
1827. Cunningham discovers the Darling Downs.
1828. Sturt discovers the Darling.
1830. Sturt explores the Murray to the sea.
1836. Mitchell explores Australia Felix.
1837–9. Grey's explorations in Western Australia.
1839–40. Macmillan's exploration of Gippsland.
1840. Strzelecki's journey through Gippsland.
1841. Eyre's overland journey to Albany.
1844. Sturt's exploration of central Australia.
1845. Leichhardt's journey to the Gulf of Carpentaria.
1848. Leichhardt's last expedition.
       E. B. Kennedy's exploration of York Peninsula.
1855–6. A. C. Gregory's expedition in search of Leichhardt.
1860. McDouall Stuart reaches the centre of the continent.
1861. Burke and Wills expedition.
1861–2. McKinlay's journey from Adelaide to the Gulf of Carpentaria.
1862. Stuart traverses the continent from south to north.
1869. John Forrest's expedition in search of traces of Leichhardt.
1874. Forrest's inland expedition.
1872–5. Giles's inland expeditions.

CONTENTS

LIST OF ILLUSTRATIONS

The portraits and drawings which illustrate this book have been chosen and arranged by Miss Kathleen Ussher

PORTRAITS

ROUTE MAPS AND DRAWINGS

LIST OF BOOKS

THE best general work dealing systematically with explorations described by the original narratives in this volume is Ernest Favenc's *History of Australian Exploration* (1888). An older work by J. E. Tenison Woods, *History of the Discovery and Exploration of Australia* (1865), is still useful. There are short biographies of the various explorers in *The Australian Encyclopædia* edited by A. W. Jose and H. J. Carter (1925), as well as a long article dealing with the whole subject.

The following books are (or contain) original stories of the several journeys of exploration : J. Davis, *Tracks of McKinley and Party across Australia*; E. J. Eyre, *Journals of Expeditions of Discovery into Central Australia*; John Forrest, *Explorations in Australia*, and *Journal of an Expedition to explore the Country from West Australia to Port Eucla and thence to Adelaide*; Ernest Giles, *Australia Twice Traversed, Geographical Travels in Central Australia*, and *Journey of Exploration from South to West Australia*; A. C. and F. T. Gregory, *Journals of Australian Exploration*; W. Landsborough, *Exploration of Australia from Carpentaria to Melbourne*, and *Journal of Expedition from Carpentaria in search of Burke and Wills*; Leichhardt, *Journal of an Overland Expedition from Moreton Bay to Port Essington*; J. McKinlay, *Journal of Exploration in the Interior of Australia*; T. L. Mitchell, *Journal of an Expedition into the Interior of Tropical Australia*, and *Three Expeditions into the Interior of Eastern Australia*; C. Sturt, *Narrative of an Expedition into Central Australia*, and *Two Expeditions into the Interior of Southern Australia*; J. M. Stuart, *Exploration of the Interior of Australia*, and *Explorations in Australia, being Journals during the years* 1858 *to* 1862; Oxley, *Journals of Two Expeditions*; Strzelecki, *Physical Description of New South Wales*; W. J. Wills, *Exploration through the Interior of Australia*; G. Blaxland, *Journal of a Tour of Discovery across the Blue Mountains* (in facsimile as well as in original edition).

AUSTRALIAN DISCOVERY
BY LAND

I. BLAXLAND'S STORY OF THE CROSSING OF THE BLUE MOUNTAINS

[GREGORY BLAXLAND printed his account of the journey of 1813, in which he succeeded in crossing the Blue Mountains in company with Lawson and Wentworth, during a visit to England in 1823. He dedicated the little book to an uncle for whom he had "feelings of gratitude for your kind attention to me during the early part of my life." The book has been twice reprinted—in a limited facsimile edition in 1923, and more recently with explanatory notes by F. Walker.]

On Tuesday, May 11, 1813, Mr. Gregory Blaxland, Mr. William Wentworth, and Lieutenant Lawson, attended by four servants, with five dogs, and four horses laden with provisions, ammunition, and other necessaries, left Mr. Blaxland's farm at the South Creek, for the purpose of endeavouring to effect a passage over the Blue Mountains, between the Western River and the River Grose. They crossed the Nepean, or Hawkesbury River, at the ford, on to Emu Island, at four o'clock, P.M., and having proceeded, according to their calculation, two miles in a south-west direction, through forest land and good pasture, encamped at five o'clock at the foot of the first ridge. The distance travelled on this and on the subsequent days was computed by time; the rate being estimated at about two miles per hour. Thus far they were accompanied by two other gentlemen.

On the following morning, (May 12,) as soon as the heavy dew was off, which was about nine, A.M., they proceeded to ascend the ridge at the foot of which they had encamped the preceding evening. Here they found a large lagoon of good water, full of very coarse rushes. The high land of Grose Head appeared before them at about seven miles distance, bearing north by east. They proceeded this day about three miles and a quarter, in a direction varying from south-west to west-north-west; but, for a third of the way, due west. The land was covered with scrubby brushwood, very thick in places, with some trees of ordinary timber, which much incommoded the horses. The greater part of the way they had deep rocky gulleys on each side of their track, and the ridge they followed was very crooked and intricate. In the evening they encamped at the head of a deep gulley, which they had to descend for water; they found but just enough for the night, contained in a hole in the rock, near which they met with a kangaroo, who had just been killed by an eagle. A small patch of grass supplied the horses for the night.

They found it impossible to travel through the brush before the dew was off, and could not, therefore, proceed at an earlier hour in the morning than nine. After travelling about a mile on the third day, in a west and northwest direction, they arrived at a large track of forest land, rather hilly, the grass and timber tolerably good, extending, as they imagine, nearly to Grose Head, in the same direction nearly as the river. They computed it at two thousand acres. Here they found a track marked by a European, by cutting the bark of the trees. Several native huts presented themselves at different places. They had not proceeded above two miles, when they found themselves stopped by a brush-wood much thicker than they had hitherto met with. This induced them to alter their course, and to endeavour to find another passage to the westward; but every ridge which they explored, proved to terminate in a deep rocky precipice; and they had no alternative but to return to the thick brush-wood, which appeared to be the main ridge, with the determination to cut a way through for the horses on the next day. This day some of the horses, while standing, fell several times under their loads. The dogs killed a large kangaroo. The party encamped in the forest track, with plenty of good grass and water.

On the next morning, leaving two men to take care of the horses and provisions, they proceeded to cut a path through the thick brush-wood, on which they considered as the main ridge of the mountain, between the Western River and the River Grose; keeping the heads of the gulleys, which were supposed to empty themselves into the Western River on their left hand, and into the River Grose on their right. As they ascended the mountain, these gulleys became much deeper, and more rocky on each side. They now began to mark their track by cutting the bark of the trees on two sides. Having cut their way for about five miles, they returned in the evening to the spot on which they had encamped the night before. The fifth day was spent in prosecuting the same tedious operation; but, as much time was necessarily lost in walking twice over the tract cleared the day before, they were unable to cut away more than two miles further. They found no food for the horses the whole way. An emu was heard on the other side of the gulley, calling continually in the night.

On Sunday they rested, and arranged their future plan. They had reason, however, to regret this suspension of their proceedings, as it gave the men leisure to ruminate on their danger; and it was for some time doubtful, whether, on the next day, they could be persuaded to venture farther. The dogs this day killed two small kangaroos. They barked and ran off continually during the whole night; and at day-light, a most tremendous howling of native dogs was heard, who appeared to have been watching them during the night.

On Monday, the 17th, having laden the horses with as much grass as could be put on them, in addition to their other burdens, they moved forward along the path which they had cleared and marked, about six miles and a half. The bearing of the route they had been obliged to keep along the ridge, varied exceedingly; it ran sometimes in a north-north-west, direction, sometimes south-east, or due south, but generally south-west, or south-south-west. They encamped in the afternoon between two very deep gulleys, on a narrow ridge, Grose Head bearing north-east by north; and Mount Banks north-west by west. They had to fetch water up the side of the precipice, about six hundred feet high, and could get scarcely enough for the party. The horses had none this night; they performed the journey well, not having to stand under their loads.

The following day was spent in cutting a passage through the brush-wood, for a mile and a half farther. They returned to their camp at five o'clock, very much tired and dispirited. The ridge, which was not more than fifteen or twenty yards over, with deep precipices on each side, was rendered almost impassable by a perpendicular mass of rock, nearly thirty feet high, extending across the whole breadth, with the exception of a small broken rugged track in the centre. By removing a few large stones, they were enabled to pass.

On Wednesday, the 19th, the party moved forward along this path; bearing chiefly west, and west-south-west. They now began to ascend the second ridge of the mountains, and from this elevation, they obtained for the first time an extensive view of the settlements below. Mount Bank bore north-east;* Grose Head, north-east; Prospect Hill, east by south; the Seven Hills, east-north-east; Windsor, north-east by east. At a little distance from the spot at which they began the ascent, they found a pyramidical heap of stones, the work, evidently, of some European, one side of which the natives had opened, probably in the expectation of finding some treasure deposited in it. This pile they concluded to be the one erected by Mr. Bass,† to mark the end of his journey. That gentleman attempted, some time ago, to pass the mountains, and to penetrate into the interior; but having got thus far, he gave up the undertaking as impracticable; reporting, on his return, that it was impossible to find a passage even for a person on foot. Here, therefore, the party had the satisfaction of believing that they had penetrated as far as any European had been before them.

They encamped this day to refresh their horses, at the head of a swamp covered with a coarse rushy grass, with a small run of good water through the middle of it. In the afternoon, they left their camp to mark and cut a road for the next day.

They proceeded with the horses on the 20th nearly five miles, and encamped at noon at the head of a swamp about three acres in extent, covered with the same coarse rushy grass as the last station, with a stream of water running through it. The horses were obliged to feed on the swamp grass, as nothing better could be found for them. The travellers left the camp as before, in the afternoon, to cut a road for the morrow's journey. The ridge along which their course lay, now became wider and more rocky, but was still covered with brush and small crooked timber, except at the heads of the different streams of water which ran down the side of the mountain, where the land was swampy and clear of trees. The track of scarcely any animal was to be seen, and very few birds. One man was here taken dangerously ill with a cold. Bearing of the route at first, south-westerly; afterwards, north-north-west and west-north-west.

Their progress, the next day, was nearly four miles, in a direction still varying from north-west by north, to south-west. They encamped in the middle of the day, at the head of a well-watered swamp, about five acres in extent; pursuing, as before, their operations in the afternoon. In the beginning of the night, the dogs ran off, and barked violently. At the same time, something was

* So in Journal, but it should be " north-west."
† The guess was incorrect.

distinctly heard to run through the brush-wood, which they supposed to be one of the horses got loose; but they had reason to believe afterwards, that they had been in great danger—that the
natives had followed their track, and advanced on them in the
night, intending to have speared them by the light of their fire,
but that the dogs drove them off.

On Saturday, the 22nd instant, they proceeded in the track
marked the preceding day, rather more than three miles in a
south-westerly direction, when they reached the summit of the
third and highest ridge of the mountains southward of Mount
Banks. From the bearing of Prospect Hill, and Grose Head, they
computed this spot to be eighteen miles in a straight line from the
River Nepean, at the point at which they crossed it. On the top of
this ridge, they found about two thousand acres of land clear of
trees, covered with loose stones, and short coarse grass, such as
grows on some of the commons in England. Over this heath they
proceeded for about a mile and a half, in a south-westerly direction, and encamped by the side of a fine stream of water, with just
wood enough on the banks to serve for firewood. From the summit, they had a fine view of all the settlements and country eastward, and of a great extent of country to the westward and south-
west. But their progress in both the latter directions was stopped
by an impassable barrier of rock, which appeared to divide the
interior from the coast as with a stone wall, rising perpendicularly
out of the side of the mountain.

In the afternoon, they left their little camp in the charge of
three of the men, and made an attempt to descend the precipice,
by following some of the streams of water, or by getting down at
some of the projecting points where the rocks had fallen in; but
they were baffled in every instance. In some places, the perpendicular height of the rocks above the earth below, could not be
less than four hundred feet. Could they have accomplished a
descent, they hoped to procure mineral specimens which might
throw light on the geological character of the country, as the
strata appeared to be exposed for many hundred feet, from the
top of the rock, to the beds of the several rivers beneath. The
broken rocky country on the western side of the cow pasture, has
the appearance of having acquired its present form from an
earthquake, or some other dreadful convulsion of nature, at a
much later period than the mountains northward, of which
Mount Banks forms the southern extremity. The aspect of the
country, which lay beneath them, much disappointed the travellers; it appeared to consist of sand and small scrubby brush-wood,

intersected with broken rocky mountains, with streams of water running between them to the eastward, towards one point, where they probably form the Western River, and enter the mountains.

They now flattered themselves that they had surmounted half the difficulties of their undertaking, expecting to find a passage down the mountain more to the northward.

On the next day they proceeded about three miles and a half; but the trouble occasioned by the horses when they got off the open land, induced them to recur to their former plan of devoting the afternoon to marking and clearing a tract for the ensuing day, as the most expeditious method of proceeding, notwithstanding that, they had to go twice over the same ground. The bearing of their course this day, was, at first, north-east and north; and then changed to north-west, and north-north-west. They encamped on the side of a swamp, with a beautiful stream of water running through it.

Their progress on the next day was four miles and a half, in a direction, varying from north-north-west, to south-south-west; they encamped, as before, at the head of a swamp. This day, between ten and eleven, A.M., they obtained a sight of the country below, when the clouds ascended. As they were marking a road for the morrow, they heard a native chopping wood very near them, who fled at the approach of the dogs.

On Tuesday, the 25th, they could proceed only three miles and a half in a varying direction, encamping at two o'clock at the side of a swamp. The underwood being very prickly and full of small thorns, annoyed them very much. This day they saw the track of the Woombat for the first time. On the 26th, they proceeded two miles and three quarters. The brush still continued to be very thorny. The land to the westward appeared sandy and barren. This day they saw the fires of some natives below : the number they computed at about thirty, men, women, and children. They noticed also more tracks of the Woombat. On the 27th, they proceeded five miles and a quarter; part of the way over another piece of clear land, without trees; they saw more native fires, and about the same number as before, but more in their direct course. From the top of the rocks, they saw a large piece of land below, clear of trees, but apparently a poor reedy swamp. They met with some good timber in this day's route. The bearing of the route for the last three days, has been chiefly north and north-west.

On the 28th, they proceeded about five miles and three-quarters. Not being able to find water, they did not halt till five o'clock, when they took up their station on the edge of the precipice. To their great satisfaction, they discovered that what they had supposed to be sandy barren land below the mountain was forest land, covered with good grass, and with timber of an inferior quality. In the evening, they contrived to get their horses down the mountain, by cutting a small trench with a hoe, which kept them from slipping, where they again tasted fresh grass for the first time since they left the forest land on the other side of the mountain. They were getting into miserable condition. Water was found about two miles below the foot of the mountain. The second camp of natives moved before them about three miles. In this day's route, little timber was observed fit for building.

On the 29th, having got up the horses, and laden them, they began to descend the mountain at seven o'clock, through a pass in the rock, about thirty feet wide, which they had discovered the day before, when the want of water put them on the alert. Part of the descent was so steep, that the horses could but just keep their footing without a load, so that, for some way, the party were obliged to carry the packages themselves. A cart road might, however, easily be made by cutting a slanting trench along the side of the mountain, which is here covered with earth. This pass is, according to their computation, about twenty miles north-west in a straight line from the point at which they ascended the summit of the mountain. They reached the foot at nine o'clock, A.M., and proceeded two miles, north-north-west, mostly through open meadow land, clear of trees, the grass from two to three feet high. They encamped on the bank of a fine stream of water. The natives, as observed by the smoke of their fires, moved before them as yesterday. The dogs killed a kangaroo, which was very acceptable, as the party had lived on salt meat since they caught the last. The timber seen this day, appeared rotten and unfit for building.

Sunday the 30th, they rested in their encampment. One of the party shot a kangaroo with his rifle, at a great distance across a wide valley. The climate here was found very much colder than that of the mountain, or of the settlements on the east side, where no signs of frost had made its appearance when the party set out. During the night, the ground was covered with a thick frost, and a leg of the kangaroo was quite frozen. From the dead and brown appearance of the grass it was evident that the weather had been severe for some time past. We were all much surprised at this degree of cold and frost, in the latitude of about 34. The track of the emu was noticed at several places near the camp.

On the Monday, they proceeded about six miles, south-west and west, through forest land, remarkably well watered, and several open meadows, clear of trees, and covered with high good grass. They crossed two fine streams of water. Traces of the natives presented themselves in the fires they had left the day before, and in the flowers of the honey-suckle tree scattered around, which had supplied them with food. These flowers, which are shaped like a bottle-brush, are very full of honey. The natives on this side of the mountains, appear to have no huts like those on the eastern side, nor do they strip the bark, or climb the trees. From the shavings and pieces of sharp stones which they had left, it was evident that they had been busily employed in sharpening their spears.

The party encamped by the side of a fine stream of water, at a short distance from a high hill, in the shape of a sugar loaf. In the afternoon, they ascended its summit, from whence they descried all around, forest or grass land, sufficient in extent, in their opinion, to support the stock of the Colony for the next thirty years. This was the extreme point of their journey. The distance they had travelled, they computed at about fifty-eight miles nearly north-west; that is, fifty miles through the mountain, (the greater part of which they had walked over three times,) and eight miles through the forest land beyond it, reckoning the descent of the mountain to be half a mile to the foot.

The timber observed this day, still appeared unfit for building. The stones at the bottom of the rivers appeared very fine large-grained dark-coloured granite, of a kind quite different from the mountain rocks, or from any stones which they had ever seen in the Colony. Mr. Blaxland, and one of the men, nearly lost the party to-day, by going too far in the pursuit of a kangaroo.

They now conceived that they had sufficiently accomplished the design of their undertaking, having surmounted all the difficulties which had hitherto prevented the interior of the country from being explored, and the Colony from being extended. They had partly cleared, or, at least marked out, a road by which the passage of the mountain might easily be effected. Their provisions were nearly expended, their clothes and shoes were in very bad condition, and the whole party were ill with bowel complaints. These considerations determined them, therefore, to return home by the track they came. On Tuesday, the 1st June, they arrived at the foot of the mountain which they had descended, where they encamped for the night. The following day, they began to ascend the mountain at seven o'clock, and reached the summit at ten; they were obliged to carry the packages themselves part of the ascent. They encamped in the evening at one of their old stations. One of the men had left his great coat on the top of the rock, where they re-loaded the horses, and it was found by the next party who traversed the mountain. On the 3rd, they reached another of their old stations. Here, during the night, they heard a confused noise arising from the eastern settlements below, which, after having been so long accustomed to the death-like stillness of the interior, had a very striking effect. On the 4th, they arrived at the end of the marked track, and encamped in the forest land where they had cut the grass for their horses. One of the horses this day fell with his load, quite exhausted, and was with difficulty got on, after having his load put on the other horses. The next day, the 5th, was the most unpleasant and fatiguing they had experienced. The track not being marked, they had great difficulty in finding their way back to the river, which they did not reach till four o'clock, P.M. They then once more encamped for the night, to refresh themselves and the horses. They had no provisions now left, except a little flour, but procured some from the settlement on the other side of the river. On Sunday, the 6th of June, they crossed the river after breakfast, and reached their homes, all in good health. The winter had not set in on this side of the mountain, nor had there been any frost.

II. EVANS'S JOURNAL OF HIS JOURNEY TO THE BATHURST PLAINS

[GOVERNOR MACQUARIE despatched Assistant Land Surveyor George W. Evans to follow up the trail across the Blue Mountains, opened by Blaxland and his companions in 1813. Evans's Journal, a copy of which was forwarded as an enclosure in a despatch to the Secretary of State, Lord Bathurst, is printed in the *Historical Records of Australia*, Vol. VIII.]

Friday, November 19th, 1813.—I directed the Provisions and other necessarys to be conveyed across the Nepean to the N.E. Point of Forest Land, commonly called Emu Island, which was done, and by the time every thing was arranged evening approached.

Saturday, 20th.—The Night was most uncomfortable, and the Morning being wet prevented our departing so early as I meant; feeling anxious to proceed, I made up my mind to make the best of our way to the end of the Mountains, and on my return to measure the distance of Messrs. Blaxlands, Wentworths and Lawsons recent excursion; it appeared to me that while the Horses were fresh it was a plan likely to meet with approbation, as I could then refresh them on good grass, and take my time in exploring to the Westward, which I conceived the object of the greatest importance; on returning should I not have sufficient provisions to subsist on to complete measuring the track of the above named Gentlemen, I could send in a Man and Horse to meet me with a small supply.

Monday, 22nd.—The Weather bad; determined to proceed we loaded the Horses when one of them turned stubborn having laid down and rolled several times over his load; he at length became steady; our track was through a thick brush; at 9 o'Clock we were on a very high Mountain but could not see any of the low Country; it is now disagreeable travelling; the Brush is so very thick, and the surface of the ridges are covered with pieces of sharp Granite intermixed with Quartz; the Horses seemed to step with caution; we stopped at 1 o'Clock, where there was a spacious Valley covered with grass and Rushes, a stream of water running through it.

Wednesday, 24th.—We all rested, which was a preservation to us, not having done so since our departure, and which we felt the effects of, as nothing could be procured for shelter but green Boughs, that was not sufficient to screen us from rain; we start quite refreshed; at 9 o'Clock came to the end of the Range from which the Prospect is extensive and gives me sanguine hopes; the descent is rugged and steep; I stowed away here a week's provisions in some hollow Cliffs in hopes of it being sufficient for our use back from this place; it was 12 o'Clock when we got into a Valley of good feed and appears a fine part of the Country; I have no doubt but the points of Ridges or Bluffs to the N.W. and S. (the Country seems to open in the form of this Angle) are the termination of what is called the *Blue Mountains* and that we are now over them; at 1 o'Clock I stopped on the bank of a Riverlett, which is a rapid stream from the N.E., its source springing from very high Mountainous; the two dogs went off after game without success and came to us severely cut.

Friday, 26th.—My Course is along the Stream; the banks are sandy and appear to be overflowed at times by heaps of Timber being lodged at the foot of some of the Trees; when I had proceeded about 2 miles the Forest ground rises and forms a steeper Bank; in places the Water has a great fall over Rocks; the numerous Valleys carry off the Water in rainy seasons into the riverlett; on one of the small ridges is a Rock resembling *White Marble* with Yellow Veins; we could not break it but from small Crevices I scraped out small pieces much like Crystal (Paper No. 1); at 4 Miles the stream alters its direction to the South, at which place the main Run joins from the West forming a considerable rapid Riverlett; the land here gets better and the Country has a fine appearance; it resembles the hills to the Eastward of the *Cori Linn* at Port Dalrymple, and put me in mind particularly of that part; the Trees being thin and light, the flats clear of Timber, a few Honeysuckles on the Banks of the Ridges, the Lockett Bird singing, and the seed of the wild Burnett sticking to our legs, neither of the two last are to be seen on the East side of the Mountains; the soil still continues sandy but the feed is good, and better than any I have seen in New South Wales; I stopped this evening near the foot of a very handsome Mount, which I take the liberty to call *Mount Blaxland*, also two Peaks rather North of it, and which the Riverlett separates *Wentworths and Lawsons Sugar Loaves*. I am at a loss to describe the pleasant appearance of this place, the Grass being quite green and good makes it look a pleasing scene, this is the termination of the excursion of the above named Gentlemen; be assured it was not without much labour, perseverance and fatigue that enabled them to reach thus far; I am certain that it is at least 50 Miles, and as the present track is, no person in the Colony on the Choicest Horse could reach this and return to the Nepean in four days; you may rely on what I say in this respect; the Mountains being covered with sharp Granite, would be dangerous to put any Horse out of a walk, and impossible so to do through the Brushes; Kangaroos are numerous, we caught one this day altho' the dogs are so much hurt.

Monday, 29th.—I stopped in very bad Spirits, not being able to get on, being completely entangled among the hills, and our Course being so little Westling; were it not for the Horses the difficulty to ourselves would be nothing; they are sometimes bad to manage, and soon tire among the high Lands; when so they will not move; after travelling 2½ Miles we were on a lofty hill, from whence the Country N.W. is all Forest hills as far as I could see, which I suppose about 15 Miles, every other direction was obscured by high Ranges; impossible there can be a better grazing Track of land, and has the same good appearance as far as I have been able to get a sight of it to the Westward; I hope I will be able to do better tomorrow, and that in a few days my account will be more interesting.

Tuesday, 30th.—I have at length reached the Ridge I so much wished to do after walking about 2 Miles, where I had a prospect to the North for a great distance; A Mist arises from a part I suppose to be a River or a large Lagoon about 20 Miles off; the Country in this direction has a fine appearance, the Trees being thin and the hills covered with Grass; A ¼ of Mile farther along the Range, I came to a very high Mount, when I was much pleased with the sight Westward; I think I can see 40 Miles which had the look of an open Country. To the South of me there are large hills much higher than the one I am on, with pasture to their tops; This Range is rather overrun with underwood and larger Timber growing thereon, but the sides are as green as possible; in descending for 2 Miles the verdure is good; the descent then becomes steep for a ¼ of a Mile, leading into a fine valley at the end I met a large Riverlett arising from the Southern Hills. We shot Ducks and caught several trout weighing at least 5 or 6 Pounds each.

Wednesday, December 1st, 1813.—My Course is down the Riverlett; it appears to lead me North of West; on the North side of it at this place is a remarkable Sugar Loaf Hill having a

Stone on the *Peak* of it, which I have named after myself; I am more pleased with the Country every day; it is a great extent of Grazing land without being divided by barren spaces as on the East side of the Mountains, and well watered by running streams in almost every Valley; I took a walk to the top of a very high Mount where I can see at least 50 Miles West, which gives me great Spirits.

Saturday, 4th.—My Progress is through an exceeding good Track of Country; it is the handsomest I have yet seen with gentle rising hills and dales well watered; the distant hills, which are about 5 Miles South, appear as Grounds laid out divided into fields by edges, there are few Trees on them and the Grass quite green; I still keep the river, and at times I walk a few Miles South or North as seems to me most requisite. The Dogs killed a Kangaroo and the river supplies us *with abundance of Fish.*

Sunday, 5th.—We remained near the River as it is Sunday. The Horses are getting fat but am Sorry to observe their backs are sore; the Saddles should have been lined; straw stuffing is too hard to render it easy we put our Blankets under them; I walked out this Evening some Miles; I cannot speak too highly of the Country, indeed I am now at a loss what to say as it exceeds my expectations and daily gets better. We are on an Allowance of Bread having lost so much by the bad Weather on the Mountains, we require little pork in this part, a Kangaroo can be procured at any time, there are also Emu's, we killed some Ducks this day.

Monday, 6th.—The river now forms large ponds; at the Space of about a Mile I came on a fine Plain of rich Land, the handsomest Country I ever saw; it surpasseth Port Dalrymple; this place is worth speaking of as good and beautiful; the Track of clear land occupies about a Mile on each side of the River; I have named it after the Lieut. Governor, "O'Connell Plains," on which we saw a number of wild Geese but too shy to let us near them; the Timber around is thinly scattered, I do not suppose there are more than ten Gum Trees on an Acre, their Bark is amazing thick at least 2 Inches; At 3 o'Clock I stopped at the commencement of a Plain still more pleasing and very Extensive; I cannot see the termination of it North of me; the soil is exceeding rich and produces the finest grass intermixed with variety of herbs; the hills have the look of a park and Grounds laid out; I am at a loss for Language to describe the Country; I named this part "Macquarie Plains."

Thursday, 9th.—I have called the Main Stream " Macquarie

River." At 2½ Miles commences a most extensive Plain, the
hills around are fine indeed; it requires a clever person to describe
this Country properly, I never saw any thing equal to it; the soil
is good; I think the lower parts of the Plains are overflowed at
times, but do not see marks to any height; the small Trees on the
lower banks of the River stand straight, not laying down as you
see them on the banks of the river and Creeks at Hawkesbury.
The grass here might be mowed it is so thick and long, particularly on the flat lands.

Friday, 10th.—Yesterdays trace led me much North of West;
today it is South of it. The extent of the Plain following the
River is 11 Miles and about 2 wide on each side, the whole
excellent good land, and the best Grass I have seen in any part
of New South Wales; the hills are also covered with fine pasture,
the Trees being so far apart must be an acquisition to its Growth;
it is in general the sweetest in an open Country. At the termination of the Plain is a very handsome Mount; I named it "Mount
Pleasant" from the Prospect it commands to the N.E. The
River now winds itself round the Points of Forest hills nearly the
same as described some days since.

Emues are numerous; the Dogs will not give chase; I imagine
they are bad ones; we have not been able to get a shot at any
of the Geese, altho' plentiful, they are so shy; but frequently
shoot Ducks. Nothing astonished me more than the amazing
large Fish that are caught; one is now brought me that weighs
at least 15 lb., they are all the same species. I call the Plains
last passed over "Bathurst Plains."

Saturday, 18th.—We departed for our Journey homewards,
keeping as far from the River as we conveniently could, and
find the feed for Stock exceeding good; the farther back among
these hills the better it is; the Valleys are beautiful, as also the
intervening ridges that divide them, being thickly covered with
herbage; Grazers may keep stock here to great advantage,
particularly sheep, as they like dry healthy parts.

Tuesday, 21st.—Fine weather very warm; halted at the commencement of *Bathurst Plains* early, as I was desirous to examine
this part; I ascended *Mount Pleasant,* the West end led me on a
Ridge of Beautiful hills, along which I travelled 3 Miles, a small
stream of Water forming ponds run at their foot; I was gratified
with a pleasing sight of an open Country to the S.W. of them;
at the space of 7 or 8 Miles I could discern *the Course of a River
winding to the West;* I saw three or four large Plains; the first of
them I was on, the Chain of Ponds before mentioned running

through it; I feel much regret I am not able to Travel a week or more in that direction; I imagine the flat open Country extends 30 or 40 Miles; at the termination I can only discern one Mountain quite Pale with three Peaks; I suspected an open Country lay about the S.W. point, as I passed, the Range of hills then obscured it from me, nor had I time to examine it; I cannot speak too much of the Country, the increase of Stock for some 100 Years cannot overrun it; the Grass is so good and intermixed with variety of herbs. Emu's and Geese are numerous, but cannot get any; we counted 41 Emu's this day; our dogs will not follow them. Returning we saw smoke on the North side of the River, at Sun sett as we were fishing I saw some Natives coming down the Plain; they did not see us untill we surprized them; there was only two Women and four Children, the poor Creatures trembled and fell down with fright; I think they were coming for Water; I gave them what Fish we had, some Fish Hooks, Twine and a Tomahawk, they appeared glad to get from us; two Boys ran away; the other small Children cried much at first; a little while after I played with them they began to be good humoured and laugh, both of the Women were blind of their Right Eye.

Thursday, 23rd.—About 9 o'clock crossed Campbell's River; the Water has fallen so much that it was fordable in many places, which saved us a Journey of 6 Miles round to our Bridge; Macquaries River is likewise fordable between the large sheets of Water; these rivers resemble the *Esks* in Van Diemans Land, being fine streams running over hard gravel Bottoms, I kept some distance back from the River and find the Country as usual, fine pasture and distant hill North and South are Forest lands thinly wooded; we stopped at the West end of O'Connell Plains.

Saturday, 25th.—Being Christmas day we remained for a day's rest; yet we walked about as much as a day's journey looking around us, and ascending Hills to see the Country, which is excellent pasture, the soil is light, but exceeds the Forest Lands in general on the East side of the Mountains. The day is so hott the Fish will not bite; it is the only time they have missed; therefore I opened my tin case of Roasted Beef.

III. GOVERNOR MACQUARIE'S REPORT ON THE COUNTRY BEYOND THE MOUNTAINS

Government and General Orders.

Government House, Sydney, 10th June, 1815.

THE Governor desires to communicate, for the information of the public, the result of his late tour over the Western or Blue Mountains, undertaken for the purpose of being enabled personally to appreciate the importance of the Tract of Country lying Westward of them, which had been explored in the latter end of the year, 1813, and the beginning of 1814, by Mr. G. W. Evans, Deputy Surveyor of Lands.

To those, who know how very limited a tract of country has been hitherto occupied by the colonists of New South Wales, extending along the eastern coast, to the north and south of Port Jackson, only 80 miles, and westward about 40 miles to the foot of the chain of mountains in the interior, which forms its western boundary, it must be a matter of astonishment and regret that amongst so large a population no one appeared, within the first 25 years of the establishment of this settlement, possessed of sufficient energy of mind to induce him fully to explore a passage over these mountains; but, when it is considered that, for the greater part of that time, even this circumscribed portion of country afforded sufficient produce for the wants of the people, whilst on the other hand the whole surface of the country beyond those limits was a thick, and in many places nearly an impenetrable, forest, the surprise at the want of effort to surmount such difficulties must abate very considerably.

The records of the Colony only afford two instances of any bold attempt, having been made to discover the country to the westward of the Blue Mountains. The first was by Mr. Bass, and the other by Mr. Cayley; and both ended in disappointment; a circumstance, which will not be much wondered at by those, who have lately crossed those mountains.

To G. Blaxland and W. Wentworth, Esqs., and Lieutenant Lawson, of the Royal Veteran Company, the merit is due of having, with extraordinary patience and much fatigue, effected

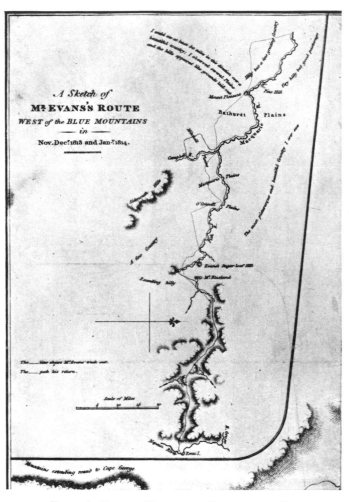

EVANS'S ROUTE, NOVEMBER–DECEMBER, 1813,
AND JANUARY, 1814.

the first passage over the most rugged and difficult part of the Blue Mountains.

The Governor, being strongly impressed with the importance of the object, had early after his arrival in this colony, formed the resolution of encouraging the attempt to find a passage to the Western Country, and willingly availed himself of the facilities, which the discoveries of these three gentlemen afforded him. Accordingly on the 20th of November, 1813, he entrusted the accomplishment of this object to Mr. G. W. Evans, Deputy Surveyor of Lands, the result of whose journey was laid before the public through the medium of the *Sydney Gazette* on the 12th of Feb., 1814.

The favourable account, given by Mr. Evans of the country he had explored, induced the Governor to cause a road to be constructed for the passage and conveyance of cattle and provisions to the interior; and men of good character, from amongst a number of convicts who had volunteered their services, were selected to perform this arduous work, on condition of being fed and clothed during the continuance of their labour, and being granted emancipation, as their final reward, on the completion of the work.

The direction and superintendence of this great work was entrusted to W. Cox, Esq., the chief magistrate of Windsor; and to the astonishment of every one, who knows what was to be encountered and sees what has been done, he effected its completion in six months from the time of its commencement, happily without the loss of a man or any serious accident. The Governor is at a loss to appreciate fully the services rendered by Mr. Cox to this colony in the execution of this arduous work, which promises to be of the greatest public utility by opening a new source of wealth to the industrious and enterprising. When it is considered that Mr. Cox voluntarily relinquished the comforts of his own house and the society of his numerous family, and exposed himself to much personal fatigue with only such temporary covering, as a bark hut could afford, from the inclemency of the season, it is difficult to express the sentiments of approbation to which such privations and services are entitled.

Mr. Cox having reported the road as completed on the 21st of January, the Governor, accompanied by Mrs. Macquarie and that gentleman, commenced his tour on the 25th of April over the Blue Mountains, and was joined by Sir J. Jamieson at the Nepean, who accompanied him during the entire tour.

The following gentlemen composed the Governor's suite:—

I. D.   e

Mr. Campbell, secretary; Captain Antill, major of brigade; Lieutenant Watts, aide-de-camp; Mr. Redfern, assistant surgeon; Mr. Oxley, surveyor-general; and Mr. G. W. Evans, deputy surveyor of lands, who had been sent forward for the purpose of making further discoveries and rejoined the party on the day of arrival at Bathurst plains.

The commencement of the ascent from Emu Plains to the first depot, and thence to a resting place, now called "Spring Wood," distant 12 miles from Emu Ford, was through a very handsome open forest of lofty trees, and much more practicable and easy than was expected. The facility of the ascent for this distance excited surprise, and is certainly not well calculated to give the traveller a just idea of the difficulties he has afterwards to encounter. At the further distance of 4 miles, a sudden change is perceived in the appearance of the timber and the quality of the soil, the former becoming stunted, and the latter barren and rocky. At this place, the fatigues of the journey may be said to commence. Here the country became altogether mountainous and extremely rugged. Near the 18th mile mark (it is observed that the measure commences from Emu Ford) a pile of stones attracted attention; it is close to the line of the road on the top of a rugged and abrupt ascent, and is supposed to have been placed there by Mr. Cayley, as the extreme limit of his tour; hence the Governor gave that part of the mountain the name of "Cayley's Repulse." To have penetrated even so far was at that time an effort of no small difficulty. From hence, forward to the 26th mile, is a succession of steep and rugged hills, some of which are almost so abrupt as to deny a passage altogether; but at this place an extensive plain is arrived at, which constitutes the summit of the Western Mountain; and from thence a most extensive and beautiful prospect presents itself on all sides to the eye. The town of Windsor, the river Hawkesbury, Prospect Hill, and other objects within that part of the colony now inhabited, of equal interest, are distinctly seen from hence. The majestic grandeur of the situation, combined with the various objects to be seen from this place, induced the Governor to give it the appellation of "The King's Table Land."

On the S.W. side of the King's Table Land, the mountain terminates in abrupt precipices of immense depth; at the bottom of which is seen a glen as romantically beautiful as can be imagined, bounded on the further side by mountains of great magnitude, terminating equally abruptly as the others, and the whole thickly covered with timber. The length of this picturesque and remarkable tract of country is about 24 miles, to which the Governor gave the name of "The Prince Regent's Glen." Proceeding hence to the 33rd mile on the top of a hill, an opening presents itself on the S.W. side of the Prince Regent's Glen from whence a view is obtained particularly beautiful and grand. Mountains rising beyond mountains, with stupendous masses of rock in the foreground, here strike the eye with admiration and astonishment. The circular form, in which the whole is so wonderfully disposed, induced the Governor to give the name of "Pitt's Amphitheatre," in honour of the late Right Hon. Wm. Pitt, to this first branch from the Prince Regent's Glen. The road continues from hence for the space of 17 miles on the ridge of the mountain, which forms one side of the Prince Regent's Glen; and it suddenly terminates in nearly a perpendicular precipice of 676 feet high, as ascertained by measurement. The road constructed by Mr. Cox down this rugged and tremendous descent through all its windings is no less than three fourths of a mile in length, and has been executed with such skill and stability, as reflects much credit on him. The labour here undergone and the difficulties surmounted can only be appreciated by those who view the scene. In order to perpetuate the memory of Mr. Cox's services, the Governor deemed it a tribute justly due to him to give his name to this grand and extraordinary Pass, and he accordingly called it "Cox's Pass." Having descended into the valley at the bottom of this pass, the retrospective view of the overhanging mountain is much higher than those on either side of it; from whence it is distinguished at a considerable distance, when approaching it from the interior, and in this point of view it has the appearance of a very high distinct hill, although it is in fact only the abrupt termination of a ridge. The Governor gave the name of "Mount York" to this termination of the ridge in honour of his Royal Highness the Duke of York.

On descending Cox's Pass, the Governor was much gratified by the appearance of good pasture land, and soil fit for Cultivation, which was the first he had met with since the commencement of his tour. The valley at the base of Mount York, he called "the Vale of Clwyd" in consequence of the strong resemblance it bore to the vale of that name in North Wales. The grass in this vale is of a good quality and very abundant, and rivulet of fine water runs along it from the eastward, which unites itself at the western extremity of the vale with another rivulet containing still more water. The junction of these two streams forms a very handsome river, now called by the Governor "Cox's River," which takes its course, as has been ascertained, through the Prince Regent's Glen, and empties itself into the Nepean River; and it is conjectured from the nature of the country, through which it passes, that it must be one of the principal causes of the floods, which have been occasionally felt on the low banks of the river Hawkesbury into which the Nepean discharges itself. The vale of Clwyd from the base of Mount York extends six miles in a westerly direction, and has its termination at Cox's River. West of this river the country again becomes hilly; but is generally open forest land and very good pasturage.

Three miles to the Westward of the Vale of Clwyd, Messrs. Blaxland, Wentworth, and Lawson had formerly terminated their excursion; and when the various difficulties are considered, which they had to contend with, especially until they had effected the descent from Mount York, to which place they were obliged to pass through a thick brush wood, where they were under the necessity of cutting a passage for the baggage horses, the severity of which labour had seriously affected their healths, their patient endurance of such fatigue cannot fail to excite much surprise and admiration. In commemoration of their merits, three beautiful high hills, joining each other at the end of their tour at this place, have received their names in the following order, viz.; "Mount Blaxland," "Wentworth's Sugar Loaf," and "Lawson's Sugar Loaf." A range of very lofty hills and narrow vallies alternately form the tract of country from Cox's River for a distance of 16 miles, until the Fish River is arrived at; and the stage between these rivers is consequently very severe and oppressive on the cattle. To this Range, the Governor gave the name of "Clarence Hilly Range."

Proceeding from the Fish River, and at a short distance from it, a very singular and beautiful mountain attracts the attention, its summits being crowned with a large and very extraordinary looking rock, nearly circular in form, which gives to the whole very much the appearance of a hill or fort, such as are frequent in India. To this lofty hill, Mr. Evans, who was the first European discoverer, gave the name of "Mount Evans." Passing on from hence, the country continues hilly, but affords a good pasturage, gradually improving to Sidmouth Valley, which is distant from the pass of the Fish River 12 miles. The land here is level, and the first met with unincumbered with timber; it is not of very considerable extent, but abounds with a great variety of herbs and plants, such as would probably highly interest and gratify the scientific botanists. This beautiful little valley runs north-west and south-east between hills of easy ascent, thinly covered with timber. Leaving Sidmouth Valley, the country becomes again hilly, and, in other respects, resembles very much the country to the eastward of the valley for some miles. Having reached Campbell River, distance 13 miles from Sidmouth Valley, the Governor was highly gratified by the appearance of the country, which there began to exhibit an open and extensive view of gently rising grounds and fertile plains. Judging from the height of the banks and its general width, the Campbell River must be on some occasions of very considerable magnitude; but the extraordinary drought, which has apparently prevailed on the western side of the mountains, equally as throughout this colony for the last three years, has reduced this river so much, that it may be more properly called a chain of pools than a running stream at the present time. In the reaches or pools of the Campbell River, the very curious animal called the Paradox, or Water-mole is seen in great numbers. The soil on both banks is uncommonly rich, and the grass is consequently luxuriant. Two miles to the southward of the line of road which crosses the Campbell River, there is a very fine tract of low lands, which has been named Mitchell Plains. Flax was found growing in considerable quantities. The Fish River, which forms a junction with the Campbell River a few miles to the northward of the road and bridge over the latter, has also two very fertile plains on its banks, the one called O'Connell Plains, and the other Macquarie Plains, both of very considerable extent and capable of yielding all the necessaries of life.

At the distance of seven miles from the bridge over the Campbell River, Bathurst Plains open to the view, presenting a rich tract of campaign country of 11 miles in length, bounded on both sides by gently rising and very beautiful hills, thinly wooded. The Macquarie River, which is constituted by the junction of the Fish and Campbell River, takes a winding course through the plains, which can be easily traced from the high lands adjoining by the particular verdure of the trees on its banks, which are likewise the only trees throughout the extent of the plains. The level and clear surface of these plains gives them at first view very much the appearance of lands in a state of cultivation.

It is impossible to behold this grand scene without a feeling of admiration and surprise, whilst the silence and solitude, which reign in a space of such extent and beauty as seems designed by nature for the occupancy and comfort of man, create a degree of melancholy in the mind which may be more easily imagined than described.

The Governor and suite arrived at these plains on Thursday, the 4th of May, and encamped on the southern left bank of the Macquarie river; the situation being selected in consequence of its commanding a beautiful and extensive prospect for many miles in every direction around it. At this place, the Governor remained for a week, which time he occupied in making excursions in different directions through the adjoining country on both sides of the river.

On Sunday, the 7th of May, the Governor fixed on a site suitable for the erection of a town at some future period, to which he gave the name of "Bathurst," in honour of the present Secretary of State for the Colonies. The situation of Bathurst is elevated sufficiently beyond the reach of any floods which may occur, and it is at the same time so near to the river on its south bank, as to derive all the advantages of its clear and beautiful stream. The mechanics and settlers, of whatever description, who may be hereafter permitted to form permanent residences to themselves at this place, will have the highly important advantages of a rich and fertile soil, with a beautiful river flowing through it, for all the uses of man. The Governor must, however, add, that the hopes, which were once so sanguinely entertained of this river becoming navigable to the Western Sea, have ended in disappointment.

During the week that the Governor remained at Bathurst, he made daily excursions in various directions:—one of these extended 22 miles in a south-west direction, and on that occasion, as well as on all others, he found the country chiefly composed of valleys and plains, separated occasionally by ranges of low hills, the soils throughout being generally fertile and well circumstanced for the purpose of agriculture and grazing. The Governor here feels much pleasure in being enabled to communicate to the public that the favourable reports, which he had received of the country to the west of the Blue Mountains, have not been by any means exaggerated. The difficulties, which present themselves in the journey from hence, are certainly great and inevitable; but those persons, who may be inclined to become permanent settlers there, will probably content themselves with visiting this part of the colony but rarely, and of course will have them seldom to encounter. Plenty of water and a sufficiency of grass are to be found in the mountains for the support of such cattle as may be sent over them; and the tracts of fertile soil and rich pasturage, which the new country affords, are fully extensive enough for any increase of population and stock, which can possibly take place for years.

Within a distance of ten miles from the site of Bathurst, there is not less than 50,000 acres of land clear of timber, and fully one half of that may be considered excellent soil, well calculated for cultivation. It is a matter of regret, that, in proportion as the soil improves, the timber degenerates; and it is to be remarked, that every where to the westward of the Mountains, it is much inferior both in size and quality to that within the present colony; there is, however, a sufficiency of timber of tolerable quality, within the district around Bathurst, for the purpose of housebuilding and husbandry.

The Governor has here to lament, that neither coals or limestone have yet been discovered in the western country, articles in themselves of so much importance that the want of them must be severely felt whenever that country shall be settled.

Having enumerated the principal and most important features of this new country, the Governor has now to notice some of its live productions. All around Bathurst abounds in a variety of game; and the two principal rivers contain a great quantity of fish, but all of one denomination, resembling the perch in appearance and of a delicate and fine flavour, not unlike that of a rock-cod; this fish grows to a large size, and is very voracious. Several of them were caught during the Governor's stay at Bathurst, and at the halting-place of the Fish River. One of those caught weighed 17 lb., and the people stationed at Bathurst stated, that they had caught some weighing 25 lbs.

The field game are kangarooes, emus, black swans, wild geese, wild turkeys, bustards, ducks of various kinds, quail, bronze and other pigeons, etc.; the water-mole or paradox also abounds in all the rivers and ponds.

The site designed for the town of Bathurst, by observation taken at a flag-staff, which was erected on the day of Bathurst receiving that name, is situated in lat. 33° 24′ 30″ south, and in long. 149° 37′ 45″ east of Greenwich, being also 27½ miles north of Government House in Sydney, and 94½ west of it, bearing west 20° 30′ north 83 geographic miles, or 95½ statute miles; the measured road distance from Sydney to Bathurst being 140 English miles.

On Thursday, the 17th of May, the Governor and suite set out from Bathurst on their return, and arrived at Sydney on Friday, the 19th ult.

The Governor deems it expedient to notify here to the public that he does not mean to make any grant of land to the westward of the Blue Mountains, until he shall receive the commands of his Majesty's Ministers on that subject, and in reply to the report he is now about to make them upon it.

In the mean time, such gentlemen, or other respectable free persons, as may wish to visit this new country, will be permitted to do so on making a written application to the Governor to that effect, who will order them to be furnished with written passes. It is at the same time strictly ordered and directed that no person, whether civil or military, shall attempt to travel over the Blue Mountains, without having previously applied for and obtained permission in the above prescribed form. The military guard stationed at the first depot on the mountains will receive full instructions to prevent the progress of any persons, who shall not have obtained regular passes. The necessity for the establishing and strictly enforcing this regulation is too obvious to every one, who will reflect on it, to require any explanation here.

IV. EVANS'S DISCOVERY OF THE LACHLAN

[EVANS left Sydney on his second inland journey in 1815 under instructions from Governor Macquarie to pursue a western course from Bathurst "until he shall fall in with the western ocean." The Governor hoped that he might meet with some great river "which may probably fall into the sea on that part of the coast bearing in a south-easterly direction from Spencer's Gulf." Evans did not reach the sea on this journey, but he found the river Lachlan.]

Saturday, May 13th, 1815.—I should have left Bathurst yesterday; when near ready to go, one of my Horses threw his Load, which damaged some of his tackling; repairs being necessary caused my delay until the Morning; my Course was S. 30° W. or thereabouts along the fine flat, named Queen Charlotte Vale. I halted near the junction of it with the Main Creek, which bears S. 20 W., having plains on both sides; the Vale is also clear of Timber; this day's journey is over exceeding good Land, well watered.

Sunday, 14th.—I follow the Vale, which still continues very good; at about 5 Miles, a fine Valley comes into it, bearing up S. 20 W., which is well watered; at 6½ Miles, the Valley is rather contracted, and remains so a short distance, when it again opens, producing the rankest of Grass with ponds as before alternately; the Land is of the strongest nature; the hills that gradually rise on each side are covered with good pasture; the steepest of them grow serviceable Timber, namely Stringy Bark, which is a Tree most used in this part of the World.

Monday, 15th.—Lost the Horses; they were tied together, but not secured in a proper manner; the Men were in search of them, but returned without success late in the day. I then went myself, and had the good fortune to come upon their track; at length discovered them fast round a Tree in Princess Charlotte Valley; the walk afforded me an opportunity of seeing a part that was before obscured from sight by the Woods in travelling along the Ridge.

Tuesday, 16th.—The first half hour's Chaining was tolerably

25

good; but, for six Miles afterwards, it was extremely fatiguing
along a Rocky and Bushy Ridge, which led me to the Centre of
the three hills, I shewed you in our long Ride and which I have
named *"Mount Macquarie"*; the three range in a direct line,
bearing N.W. and S.E.; that to the S.E. measuring ¾ of a Mile
from Mount Macquarie, I call *"Maclaine's Peak"*; the N.W. one
is separated from the others by a small Gully, and at a distance
of about 2 Miles from Mount Macquarie, I have named "Antill's
Peak"; they are most remarkable and conspicuous hills; I see
no other in any direction of their shape; from these lofty eminences, I had a clear and perfect View of the Country. The S.W.,
West and N.W. is a series of high Mountainous hills, their tops
shewing themselves at a great distance; in the direction of E.
20° S., about 15 Miles is a fine looking Country; there are plains,
I suppose it, towards the head of Campbell River, as I can trace
it down some distance; it continues round to S.E. If I cannot
do better, or see a more satisfactory prospect Westward to-
morrow, I shall travel South for 10 or 12 Miles, where, from
present appearances, I think I may be able to wind round some
hills again to the West; the hill at the end of my last journey
is W. 12° N. about 14 Miles. I was convinced, when there, I
could not make further in a S.W. line, all my dependance is in
getting South about; I halted at some Water holes running
N.E.; they empty themselves into the River by way of Queen
Charlotte Vale.

Friday, 19th.—After a Mile and half, finding the Valley bend
off East of South, I followed a ridge; in the space of two Miles,
I had asscended a very high Conical hill; the sight from it quite
astonished me; the whole Country I suppose from 30 to 40
Miles from S.E. to S.W. is covered with Conic hills, which are
lost to me in distant Mountains. I took a Man to examine a few
Miles, and found that between each Chain of these pointed hills
are ponds; in one of the Gullies is a small stream; with much
difficulty I travelled down it to a Main one from the S.E.; to
climb up the hills we were obliged to crawl upon our hands and
knees: the whole of them are thinly wooded with small Crooked
Gums and covered with good Grass; but the sharp Rocks render
travelling disagreeable and bad. I went among them, so far as
to convince me that the principal Stream runs through a break,
bearing near West; the last two Miles Chaining took me close
upon three hours, nor could the Horses travel faster from sliping
about; besides this is not half the difficulties, that appears before
us, which I unavoidably experienced to make myself certain of

the direction the Stream led. *Appledore* and myself returned much fatigued, I never was more so in my life; from a sudden slip in climbing the hills, I am quite unwell with a pain in my left side; I thought it would be labour in vain to penetrate into a Country, where I could not see a possibility for a Road to be made, or Horses to travel with loads in safety.

Monday, 22nd.—I took a W. 20° S. direction through a fine Grazing Country, most part a thick Forest of various description of good grown timber; at five Miles is a Valley, which bears down West. A remarkable round top'd high hill is now North of me, about 4 Miles, I have taken the liberty to name it *"Mount Lachlan."*

Tuesday, 23rd.—There are hills a-head. I thought a West Course would avoid them, but found I was necessitated to asscend, and the Ridge led me onward for Four Miles, when a prospect appear'd at which I was highly gratified. I never saw a more pleasing Country. I cannot express the pleasure, I feel, in going forward; the hills we have passed are excellent land, well wooded; to the South distant objects are obscured by high hills; in the S.W. are very distant Mountains; under them appear a Mist as tho' rising over a River; it has the like look round to West; but, beyond, the loom of low hills are very faintly distinguished; in the N.W. are high distant Mountains; one with a flat top bearing N. 70° W., I name "Jamison's Table Mountain." The intermediate space is a grassy Country, thinly wooded; there are hills and dales; between some, appear Valleys clear of Timber; at a great distance is a remarkable Peaked hill standing alone, as it were, in the Centre of an immense flat Country. Finding a Valley with ponds led near N.W., my anxiety obliges me to deviate from the intended course to follow them; at a Mile and half is a clear hill on my right hand, which I have named "Mount Molle," and the fine Valley under it "Redfern Valley"; the end of Four Miles ponds form a junction from an E. 20° S. point down a spacious flat, I have called it "Meehan Valley." I then travel near West; at about a Mile other Ponds join the Main ones from the N.E., and at the end of to-day's journey they have almost the appearance of a River; there is no perceptible Stream, but some of the ponds are a ¼ and ½ a Mile long.

Wednesday, 24th.—My Course was West for three Miles; it led me to the top of an high hill; the Water shewed itself about ½ Mile North of me; on the South is an extensive flat; from the hill I travelled W. 20° S. two Miles; at one and half, I crossed a small Creek coming from the South leading to the Ponds; I then went on again West for 5½ Miles, which brought me on a second hill; in following it down, I was rather North of West for upwards of a Mile, and there found a Creek bearing up South; I resolved on tracing it, which I did for three Miles North; here the points of the hills end in perpendicular heads 30 or 40 feet high, which is pure Lime Stone of a Misty Grey Colour; this Creek joins the bed of a River, rising in a N. 30° E. direction, now dry except in hollow places; it is full 70 ft. wide, having a pebbly bottom; on each side grow large swamp Oaks; I travelled down in the bed of it ¾ of a Mile near West, and halted greatly fatigued. The open Country and falling on the Water courses encouraged me so much that I made every exertion to push forward, besides being full of anxiety hoping soon to reach a River of some consequence. Every steep hill, between the Lime Rocks and Bathurst, may be avoided except two, and they are not worse than that at the Fish River. An handsomer and finer Country I never saw than what I have been over these last two Days; greatest part of the Land is good; Timber is its worst production; Kangaroos Emu and Wild Ducks are very numerous.

Thursday, 25th.—The Lime Cliffs having the appearance of being very steep down the run, I thought it prudent to let the Horses have a day's rest; in the mean time I took Appledore with me to examine the Country; large Ponds of Water are now in the River Bed; they connect with each other by a small stream that I distinctly see to rise up between the Stones; its general course is W. 15° N. I walked down about Five Miles; it was impossible to proceed further as perpendicular Cliffs of Slate Rock prevents me; with much difficulty I got so far. The Stream is now equal to Macquarie River. On leaving the Water, I made for the high Peak, which bore S. 40° E. about three Miles; it was a fatiguing matter to reach the top and feel happy I did so, as it convinced me I could not go on in a West direction, as I should be impeded by high head lands and Gullies. I named the Peak "Mount Lewin."

Sunday, 28th.—Being determined to see the Plains, I started at day break with a Man; in the space of an hour, we arrived on one this side of the River; it reached about a Mile, and is at least 1½ deep. I suppose I went up the River six Miles; the Plains are alternately on each, and nearly the same size; opposite to the Plains are Woodlands, and appeared to continue so for a great distance S. 30° W.; the River comes from about that point, and to the best of my Judgment the Stream empties into it that I mention on the 19th Instant; the Soil on the plains is very rich, and the woodlands are equally so; when about to return we saw a number of Natives; on making towards them, they run from us; all that I could do had no avail in having communication with them; it was past One O'Clock when we got back, and I was too fatigued to go down the River any distance, therefore remained to wash and clean ourselves; I have named the Plains "Oxley's Plains."

Wednesday, 31st.—The River took the direction I supposed N.W.; points of Rocky hills, every Mile or Mile and half, lead down to it; the flats continue rich Soil; on the S.W. side are no hills, but a continued space of level Rich Land, thinly wooded, except near the Water's edge, where the timber is good and very large; they are what is called Black Butted Gums; some of them are 8 and 10 feet in diamiter. We see Natives two or three times a day; I believe we are a great terror to them; a Woman with a young Child fell in our way this afternoon, to whom I gave a Tomahawk and other trifles; she was glad to depart; soon after we suddenly came upon a Man, who was much frightened; he run up a Tree in a moment, carrying with him his Spear and Crooked throwing Stick; he hallowed and cryed out so much and loud, that he might have been heard half a Mile; it was useless entreating him to come down, therefore stuck a Tomahawk in the Tree, and left him; the more I spoke, the more he cryed out. 7 Miles.

Thursday, 1st June, 1815.—The River to-day is near West, and am clear of the points of hills; the Country is good indeed; these fine flats are flooded; there are rising Lands clear of it as I before stated, but no hill that will afford a prospect; to-morrow I am necessitated to return, and shall asscend a very high hill, I left on my right Hand early this Morning. I could leave no mark here more than cutting Trees; on one situated in an Angle of the River and a wet Creek, bearing up North, I have deeply carved "Evans 1st June 1815." The Country continues good, and better than ever I expected to discover.

Friday, 2nd June.—In travelling back, I left the River; at about a Mile from it, the Land is not so Rich; the Soil changed to red loom, as deep colour'd as a burnt Brick, wherein the Grass is poor and the Box Trees small. I am glad to observe that the deficiency is made up by useful Pine Trees from one Inch to three feet in Diamiter, as straight as Arrows, some of them at least 40 feet high before the Branches begin to shoot out;

those, growing on what I term Pine hills, are stinted; the trunks of them rise but a few feet from the Ground before their Branches spread, which I think may be accounted for by those hills being chiefly a Mass of Granite Rock. I asscended the Height; no Country can possibly have a more interesting aspect; so much so that, if a further trace into the interior is required at a future period, I respectfully beg leave to offer myself for the Service. I see no end of travelling. I am deficient in abilities to describe it properly, but shall endeavour to do so by compareing the Country to an Ocean, as it is nearly level, with the Horizon from N.W. to S.W.; small Hillocks are seen at great distance of a pale Blue, shewing as Land appears when first discovered at Sea; Spaces clear of Trees may be imagined Islands, and the Natives Smokes, rising in various points, vessels; it is a clear calm Evening near Sunsetting, which shewed every part advantageously. The River I can distinctly discover to continue near due West, and rest confident that, when it is full, Boats may go down it in safety; my meaning of being full is its general height in moderate Seasons, which the banks shew, about Five feet above the present level; it would then carry Boats over Trees and Narrows that now obstruct the Passage; no doubt the Stream connects with Macquarie or some other River further West; the Channel then sure is of great magnitude; I should think so to carry off the body of Water that must in time of Floods cover these very extensive flats.

Monday, 5th June.—Left the River, which I have now called *"The River Lachlan."* The Rain has fallen very heavy; we were completely wàshed up last Night; it extinguished our Fire, which made us still more uncomfortable, besides damaging my papers. I am fearful we shall experience the like this Evening, but have taken every precaution to prevent it.

Tuesday, 6th June.—We reached Lime Stone Creek; the descent was not down so bad a hill as I expected; I cutt off about 6 Miles, and find abundance of Lime Stone more convenient upwards without going down the Creek at all, by which means a difficult road is avoided; there is also good Water and fine bottoms of Land, containing in each from 5 to 10 Acres, surrounded with Lime Stone Rocks; This is a fine Grazing Country with plenty of Wood.

Wednesday, 7th June.—The ascent from Lime Stone Creek is the steepest part in my way; I examined it particularly, and do not think it near so bad as the Fish River hill. I left the height, mentioned on the 24th Ulto., about a Mile North of me, and crossed the flat then spoken of, which is very extensive; it bears up South for some distance, then bends to the East and S.E. The Soil is Rich, and well watered by large Ponds; I have named this place "Warwick Plains."

Monday, 12th June.—Arrived at Bathurst, having experienced for these last six days extremely cold uncomfortable Weather, with Misty rain. My journal is short; but have endeavoured to state every thing, as it actually is, in as plain and correct a manner as I am capable of doing, that it should be clearly understood by any person, who may hereafter follow my Track.

V. OXLEY'S EXPLORATION OF THE LACHLAN

[JOHN OXLEY's exploration of the Lachlan in 1817, and of
the Macquarie in 1818, revealed for the first time the peculiar
character of the inland rivers, and furnished a more detailed
account of the territory between the rivers than had hitherto
been available. Oxley was greatly puzzled, and in submitting
his first narrative to the public, expressed himself as doubtful
whether Australia, with a surface nearly as extensive as Europe,
possessed rivers which terminated in interior seas, or whether
they made their way to estuaries on the coast. It did not occur
to him that these rivers were part of a great riparian system,
that of the Murray–Darling watershed. This narrative is taken
from the *Journals of Two Expeditions into the Interior of New
South Wales*, by Oxley, published at London, 1820.]

On the twenty-fourth of March, 1817, I received the instructions of his excellency the Governor to take charge of the
expedition which had been fitted out for the purpose of ascertaining the course of the Lachlan River, and generally to prosecute the examination of the western interior of New South
Wales.

On the sixth of April I quitted Sydney, and after a pleasant
journey arrived at Bathurst on the fourteenth, and found that
our provisions and other necessary stores were in readiness at
the depot on the Lachlan River. We were detained at Bathurst
by rainy unfavourable weather until the nineteenth, when the
morning proving fine, the *bât* horses, with the remainder of the
provisions, baggage, and instruments, were sent off, we intending
to follow them the ensuing morning.

Bathurst had assumed a very different appearance since I first
visited it in the suite of his excellency the Governor in 1815.
The industrious hand of man had been busy in improving the
beautiful works of nature; a good substantial house for the
superintendant had been erected, the government grounds fenced
in, and the stackyards showed that the abundant produce of the
last harvest had amply repaid the labour bestowed on its culture.
The fine healthy appearance of the flocks and herds was a con-

JOHN OXLEY.

From a signed portrait in the possession of Mrs. Oxley.

vincing proof how admirably adapted these extensive downs and thinly wooded hills are for grazing, more particularly of sheep. The mind dwelt with pleasure on the idea that at no very distant period these secluded plains would be covered with flocks bearing the richest fleeces, and contribute in no small degree to the prosperity of the eastern settlements.

The soil, in the immediate neighbourhood of Bathurst, is for the first six inches of a light, black, vegetable mould, lying on a stratum of sand, about eighteen inches deep, but of a poor description, and mixed with small stones, under which is a strong clay. The surface of the hills is covered with small gravel, the soil light and sandy, with a sub-soil of clay. The low flats on the immediate borders of the river are evidently formed by washings from the hills and valleys deposited by floods, and the overflowings of the water-courses.

Sunday, April 20.—Proceeded on our journey towards the Lachlan River. At two o'clock we arrived at the head of Queen Charlotte's Valley, passing through a fine open grazing country; the soil on the hills and in the vale a light clayey loam, occasionally intermixed with sand and gravel: the late rains had rendered the ground soft and boggy. The trees were small and stunted, and thinly scattered over the hills, which frequently closed in stony points on the valley. The rocks a coarse granite.

April 25.—Our course for the first seven or eight miles was through a level open country, the soil and grass indifferently good. We now ascended a hill a little to the left of the road, for the purpose of viewing the country through which the river ran: it appeared a perfect plain encompassed by moderately high hills, except in the south-east and west quarters, these being apparently the points whence and to which the river flows. The whole country a forest of eucalypti, with occasionally on the banks of the river a space clear of timber: there was nothing either grand or interesting in the view from this hill, neither did I see in any direction such high land as might be expected to give source to a river of magnitude. When we quitted the hill, we went west, to make the Lachlan River, passing for nearly six miles over a perfect level, the land poor, and in places scrubby. At two o'clock saw the river, which certainly did not disappoint me: it was evidently much higher than usual, running a strong stream; the banks were steep, but not so as to render the water inaccessible; the land on each side quite flat, and thinly clothed with small trees; the soil a rich light loam: higher points occasionally projected on the river, and on those the soil was by no

I. D.   *f* means so good. The largest trees were growing immediately at the water's edge on both sides, and from their position formed an arch over the river, obscuring it from observation, although it was from thirty to forty yards across. At four o'clock we arrived at the depot.

We had scarcely alighted from our horses, when natives were seen in considerable numbers on the other side of the river. I went down opposite to them, and after some little persuasion about twenty of them swam across, having their galengar or stone hatchet in one hand, which on their landing they threw at our feet, to show us that they were as much divested of arms as ourselves. After staying a short time they were presented with some kangaroo flesh, with which they re-crossed the river, and kindled their fires. They were very stout and manly, well featured, with long beards: there were a few cloaks among them made of the opossum skin, and it was evident that some of the party had been at Bathurst, from their making use of several English words, and from their readily comprehending many of our questions.

April 26.—Fine clear warm weather. The natives were still on the opposite bank, and five of them came over to us in the course of the morning; but remained a very short time. During the last night a few fine shrimps were caught; the soldiers stationed at the depot said they had frequently taken them in considerable numbers. During the day arranged the loads for the boats and horses, that they might be enabled to set off early the next morning.

April 27.—Loaded the boats with as much of the salt provisions as they could safely carry, and despatched them to wait at the first creek about seven or eight miles down the river until the loaded horses came, and then to assist in taking their loads over the creek; intending myself to follow with the remainder of the baggage early to-morrow morning.

April 29.—Proceeded on our journey down the river, directing the boats to stop at the creek which terminated Mr. Evans's former journey. The country through which we passed this day in every respect resembles the tracts we have already gone over. The crowns and ridges of the hills are uniformly stony and barren, ending as before alternately on each side of the river; the greater proportion of good flat land lies on the south side of the river; there are however very rich and fertile tracts on this side. After riding about eight miles, we ascended a considerable hill upon our right, from the top of which we could see to a considerable distance; between the south-west and north north-west, a very low level tract lay west of us, and no hill whatever bounded the view in that quarter. Three remarkable hummocks bore respectively S. 72 W., S. 51½ W. and S. 34½ W., within which range of bearing the country was uniformly level, or rising into such low hills as not to be distinguished from the general surface. The tops of distant ranges could be discerned over low hills in the north-west, whilst, from north by the east to south, the country was broken into hill and valley. The whole of this extensive scene was covered with eucalypti, whilst on the rocky summits of the hills in the immediate neighbourhood a species of callitris was eminently distinguished. From this extensive view I named the hill Mount Prospect.

At five o'clock in the afternoon we arrived at the place where the horses had been directed to wait for the boats, but they had not arrived; the distance is at least doubled by following the immediate course of the stream, but I had calculated that its rapidity would make up for the distance, and enable the boats to keep pace with the horses.

At six o'clock the boats arrived safe, the men having had a very fatiguing row, and been obliged to clear the passage of fallen trees, and other obstructions; so that we determined to give them some repose, and halt here for the night. At half past eight o'clock proceeded down the river, intending to stop at the termination of Mr. Evans's journey in 1815, about five miles further, for the purpose of repairing the small boat, which had sustained some slight damage in coming down the river yesterday. I rode about three miles back into the country; the cupressus was here more frequent, though not of large growth; the soil is not good. In returning to the river we came upon the creek which terminated Mr. Evans's journey, down which we travelled until we came to the river, about half a mile from which is a large shallow lagoon, full of ducks, bustards, black swans, and red-bills. At twelve o'clock the horses arrived at the mouth of the creek, and the boats half an hour afterwards. The banks of the creek were very steep, and it was three o'clock before all the provisions were got over. The creek was named Byrne's Creek, after one of the present party, who had accompanied Mr. Evans in his former journey.

May 1.—The creek fell upwards of a foot during the night, by which some of the articles in the large boat received damage. Commenced the survey of the river from this point. The flats on both sides the river were very extensive, and in general good;

the same timber and grass as usual; the stream was from thirty to forty yards broad on an average.

May 2.—Our journey this day was very fatiguing, the grass being nearly breast high, thick, and entangled. The soil is tolerably good within a mile and a half of the banks: I rode five or six miles out, in hopes of finding some eminence on which to ascend, but was disappointed, the country continuing a dead level, with extensive swamps, and barren brushes.

May 3.—Proceeded down the river. We passed over a very barren desolate country, perfectly level, without even the slightest eminence, covered with dwarf box-trees and scrubby bushes; towards the latter part of the day a few small cypresses were seen. I think the other side of the river is much the same. We have hitherto met with no water except at the river, and a few shallow lagoons, which are evidently dry in summer. I do not know how far this level extends north and south, but I cannot estimate it at less than from ten to twelve miles on each side; but this is mere conjecture, since for the last three days I have been unable to see beyond a mile: I have, however, occasionally made excursions of five or six miles, and never perceived any difference in the elevation of the country.

May 4.—As soon as it was light I sent two men up the river to search for the boat: at nine o'clock one of them returned, having found it about four miles back. It appeared that the large boat had got stoved against a tree under water, and that the people were obliged to unload and haul her on shore to undergo some repairs, which they had effected; but the rain prevented them from paying her bottom. They expected to be able to proceed in an hour or two, as the weather had begun to clear up. It was fortunate that no damage had befallen any part of the boat's lading. At twelve proceeded about three quarters of a mile down the river, and from a small eminence half a mile north of it, an extensive tract of clear country was seen, bearing N. 50 W., about two or three miles from us, having a low range of hills bounding them in the direction of S. 65 W. and N. 65 E. The river wound immediately under the hill, taking a westerly direction as far as I went, which was about three miles; its windings were very sudden, and its width and depth much the same as before.

May 5.—Proceeded down the river, ascended the eminence mentioned yesterday, and from the top of a cypress tree a very distant view of the whole country was obtained. The country was in general poor, with partial tracts of better ground; the hills were slaty, and covered as well as the levels with small eucalypti, cypresses, and camarinas. About a mile from this place we fell in with a small tribe of natives, consisting of eight men; their women we did not see. They did not appear any way alarmed at the sight of us, but came boldly up: they were covered with cloaks made of opossum skins; their faces daubed with a red and yellow pigment, with neatly worked nets bound round their hair: the front tooth in the upper row was wanting in them all: they were unarmed, having nothing with them but their stone hatchets. It appeared from their conduct that they had either seen or heard of white people before, and were anxious to depart, accompanying the motion of going with a wave of their hand.

About three miles from our last night's halting-place we had to cross a small creek, the banks of which were so steep that we were obliged to unload the horses. I rode up the creek about three quarters of a mile, and came upon those extensive plains before-mentioned; the soil of this level appears a good loamy clay, but in some places very wet: it was far too extensive to permit us to traverse much of it; we saw sufficient to judge that the whole surface was similar to that we examined; it was covered with a great variety of new plants, and its margin encircled by a new species of acacia, which received the specific name of *pendula*, from its resembling in habit the weeping willow. Low hills to the north bounded this plain, whilst a slip of barren land, covered with small trees and shrubs, lay between it and the river.

It appeared to me that the whole of these flats are occasionally overflowed by the river, the water of which is forced up the creek before-mentioned, and which again acts as a drain on the fall of the water.

At four o'clock we halted for the evening, after a fatiguing day's journey; the boats were obliged to cut their passage three or four times, and the whole navigation was difficult and dangerous: the current ran with much rapidity, and the channel seemed rather to contract than widen. We were obliged to stop on a very barren desolate spot, with little grass for the horses; but further on the country appeared even worse. The south bank of the river (as far as I could judge) is precisely similar to that which we are travelling down. The clear levels examined to-day were named the Solway Flats. Many fish were caught here, one of which weighed upwards of thirty pounds.

May 6.—Proceeded down the river. It is impossible to fancy a worse country than the one we were now travelling over, intersected by swamps and small lagoons in every direction; the soil a poor clay, and covered with stunted useless timber. It was excessively fatiguing to the horses which travelled along the banks of the river, as the rubus and bromus were so thickly intermingled, that they could scarcely force a passage. After proceeding about eight miles, a bold rocky mount terminated on the river, and broke the sameness which had so long wearied us: we ascended this hill, which I named Mount Amyot, and from the summit had one of the most extensive views that can be imagined. On the opposite side of the river was another hill precisely similar to Mount Amyot, leaving a passage between them for the river, and the immense tract of level country to the eastward; this hill was named Mount Stuart. Vast plains clear of timber lay on the south side of the river, and which, from our having travelled on a level with them, it was impossible for us to distinguish before. These plains I named Hamilton's Plains, and they were bounded by hills of considerable elevation to the southward; whilst the whole level country thus bounded was honoured with the designation of Princess Charlotte's Crescent.

To the west of Mount Amyot the view was equally extensive, being bounded only by the horizon; some high detached hills, rising like islands from the ocean, broke, in some measure, the sameness of the prospect. I estimated that in the west northwest I could see at least forty miles, and in the south south-west as far; the view in other points being slightly interrupted by low ranges of hills, rising occasionally to points of considerable elevation: none of those elevated spots was nearer than twenty-five or thirty miles, and considerable spaces of clear ground could, by the assistance of the telescope, be distinguished, interspersed amidst the ocean of trees whence those hills arise: a long broken mountain, bearing W. 32½ N., was named Mount Melville; one W. 24 N. Mount Cunningham; and another, bearing S. 70 W. Mount Maude. Smoke, arising from the fires of the wandering inhabitants of these desolate regions, was seen in several quarters. At four o'clock we stopped for the evening, about three miles west of Mount Amyot.

I have reason to believe that the whole of the extensive tract named Princess Charlotte's Crescent is at times drowned by the overflowing of the river; the marks of flood were observed in every direction, and the waters in the marshes and lagoons were all traced as being derived from the river. During a course of upwards of seventy miles not a single running stream emptied itself into the river on either side; and I am forced to conclude that in common seasons this whole tract is extremely badly watered, and that it derives its principal if not only supply from the river within the bounding ranges of Princess Charlotte's Crescent. There are doubtless many small eminences which might afford a retreat from the inundations, but those which were observed by us were too trifling and distant from each other to stand out distinct from the vast level surface which the crescent presents to the view. The soil of the country we passed over was a poor and cold clay; but there are many rich levels which, could they be drained and defended from the inundations of the river, would amply repay the cultivation. These flats are certainly not adapted for cattle; the grass is too swampy, and the bushes, swamps, and lagoons, are too thickly intermingled with the better portions to render it either a safe or desirable grazing country. The timber is universally bad and small; a few large misshapen gum trees on the immediate banks of the river may be considered as exceptions. If however the country itself is poor, the river is rich in the most excellent fish, procurable in the utmost abundance. One man in less than an hour caught eighteen large fish, one of which was a curiosity from its immense size, and the beauty of its colours. In shape and general form it most resembled a cod, but was speckled over with brown, blue, and yellow spots, like a leopard's skin; its gills and belly a clear white, the tail and fins a dark brown. It weighed entire seventy pounds, and without the entrails sixty-six pounds: it is somewhat singular that in none of these fish is any thing found in the stomach, except occasionally a shrimp or two.

May 8.—Proceeded down the river. Our general course was westerly, and the country, though equally level with any we had passed, improved in the quality of the soil, which, during the greater part of to-day's route, was a good vegetable mould, the land thickly covered with small acacia and dwarf trees. The banks of the river were, I think, much lower, not exceeding fifteen or twenty feet high, and they were rather clearer of timber than before. The camarina, which used to line the banks, was now seldom seen, the acacia pendula seeming to take its place. We stopped for the night on a plain of good land, flooded, but clear of timber: large flocks of emus were feeding on it, and we were fortunate enough to kill a very large one after a fine chase.

May 9.—The country we passed through during this day's route was extremely low, consisting of extensive plains divided by lines of small trees: the banks of the river, and the deep bights formed by the irregularity of its course, were covered with acacia bushes and dwarf trees. The river, at the spot where we stopped, wound along the edge of an extensive low plain, being at least six miles long and three or four broad; these I called Field's Plains, after the judge of the supreme court of this territory; they are the same which we saw from the top of Mount Amyot.

May 10.—The horses having strayed in the night, and it being nearly noon before they were found, I determined to make this a halting day. These plains are much more extensive than I supposed yesterday, and many new plants were found on them. The river rose upwards of a foot during the night, and still continues to rise; a circumstance which appears very singular to me, there having been no rains of any magnitude for the last five weeks, and none at all for the last ten days. We are also certain that no waters fall into it or join it easterly for nearly one hundred and fifty miles. This rise must therefore be occasioned by heavy rains in the mountains, whence the river derives its source; but it is not the less singular, that during its whole course, as far as it is hitherto known, it does not receive a single tributary stream. Observed the latitude 33. 16. 33. S.

May 11.—The river rose about four feet during the night, and still continues to rise. Set forward on our journey down the river. About four miles and a half from this morning's station, the river began to wash the immediate edge of the plain, and so continued to do all along. My astonishment was extreme at finding the banks of the river not more than six feet from the water: it at once confirmed my supposition that the whole of this extensive country is frequently inundated; the river was here about thirty yards broad. The soil of these extensive plains is for the most part extremely rich, as indeed might be expected, from the deposition of the quantities of vegetable matter that must take place in periods of flood.

May 12.—The fine weather still continues to favour us. The river rose in the course of the night upwards of a foot. It is a probable supposition that the natives, warned by experience of these dangerous flats, rather choose to seek a more precarious, but more safe subsistence in the mountainous and rocky ridges which are occasionally to be met with. The river and lagoons abound with fish and fowl, and it is scarcely reasonable to suppose that the natives would not avail themselves of such store of food, if the danger of procuring it did not counterbalance the advantages they might otherwise derive from such abundance. About three quarters of a mile farther westward we had to cross another small arm of the river, running to the northward, which although now full, is, I should think, dry when the river is at its usual level. It is probable that this and the one which we first crossed join each other a few miles farther to the westward, and then both united fall into the stream which gave them existence. We had scarcely proceeded a mile from the last branch, before it became evident that it would be impossible to advance farther in the direction in which we were travelling. The stream here overflowed both banks, and its course was lost among marshes: its channel not being distinguishable from the surrounding waters.

Observing an eminence about half a mile from the south side, we crossed over the horses and baggage at a place where the water was level with the banks, and which when within its usual channel did not exceed thirty or forty feet in width, its depth even now being only twelve feet.

We ascended the hill, and had the mortification to perceive the termination of our research, at least down this branch of the river: the whole country from the west north-west round to north was either a complete marsh or lay under water, and this for a distance of twenty-five or thirty miles, in those directions; to the south and south-west the country appeared more elevated, but low marshy grounds lay between us and it, which rendered it impossible for us to proceed thither from our present situation. I therefore determined to return back to the place where the two branches of the principal river separated, and follow the south-west branch as far as it should be navigable; our fears were however stronger than our hopes, lest it would end in a similar manner to the one we had already traced, until it became no longer navigable for boats.

In pursuance of this intention we descended the hill, which was named Farewell Hill, from its being the termination of our journey in a north-west direction at least for the present, and proceeded up the south bank of the stream. We were able to reach only a short distance from the spot where we stopped last night, having been obliged to unload the horses no less than four times in the course of the day, added to which, the travelling loaded through those dreadful marshes had completely exhausted them: my own horse, in searching for a better track, was nearly lost, and it consumed four hours to advance scarcely half a mile.

My disappointment at the interruption of our labours in this quarter was extreme, and what was worse, no flattering prospect appeared of our succeeding better in the examination of the south-west branch. I was however determined to see the present end of the river in all its branches, before I should finally quit it, in furtherance of the other objects of the expedition.

May 13.—Returned to the point whence the river separates into two branches; intending. first to descend the south-west branch for some distance before the boats and baggage should move down, being unwilling the horses should undergo an use-less fatigue in traversing such marshy ground, unless the branch should prove of sufficient magnitude to take us a considerable distance; conceiving it an object of the first importance that the horses should start fresh, if I should find it necessary to quit the river at this point of the coast.

May 14.—My present intention is to take a south-west direction for Cape Northumberland, since should any river be formed from those marshes, which is extremely probable, and fall into the sea between Spencer's Gulf and Cape Otway, this course will intersect it, and no river or stream can arise from these swamps without being discovered. The body of water now running in both the principal branches is very considerable, fully sufficient to have constituted a river of magnitude, if it had constantly maintained such a supply of water, and had not become separated into branches, and lost among the immense marshes of this desolate and barren country, which seems here to form a vast concavity to receive them. It is impossible to arrive at any certain opinion as to what finally becomes of these waters, but I think it probable, from the appearance of the country, and its being nearly on a level with the sea, that they are partly absorbed by the soil, and the remainder lost by evaporation.

May 18.—At nine o'clock we commenced our journey towards the coast; at three stopped within four miles of Mount Maude, on a dry creek, with occasional pools of very indifferent water. The country through which we passed from the branch was for the first three miles very low and wet, with large lagoons of water. During the latter part of the journey the country was more elevated though still level, the soil light and rotten, and overrun with the acacia pendula. The horses being very heavily laden fell repeatedly during the early part of the day. Our course was nearly south-west, and we performed about ten miles.

June 14.—Fine clear weather. Proceeded on our journey northwards: the first four or five miles was over a rocky broken country, consisting of low hills, rising westerly of Peel's range.

After going about six miles and a half the country became more open and less rocky; as the grass was here better than at our last night's halting-place, and the water convenient and tolerable, we resolved upon stopping, particularly as I intended resting the horses to-morrow; and I was fearful if I proceeded farther I might meet with neither, and thus be obliged to continue travelling to-morrow; an exertion which the horses were not in a condition to make. Nothing can be more irksome than the tedious days' journeys we are obliged to make through a country in which there is not the smallest variety, each day's occurrences and scenes being but a recapitulation of the former: our patience would frequently be exhausted, were we not daily reanimating ourselves with the hopes that the morrow will bring us to a better country, and render a journey, the labour of which has hitherto been ill repaid, of some service to the colony, and of some satisfaction to the expectations which had been formed of its result.

June 23.—After going about eight miles and a quarter, we suddenly came upon the banks of the river; I call it the river, for it could certainly be no other than the Lachlan, which we had quitted nearly five weeks before. Our astonishment was extreme, since it was an incident little expected by any one. It was here extremely diminished in size, but was still nearly equal in magnitude to the south-west branch which we last quitted. The banks were about twelve or fourteen feet above the water, and it was running with a tolerably brisk stream to the westward. The banks were so thickly covered with large eucalypti, that we did not perceive it until we were within a very few yards of it; it appeared about thirty feet broad, running over a sandy bottom. I think it extremely probable that the waters of both the main branches, after losing a very considerable portion over the low grounds in the neighbourhood of Mount Cunningham and Field's Plains, have again united and formed the present stream.

Our future course did not admit of any hesitation, and it was resolved to go down the stream as long as there was a chance of its becoming more considerable, and until our provisions should be so far expended as barely to enable us to return to Bathurst.

It is a singular phenomenon in the history of this river, that, in a course of upwards of two hundred and fifty miles, in a direct line from where Mr. Evans first discovered it, not the smallest rivulet, or, in fact, water of any description, falls into it from either the north or south; with the exception of the two small occasional streams near the depot, which flow from the north.

June 30.—The first two or three miles were somewhat harder travelling than the greater part of yesterday. Immense plains extended to the westward, as far as the eye could reach. These plains were entirely barren, being evidently in times of rain altogether under water, when they doubtless form one vast lake: they extended in places from three to six miles from the margin of the stream, which on its immediate borders was a wet bog, full of small water holes, and the surface covered with marsh plants, with a few straggling dwarf box-trees. It was only on the very edge of the bank, and in the bottoms of the bights, that any eucalypti grew; the plains were covered with nothing but gnaphalium: the soil various, in some places red tenacious clay, in others a dark hazel-coloured loam, so rotten and full of holes that it was with difficulty the horses could travel over them. Although those plains were bounded only by the horizon, not a semblance of a hill appeared in the distance; we seemed indeed to have taken a long farewell of every thing like an elevation, whence the surrounding country could be observed. To the southward, bounding those plains in that direction, barren shrubs and dwarf box-trees, with numberless holes of stagnant water, too clearly proclaimed the nature of the country in that quarter. We could see through the openings of the trees on the river that plains of similar extent occupied the other side, which has all along appeared to us to be (if any thing) the lower ground. We travelled in the centre of the plains, our medium distance from the river being from one to two miles; and although we did not go above thirteen miles, some of the horses were excessively distressed from the nature of the ground.

There was not the least appearance of natives; nor was bird or animal of any description seen during the day, except a solitary native dog. Nothing can be more melancholy and irksome than travelling over wilds, which nature seems to have condemned to perpetual loneliness and desolation. We seemed indeed the sole living creatures in those vast deserts.

The plains last travelled over were named Molle's Plains, after the late lieutenant-governor of the territory; and those on the opposite side, Baird's Plains, after the general to whom he once acted as aide-de-camp, and whose glory he shared. The naming of places was often the only pleasure within our reach; but it was some relief from the desolation of these plains and hills to throw over them the associations of names dear to friendship, or sacred to genius.

July 5.—Our route lay over the same unvarying plain surface as on the preceding days, and after travelling about five miles, we again saw the line of trees growing on the banks of the stream; and having performed about ten miles more, we halted on the immediate banks of it. These were considerably lower, being about six feet above the water; the current was almost imperceptible, and the depth did not exceed four feet, and was extremely muddy; the trees growing on the banks were neither so large nor so numerous as before, and a new species of eucalyptus prevailed over the old blue gum. The north-east side was precisely of the same description of country as the south-east. A very large sheet of water or lake lay on the north-west side, opposite to the place where we made the river. The horizon was clear and distinct round the whole circle, the line of trees on the river alone excepted. From the marks of these trees, the waters appear to rise about three feet above the level of the bank; a height more than sufficient to inundate the whole country. This stream is certainly in the summer season, or in the long absence of rain, nothing more than a mere chain of ponds, serving as a channel to convey the waters from the eastward over this low tract. It is certain that no waters join this river from its source to this point; and passing, as it does, for the most part, through a line of country so low as to be frequently overflowed, and to an extent north and south perfectly unknown, but certainly at this place exceeding forty miles, it must cause the country to remain for ever uninhabitable, and useless for all the purposes of civilized man.

These considerations, added to the state of our provisions, of which, at the reduced ration of three pounds of flour per man per week, we had but ten weeks remaining, determined me to proceed no farther westward with the main part of the expedition; but as the state of the greater part of our horses was such as absolutely to require some days' rest and refreshment, before we attempted to return eastward, I considered that it would be acting best up to the spirit of my instructions to proceed forward myself with three men and horses, and as we should carry nothing with us but our provisions, we should be enabled to proceed with so much expedition, as to go as far and see as much in three days as would take the whole party at least seven to perform.

My object in thus proceeding farther was to get so far to the westward as to place beyond all question the impossibility of a river falling into the sea between Cape Otway and Cape Bernouilli. In my opinion, the very nature of the country altogether precludes such a possibility, but I think my proceeding so far will be conclusive with those who have most strongly imbibed the conviction that a river enters the sea between the Capes in question, which was certainly an idea I had also entertained, and which nothing but the survey of a country, without either hills or permanent streams, could have destroyed.

I must observe as a remarkable feature in this singular country, that for the last fifty miles we have not seen a stone or pebble of any kind, save two, and they were taken out of the maws of two emus. I am now firmly persuaded that there are no eminent grounds in this part of the country, until these low sandy hills which bound the south-western coast-line are reached; and these, in my judgment are the only barriers which prevent the ocean from extending its empire over a country which was probably once under its dominion.

July 7.—At eight o'clock, taking with me three men, I proceeded to follow the course of the stream; I attempted in the first instance to keep away from the banks, but was soon obliged to join them, as the morasses extended outwards and intersected my proposed course in almost every direction. About three miles and a half from the tent, a large arm extended from the north bank to a considerable distance on that side; the banks continually getting lower, and before we had gone six miles it was evident that the channel of the stream was only the bed of a lagoon, the current now being imperceptible, with small gum trees growing in the middle. Three miles farther the morasses closed upon us, and rendered all farther progress impossible. The water was here stagnant. The large trees that used to be met with in such numbers up the stream were entirely lost, a few diminutive gums being the only timber to be seen: the height of the bank from the water-line was three feet six inches; and the marks of floods on the trunks of the trees rose to the height of four feet six inches, being about one foot above the level of the surrounding marshes. It would appear that the water is frequently stationary at that height for a considerable time, as long moss and other marks of stagnant waters were remaining on the trunks and roots of the trees, and on the long-leaved acacia, which was here a strong plant. There could not be above three feet water in this part of the lagoon, as small bushes and tufts of tea grass were perceptible. The water was extremely muddy, and the odour arising from the banks and marshes was offensive in the extreme. There were only four different kinds of plants at this terminating point of our journey, viz., the small eucalyptus, the long-leaved acacia, the large tea grass, and a new diaeceous plant which covered the marshes, named polygonum junceum. It is possible that the bed of the lagoon might extend eight or ten miles farther, but I do not think it did, as the horizon was perfectly clear in all directions, a few bushes and acacia trees, marking the course of the lagoon, excepted.

Had there been any hill or even small eminence within thirty or forty miles of me they must now have been discovered, but there was not the least appearance of any such, and it was with infinite regret and pain that I was forced to come to the conclusion, that the interior of this vast country is a marsh and uninhabitable. How near these marshes may approach the south-western coast, I know not; but I do not think that the range of high and dry land in that quarter extends back north-easterly for any great distance; it being known, that the coast from Cape Bernouilli to the head of Spencer's Gulf is sandy and destitute of water.

Perhaps there is no river, the history of which is known, that presents so remarkable a termination as the present: its course in a straight line from its source to its termination exceeds five hundred miles, and including its windings, it may fairly be calculated to run at least twelve hundred miles; during all which passage, through such a vast extent of country, it does not receive a single stream in addition to what it derives from its sources in the eastern mountains.

I think it a probable conjecture that this river is the channel by which all the waters rising in those ranges of hills to the westward of Port Jackson, known by the name of the Blue Mountains, and which do not fall into the sea on the east coast, are conveyed to these immense inland marshes; its sinuous course causing it to overflow its banks on a much higher level than the present, and in consequence, forming those low wet levels which are in the very neighbourhood of the government depot. Its length of course is, in my opinion, the principal cause of our finding any thing like a stream for the last one hundred miles, as the immense body of water which must undoubtedly be at times collected in such a river must find a vent somewhere, but being spent during so long a course without any accession, the only wonder is, that even those waters should cause a current at so great a distance from their source; every thing however indicates, as before often observed, that in dry seasons the channel of the river is empty, or forms only a chain of ponds. It appears to have been a considerable length of time since the banks were over-flowed, certainly not for the last year; and I think it probable they are not often so: the quantity of water must indeed be immense, and of long accumulation, in the upper marshes, before the whole of this vast country can be under water.

August 29.—At eight o'clock we proceeded towards Bathurst, hoping to reach it by the evening; this we effected between eight and nine o'clock, passing over a very hilly country with numerous running streams, joining the river near Pine Hill, and afterwards keeping along its banks.

VI. OXLEY'S EXPLORATION OF THE MACQUARIE

[THIS Journal was included in Oxley's book of 1820.]

May 20, 1818.—Having received his Excellency the Governor's instructions for the conduct of the expedition intended to examine the course of the Macquarie River, and every preparation having been made at the depot in Wellington Valley for that purpose, I quitted Sydney in company with Dr. Harris (late of the 102d foot), and after a pleasant journey arrived at Bathurst on the 25th. Our little arrangements having been completed by the 28th, we again set forward with the baggage horses and men that were to compose the expedition.

We at first kept nearly upon the track pursued by us on our return from the first expedition in August last; but on approaching Wellington Valley, keeping a little more to the westward, we avoided much of that steep and rugged road which we then complained of; the country being quite open, the valleys and flats good, the hills limestone rock. We did not meet with the slightest interruption, and arrived at the depot on the 2d of June, where we found the boats, etc., in perfect readiness for our immediate reception.

June 6.—Proceeded down the river about four miles, when the boats were finally laden. The river in Wellington Valley had been swelled by the late rains, insomuch that the water below its junction with the Macquarie was quite discoloured. From the fineness of the soil, the rain had made the ground very soft, rendering it difficult for the horses to travel.

June 7.—Proceeded on our journey, both boats and horses being very heavily laden with our stores and provisions. The river rose but little. Our day's journey lay generally over an open forest country, with rich flats on either side of the river: high rocky limestone hills ended occasionally in abrupt points, obliging the horses to make considerable detours. The hills were very stony, and so light was the soil upon them, that the rain rendered the ground very soft. The river had many fine reaches, extending in straight lines from one to three miles, and of a corresponding breadth. The rapids, although frequent, offered no material obstruction to the boats. The current in the long reaches was scarcely perceptible, and it appears to me that the difference of elevation between this station and the last is not considerable.

June 8.—The river expanded into beautiful reaches, having great depth of water, and from two to three hundred feet broad, literally covered with water-fowl of different kinds: the richest flats bordered the river, apparently more extensive on the south side. The vast body of water which this river must contain in times of flood is confined within exterior banks, and its inundations are thus deprived of mischief. About six miles down the river, a freestone hill ended on the north side of the river: I mention this, as the only stone of that description I had yet seen. The trees were of the eucalyptus (apple tree), and on the hills a few of the cupressus macrocarpa were seen: the trees would furnish large and useful timber.

June 26.—The country this day was as various as can be imagined; low but not level; in some places covered with the acacia pendula, chenopodeae, and polygonum juncium; in others, with good gum and box trees. The whole, with few exceptions, appeared liable to flood. Four or five miles back the country imperceptibly rises, and is free from river floods; but the hollows, proceeding from the inequalities of its surface, are in rainy seasons the reservoirs of the land floods. The whole country was now perfectly dry, and must have been so for a long period: it would indeed have been impossible, had the season been wet, to have kept company with the boats. The river itself continues undiminished, and is a fine stream, with nothing to impede the navigation; its windings, however, are very considerable.

June 30.—After making every arrangement that we could devise to ensure our keeping company with the boats, we proceeded down the river. Our progress was, however, interrupted much sooner than I anticipated; for we had scarcely gone six miles, and never nearer to the river than from one to two miles, when we perceived that the waters which had overflowed the banks were spreading over the plains on which we were travelling, and that with a rapidity which precluded any hope of making the river again to the north-west by north, in which direction we imagined it to run for some distance, when its course appeared to take a more northerly direction. Our situation did not admit of hesitation as to the steps we were to pursue. Our journey had, in fact, been continued longer than strict prudence would have warranted, and the safety of the whole party was now at stake: no retreat presented itself except the station we left in the morning, and even there it was impossible that we could, with any regard to prudence, remain longer than to carry the arrangements which I had in contemplation into effect. The horses were therefore ordered back, and two men succeeded, after wading through the water to the middle, in making the river about three miles below the place they set out from. Fortunately the boats had not proceeded so far, and on their coming up were directed to return. The boats arrived at sunset, having had to pull against a strong current. The river itself continued, as usual, from fifteen to twenty-five feet deep, the waters which were overflowing the plains being carried thither by a multitude of little streams, which had their origin in the present increased height of the waters above their usual level. The river continued undiminished, and presented too important a body of water to allow me to believe that those marshes and low grounds had any material effect in diffusing and absorbing it: its ultimate termination, therefore, must be more consonant to its magnitude. These reflections on the present undiminished state of the river would of themselves have caused me to pause before I hastily quitted a pursuit from the issue of which so much had naturally been expected. For all practical purposes, the nature of the country precluded me from indulging the hope, that even if the river should terminate in an inland sea, it could be of the smallest use to the colony. The knowledge of its actual termination, if at all attainable, was, however, a matter of deep importance, and would tend to throw some light on the obscurity in which the interior of this vast country is still involved. My ardent desire to investigate as far as possible this interesting question, determined me to take the large boat, and with four volunteers to proceed down the river as long as it continued navigable; a due regard being had to the difficulties we should have to contend with in returning against the stream. I calculated that this would take me a month; at all events, I determined to be provided for that period, which indeed was the very utmost that could be spared from the ulterior object of the expedition.

July 2.—I proceeded down the river, during one of the wettest and most stormy days we had yet experienced. About twenty miles from where I set out, there was, properly speaking, no country; the river overflowing its banks, and dividing into streams which I found had no permanent separation from the main branch, but united themselves to it on a multitude of points. We went seven or eight miles farther, when we stopped for the night upon a space of ground scarcely large enough to enable us to kindle a fire. The principal stream ran with great rapidity, and

its banks and neighbourhood, as far as we could see, were covered
with wood, inclosing us within a margin or bank. Vast spaces of
country clear of timber were under water, and covered with the
common reed, which grew to the height of six or seven feet about
the surface. The course and distance by the river was estimated
to be from twenty-seven to thirty miles, on a north north-west
line.

July 3.—Towards the morning the storm abated, and at daylight we proceeded on our voyage. The main bed of the river was
much contracted, but very deep, the waters spreading to the
depth of a foot or eighteen inches over the banks, but all running
on the same point of bearing. We met with considerable interruption from fallen timber, which in places nearly choked up the
channel. After going about twenty miles, we lost the land and
trees: the channel of the river, which lay through reeds, and was
from one to three feet deep, ran northerly. This continued for
three or four miles farther, when although there had been no previous change in the breadth, depth, and rapidity of the stream
for several miles, and I was sanguine in my expectations of soon
entering the long sought for Australian sea, it all at once eluded
our farther pursuit by spreading on every point from north-west
to north-east, among the ocean of reeds which surrounded us, still
running with the same rapidity as before. There was no channel
whatever among those reeds, and the depth varied from three to
five feet. This astonishing change (for I cannot call it a termination of the river), of course left me no alternative but to endeavour
to return to some spot, on which we could effect a landing before
dark. I estimated that during this day we had gone about twenty-
four miles, on nearly the same point of bearing as yesterday. To
assert positively that we were on the margin of the lake or sea into
which this great body of water is discharged, might reasonably be
deemed a conclusion which has nothing but conjecture for its
basis; but if an opinion may be permitted to be hazarded from
actual appearances, mine is decidedly in favour of our being in
the immediate vicinity of an inland sea, or lake, most probably a
shoal one, and gradually filling up by immense depositions from
the higher lands, left by the waters which flow into it. It is most
singular, that the highlands on this continent seem to be confined
to the sea-coast, or not to extend to any great distance from it.

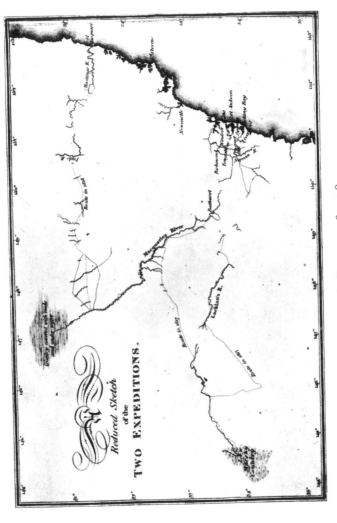

Oxley's Routes, 1817–18.

From "Journals of Two Expeditions into the Interior of New South Wales, 1817–18."

VII. EVANS'S DISCOVERY OF THE CASTLEREAGH

[This narrative is embodied in Oxley's " Journals."]

July 18, 1818.—In the evening Mr. Evans returned, after an interesting though disagreeable journey. His horses were completely worn out by the difficulties of the country they had travelled over. His report decided me as to the steps that were now to be pursued; and I determined on making nearly an easterly course to the river which he had discovered, and which was now honoured with the name of Lord Castlereagh. This route would take us over a drier country, and the river being within a short distance of Arbuthnot's range, would enable me to examine from those elevated points the country to the north-east and east; and to decide how far it might be advisable to trace the river, which it is my present inclination to do as long as its course continues to the eastward of north.

July 27.—This morning the weather cleared up just in time to enable us to retreat to the river banks in safety, for we were washed out of the tent. The provisions and heavy baggage were carried by the people to a firmer spot of ground, at which place the horses being lightly laden, we got every thing transported to the river by one o'clock. Castlereagh River is certainly a stream of great magnitude; its channel is divided by numerous islands covered with trees: it measured in its narrowest part one hundred and eighty yards, and the flood that had now risen in it was such as to preclude any attempt to cross it. The outer banks were good firm land, apparently free from floods, and extending not more on this side than a quarter of a mile, when it became wet and marshy: the banks were twelve to seventeen feet high, and gradually sloped to the water. The trees on this firm margin of land were a species of eucalyptus, cypresses, and the sterculia heterophylla, with a few camarinae. This river doubtless discharges itself into that interior gulf, in which the waters of the Macquarie are merged: to that river it is in no respect inferior, and when the banks are full, the body of water in it must be even still more considerable. Towards evening I thought the waters were falling, which was an event we anxiously looked for, to enable us to proceed to Arbuthnot's Range, fro n the heights of which we hoped for an interesting view. Natives appear to be numerous; the guniahs (or bark-huts) are in every direction, and by their fire-places several muscle-shells of the same kind as those found on the Lachlan and Macquarie Rivers were seen. Game (kangaroos and emus),frequenting the dry banks of the river,were procured in abundance.

July 28.—The river during the night had risen upwards of eight feet; and still continued rising with surprising rapidity, run-ing at the rate of from five to six miles per hour, bringing down with it great quantities of driftwood and other wreck. The islands were all deeply covered, and the whole scene was peculi-arly grand and interesting. The sudden rise probably was caused by the heavy rains of the preceding days; but great must be the sources from whence so stupendous a body of water is supplied, and equally grand must be that reservoir, which is capable of containing such an accumulation of water as is derived from this and the Macquarie Rivers; not to mention the supplies from the occasional streams which had their sources in the marshes which we have crossed. The water was so extremely thick and turbid, that we could not use it; but were forced to send back to the marshes for what we wanted. At night, the river seemed at its greatest height.

July 29.—The waters this day subsided rapidly. It is evident that there has been no flood in the river for a very considerable period prior to the present one, there being no marks of wreck or rubbish on the trees or banks. Now the quantity of matter is astonishing, and such as must take some years to remove. The rapid rise and fall in the water would seem to indicate that neither its source nor its embouchure can be at any great distance. The former is probably not far east of Arbuthnot's Range.

August 2.—It was not until this morning that the river had fallen sufficiently to allow us to ford it.

August 3.—A dark cloudy morning. At nine o'clock proceeded on our eastern course towards Arbuthnot's Range. The river had risen in the night so considerably, that had we delayed until this morning, we should have been unable to pass it. The rain had rendered the ground so extremely soft and boggy, that we found it impossible to proceed above three-quarters of a mile on our eastern course. We therefore returned, resolving to keep close to the river's edge, until we should be enabled to sound the vein of quagmire, with which we appeared to be hemmed in. In this attempt we were equally unfortunate, the horses falling repeatedly: one rolled into the river, and it was with difficulty we saved him: my baggage was on him, and was entirely spoiled; the chartcase and charts were materially damaged, and our spare thermometer broken: we therefore unladed the horses where they stood, and the men carried the provisions to a firmer spot, where they were reladen. We again proceeded easterly, and for upwards of a mile we travelled up to our knees in water and mud : the horses were here stopped by running waters from the marshes, encircling a spot of comparatively dry ground; they were again unladen, and with the utmost difficulty we got every thing safe over. Both men and horses were so much exhausted by the constant labour they had undergone, that I determined to halt, in order to restore our baggage to some order. Our ardent hopes are fixed upon the high lands of Arbuthnot's Range, which I estimate to be about twenty miles off. The intermediate country, we fear, will be one continued morass.

August 4.—Proceeded on our journey. In the seven miles and a half which we accomplished to-day, the water and bog were pretty equally divided; and a plain covered with the former was a great relief both to men and horses, since an apparently dry brush, or forest, was found a certain forerunner of quicksands and bogs. The natives appear pretty numerous: one was very daring, maintaining his ground at a distance armed with a formidable jagged spear and club, which he kept beating against each other, making the most singular gestures and noises that can be imagined: he followed us upwards of a mile, when he left us, joining several companions to the right of us. Emus and kangaroos abound, and there is a great diversity of birds, some of which have the most delightful notes, particularly the thrush.

VIII. ALLAN CUNNINGHAM'S EXPLORATIONS

[ALLAN CUNNINGHAM contributed the following account of his explorations to the *Geographical Journal, 1832.*]

Amidst the ardour with which geographical research has been patronized and prosecuted in almost every other portion of the globe, it is a subject of surprise and regret that so little anxiety should have been shown by geographers, and even by men of science in general, to increase our knowledge of the interior of the Australian continent. But so it is,—that land of anomalies may still be said to be almost a terra incognita; and, limited as may be the information which we possess of its internal features, yet, with the conviction that some concise notice of the way in which that knowledge has been progressively acquired will not prove altogether uninteresting to the Geographical Society, I beg to lay before it, in a brief view, the results of the several expeditions which have been employed in inland discovery since the first settlement was formed at Port Jackson; to which I have added, a few occasional remarks on the different routes which have been pursued, and which will be further illustrated by the accompanying map.

To that fine settlement, in whose internal prosperity and advancement I have, during my long residence among its inhabitants, ever felt a lively interest, I shall consider myself as having rendered no small service, if what may appear in the following pages should induce this society to promote, by such means as it may have at command, the more extensive examination of the interior of New South Wales. We possess colonies, on its eastern and western shores, which are daily exciting more and more interest in this country; and, should the tide of emigration continue to flow, as it has done for some years past, new land must be thrown open to meet the wants of the settlers.

Up to that period (1819), the colonists knew nothing of the southern country, beyond the cow-pastures, where that extensive patch of thicket, called the "Bargo-brush," formed a boundary, which had not been penetrated. At length, about this time, both that and the Wombat-brush, in Argyle, were

56

passed, and a third river flowing inland, and called by the aborigines "Morrumbidgee," was discovered. Minor excursions were immediately afterwards made by individuals into that interesting country, where many fine tracts of land were found, which have since proved of great value to the grazier. It was not, however, until the winter of 1823, that an extensive tract of undulated country, clear of timber, and watered by the Morrumbidgee, was discovered by a party, conducted by an officer of the navy, at a point nearer to its source than had before been seen. This open country, which was named, upon its discovery, "Brisbane Downs," the travellers learnt from a tribe of natives was called in aboriginal language, "Monaroo"; and its extent was described by the Indians as very considerable. These fine sheep-walks were ascertained, by accurate observations, to lie immediately to the eastward of the meridian of 149°, and were found to extend upwards of forty miles to the southward of the parallel of 36° 15', which appears to be the latitude of their northern skirts. They are further described as being bounded on the east by the coast range of hills, which give an interior direction to the course of the streams, by which they are permanently watered; and on their western side, by those lofty mountains, now known by the native name Warragong.

The elevation of Brisbane Downs, above the sea-shore (distant from them to the eastward about seventy miles), although it has never been measured, cannot be less than two thousand feet; and as they are in higher latitude than other portions of land, within the present boundaries of the colony, the climate may probably be found more congenial to the growth of wool and the constitution of sheep, than that of those extensive tracts of pastoral country, from which the colonists are annually obtaining so many thousand fleeces for the English market. The mean height of any one point of the great Warragong Chain, which appears to extend without interruption to Wilson's Promontory (the southernmost extremity of the Australian continent), has not yet been determined. That portion, however, of which may be called the backbone of the country, is, probably, of greater elevation above the level of the ocean than any other range of mountains along the eastern coast, either within or beyond the tropic, since its summit is not simply covered with snow during the winter months, but has been seen perfectly white at other seasons of the year.

At the same time that these important geographical researches were carrying on in the southern parts of the colony, I was occupied with a party in the elevated country on the north of Bathurst, in which direction, at a distance of fifty miles from that settlement, the Cudgeegong, a tributary to the Macquarie, had been previously discovered, and stock stations erected on its banks.

In my excursion through that mountainous country, I succeeded not only in effecting a clear, well-defined route for the grazier to Liverpool Plains from Bathurst, but also in bringing the settlers of the latter district in direct communication with those farmers, who had taken their lands on Hunter's River.

With the exception of my examination of the western and northern sides of Liverpool Plains in the month of May, 1825, which enabled me to furnish something more than what had been previously known of those extensive levels, our stock of geographical knowledge received no accession during either that or the following year. The year 1827, however, a new scene opened to the colonists; for a journey which the late Mr. Oxley had himself at one period contemplated, was determined on, viz., to explore the entire unknown country, lying on the western side of the dividing range, between Hunter's River in latitude 32° and Moreton Bay in latitude 27° S. For this purpose a well-appointed expedition, equipped fully for an absence of five months, was placed by the Colonial Government under my direction.

On the 30th of April of that year (1827), having provided myself with the necessary instruments, and with an escort of six servants and eleven horses, I took my departure from a station on an upper branch of Hunter's River, and upon crossing the dividing range to the westward, at a mean elevation above the level of the sea of three thousand and eighty feet, I pursued my journey northerly, through an uninteresting forest country, skirting Liverpool Plains on the eastern side. As it is my intention to lay before the public, ere long, a narrative of this journey, which, in consequence of the long drought by which this part of the country had suffered, cost my party no ordinary exertions, I trust that an outline of it will now be sufficient.

On the 11th of May, we crossed (in latitude 31° 2') Mr. Oxley's track easterly towards Port Macquarie in 1818, and from that point the labours of the expedition commenced on ground previously untrodden by civilized man. It was my original design to have taken a fresh departure to the northward, from the point at which the late Surveyor-General had passed the

river named by him the "Peel," upon our reaching the above-
mentioned parallel, and which bore from a spot on which we
had encamped, due east about twelve miles: however, the intermediate country, although Mr. Oxley had passed it, proved too
elevated and rocky for my heavily-burdened horses; and I was,
therefore, obliged to continue the course of the expedition to
the north under the meridian of our tents, (viz. 150½°) being
well aware that as the final course of that river was towards the
interior, we should cross its channel whenever the chain of lofty
hills which bounded us on the east, and which appeared to
stretch far to the north, should either terminate or become so
broken as to allow of its escape through them to a lower level.
Thus we continued our journey to the north through a barren,
but densely-timbered country, of frequently brushy character,
and altogether very indifferently watered. Each day as we
advanced, our barometer showed us that these poor forest-
grounds, which, to add to the difficulty of penetration, were
occasionally traversed by low arid ridges of argillaceous iron-
stone and clayslate, rose in elevation from the low level of the
northern margin of Liverpool Plains, which I found to be only
eight hundred and forty feet above the level of the sea. This
rise of surface was, however, most gradual; for, after a march
of forty miles directly to the north, we found, on reaching the
bank of a small stream, a branch evidently of the Peel, that we
had attained but a mean height of one thousand nine hundred
feet above the sea-coast—an elevation which was too inconsiderable to produce any obvious change for the better, either
in the growth of the timber, the nature of the soil, or of the
scanty herbage. Through those gloomy woods, with scarcely a
trace of either Indian or kangaroo, we patiently pursued our way
until the 19th of May, when upon passing the parallel of 30°, we
descended from some stony hills to the head of a beautiful well-
watered valley, affording abundance of the richest pasturage,
and bounded, on either side, by a bold and elevated rocky range.
This grassy vale we followed northerly about sixteen miles to its
termination at the left bank of a large river, which, in seasons
less unfavourable to vegetation, appeared evidently a stream of
considerable magnitude. This was the Peel of Mr. Oxley; which,
after pursuing its course to the north for upwards of a degree
of latitude from the point at which that officer had passed it in
1818, had at length forced its passage through a break in the
eastern ranges, and, passing the lower extremity of the valley
in latitude 29° 51′, flowed on towards an open country observed

beyond it at north-west. So considerable was the dip of the vale along which our route had extended, that we found ourselves in the channel of this river, again nearly on the level of the northern or lower sides of Liverpool Plains—the mean of the results of our morning and evening observations of the barometer giving us only nine hundred and eleven feet. The channel of the Peel, which, at this period, exhibited a bed of gravel two hundred and fifty yards in breadth, is, in seasons of long rains, entirely filled by floods to the depth of twelve and fifteen feet, as was obvious from the marks of those freshes on the upper banks. The long continuance of dry weather, which had alike distressed the colony and these distant parts of the interior, had, however, reduced its stream to a mere rill, which we forded without difficulty. Passing the channel of this river, by which a considerable tract of broken mountainous country to the S.E. is drained, we resumed our journey to the north, between the meridian of 150° and 151°. Our course led us through a variety of country; for, on quitting the river, we traversed a barren, brushy tract, which extended more or less for fourteen miles; beyond, however, the land materially improved, and, as it was less encumbered with small timber and more open to the action of the atmosphere, a considerable growth of grass was produced. A succession of open forest hills of moderate elevation, and narrow intermediate valleys, with an occasional patch of plain, of a good soil, characterised the line of country, which the expedition afterwards crossed; and although the land (the mean elevation of which did not exceed eleven hundred feet) was, generally speaking, rich, and productive of much grass, it was, nevertheless, distressing to meet with tracts, many miles in extent, entirely destitute of water. Traces of the natives were frequent, although not of recent date. We met, however, with neither the wandering Indian nor any description of animal, for the parched state of vegetation and the distressed condition of the country generally, had evidently driven both to other parts of the interior, where the means of sustaining life were less precarious, or, at least, where a permanent supply of water, although it might be in a stagnant state, was to be obtained. Hitherto our view towards the west had been circumscribed by a continued chain of thinly-wooded ridges, which had extended, northerly, parallel to the course we were daily pursuing. On reaching the latitude of 29° 10', which we did on the 25th of the month, all the hills to the westward of our line of route terminated, and a level, open interior, of vast expanse, bounded on the north and

CUNNINGHAM'S ROUTE, APRIL–MAY–JUNE, 1823.
From " Geographical Memoirs of New South Wales," 1825.

north-west by a distant horizon, broke suddenly on our view!
At north-west, more particularly, it was evident to all of us that
the country had a most decided dip, and on that bearing, the
line of sight extended over a great extent of densely wooded, or
brushed, land, the monotonous aspect of which was here and
there relieved by a brown patch of plain: of these some were so
remote as to appear a mere speck on the ocean of land before us,
on which the eye sought anxiously for a rising smoke, as indicative of the presence of the wandering aborigines; but in vain:
for, excepting in the immediate neighbourhood of a river of the
larger magnitude, these vast solitudes may be fairly said to be
almost entirely without inhabitants. We had now all the high
grounds on our right hand, or to the east of us, and before us,
at north, a level, wooded country. With an anxious curiosity to
explore so extraordinary a region, we continued our route on
the 26th of May, from a rocky creek, where we had rested upon
some tolerable pasture. Our elevation above the sea-shore, we
found by our barometer to be one thousand two hundred and
twenty-eight feet, and we soon discovered that we had entered
a barren waste, over which was spread a loose sand, (the debris
of the prevalent rock formation of the eastern hills,) which gave
it a desert-like aspect. A blighted kind of the iron-bark tree,
(apparently Eucalyptus resinifera,) scarcely twenty-five feet
high, clothed its surface, on which were here and there interspersed dense patches of underwood, composed of plants formerly
observed on the western skirts of Liverpool Plains. In this stage
of our journey we crossed the parallel of 29°, in about the
meridian of 150° 40'; and having very little expectation of meeting with water, in any state, in so arid a region, we were most
agreeably surprised to find the channel of a river from eighty to
one hundred yards in width, winding its course to the westward.
This stream, which received the name of Dumaresq's River,
although greatly reduced by drought, presented, nevertheless,
a handsome piece of water, half a mile in length, about thirty
yards in width, and evidently very deep. My barometer, which
I set up on the gravelly bed of the river, gave me only eight
hundred and forty feet of elevation above the sea-coast, from
which we were distant to the westward about one hundred and
seventy English miles.

It was my full intention to have continued my course in the
direction of the meridian, at least to the parallel of 27°, before
I made the least easting towards the coast-line; this design,
however, the existing circumstances of the country we had

penetrated compelled me to abandon; for the great debility to which the whole of my horses were reduced, by the labours of the journey through a line of country parched up by the drought, at once obliged me to pursue a more eastern course; in which direction, upon gaining the higher lands, I could alone expect to meet with a better pasture than that on which they had for some time subsisted.

On our new course to the northward and eastward, we had to struggle through a desert waste for many miles, before we gained a more undulated surface to the eastward of 151°, when the country through which we journeyed for about thirty miles, presented a succession of thinly wooded stony hills, or low ridges of sandstone rock, separated from each other by narrow valleys, in which my half-famished horses met with but scanty subsistence. At length, on the 5th of June, having gained an elevation of about nine hundred feet above the bed of Dumaresq's River, we reached the confines of a superior country. It was exceedingly cheering to my people, after they had traversed a waste often times of the most forbiddingly arid character, for a space, more or less, of eighty miles, and had borne, with no ordinary patience, a degree of privation to which I had well-nigh sacrificed the weaker of my horses—to observe, from a ridge which lay in our course, that they were within a day's march of open downs of unknown extent, which stretched, easterly, to the base of a lofty range of mountains, distant, apparently, about twenty-five miles. On the 6th and following day, we travelled throughout the whole extent of these plains, to the foot of the mountains extending along their eastern side, and the following is the substance of my observations on their extent, soil, and capability.

These extensive tracts of clear pastoral country, which were subsequently named Darling Downs, in honour of his Excellency the Governor, are situated in, or about, the mean parallel of 28° S., along which they stretch east, eighteen statute miles to the meridian of 152°. Deep ponds, supported by streams from the highlands, immediately to the eastward, extend along their central lower flats; and these, when united, in a wet season, become an auxiliary to Condamine's River—a stream which winds its course along their south-western margin. The downs, we remarked, varied in breadth in different parts of their length-ened surface: at their western extremity they appeared not to exceed a mile and a half, whilst towards their eastern limits, their width might be estimated at three miles. The lower grounds, thus permanently watered, present flats, which furnish an almost inexhaustible range of cattle pasture at all seasons of the year—the grasses and herbage generally exhibiting, in the depth of winter, an extraordinary luxuriance of growth. From these central grounds, rise downs of a rich, black, and dry soil, and very ample surface; and as they furnish an abundance of grass, and are conveniently watered, yet perfectly beyond the reach of those floods, which take place on the flats in a season of rains, they constitute a valuable and sound sheep pasture. We soon reached the base of some hills, connected laterally with that stupendous chain of mountains, the bold outline of which we had beheld with so much interest during the three preceding days. These hills we found clothed, from their foot upwards, with an underwood of the densest description, in the midst of which, and especially on the ridges, appeared a pine, which I immediately discovered to be the same species as that observed in 1824, on the Brisbane River. Encamping, I ascended a remarkable square-topped mount, which formed the western termination of one of these ridges; and from its summit had a very extensive view of the country lying between north and south, towards the west. At N. and N.N.W. we observed a succession of heavily-timbered ridges, extending laterally from the more elevated chain of mountains immediately to the east, which evidently forms the main dividing range in this part of the country; whilst from north-west to west, and thence to south, within a range of twenty miles, a most beautifully diversified landscape, made up of hill and dale, woodland, and plain, appeared before us.

Large patches of land, perfectly clear of trees, lying to the north of Darling Downs, were named Peel's Plains, whilst others, bearing to the south and south-east, and which presented an undulated surface with a few scattered trees, were called after the late Mr. Canning. Directing our view beyond Peel's Plains to the north-west, an expanse of flat, wooded country met the eye, being evidently a continuation of those vast levels, which we had frequently observed, in the progress of our journey, extending to the westward of our line of route, and which, it was now perceived, were continued northerly at least to the parallel of 27°.

In a valley which led to the immediate base of the mountain-barrier, I fixed my northernmost encampment, determining, as I had not the means of advancing further in consequence of the state of my provisions and the low condition of my horses, to employ a short period in a partial examination of the principal range, to the western base of which we had penetrated from the southward, through a considerable portion of barren interior. In exploring the mountains immediately above our tents, with a view more especially of ascertaining how far a passage could be effected over them to the shores of Moreton Bay, a remarkably excavated part of the main range was discovered, which appeared likely to prove a very practicable pass through these mountains from the eastward. Its more particular examination, however, I left to the period of a visit, by sea, to Moreton Bay, which I had already contemplated, and which I was enabled to effect in the course of the succeeding year (1829). And the brief notice of my having thus, in a most satisfactory manner, connected my sketch of the Brisbane River country with this pass, and with the lands to the westward, will be seen in another part of this paper.

The situation of my tents in the valley was determined to be as follows. Latitude, by meridional altitudes of the sun, being the mean of five observations, 28° 10′ 45″ south. Longitude, by account corrected by bearings taken to fixed points on or near the coast-line, and compared with the mean results of several sets of distances of the sun and star Antares from the moon, 152° 7′ 45″ E. The variation of the compass was found by azimuths to be 8° 18′ E. The mean height of the spot above the level of the sea, by the mercurial column noted morning and evening, was one thousand eight hundred and seventy-seven feet; and its distance from the penal settlement on the Brisbane River, which bore by compass about north-east from us, was estimated at about seventy-five statute miles. Circumstances now urged me to commence my journey homewards, and this I determined to prosecute with as much despatch as the condition of my horses and the nature of the country would admit of. I had also resolved to pursue my course to the southward, under the meridian of our encampment, as that would lead us through a tract of perfectly unknown country, lying nearly equidistant between our outward-bound track and the coast-line.

On the 16th of June, therefore, I again put my people in motion, and quitting the vale in which we had rested, (and which I had named after the late Captain Logan, at that period commandant of Moreton Bay,) I shaped my course to the southward; and after passing through a fine, open, forest tract, abounding in excellent pasturage, in nine miles gained the north-eastern skirts of Canning Downs, of which I had had a view from a station on the hills which we had left.

At the close of the 18th, after penetrating an uninteresting forest, chiefly of red gum (Eucalyptus robusta), we reached the borders of a broken mountainous country, which exhibited a geological structure that had not been previously met with in any part of our journey. The rock was a very hard granite, in which the quartz, greatly preponderating, was unusually large; and at this stage of our homeward-bound journey our difficulties commenced. During the succeeding week, our daily journeys were attended with great fatigue both to my people and horses; for being surrounded by high lands, we had no alternative but to pursue our way southerly, from one rocky range to another of greater elevation; until at length we found ourselves upon an open heath, totally devoid of trees, but covered with a low, scrubby vegetation, and interspersed with small patches of spongy swamp, in aspect similar to parts of the Blue Mountains to the westward of Port Jackson. And although the base continued of granite, and the difference of latitude was nearly 5°, yet the same species of plants as are to be observed upon those elevated ranges of the colony were, for the most part, to be found. At noon of the 25th, our latitude, observed on a very bleak sterile spot on those mountains, (two thousand nine hundred and sixty-nine feet above the sea-shore,) was 28° 45′ S., and our longitude, reduced from the meridian of our encampment in Logan Vale, was about 151° 59′ E. From that point, notwithstanding our elevation, our view towards the east was altogether circumscribed by lofty ranges, whose summits towered far above the height we had attained. In the course of the succeeding day, the progress of the expedition to the south was arrested by a most wild and frightful region, which obliged me at once to seek a more practicable country, by directing the course of my party to the westward, in which direction we, with difficulty, gained a lower level, and thence prosecuted our journey to the south-west, by such stages as the reduced strength of my horses was able to accomplish. On passing to the southward of the parallel of 29°, which we did in longitude 151° 32′ E., we again forded Dumaresq's River about fifty miles nearer its source, or to the eastward of the point at which we had discovered it on our outward-bound journey. Here our barometer gave us an elevation of one thousand and forty feet above the level of the sea, which showed a mean fall of four feet per mile, between the two fords.

I. D. *h*

On the 9th of July, after having traversed in a south-western direction a great diversity of country, in general of broken, rocky surface, we fell in with our former track, and on the following day crossed the channel of what I had considered the Peel, but which I subsequently named the Gwydir, upon finding it formed by a junction of Mr. Oxley's River with another as large, to which I gave the title of Horton's River. This latter has a course parallel to the Peel, through a valley lying to the westward of it, along which I was again enabled to direct my party to the south many miles, before a series of elevated forest ridges, stretching laterally from Hardwicke's range of Mr. Oxley, once more obliged us to climb the hills. These we ascended from the head of the vale, by a steep acclivity, and, at an elevation of one thousand three hundred feet above its level, resumed our course to the south. Among these hills we again observed granite, but of a reddish appearance, in consequence of the quantity and colour of the felspar which might be seen disseminated through the rock, of which Hardwicke's range is evidently formed; the elevation, above the level of the sea, of whose curiously formed cubical and chimney-shaped summits cannot be less than three thousand five hundred feet. The vegetation of this group of hills exhibited nothing remarkable; the ridges were generally grassy, but the Gramineae, as well as the timbers, which were of Eucalyptus, were of species frequent in the colony. At the close of our second day's journey, we had traversed these lateral ranges to their southern side, which overlooked an apparently level, wooded country, extending to Liverpool Plains, the greater body of which at length appeared before us to the south-west, at a distance of forty miles. Repeatedly, in our attempts to descend to the lower country, were we stopped by rocky ravines several hundred feet in depth; and it was not without considerable difficulty and danger to the horses that we gained the levels beneath us, having actually descended a wooded ridge, from which there was an abrupt declivity of one thousand five hundred and forty feet. After a severe march of thirty miles through a barren forest, for the most part of blighted Iron-bark, furnishing but little pasturage and still less water, we at length arrived at Barrow's Valley of Mr. Oxley, which, in seasons of long rains, is evidently laid under water by the overflow of Field's River, which, in its course inland, we met meandering north-west, through the adjacent forest. On the bank of this river, where I gave my horses a day's rest upon the richest meadow-land we had seen in the whole tour, it was with pleasure that I hailed the colonial blue gum (Eucalyptus piperita) of stupendous size, the alluvial grounds on each bank producing also the herbage of the flooded flats of the Hawkesbury River in the colony. On the 20th of July, we resumed our route to the southward, and after pursuing a steady course for about twenty-seven miles through a barren, brushy country, not nine hundred feet above the level of the sea, we passed the northern margin of Liverpool Plains, throughout which, such had been the effect of drought, that we crossed their extensive surface almost to the foot of the dividing range (a space of twenty-five miles) before we found water for the horses or ourselves. On the 28th my party repassed the Mountain Range, and after an absence of thirteen weeks, we returned to the station from which we had departed, on the Hunter, having, in that period, traversed upwards of eight hundred miles of every description of country.

My report to the Colonial Government of this journey—of the spacious downs we had discovered in latitude 28°—and the considerable tract of very indifferent country, in part actual desert, that lay between the colony and those extensive pastoral lands, immediately suggested the importance of examining the space between those downs and the sea-coast at Moreton Bay; since, should the Gap, which had been discovered in the main dividing range in the above parallel, prove, on actual survey, to admit of a passage through that chain of mountains, the readiest point of access to the very desirable country on their western side would be from the shores of Moreton Bay and Brisbane River,—on the banks of the latter of which a penal settlement had already been established for several years. This inquiry became one of the objects of my voyage from Port Jackson the following year; and its results proved every way most satisfactory to the colonial government, and the colonists generally.

As I propose to make some general remarks elsewhere on the character of the country around Moreton Bay—a country alike interesting to the botanist and geologist—I will here simply remark, that in exploring the intermediate tract between the Brisbane River and the point where my overland journey of the preceding year had terminated, I ascertained that a line of road could be easily constructed from the western downs, easterly through the mountain pass, and thence in a north-eastern direction to the head of the navigation of a branch of the Brisbane River, named the Bremer; to which point evidently the future produce of the interior beyond those mountains will be conveyed, since from it the means of water-carriage to shipping in the bay will be found practicable at all seasons of the year, whatever may be the effect of drought on the land; the tide, which daily sets into the Brisbane for fifty miles above its mouth, flowing also up the channel of the Bremer, the depth of water in which it augments eight or more feet.

I was happy on this occasion of my visit to the Brisbane River, with in part other objects in view, to be enabled to carry on my survey from Darling Downs to the very shores of Moreton Bay; and in effecting it, I derived an additional pleasure, in closing my sketch of an extent of intricate country, comprehending from Hunter's River to Brisbane Town, 5° of latitude, to find out a very small error in my longitude. In the winter of the following year (1829), I again made a voyage to Moreton Bay, where I was engaged more particularly in botanical research. From that most interesting occupation, in so novel and ample a field as the banks of the Brisbane River afforded me, I found a short period of leisure to devote to geographical inquiry; and, accordingly, in an excursion to the north-west, I explored that stream far towards its source, through an irregular country, which presented much diversity of surface to interest the geographer. During that short journey, in which I employed a small party about six weeks, I traced the principal branch of the river as far north as latitude 26° 52', until its channel assumed merely the character of a chain of very shallow stagnant pools. In this excursion I made such observations as fully established two facts, viz.:—That the Brisbane River, at one period supposed to be the outlet of the marshes of the Macquarie, etc., originates on the eastern side of the dividing range, its chief sources being in elevated lands, lying almost on the coast line, between the parallels of 26° and 27° ; and that the main ranges, which separate the coast-waters from those that flow inland, continue to the north in one unbroken chain as far as the eye could discern, from a commanding station near my most distant encampment up the river, and present no opening or hollow part in their elevated ridge, through which to admit of a road being made, to the interior beyond them. My pass, therefore, through those lofty mountains (the mean elevation of which above the shores of Moreton Bay cannot be less than four thousand feet), seems thus the only opening to the interior country from the coast between the parallels of 26° and 29° south.

Whilst I was engaged at Moreton Bay, the long droughts to which our distant colony has been repeatedly subjected since its foundation, and which, again visiting that country in 1826, had continued with most distressing severity for upwards of three years, led the colonial government to inquire into the state of the interior, to the westward of the termination of the Macquarie River, with the view of attempting to make some discoveries in that quarter. Whilst the drought continued, an expedition was despatched under the direction of Captain Sturt, an officer of his Majesty's 39th regiment, to Mount Harris, a detached hill upon the Macquarie River, where Mr. Oxley had left his boats upon proceeding easterly towards the coast. Upon reaching that remarkable eminence, which Captain Sturt and the party forming his expedition were enabled to do on the 20th of December, he ascended the summit to survey the country below. But how much had the evaporation of the sun, which, in its operation, had continued during a period of three years, changed the face of those regions! The plains which Mr. Oxley had left entirely under water in 1818, now presented an expanse of dried-up surface, which to all appearance extended northerly, without the slightest semblance of rising ground, to a distant "clear unbroken horizon." Encouraged by these appearances, the expedition traced the Macquarie, through the last stage of its existence, to the woodlands below Mount Harris, where its channel becoming broken and in parts having altogether disappeared on the common level, ceased "to exist in any shape as a river." In exploring the country beyond this point, the party traversed the bed of that extensive morass, into which the late surveyor-general had ten years previously descended in his boat: this they now found "a large and blasted plain, on which the sun's rays fell with intense heat"; the ground itself, parched to an extreme, exhibiting in many places deep and dangerous clefts, which clearly demonstrated the long existence of those droughts, to which every known part of New South Wales was at that period exposed. On these inhospitable levels, Captain Sturt passed a week; and in that period he skirted three distinct patches of marsh, in which were found broken channels of the river, forming so many stagnant lagoons or canals, surrounded by reeds.

In whatever direction they advanced to satisfy themselves as to the fate of the Macquarie, whether on the plains or wooded grounds, reeds of gigantic stature (the clearest indication of what such a country is in a regularly wet season) encompassed them, and greatly obstructed their progress. Mr. Hume, whose enterprising disposition was abundantly manifested in his journey to the south coast, which has been already noticed in this paper, was associated with Captain Sturt on this occasion. With such aid, the latter proposed to divide the party, in order to undertake at the same time two distinct excursions, to ascertain more fully the nature and extent of those marshy flats, and set at rest any doubts which might be entertained as to the mode in which that river terminated—that is, of its non-existence in that low country, after the devastating operation of a drought of three years. Accordingly, one party, conducted by Mr. Hume, proceeded in a north-easterly direction, towards the Castlereagh, whilst Captain Sturt himself pursued a course to the north-west.

It would indeed have been most interesting, at this stage of the expedition, had Captain Sturt been provided with good barometers, to have ascertained the mean height above the level of the sea, not only of the lowlands over which the party had so patiently borne the burden and heat of the day, but also of the country which Captain Sturt traversed in his excursion to the north-west, and which he found, "after travelling between twenty and thirty miles," began to rise; also his level at the end of his journey, which was extended to an estimated distance of one hundred miles, where he "made a hill of considerable elevation," from the summit of which he had "a view of other high lands"; one in particular to the south-west, which he describes as "being a very fine mountain"; and which he afterwards visited, and found "of sandstone formation," elevated above the "desert waste" on which it stands, one thousand three hundred feet. Captain Sturt, however, had no barometer on which he could in the least depend; the instrument with which he had been provided on his quitting Sydney having sustained an injury on the Macquarie, four days before the expedition reached Mount Harris.

The observations made during these short excursions satisfied the party, that the river had no existence in any shape beyond the "third marsh" previously explored. Mr. Hume passed from east to west, along the northern skirts of those extensive reedy flats, without either meeting with a further trace of a channel northerly, or finding water enough to supply his daily wants. And the character and direction of those vast flats, as well as the points to which the waters discharged upon them by the Macquarie in seasons of prolonged rains, tend, were now fully determined.

From the report of Captain Sturt's examination of those lowlands, then, affected as they were at the time by drought, these facts may be gathered. At a distance of about twenty-eight

miles below Mount Harris, the flat lands commence, and there
the Macquarie itself ceases to be a river, having no banks, or
continued channel, by which to prevent the dispersion of its
waters when they rise in rainy seasons. The surface of those
flats, however, has not one continued dip, but presents a succession of levels and inclinations, with each a detached lagoon-like
channel, hemmed in on all sides by high reeds which catch the
waters as they spread; and it is only when these are overflowed
that the floods spread over the level, "until," as Captain Sturt
observes, "a slight declivity giving them fresh impulse," they
arrive at a second channel, and so spread to a third, until a
considerable extent of surrounding country is laid under water.
When such a general inundation takes place, as that witnessed
in 1818, there is a current through the body of these marshes,
setting, agreeably to configuration of the ground (as at length
shown to us by Captain Sturt), to the north and north-north-east,
where, uniting with the waters of Morissett's ponds, the whole
is thrown into the channel of the Castlereagh River.

To the north-west of those marshy grounds, Captain Sturt
described the country as rising, and therefore preventing any
flow of the waters of the morass to that point of the compass.
This rise of the surface, which I observe is elsewhere described
as a "table-land with scarcely water to support its inhabitants,"
may be clearly understood as meaning a series of low terraces
of dry forest-land, which present a level tract of ground, or one
but slightly undulated, extending, probably, a considerable
distance, until a second rise of the ground takes place. And the
extreme perpendicular elevation of such a tract above the plane
of the marshes is far too inconsiderable to justify its being considered a rising hilly country; nor is its actual mean height above
the level of the sea raised in the least, because it has been ascertained that there are upon its desert-like surface a few rocky
hills, which, standing far detached from each other, appear,
when viewed with the country surrounding the base of each,
like so many islands in the ocean. This view of the face of the
country bounding the marshes of the Macquarie on the north-
west will assuredly be verified, whenever a barometer is carried
to that part of the interior.

Finally, before I quit the subject of those low marshy grounds,
which have excited so much interest and speculation among
geographers since the report of them given by Mr. Oxley, I would
briefly remark, that although a drought of unparalleled duration
had disposed of their waters, so as to enable Captain Sturt and

his party to traverse their bed in a dried-up, hardened state, still, whenever a wet season sets in, and rain falls upon the mountainous districts of that colony, in the same quantity that it did in the years 1817 and 1818, it can scarcely be doubted that a like considerable inundation will again take place in that part of the interior; and when it is considered (as Captain Sturt informs us) that a space, twenty miles in breadth, and more than fifty in length, is subject to be thus deluged, can it be a subject of surprise that the late indefatigable surveyor-general, when he descended in his boat to such an expanse of water, to which he could perceive neither boundary nor shore, should, with no previous knowledge of such a water, or of the features of the surrounding country, have conceived himself in the "vicinity of an inland sea or lake," of the temporary or more permanent existence of which he did not, nor could he have offered an opinion?

Captain Sturt now directed his expedition to the north-west, with a view to further discoveries, aware as he was, from the observations he had previously made during his own short excursion, that a clear open country was before him in that direction. In their route his party traversed plains "covered with a black scrub," yet furnishing in parts some good grass. The detached hills, already spoken of, as relieving the otherwise monotonous aspect of that part of the interior, and in the neighbourhood of which Captain Sturt had directed his course, he described "as gentle picturesque elevations, for the most part covered with verdure." Of two of these isolated spots, the one "Oxley's Table Land," the other "New Year's Range," it appears our indefatigable officer determined the positions; these were as follows:

Oxley's Table Land, lat. 29° 57' 30" S., long. 145° 43' 30" E.
New Year's Range   ,,   30° 21' 00"   ,,   146°.33' 30"

In continuing their journey westerly over this level country, its total want of water, excepting in creeks where the supply was both bad and uncertain, became a source of considerable annoyance to the party; who ultimately were obliged to follow one of the water-courses, which, when tracing it to the north-west, brought them (on the 2nd of February) to the left bank of a large river, the appearance of which "raised their most sanguine expectations." To the utter disappointment of the travellers, however, its waters were found perfectly salt; and this circumstance was the more severely felt, as the horses of the expedition had travelled long in an excessively heated atmosphere, and had been without water a considerable time. After making some arrangement in favour of his exhausted animals, Captain Sturt, accompanied by Mr. Hume, proceeded to explore this river, to which he gave the name of Darling. They followed it in the direction of its course (south-westerly) about forty miles, and throughout found its waters not only not drinkable, but rather becoming, as they advanced, more considerably impregnated with salt. In one part they observed "brine-springs," and the banks throughout were encrusted with "salt," or, probably, with aluminous particles. The breadth of the river, at the point they first made it, was estimated at sixty yards, and its boundary banks were from thirty to forty feet in height—dimensions which they maintained as far as it was possible to explore the river.

At length the want of "drinkable water" along its bank, and the appearance of a loose red sandy soil, at the point to which the patience and perseverance of the travellers had induced them to trace the river, at once destroying all hope of meeting with the most scanty supply in the back country, obliged them to give up its further examination. The extreme point to which the Darling was traced, and from which it continued its course through a level country to the south-west, Captain Sturt marks on his map, in latitude 30° 16' south, and longitude 144° 50' east.

Thus was a portion of the interior of New South Wales, comprehending two degrees of longitude to the westward of the part to which Mr. Oxley had penetrated in the marshes, explored; and although the country is little better than a desert waste, and, therefore, can hold out no prospect of an advantageous "extension of the colony in that direction," its character, nevertheless, was ascertained, and so much of the map of the country, previously a blank, was at length filled up.

The expedition had daily intercourse with the natives who inhabit the river and adjacent country, which it would seem is, comparatively speaking, well peopled; for Captain Sturt estimates that he could not have seen fewer than two hundred and fifty of these Indians, among whom his party passed on the most friendly terms, and, indeed, were frequently indebted to them for kindly acts.

Captain Sturt, however, draws a most melancholy picture of these distant regions, which, notwithstanding the population found on their surface, were rendered, by the distress of the season, scarcely habitable. "The natives," he observed, "were remarked wandering in the desert, and from the badness of the water which they were obliged to drink, had contracted a cutaneous disease, which was fast carrying them off. Birds, which were noticed sitting on the trees, appeared to be gasping for existence, amidst the glare of torrid heat. The wild dog, or dingo, was seen prowling about in the day-time, being unable from debility to avoid the party; and while minor vegetation was altogether burnt up, the very trees were absolutely drooping from the depth to which the drought had penetrated the soil. Several of the party were affected by ophthalmia, produced by the reverberated heat from the plains which they had traversed, where the thermometer stood in the shade at three P.M. at 122°, or from 98° to 102° Fahrenheit, at sunset."

The Darling may be justly considered the largest river which has been discovered in New South Wales, since it is formed by a junction of all the streams which were discovered by Mr. Oxley in 1818 (and these were five in number, each of considerable magnitude), as well as of those I met with in my journey of 1827; and thus it constitutes the great drain of a tract of mountainous country lying between the parallels of 27° and 33½°. But what ultimately becomes of this river so sustained, to what other channels it becomes united, what course it eventually pursues, beyond the spot where Captain Sturt and his comrade left it flowing through a desert country to the south-west, or on what coast it is discharged, if it really does make the sea at any point, remains wholly unknown, and is therefore still to be discovered.

The party were now glad to direct their steps towards Bathurst; but before they finally quitted these parched levels, they shaped a course to the eastward, with the view of meeting with the Castlereagh, the channel of which (one hundred and eighty yards in width) Mr. Oxley experienced no small difficulty in crossing, as the rains which had fallen on the mountains to the south-east, whence it derives its principal sources, had swollen its waters to the level of its upper banks. On making this river they traced it down full one hundred miles to its junction with another part of the Darling, the water of which they found even salter than it was at the point at which the expedition had originally fallen in with it; nor did they find a sufficiency in the Castlereagh to meet their daily demands, for its bed was laid bare "for a distance of thirty miles at a stretch," which obliged our travellers to "search the country round" for the little water which it had to yield them.

Surrounded as the party were by difficulties in a region "deserted by the native tribes," scarcely capable of sustaining animal life, and in which all the dogs of the expedition fell a sacrifice, still Captain Sturt appears to have been unwilling to quit his ground; for although the briny waters of the Darling were in themselves quite enough to have induced him to have made a hasty retreat southerly, to higher grounds and a better country, we, nevertheless, find him crossing the Salt River, to see what the country was in a north-westerly direction; nor does it appear that the curiosity of our travellers was at all satisfied, until they had penetrated a considerable distance on that course, where they found the ground uniformly level, and the surface in no part broken by either creek or minor water-course, the entire country around being, as far as could be seen from the highest tree, "a boundless flat," the elevation of which.above the level of the sea was, probably, not more than five hundred feet. Captain Sturt had at length done his utmost; he, therefore, very wisely directed his party to the southward, and soon reached Bathurst.

Thus, much of our knowledge of the internal parts of New South Wales in the parallel of 30°, was derived from the labours of this indefatigable officer; to whom was entrusted, at the close of 1829, the direction of a second expedition, destined to trace the course of the Morrumbidgee, another western stream, rising in a range of mountains situated to the southward of the parallel of 35°, and under the meridian of 149°, at a distance of about eighty miles inland from the eastern coast line, and within what is now denominated the county of Murray. Of the character of this river it may be here briefly remarked, that its bed forms a succession of planes, of which some are of great inclination; along these its waters flow with considerable velocity in nearly a west direction.

After receiving the Yass River and some other minor streams, all of which fall into it at an early stage of its progress, namely, in longitude 148½°, the Morrumbidgee pursues a long and tortuous course for upwards of three hundred statute miles, without deriving the slightest increase from the country it waters; and thus in this respect it resembles the Lachlan, which maintains a parallel course through the low interior to the northward. From this fact may be inferred the generally sterile character of a considerable portion of the country lying between the channels of these two rivers, and which was in part ascertained by Mr. Oxley in 1817. As its course extends to the westward of the meridian 147°, the Morrumbidgee falls on a low level; the hills of sandstone rock, which give a picturesque appearance to the lands on its banks, higher up the stream, disappear; and flats of alluvial deposit occupy their place.

Thus far the river had been followed down some years ago, by stock-keepers in pursuit of strayed cattle, who also ascertained, in their long rides along its banks, the extent to which the country westerly, from its elevation above inundation, might be safely occupied as grazing stations. The direction which this river was also at that period known to take towards the marshes of the Lachlan, led to the conclusion, that both streams were united in those morasses; and on so low a level, (as was ascertained by Mr. Oxley in 1817), as to favour the opinion that their confluent waters were rather dissipated over an extensively flat surface, than carried on in one body to the ocean, distant at least three hundred miles. And this opinion, gratuitous as it was, would nevertheless have proved to have been correct, had the Morrumbidgee not pursued its course so far to the westward as to reach the channel of a much larger river; since, as will presently be seen, it has neither magnitude nor velocity sufficient to force its way two hundred and sixty miles to the sea-coast; but which the principal stream, by its volume and strength, has the power to effect.

The second expedition conducted by Captain Sturt proceeded from Sydney to explore the Morrumbidgee, in December, 1829. Tracing it down on its right bank, until he had passed every rapid or fall that might impede its navigation, he established a depot—launched a boat, which he had conveyed overland from Sydney, and having, by dint of great exertion, built another on the spot, he lost no time in commencing his examination of the river to the westward. Before we follow the enterprising party on their voyage, it may be interesting to give the height of the river at the depot, above the sea-coast, as derived from the observations of the late surveyor-general many years ago, on the adjacent country, which results it would have been very satisfactory had Captain Sturt been possessed of the means of verifying. This will show not only how slight is the inclination of its bed to give an impetus to its stream westerly towards the ocean, but also how perfectly unavailable to the colony are those vast flats of low country, which were observed to extend along its banks. The situation of his depot Captain Sturt found to be in latitude 34¼° south, and longitude 143° 57' east, or about twenty-seven geographic miles south-west from Mr. Oxley's extreme point of penetration on the steppes of the Lachlan, in July 1817, the mean elevation of which above the level of the sea, that accurate traveller had determined, by barometrical admeasurement, to be not more than two hundred and fifty feet. Now, as Captain Sturt informs us that the dispersed waters of those morasses again unite, and drain into the Morrumbidgee by a "large creek," which he passed about twelve miles west from his depot, it is very evident that the bed of this latter river, and the country immediately adjacent, are at a somewhat lower level than Mr. Oxley's last or westernmost encampment.

On the 7th January, the expedition moved forward down the river, and on the fourth day, having passed extensive alluvial flats, on which were patches of reeds, the navigation became much interrupted by "fallen timber," and as the current was frequently very rapid, particularly in those parts of the river where its channel had become contracted, the boats were oftentimes in great danger from sunken logs. After advancing on their voyage about ninety miles to the westward, through a country of level, monotonous aspect, the party were relieved from the state of anxiety which a week's most difficult and dangerous navigation had caused, by their arrival at (to use Captain Sturt's words) "the termination of the Morrumbidgee," for its channel, much narrowed and partially choked by driftwood, delivered its waters "into a broad and noble river," the current of which was setting to the westward at the rate of two miles and a half per hour, with a medium width from bank to bank of from three to four hundred feet. This "new river," which was called the Murray, and into which the diminished waters of the Morrumbidgee fall, is evidently formed by a junction of the "Hume," and "Ovens,"—which streams, taking their rise in the great Wanagong Chain, were first made known to us by the travellers Messrs. Hovell and Hume, who crossed them, two hundred and fifty statute miles nearer their sources, in their excursion to Port Philip in 1824. Pursuing the course of the Murray, on the 14th January, the voyagers made "rapid progress to the W.N.W.," noticing, as they passed on, a low "unbroken and uninteresting country of equal sameness of features and vegetation," to that observed whilst descending the intricate Morrumbidgee on quitting their depot.

After nine days' voyage down the Murray, in which period they made about one hundred miles of westing, without observing the slightest change of country for the better, or the least rise in its surface, the expedition passed the mouth of a stream flowing from the north by east, with a strong current, and in point of magnitude but "little inferior" to the Murray itself. Ascending it, Captain Sturt found it preserved a breadth of one hundred yards, and its banks, on which were many natives, "were overhung with trees of finer and larger growth" than those of the Murray. Its waters were, moreover, ascertained to be two fathoms in depth; of turbid appearance, but "perfectly sweet to the taste." The confluence of these two rivers takes place, it appears, (by Captain Sturt's reckoning), in exactly longitude 141° east, and immediately to the south of the parallel of 34°. It was at this stage of the expedition that the face of the country began to assume (comparatively speaking) an interesting appearance; and the first rise of ground which had been seen in the advance of the party to the westward in a direct line of more than two hundred miles, was observed at a moderate distance from the river to the north-west. Previous to his reaching the point of confluence of the two rivers, Captain Sturt, it would appear, had entertained a doubt as to the "decline of the vast plain through which the Murray flows," as well as of "the probable fall of the waters of the interior" to the north of it; but on observing a new stream flowing into the Murray, the circumstance of the "parallel" (meridian doubtless) in which he had struck it, "and the direction from which it came," combined to satisfy him, "that it could be no other than the Darling." It was therefore concluded that the whole of the internally formed streams, at present known in that country, from my Dumaresq's River, (discovered in 1827 in lat. 29°) to the Murray in 34°, are discharged into the ocean on the south coast—the dip of the continent within the parallels of 28° and 35½°, being of course to that point. However, the identity of this tributary to the Murray with the Darling, remains still to be ascertained, before the declension of so considerable portion of the interior can be said to be southerly, and before one can positively assert, with the president of a society in New South Wales, either that an interesting fact has been established—viz., "that all the waters from the Bathurst country, owing to the dip of the earth, run to the south-west extremities of eastern Australia,"—or that these discoveries have opened a water communication from the south coast, " one thousand miles through a variety of agricultural and pastoral country, in one of the finest climates which the world can boast of," and capable of sustaining " millions of emigrants."

The character of the Darling, as also the general direction of its course, beyond the point to which it has been traced, we have yet to ascertain. Since, however, it is by far the most considerable inland stream at present known in that country, it is to be hoped, that its further examination, which may furnish much interesting information respecting the actual features of the more remote regions of the interior to the north-west, will ere long be prosecuted. But to follow the expedition down the Murray.

That river, after it receives the supposed Darling, continues its course upwards of a degree farther to the westward, and in that space received a second stream, which falls in on its left bank from the south-east. This tributary stream, which is described as a river of "considerable importance," and was named the "Lindesay," is most probably the "Goulburn" of the same indefatigable explorers, whose journey overland to the south coast in 1824 I have already adverted to, and who, in fording their river at a part where its channel presented a breadth of eighty yards, left it winding its course to the north-west. From this point, the Murray assumed a new feature, and along its northern bank extended a range of cliffs, which appeared to the party, as they passed beneath them, to be of "partial volcanic origin." The navigation at length became rather intricate, for those cliffs being immediately succeeded by others on each bank, of limestone, the river was found to force its way through a glen of that rock, in its passage frequently striking bases of precipices of the same formation, which rose to a perpendicular elevation of two hundred feet, and in which "coral and fossil remains" were remarked to be plentifully imbedded. At this stage of their passage, those long ranges of forest hills, which extend along the eastern shore of the Gulf of St. Vincent, became discernible, indicating to the exploring party their approach to the coast. On the 3d February, the river having reached the meridian of $139\frac{3}{4}°$, the disposition of the bounding cliffs gave its course a decided bend to the southward, through a continuation of the glen, which at length opened into a valley.

Here the river was observed to have lost the sandy bottom which it had exhibited throughout its long course from the eastward, for its bed having now dipped to almost the level of the sea, its waters had become "deep, still, and turbid." Its course to the south was followed by the voyagers along reaches of from two to four miles in length; and upon their passing the parallel of $35°$, a more open country appeared before them, for the cliffs having partially ceased, had given place to picturesque hills and lower undulations, beneath which extended "thousands of acres of the richest flats"; but, as Captain Sturt adds that these were covered with reeds, and were evidently liable to inundation from the river, the value to the agriculturist of such marshy grounds, scarcely at all elevated above the sea-shore, may be easily estimated.

On the 8th of February (the thirty-second day of the voyage from the depot) the hills "wore a bleak appearance," and the few trees which had at one period fringed their ridges, were for the most part broken off, "as if by the prevalent winds." At noon, upon entering the river's last reach, no land could be discerned at its extremity; some low hills continued, however, along its left bank, whilst its right was hid by high reeds. Immediately afterwards, these enterprising voyagers entered an extensive lake, the body of which stretched away far to the south-west, in which direction "the line of water met the horizon." This lake, which received the name of "Alexandrina," was estimated at from fifty to sixty miles in length, and from thirty to forty in breadth. A large bight was observed in it to the south-east, and an extensive bay at the opposite point; still, notwithstanding these dimensions, this very considerable sheet of water appears to be but a mere shoal throughout, since Captain Sturt states, "its medium depth" is but "four feet"!

Upon this vast but shallow lake, he pursued his voyage to the southward, remarking that its waters, which at seven miles from the point of discharge of the Murray into it were brackish, were at twenty-one miles across perfectly salt, and there the force of the tide was perceived. As the party approached the southern shore, the navigation of the boats was interrupted by mud flats, and soon their further progress was effectually stopped by banks of sand. Captain Sturt therefore landed, and walking over some sandy hummocks, beyond which he had, from his morning's position, seen the sea, almost immediately came out upon the coast of Encounter Bay of the charts, whence he took bearings to Cape "Jarvoise," (rather Jervis of Captain Flinders), and the South-east point of Kangaroo Island. At the lower part of the lake seals were observed, and near the spot on the southern shore, where the party had effected a landing, some natives were seen grouped together, but as they bore arms and had their bodies painted, it was obvious that their intentions were far from being friendly; nor did they, although they saw the party were peaceably disposed, attempt to visit the encampment of the travellers during their stay on the margin of the lake.

Having thus seen the termination of the Murray and the

outlet of the lake into which it fa ls upon the south coast, Captain Sturt lost as little time as possible in conducting his party back by water to his depot—circumstances not permitting of a more perfect examination of that extensive piece of water, from the north-western extremity of which, some hopes had been entertained of there being a clear and open communication with the Gulf of St. Vincent.

Now we gather from the results of this second tour of discovery of Captain Sturt, simply this, and no more, viz.—in what way the Morrumbidgee, as well as the several streams which were crossed by Messrs. Hovell and Hume in 1824, and the waters of the Lachlan of Oxley in 1817 (all which unite), are disposed of; as also the nature of the "unbroken, uninteresting country," lying to the westward of the marshes of the latter. It must, however, be acknowledged that, in effecting this service, Captain Sturt has added largely to the geographical knowledge which we previously possessed, since the facts ascertained by him during the progress of his expedition have enabled him to fill up no inconsiderable blank on the map of that part of New South Wales lying to the west and south-west of Port Jackson. That the expedition of this enterprising officer has opened to the settler "unmeasurable tracts of well-watered" country previously unknown, as stated in the report of a society in the colony already referred to, his dispatch to the local government does not in the slightest degree support; nor does it contain the announcement to the colonists, that a river, navigable for commercial purposes, has been discovered in that country, which can be available at some future day "to convey to the coast the wools and other exportable produce" of the settlers, who may hereafter be established in those parts of the interior which lie in the neighbourhood of its banks. The reverse is the fact. The Murray, when flooded from the eastward, will doubtless carry a boat safely down its channel, but as a navigable river at all seasons, it is, like the Macquarie, and indeed every other western stream, useless to the colonists. Even if the Murray were throughout the year, and during the driest seasons, a deep navigable river, its waters could not be rendered of use for the purposes of commerce, since it discharges itself into a shoal lake, and that again into the sea at Encounter Bay, where, although the passage is, as Captain Sturt states, "at all periods of the tide, rather more than a quarter of a mile in width, and of sufficient depth for a boat to enter," still, as he also observes, and the master of every coaster well knows, "a line of dangerous breakers," which are constantly rolling against the sand-bars thrown up by the prevalent winds, "will always prevent an approach to the lake from the sea, excepting in the calmest weather; whilst the bay itself will at all times be a hazardous place for any vessel to enter under any circumstance." The opinion also, which has been entertained, that a more practicable communication with the lake might be found from the Gulf of Saint Vincent is wholly gratuitous, for a reference to the voyage of Captain Flinders, who closely examined the shores of that deep bight, and an inspection of the chart of that able navigator (the accuracy of which, generally, no seaman ever doubted who had sailed by it), on which is laid down a range of wooded hills, extending from the promontory of Cape Jervis northerly, along the whole of the eastern shore of the gulf, are sufficient for us rather to entertain every doubt of the existence of such a channel of communication with the north-western bay of the lake, which is itself, in all probability, nothing else than an extensive mud-shoal.

I have now given the sum of our geographical knowledge of New South Wales up to the present period; and dividing the map of that vast country into seven equal parts, one division will fully include the tracks of all the journeys which have been undertaken since 1817, with a view to discovery, by Oxley, Sturt, Hovell and Hume, myself, and others; whilst the remaining six portions, which comprehend a great expanse of interior beyond the tropic, and the whole of the equinoctial part of the continent, continue, at this day, a vast region, entirely unknown. The want of navigable rivers in that "Great South Land," must necessarily impede the progress of discovery in the interior of the country.

IX. HUME AND HOVELL'S JOURNEY TO PORT PHILLIP

[The following narrative of the important journey of Messrs. Hume and Hovell to Port Phillip, in 1824, is taken from the field note-book of Hovell, which is preserved in the Mitchell Library, Sydney.]

October 2, 1824.—At 1 p.m. loaded the cart with the provisions and all things necessary for our intended journey, being a supply for four months, viz., 640 lbs. flour, 200 lbs. pork, 100 lbs. sugar, 14 lbs. tea, 8 lbs. tobacco, 12 lbs. soap, salt, coffee, etc. etc., etc., for myself and three men, together with a musket and ammunition for each man. This is exclusively for ourselves, as Mr. Hume has supplied (as I understand) the same quantity.

Sunday, 3rd October.—At 1 p.m. left Mr. Hume's house in company with his cart; at 4 o'clock crossed the Cowpasture River, and commenced measuring our distance by perambulator. Weather fine, but very hot considering the time of the year.

Tuesday, 16th November.—At half an hour after sunrise we were away, and at the end of 3½ miles (7 o'clock) we suddenly arrived at the bank of a very fine river, at least two hundred feet wide, apparently deep, with the bank about eight or nine feet above the level which is overflowed at the time of a flood, and the stream running about three knots per hour. On both sides the land is low and level, and consists of a fine alluvial soil, with grass up to our middle. This I named Hume's River, he being the first that saw it. As we could not cross here, we followed its course to the distance of 3½ miles, making seven miles in all, and stopped to breakfast. Between 2 and 3 o'clock we set out with the intention to follow the course of the river, to find a crossing place, but we had not proceeded far before we found that impossible, as all between the river and the high land are lagoons and swamps to the distance of about two miles back. We had therefore to keep back to the high land, and came to at the foot of a hill alongside the river, and, at the end of ten miles, myself and Mr. Hume went to the top of the hill to see if there

83

was any place down the river where it was likely there would be a fall, or crossing place. From south to west is a range, at about the distance of sixty miles, under which I think a river runs. It is all a flat level country in front of us, say, west. This river, as far as we can see it, bore W. by S., and I think I may venture to say it afterwards runs W.N.W., the land there appearing the lowest. The flax plant grows in common here, and there is also a peppermint plant, different but superior to the English. Wild duck are numerous; some we shot. Caught one fish, the same as the Lachlan River fish, and one of another description, different to any that has been seen before in the Colony (as Mr. Hume informs me). I think, from what I can recollect of the tench, these and they are sworn brothers. Got the skin of a very large black snake; the snake itself must have been at least eight feet long as the skin is fully six. The bell-bird is common here. The natives frequently resort here, and I have no doubt are numerous, as fish are plentiful, both in the river and lagoons. It appears they are caught in dams where there is a running stream, as there is one they have made now in front of us. They are driven into the dam by the natives at one end, which is closed up when they think they have got sufficient. They are made intoxicated (as is usually done near to the sea coast about the Five Islands) by the bark of the willow tree, which they throw on to the place. By this they are supposed to be brought to the top. The natives then get into the water and throw them out. Variation pr. west 72 deg. 33 min. In the solid wood of a healthy tree I cut my name, "Hovell, Novr. 17/24."

Wednesday, 17th November.—As we did not know where we could cross the river, we thought it advisable to let the cattle remain, and myself, Mr. Hume, and two men to follow the course of the river down, to seek for a crossing place. We therefore started about 7 o'clock for that purpose; but we found that to keep along its banks was impossible, as the lagoons and swamps in most places completely shut us out, some of them forming a half circle, the centre part extending to a distance of two miles and the two ends coming to this river. Many of these creeks are as wide as the river itself, therefore we only got to the river in two places until we got to the distance of about eight or nine miles. Here the river appeared to us as it did when we first saw it, but if at all different, it is with a more majestic appearance, it being rather wider, the banks more open and regular, and their height being about eight feet, over which I think the flood seldom comes (at least I saw no appearance of it here, but

I may be mistaken). The timber near the river is blue gum (as Hume assures me). But the timber at a distance from the river, where the soil is not so good, is box tree; the whole is very thin. In many parts there is very little more than sufficient to give it a handsome appearance. The grass is of a good quality, as well as the soil, and of all parts of the Colony I have seen, this has the advantage for feeding pigs or cattle, and if the banks are overflowed at times, there is high land at a short distance for them to retire to. This river, like the last two, is deficient in either swamp oak or appletree. As we found that it would be impossible to cross the river in any part we had seen without a good boat, sufficient to keep up the heads of the cattle, we propose going towards the mountains, where perhaps we may find it practicable to cross, as it is not unlikely but we may find two rivers instead of one. If it so happens that we cannot cross it at all, it is our intention to follow it down for at least one hundred miles. If circumstances will admit, I should like much to start from where we now are for that purpose, but as we have one object now in view, and which we set out for the purpose of carrying into effect, if at all possible, we are anxious to accomplish that desire, if *practicable*. If not, we will endeavour to follow his Excellency's directions, viz., that should we on our journey fall in with any extensive river (which he had no doubt we should) that we could not cross, to trace it down for some distance. But which of the two objects hereafter may attend to the greatest advantage, time must show.

Thursday, 18th November.—Every morning at the first dawn of day, and often before the birds themselves, we are on the move, and by the time we have everything packed up, bullocks and horses loaded, it is generally about half an hour after sunrise; by so doing we can get half our day's work over by 9 o'clock—before the heat of the day comes on, and about 2 p.m., we are ready to start again. This was the case to-day, and we arrived at the place where we first made the river on the 16th inst. Here we got breakfast. The river at this place we find to be eighty yards, according to our measurement by throwing a stone. At 2 p.m. we proceeded on to follow the course of the river up, but at the end of about three miles in an easterly direction we came to the river again. Here the river was as wide as any part we had seen, with a fine level forest on the opposite side, and with its course about N.E. and S.W. I have no doubt now, from what I could see from the top of the hill adjoining the river, but all the waters we passed hitherto running to the southward all fall into this, and that the river itself comes from an opening in the Snow Mountains. The country all around us has a very fine appearance. In some places there is not more than half a dozen trees in a hundred acres. The swamps and creeks back in the river here are the same as lower down, and in some future day will be valuable to those that may come to reside here. They are full of fish and wild ducks. We also saw two black swans on one of the creeks, being the first we have seen since leaving home.

Friday, 19th November.—Throughout the day the weather has been very pleasant. At the usual time we started, and, having arrived at a place where we thought we could cross the river, we stopped to breakfast rather earlier than usual. As this place did not appear to me to be safe for our cattle to cross, I took one man and our horses with me to trace the river higher up, to endeavour to find one more suitable for our purpose, and having gone a few miles we found a place where the current is not so strong, being more broken by rocks above us, the river not more than half the width, and the banks not so steep. But how we are to contrive to make a boat to take our provisions across (having no cart with us now) I am as yet at a loss to say, as the only tarpaulin we have with us is going to pieces, and the bark will not strip off the trees this time of the year. At 3 p.m. we started again and arrived at the crossing place (at least the place we propose for that purpose) by 5 o'clock, the whole distance we have travelled to-day being only 7½ miles.

Saturday, 20th November.—Throughout the day the weather was very pleasant, and favourable for the purpose we had to carry into effect, for having determined overnight to cross the river to-day, if practicable, we commenced first to patch up my tarpaulin, the only one we have with us; and having done it to our satisfaction, we then made a frame (neither round nor square), the bow being something narrower than the stem, and made something after the shape of one I had before made when wrecked at Kent's Group, Bass Straits, in the year 1816. We then put the tarpaulin over the frame, as we had before done by the cart. At 11 o'clock we began to send the articles across, and by 4 p.m. horses, bullocks, etc., etc., were over, but it was nearly with the loss of Mr. Hume's bullock. At 5 o'clock we left the banks of the river and travelled 2½ miles into the forest before dark. The river on this side is encircled by creeks, lagoons and swamp, the same as on the other, and it is but seldom that we can come near it. All the back land is of an excellent quality, and I think, from the little I have seen of it, I may venture to say it is superior to the soil on the other, and the grass, of course, will also have the advantage. We found in crossing all the other rivers that the waters, as well as the creeks which ran either to the northward or westward were all of them very cold, but this river, as well as the creeks which ran to the southward or eastward, are altogether as warm. How to account for it, I am not equal to the task. I should have thought this river in particular would have been cold, as we have every reason to believe that most of the streams which fall into it must come from the Snow Mountains range, which forms a part of the Australian Alps.

Sunday, 21st November.—About the usual time we started in hopes that we should be able to make up for the lost time which this river had occasioned, not even allowing ourselves a Sunday, knowing that we had no time to spare. But we had not travelled more than a mile and a half (or four miles from the other) through swamps, etc., before we came to the banks of a sixth river, its width being 110 feet from the water's edge. The stream was equally as strong as the other river, but it was not so deep, and the cattle crossed with little difficulty. But we had to make another boat, the same as before, to get our provisions, etc., etc., across, and by noon we were ready to start again. Having had some little trouble to get out from the side of the river, through the swamps, lagoons, etc., we kept a course S.W. over a range and descended on the other side, where we came to other lagoons, which plainly showed that another river was at hand. At the distance of about four miles, we had for our comforts to cross another river, its width being about the same as the other, its current the same also, but in what part of the Hume they come into I can only judge. But I think this comes in below, and the last one above, where we first made that river. The banks of both are not more than six or seven feet, and there is every proof that all the lagoons and rivers are in the time of flood one immense sheet of water, perhaps not less than two miles in some places, in others more. It is quite clear that there is only one range of mountains or hills between each of those rivers. The first appeared to come from the N.N.E., (Perhaps after N.E.) the second S.E. and this south. The one we crossed yesterday was a rocky bottom, but those two are pebbly bottom. The natives are numerous here, but we have not seen any, only their smoke. There is little doubt but they have seen us. Shot two native companions and ducks, and caught some of the Lachlan River fish out of both those. We have caught no perch, only out of the ponds.

Monday, 22nd November.—In the middle of the day the weather was very warm, but the morning and evening cool and pleasant. As it was too late last night to get everything across the river, we did not begin to do so until this morning, and as a very large tree had fallen across the river, which reached from bank to bank, with the body out of the water, we fastened a rope from one side to the other as a hand rope, and it saved us the trouble of making another boat, for upon this tree we carried everything across. As our cattle have become so used to the water, we have no trouble (to what we had at first) to cross any of the streams, unless they are very strong, as for instance the Murrumbidgee. This, and the last, they crossed at one and the same time by being strung together by one rope. By the time the first bullock has foothold on the opposite side, the last is about going in. As for my mare, she wants no rope, for she feels as much pleasure in swimming about in the water as we do ourselves when we got into the water for that purpose. By half-past eight we had everything over, got our breakfast, and were ready to proceed on our journey. After getting out from between the creeks, etc., we kept our course S.W. between two ranges, which appeared favourable for that purpose, and at the end of six miles, it being half-past eleven, we came to for two or three hours. The land is of the same quality as that which is already described, as is the grass also; but the flax plant is, in my opinion, superior to any I have seen in the Colony, the length being from 4½ to 5½ feet. I think the natives make use of it for different purposes. At the end of 10½ miles, it being 6 o'clock, we stopped for the night, having got to the end of the opening, we took the bearing in the morning. The land which we have passed through this afternoon is something of a mountain forest—I cannot call it good. In parts the grass is long and of the same description as grows on the sides of mountains; but where there is moisture, the grass is better.

We have seen no limestone since the 15th inst., at the Limestone Falls, nor have I seen any stone that contains any part of it. Nearly all the stone that we have seen since that time is granite. The timber is principally stringy-bark and very good. There is every appearance by the marks on those trees where they have taken the bark off, that it has been cut by an iron tomahawk. I suppose they have communication with the coast natives, as they can have no other way of obtaining them but through that channel, as the distance from any station is too great for them to procure them by that means. The bronzewing pigeon is not so common here as with us, but the black and white cockatoos and the parrots are, as also the quail. And where there is water, the curlew and the snipe are seen. It is now the season for the swans and other waterfowls to bring out their young ones. The flesh of the native companions, when boiled, resembles beef, both in appearance and flavour, but there is no fat. We killed one kangaroo this afternoon, being the first for several days.

Tuesday, 23rd November.—For the first three miles this morning we crossed several ends of ranges, when we came to a forest of good grass, but the ground not of a very good quality, but thinly covered with timber, which is excellent stringy bark and box gum. At 10 a.m. stopped to breakfast beside a spring of water, and at the distance of 6½ miles. At 3 p.m. we started again and travelled 5½ miles further (making in all 11½ miles, S.W.) and stopped at the foot of the last high range we had but a little before ascended and descended again, beside a fine running stream of cold water. All the land we have gone over this afternoon is of a more inferior quality than that which we passed over this morning, and in parts worse than any land we have seen since leaving home. The appearance of the country to the westward is low, with few or no hills. To the S.W. it appears like the end of ranges falling off to a level; but to the eastward immense mountains appear to view. I find, whenever we come near the mountains, we are plagued by the devil fly and the mosquito—we cannot rest for them now, unless we get into a cloud of smoke, and the remedy is nearly as bad as the evil. I think the snakes are not numerous, as we have not seen more than one these last few days.

Wednesday, 24th November.—We started about 6 this morning, our course being S.W. through a forest country nearly on a line with the mountains, till we got to the distance of about five miles, when we came to a running stream of water. We had now to ascend a very high hill, the north side of which, and another at a little distance, were quite clear of trees, growing only brushwood; but the tops were very thick of timber. On getting to the top we found it to be a dividing range, from which we had a fine view. On the east side, all mountains—I suppose a continuation of the Australian Alps—on the north, the country we had passed through; on the west, similar to what I described on the 17th instant. On the south side an opening appeared through which we shall have to pass, and which I have no doubt the waters, which we see below us, run also. This creek comes from the east, and I suppose we shall find hereafter that it runs into the Hume. All below us, from east to the foot of the mountains around, is a large open forest through the middle of which the creek runs. The land is dry and parched up by the drought; the grass is dry also. Beside this nearly dry creek, we stopped to breakfast, having travelled 7¾ miles by 10 o'clock.

At 4 p.m. proceeded on through a pleasant country, but we see it now at a great disadvantage. It is quite level, the grass tolerably good, and some very fine timber. At 6 o'clock, and at 4¼ miles from where we last started, we came to the north bank of the eighth river. The width where the river is at its usual height, is something wider than the last two we crossed, but as it is low I think we shall be able to cross it without the trouble of making a boat. I think from appearances that it is at times flooded. The land adjoining is exceedingly good, and is without the scrubs, lagoons and swamps to which the last three are subject. The timber which grows on its banks is thin, but of good quality. The land could be cleared at a very little expense. There are fine hills and grass land in the back. In my opinion it is as pretty a spot and as valuable as any I have seen since leaving home. But we cannot judge to what extent it runs, as the bush is all on fire around us. Consequently our view is obstructed. The river comes from the east. From the mountains which now appear to us in that direction, I have no doubt that the Hume and this join, but it will be at some distance to the westward from us. Which will be the leading river time must shew. I have named it the Ovens, in compliment to Major Ovens. My friend (Hume) has just ventured an opinion, that he is sure all those rivers empty themselves into the sea, but he does not say whether an inland sea or the ocean. My opinion is that they empty themselves, first into one immense lake, and the waters from the lake are carried off into the ocean in the N.E. or S.W. coasts, as part of the coast, in these directions, is low. The land in a N.W. direction, whenever we can see it to advantage from the top of a mountain, always appears the lowest part around. Whenever the journey is undertaken to determine that which now appears a mystery, and there is a problem to solve, I have no doubt but it will be pleasant one, if they follow the north side of the Hume, as there does not appear to be any mountains, as I before mentioned in that part, in the westerly direction. Mr. Hume calls the timber here the Bong Bong Gum.

Thursday, 25th November.—We found very little trouble in crossing the Ovens, as it has fallen so very low, that it was fordable in many parts. The one we took had not more than three feet of water upon it, and it being of a pebbly bottom, it occasioned little trouble or delay, as the cattle crossed it with their load upon their backs, notwithstanding the current being strong at the falls. I think the banks of the river are higher than the last two we crossed, but it is not so subject to be flooded as either of the others, although there are evident marks of its being flooded at times. The land at the back is as good as on the other side. It was here we saw the flax plant growing in perfection, its length being six or seven inches longer than a soldier's musket. It is here also we saw the honeysuckle growing. Wherever we find the honeysuckle and the grass tree in this country we find the land to be good. A mountain with snow upon it bore S.E. about fifteen or twenty miles—a singular looking mount, but on this side of the above, which we call Mount Buffalo S.E. At the distance of five miles in the same range, but further west, we had another view of a fine level country all to the west, in parts as far as the eye could reach, particularly N.W. The country south from us does not appear to be so mountainous as hitherto. All the country from where we started this morning is all burned, and in every direction the bush is all on fire.

At 4 we started and, having gone a short distance, came to a creek of fine running water which runs to the northward. For the most of the afternoon we have been crossing the ends of ranges to keep our course. Some of them, one a complete mass of stones apparently as if they had been heaped together for the purpose, which make it very bad for the feet of the poor beasts. From one of the hills we had a fine view of the country to the southward.

Friday, 26th November.—At half past 5 o'clock this morning we proceeded on again, keeping a course of about S.W. by S. for a hill of which we took the bearing yesterday, and keeping a range of forest hills on the north side of us. All the land below those hills is of a good quality, and has a good coat of grass. The timber is stringy-bark and fine gum, and a description of manna tree. At the distance of 1½ miles from where we started, we came to a creek of fine running water, and, from appearances, we were sure a river was at hand. I was not wrong in my conjecture, for at the distance of about half a mile we came to the banks of the ninth river. As we fortunately hit upon a good crossing place, we were not delayed much in doing it. The banks of this river are not more than five or six feet, the width from twenty to thirty; it has very little current, only at the falls; the water is very low at this time, but is occasionally flooded. It comes from the southward, and I have no doubt that at some distance further to the N.N.W. the Ovens and it join, but as that river is the largest it is into that it will fall. At the distance of 4¼ miles we came to the top of a range which gave us a fine view of the country to the north of us. All in that direction appeared a fine, open level country, the grass green, and here and there a plain, but seldom of any great extent.

Saturday, 27th November.—Started about 6 o'clock. From the appearance of the morning I thought we should have a change of weather, as the morning was cloudy and threatened rain; but it was all deception. For a few hours the sun was intolerably hot, and as our whole time has been employed in ascending and descending five different ranges, all stones, bad soil and brush, we felt the heat much more than we should have otherwise done had the road been good or level. By the time we had got to the distance of 6½ miles, it being half-past 10 o'clock, the cattle were quite exhausted, and the men fatigued. There being a run of water near us, but very little or no grass, we came to. Our object in crossing these ranges is, first, that we think as we get to the southward the ranges may not be so high; secondly, there appears to be a division in the ranges; and, thirdly, that a river must come from that opening, and we are anxious to ascertain its course and extent.

Sunday, 28th November.—As the place we stopped at last night did not afford enough grass for our cattle for to-day, we left it early this morning to seek a better place, and having got to the top of the range, a plain and meadow appeared in front of us, but not of any great extent. This hill also offered us a good view of the country to the N.W. It appears here, as it has always done, viz., level forest country, with here and there a plain, one of which bore N. 20 deg. W. To the S.W. the ranges lie quite across our course. We descended the range and crossed the swamp, which we before thought was a plain, and at the distance of four miles we stopped, as the place afforded good grass. This place appears to be the same as all the other meadows where the division of the ranges is of any extent, viz., always a run of water towards the top,—swampy, with reeds growing.

As the ranges run to the N.W. they fall off with a gentle slope, as they become level. And, of course, there is a greater extent of forest as the ranges come to an end; and from being a swamp, it becomes dry, good land fit for any purpose.

Monday, 29th November.—About the usual time this morning we started, keeping a course as near S.W. as circumstances would permit. Most part of the ground we passed near this morning is of a very good quality and the quality of timber always denotes it. Some of the soil is a complete scarlet colour, the stone from which it is composed is of the same colour. The trees were mostly honeysuckle, manna and cow-pasture box. At the distance of 5¾ miles we crossed a creek which runs N.W.; here we rested. At 4 o'clock got under way and crossed another range, the whole of which appears as if it had been turned topsy-turvy. There is scarcely one stone lying upon another; the whole is separated and divided, and lying in irregularly sized pieces. Nor can I tell which way the strata formerly lay; the whole is coarse granite, the soil good below. After descending the hill we crossed a creek, and came to a second, the waters of both running to the N.W. Here we remained for the night, with abundance of good grass for our cattle. It will not be improper to remark here that, whatever place we have been in, whether on the top of the highest mountain, or in any of the deepest ravines, we always find evident marks that the natives occasionally resort to them, although there does not appear to be any inducement for them to visit those secluded places. Those are the people we generally call "miserable wretches," but in my opinion the word is misapplied, for I cannot for a moment consider them so. They have neither house-rent nor taxes to provide, for nearly every tree will furnish them with a house, and perhaps the same tree will supply them with food (the opposum). Their only employment is providing their food. They are happy within themselves; they have their amusements and but little cares; and above all they have their liberty.

Wednesday, 1st December.—Towards daylight this morning the weather was very cold, so much so that we could not keep ourselves warm in bed, and with all the clothes we could put on us. It is true we were elevated much above our usual height, and the wind was at S.W. At daylight the thermometer stood at 41 deg. in the tent, but it must have been much lower before that time. At sunrise the weather, which before had threatened rain, had now altered its appearance, and we moved off at our usual time. But previous to our descending from that high range, we got a view of the country around from an adjoining hill. Towards the east there appeared to be a forest country, flat, and extending along on each side of what I suppose to be the banks of a river. There are also three plains, the nearest about four miles from us, the farthest about twelve. There is also a gap in the mountains which appear to surround this place, the which I suppose to be the opening where the river runs through to the eastward or takes its rise farther to the eastward, and comes to where we think we shall fall in with a river to the S.W. of us, as there are two ranges, in that direction (both very high, but the farthest much the highest) between which we think the river comes. The country S.E. to south is completely broken, so much so as any we have seen. It is only to the N.W. the country looks at all favourable. At the distance of one mile in descending this range, we had to unload to get the cattle across a creek. We had then to ascend another range, and descend again to another creek, where we stopped to breakfast, at the distance of 4¾ miles. As two of our dogs which went in chase of a kangaroo had not returned this morning we did not think it advisable to proceed without first sending in search of them, and three men were sent for that purpose, but returned a little before sundown without having seen the least trace of them. Our best missing dog had also been away, but just returned wounded by the feet of a kangaroo. We have now only one dog, and him so very low in condition from not having had animal food so long that he is now unable to run, but more likely to die.

Thursday, 2nd December.—We were surprised this morning on rising to find that one of the dogs had returned some time in the night. He was a little cut by a kangaroo. At half-past five this morning we set off. At two miles we came to a meadow with a creek running through the centre. We continued our course S.W. through a good forest country till we got to the distance of 5½ miles, when we were obliged to stop, as the natives had set the grass on fire in the direction we wanted to go, and we were doubtful whether we should find grass for our cattle if we passed this place, where it is plentiful, and good water. A little after we stopped the other dog returned. They had every appearance that they had killed the kangaroo, and had been lying by it till they had filled themselves. About 2 o'clock we left this place as the smoke and fire had passed by us and the weather was pleasant for travelling. On getting to the top of the hill, about one mile from where we last started, we observed that a gap, which on Tuesday last bore S.E. by S. but now bore S. 35 deg. W., would be favourable for us to pass between if we could get to it, and there was every appearance of a river passing through, and forest hills adjoining it. To this we directed our course, and, having ascended the ranges, we found the country alter, in our opinion for the better; but in this whole country the grass for miles around was burnt. Therefore we saw it at a very great disadvantage. Having travelled thirteen miles this day, and the sun being nearly set, we at length came to a spot of about two acres where the grass had escaped the fire. Here we remained all night, beside some water-holes. I should have observed before that in all the holes of water (where the stream is not strong) we have always found leeches of a very large size and fit for medical purposes.

Friday, 3rd December.—Started very early this morning, but it was not till we had got the distance of four or five miles through the burnt grass, following the course of the creek down, when we got to the end, that it brought us within a short distance of the river (eight miles) which runs N.W. On one side of the creek is a sort of meadow, but the whole is a fine pleasant country. The soil, being good, produces abundance of fine grass and the whole, both hills and lowlands, are thinly covered with timber. It is our opinion that we have not seen a more agreeable and interesting country since leaving home. At 5 p.m. we came to the banks of the river and found a place where we could cross upon a tree, without the trouble of making a boat. But it will require some trouble to make a road to the water to get the cattle over, as also to carry the provisions, as the banks are at least twelve feet and perpendicular. This river is as wide as the Hume where we first made it, say, eighty yards, but the current is not so strong. The creeks and lagoons back into the river, but in some parts the south end of the high ranges comes close to the side of the river, thereby making it impossible to pass between with cattle. Here we remained all night and prepared for carrying our things across in the morning. Caught some of the Lachlan River fish. This river we named the Goulburn, in compliment to Major Goulburn. Killed one kangaroo.

Saturday, 4th December.—Before breakfast we had all our provisions, etc., etc., across the river, and after breakfast the bullocks and horses were swum over, and at 10 o'clock we proceeded on our journey. Having got through the swamps and creeks, which were nearly one mile from the river, we ascended a range the foot of which came close to a creek, the same as on the other side. We continued our course S.W. through agreeable and picturesque country, soil good, a good coat of grass, but at present dried up in consequence of the drought, and only here and there trees, just enough to answer as a shade for cattle on a warm day. I think the fine dry hills have less timber upon them than the flats. At the distance of seven miles from the Goulburn we suddenly arrived at the banks of another river, but although it was only a small one when compared with the other, yet it gave us nearly as much trouble in getting our things across, which we did by means of a tree lying across it. But we had much more trouble with our cattle, as we had to let every one swim over separately. This was occasioned by the depth of water, broken trees, and a mud-bank to land them upon on the opposite side. After crossing it we loaded again and got to the edge of the forest distant about one mile, where we stopped for the night, it being sundown before we arrived here.

In all our travels I have seen no country better adapted for feeding sheep, the hills adjoining the Goulburn River being nearly clear of timber, grass to the top, and in the hollows below an abundance of herbage of a very excellent quality.

Tuesday, 7th December.—At the rise of the sun this morning we set off to cross some ranges which were in front of us, and at the distance of $2\frac{1}{4}$ miles we came to a creek, or river, which receives the waters from the mountains to the east of us. The stream runs very strong, but we found a good place to cross; it has a pebbly bottom and at times rises very high. It was here we first saw any king parrots since leaving home. From that circumstance we named the water King Parrot Creek. After leaving this we ascended a very high range full of stones, which made it very troublesome for the cattle to get up with their loads, and it was 9 o'clock before we got to the top; and for our trouble we found that we should have to descend it again, as there was no range leading from this to the one opposite, which was much higher than the one we were then upon. As we considered by getting upon the other, we should find a communication from range to range, by what we call cross ranges, and if so we could cross the mountains to the opposite side, we descended again, and stopped at a run of water below to breakfast. Here we remained for about two hours and then commenced our task of ascending the mountain in front of us. After two hours' hard labour, not so much for ourselves as for the cattle, we arrived at the top. Here we were put to our wit's end to know in what direction to proceed, as the brush was so thick (we could not see ten yards before us); the consequence was we were obliged to go by guess and to keep two men in front cutting away the brushwood for the cattle to pass through. This we had to do for about $1\frac{1}{4}$ miles, and as the night was fast approaching, we found it necessary to stop for the night, as both cattle and men were fatigued and could not proceed any further. As there was neither grass nor water, we had to make the beasts fast to trees, leaving them only room or rope enough to lie down. As for ourselves, I think we felt the greatest want of that necessary article, water, more than the cattle, for, having been accustomed of late to so much good water, we did not before know the value of that principal support of life. As I had given each man some spirits to drink with his bread, it was the occasion of making them more thirsty than they would otherwise have been, nor was this the only cause of their being very uncomfortable, for as the top of the range was all stones, there was not a place to be found that would admit of their lying down at all with any comfort.

Wednesday, 8th December.—It may be supposed that owing to the miserable state we were in all night we were anxious to move from the place which was the occasion of it. Therefore before it was properly daylight we were on our legs, ready to start, and having got to the distance of about $1\frac{1}{4}$ miles through the brush which had to be cut for us to pass along, we found it impossible to get any further in that direction, say, about south, because of the closeness of the brush, dead timber lying in all directions on the ground, and the large pieces of stone, which crippled the feet of the cattle. Then we found it necessary to descend the mountain again in an easterly direction, and make for the King Parrot Creek. This we did, and, by 8 o'clock, we had got nearly to the bottom. As also an agreeable run of water presented itself for our acceptance, to us as well as the cattle, it was a welcome stranger, for we had been nearly eighteen hours without such a friend. At 9 o'clock we came to the banks of the King Parrot Creek, which we crossed, and then stopped to breakfast.

Thursday, 9th December.—Before 6 o'clock this morning, myself, Mr. Hume and two men, set out, taking a sufficiency of flour, tea and sugar to last us for four or five days. About 7 we began to ascend the Forlorn Hope Range, or Doubtful Range. The reason for my giving it that name was that yesterday I had paid particular attention to the soil of this and the different mountains around, together with the timber, the scrub and the stone. By doing so I found that they had all nearly one and the same appearance. By this I judged that if the ranges and mountains are of that quality on this side, doubtless they would be the same on the other, and therefore judged it impossible to get the cattle through, even if we were able to get through ourselves. From my doubts on that head it was that I gave it that name.

I. D.   k

At 10 we got to the top and crossed our track of yesterday. We then began to descend gradually on the other side; but it was only till now that we had seen anything of the difficulty of getting through this thicket. Scrambling for about two hours, sometimes on our hands and knees, at other times on the tops of bushes and rocks, in this manner did we go on till 12 o'clock, when we arrived at a spring of water. a distance of about two miles, where we stopped to take a pot of tea and some bread. After we had finished our humble meal we set forward again with hopes to find it better on the range opposite us. But this was not the case, for, instead of getting better, we found that it got worse, and, to add to this, a grass known about the Five Islands by the name of the "Cutting Grass," became more frequent. It runs here about four or five feet long, the edges are as sharp as a butcher's knife, and its width about one and a half inches. It is tough and strong, and should it by any chance draw edgeways across the flesh, it will make a deep incision in it, which afterwards will become very troublesome. About 4 p.m. we got to the top of the other range, but without any appearance of a change for the better, and, from what we could see from a high stump where a tree had been broken 'off, the general appearance was the same all around. We now thought that to continue going forward would be madness, as we could not, in the first place, form any idea where it would end, and, in the second place, if we went on much farther, we should not have a rag left upon our backs. We therefore thought it the most advisable plan to retrace our steps towards home (the tent) and, having arrived at a small run of water a little before dark, we took up our abode for the night, having gone nearly four miles into the scrub, our whole distance from the station to where we returned to sleep being about fourteen miles. To describe this brush or scrub is almost impossible, as it cannot be compared with any that is known in the Colony. Suffice it to say that it is worse than any that is known in it, or worse than any jungle in any other country. It is much worse than the scrub at the Five Islands, for there, if you cannot get over it, you can get under it, and can see your road before you; but here we could not see either over or under, nor two yards before. Sometimes we were on the top of dead logs, lying five or six feet above the ground, at other times in holes fully as deep, and had we been seen coming into a town in the state we were in, people would have sworn that we had been in some drunken affray. Mr. Hume had his face so nearly covered with the brambles and boyers that it appeared as if it had been done by the fair hand of some Amazonian damsel; and myself had an eye that would have done honour to any young gentleman taking his first rudiments in that admirable art, pugilism. But worse than all was one of the men that had got on the only pair of trousers among three men. He had got an unfortunate tumble, which not only took away every part of his trousers, but the front flap of his shirt also, thereby leaving him in that state that, had there been any doubt of his manhood before, these doubts were now removed.

Friday, 10th December.—There is nothing will make a man forget the quality or the harshness of the bed he is lying upon more than being well fatigued. It is ten chances to one but he will lie down and fall asleep without once thinking to put on his nightcap. This was the case with me, for having made choice of the softest place I could find, I ate my piece of bread and drank my quart of tea and fixed some boughs to break off the south wind, when I laid myself down, as I thought to rest, not to sleep. But in this I was mistaken, for I fell asleep, nor did I awake till the morning. As soon as the sun was up we were up also, and set forward to reach our tent, which we did by a little after 9 o'clock. The fatigues of yesterday made our humble home acceptable to us. I have now to express my regret that we have not been able to penetrate through the brush across the range, as there would have been some hopes of our being able to get to our place of destination in time, and to have a sufficiency of flour left to return to Argyleshire with. But now those hopes are banished, unless we find a country at the west end of this range more favourable, judging from appearances, than we can possibly expect. But should we be fortunate enough to find good travelling, and at last to gain our object, this will indeed be a great relief to our mind, as that will do away with all doubts as to our exertions or endeavours to gain the intended object. Having refreshed ourselves, we set forward to our journey about 2 o'clock, following the course of the King Parrot Creek down.

Sunday, 12th December.—Before 5 o'clock this morning we were under way. Our motive for setting off so early was that, by the time the sun got up, it was likely the wind would rise also and prevent us from crossing the burning grass and scrub, which was still in the track we wanted to go. At the distance of eight miles (9 o'clock) the land began to change its appearance for the better, being gently sloping hills covered with grass, the soil good, and thinly covered with stringy-bark and gum trees. Should Fortune, that fickle-minded jade, but favour us in our one grand object, (to us it is so, having set our mind and our whole soul upon the thing,) she will then have recompensed us for all our troubles and difficulties when crossing the mountains, nor shall I care, living upon bread and water, and that but half allowance on my return, so long as I gain the object. At 5 we stopped, having travelled 12½ miles, beside a creek which we call Sunday Creek. Some part of the land we passed over this afternoon is not so good as that which we passed over a little before we stopped in the forenoon, but it produces good grass. From the hill I before mentioned, we could see that the country is on fire in all directions. This appears to be the season for their burning the old grass to get new. The country to the westward is high, inclining to the mountains; to the northward the land is low, through which the Goulburn River runs. There appears to be a river (at least from appearances of the land) ahead of us, which I have no doubt will join the above river at some distance farther northward.

Tuesday, 14th December.—Mr. Hume ascended a high but single hill, in front, from which we saw a very gratifying sight. This was a very extensive plain, extending from west to S.E. for several miles with patches of forest which appear to separate one plain from another. But the whole appeared in front, say, south, to be level, but in parts in the plains, some hills rose, of conical shape, with only here and there a few trees upon them, and all of the soil of the best quality. At eight miles we had got to the entrance of a forest and continued till we got to another hill from which we had another gratifying sight. This was plains and open forest, the latter serving to give the former a more beautiful appearance. They stretched beyond the reach of the eye and as far as we could see with the spy-glass, say, from S.E. to west, and the land fell with a gradual descent towards the south. Never did I behold a more charming and gratifying sight, at least not where it is in its natural state. I have travelled from Launceston to Hobart Town, but in the whole distance, I do not recollect seeing any one place where it can at all be compared with the spot we have passed and this before us. It perhaps may be supposed that I speak interestedly, or beyond what it really deserves, but that is not the case. I am always anxious to confine myself as near to truth as possible, and in this case in particular, as some day not far distant it might be proved that I had pictured it beyond what it deserved, thereby making me ashamed of what I had made public. After descending from the hill we went in search of water for ourselves and cattle, but we had to travel twenty-one miles from where we started this morning before we succeeded in getting any, it being nearly sundown before we arrived at the creek.

Wednesday, 15th December.—As the cattle were very much fatigued from yesterday's journey, we did not start till after breakfast, half past 8 o'clock, and having kept a course about S.S.W. four miles, we came to a very deep creek, which I suppose, lower down, becomes a river.

From where we now are, we can see at least fifty miles in any direction. It is all plains and small forests around. The whole is easy travelling. Should I be asked if I should, or would, come to reside here, which is usually the question first asked when recommending any place, my answer would be, yes, provided encouragement is given to me, as is usually given to gentlemen coming to reside among us as settlers under this Government. I have been endeavouring to bring to recollection a resemblance of this country to some counties in England, and of those I have seen the nearest of any which I can bring to mind is that of the County of Norfolk. That is supposed to be the most level county, and has the best soil; and this at first view would appear level, but after observing it closely you may perceive the gradual descent.

It has just occurred to my recollection that I have frequently heard persons express their astonishment that, in such an extensive country as this is, there is not a greater number of fine rivers along the east coast, through Bass's Straits, etc., etc., than what there is. We need not now wonder at the cause, when we come to consider that all the rain which falls within fifty miles may, in some of the places not more than twenty miles of the coast, run to the N.W. and north. This will give an idea of the height of the coast mountains, and the waters which come from the east side of the Alps are joined by those which come from the west side of the coast mountains, and are undoubtedly carried off by the Murrumbidgee, the Hume and the Ovens, and the Goulburn, all to the N.W. and north, except as far as about Cape Howe, when it is carried off by the Yar through Western Port.

Thursday, 16th December.—After breakfast we carried our provisions across the river, and afterwards crossed with the cattle, which was done with very little trouble, as they were able to walk across, and the water was only up to their bellies. This river Mr. Hume called the Arndell, in compliment to the late Dr. Arndell (the father of Mrs. Hovell) and to my son, Arndell Hovell. We continued our course through the plains, about S.W. by S. and at the distance of six miles we thought we saw the water, but at other times we thought it was the grass on fire. Sometimes we thought we could see the blaze, at other times the smoke; but this we afterwards found was occasioned by the wind blowing in hard from the N.W., which blew the heads of the billows, as it were, from us, we being to windward. But as the plain was so perfect a level, and had no high land at the back except at a very great distance, I was enabled to get a meridian altitude, which gave the latitude 38 deg. 6 min. and longitude 145 deg. 25 min. E. We bore down nearly south, and about 4 o'clock we could plainly perceive that that which we at times thought was fire and smoke was the very thing we were so very anxiously looking out for. At 5 o'clock we came to the point of land which separates the S.E. from the N.W. branches.   On this point I took several bearings of the harbour (refer to bearing book). From the place we were standing upon to the nearest land on the opposite, but S.E. side, I think is not less than eight or ten miles, and about the same distance to the west side. But higher up the S.E. branch than where we stood it was one immense sheet of water, and continued up as far as the eye could reach, and as I thought up to an opening near to the south end of the Australian Alps. Should there be water for shipping of a large tonnage up that branch it is equal to any harbour I have seen, and it will be an easy conveyance for timber for building, from those mountains, and the one most recommended is Mount Disappointment. Into this branch all the waters which we have crossed since coming upon the plains empty themselves, and it will be the conveyance for the produce coming through the Duke of York's Downs, which come up to the first river we crossed from Mount Disappointment round to the Gap in the Australian Alps. From this river to the Arndell River is Salamank (? Salamanca) Plains, in compliment to his Excellency, who distinguished himself in that action. From the Arndell up to Kennedy's Creek is the Duke of Clarence's Downs. This creek comes round the west end of Mount Wollstonecraft. I gave it that name for the respect I have for the gentleman bearing its name. It is a very conspicuous mountain, or rather it consists of a number of peaked hills adjoining each other, particularly when it bears N. 50 deg. W. (distance about five miles).

For the whole of the distance we have come since entering the plains, I find very little difference in the appearance of the country. There is a sameness throughout; the soil, generally speaking, is everywhere good. I have seen none bad, but I have seen some (I do not speak of a few acres, but of large spaces) equal to the best of any land, and the grass and herbage denotes it.

Notwithstanding it is dried and parched by the long drought which has shrivelled up the leaves, it is generally of a fine silky nature, and in places is intermixed with the long forest grass. The greatest deficiency this fair land has is that of timber. To make it a delightful spot, what nature has been very sparing of here must be supplied by artificial means. But I before observed there are places or rather patches of trees which will answer for fuel, and at the same time will be sufficient to hide its nakedness. On the sides of the rivers and creeks there is plenty of gum, etc., etc. There are parts of the plains where it is very stony, some of the stones weighing three or four cwts. Between them the grass grows best, and is always dry. But there are parts for a considerable distance where there is not a stone to be seen. From Mount Wollstonecraft there are two or three ridges of stones, which continue nearly to the water side, a distance of about six or seven miles. At the same time they are very little above the level of the other land.

On the beach are numerous beds of shells; therefore there can be no want of lime, supposing there was no limestone to be found. But in this I think there will be no deficiency, if the hills on the Jullian range are examined. But here the earth which is below the top soil may answer for the making of bricks. I am not able to judge, as we have no spade to dig down sufficiently deep to tell what quality of earth lies below.

Friday, 17th December.—A little after 5 o'clock this morning, we left this place (the place where we slept all night) and kept our course by Kennedy's Creek till we came to fresh water, a distance of about four or five miles from the extreme point, which separates the two branches. As there was good grass round the ponds, we remained here for the day, to refresh the cattle, which since the time of our first coming into this country, say, since last Monday, have had nearly double the work to do to accomplish the object by the time stipulated. To-morrow is the day fixed for our return, and we have only five weeks' ration of flour, at 8½ lbs. per man (instead of ten lbs.), and no meat, to travel back the distance which has taken us eleven weeks to come. We have to take the chances of the weather and should there be any change which would occasion the rise of ten rivers, exclusive of Muddy and King Parrot Creeks, and several others which we took no notice of at the time. They would occasion us a great deal of trouble if once filled with water. But we generally hope for the best.

A little after breakfast one of the men, Jas. Fitzpatrick, went out with his gun a little way up the creek to shoot some ducks, but he had not gone more than half a mile from our station when he suddenly came within a short distance of two natives, whom, it appeared, were either watching him, or were coming to watch us. As soon as the man saw them he began to retreat, but they, on the contrary, advanced, and having thrown off their cloak and with their arms in their hands, gave chase. When the man saw their hostile intentions, he turned round and snapped his pieces at one, but it miss-fired. The only chance then left him was his heels, which, being rather heavy, the lightness of the others gained upon him. However the short distance we were from him enabled us to hear him call for assistance, and as soon as the natives saw us they retreated as fast as they had before advanced. About two hours afterwards, as two of the men were going for a little firewood, from among some standing trees, taking their arms with them, two natives sprang from behind the tree, but seeing the men present their guns at them, they made signs of peace, at the same time calling out, as the men understood: "Good while ago, good while ago." As Mr. Hume was not far off, and knew their manners, he also made signs to them of peace. They laid down their arms, and at the same time called out to our men to lay down theirs also. When this was done they advanced, and, after a great deal of jabbering on both sides (not a word either one or the other understood), they came with us to the tent, and by degrees we began to understand each other by signs. From this we understand that a vessel had lately been in the bay, that they had been landing some things, including something like my trunk, that the commander always appeared in a bustle, and said to the men, "here, here," at the same time pointing to them to come down, or put them down. They described to us where the vessel laid. They also pointed towards Port Phillip and indicated that they had seen the men fell trees at that place; at the same time taking an axe, they described the way they used them, not forgetting the grunt or hiss which the men invariably do when they are striking anything with any force (undoubtedly alluding to the time that a settlement was about to be established there). The young man (who I understood was son-in-law to the elder man) began at last to be very inquisitive, as well as excessively troublesome, and by degrees to endeavour to secrete small articles. (I should have observed before, that a third native, son of the old man, had joined the other two) and notwithstanding there were generally one or others looking after him, yet he contrived to get away with several small but needful articles. At least he had hid them, for he had them when he left us. We afterwards found a tin pot and a spear, which he had buried in the ground at some distance. Taking their conduct generally, it appeared to all very suspicious and treacherous. They laughed about running after the man, but I have not the least doubt that had they got him they would have eaten a good part of him before we should have thought of looking for him. It was my wish, as also that of Mr. Hume, to have taken our horses to-morrow (the time the cattle rest) and have gone across to Port Phillip. But after what had passed, we did not consider it safe either to go or to leave the cattle behind, and from the different signals which were being made around us, we thought it better to abandon that plan, and to face towards home to-morrow after breakfast. I see very little difference between these men and those about Sydney, but their language is quite different. Mr. Hume knows a little of the Jervis Bay language, which he spoke to them, but they could not understand one word. Their manners are the same, and they use the same kind of weapon. By the largeness of their belly and their appearance they seem to live well. The name of the bay where they said the vessel lay is Geelong; Mount Wollstonecraft they call "Wibamanharter"; water is "Golamoo"; the name of a bird which Mr. Hume shot and skinned (something of a diver) they call "Bonering"; dog is "Narranuki"; bread is "Mumbungea." They did not appear to be astonished at the sight of the horses and bullocks, but they were very much afraid of them, much more so than they were of us, and dreadfully alarmed if they saw the bullocks look towards them, notwithstanding they were at a great distance from them. This fear we encouraged, as we considered it the greatest security against any attack. I have no doubt but this is the principal cause of our not seeing any of the natives during the whole of our journey before.

Saturday, 18th December.—By 7 o'clock this morning we had the natives with us again with the addition of another, but having shown our displeasure at their concealing the articles, they did not move from the place where they first sat down (their wives, children, and some other men remained at a little distance in the rear), they stopped until they saw the men bringing up the horses and cattle to be harnessed, when they took a hasty leave and retired. It was not till after they were gone that I missed a small bag, which contained a number of very useful articles, and such as I shall feel the want of before we get home. I had had it out the evening before to get some trifles as presents to give them, but not being satisfied with what I had given them, they watched where I had laid it down, and took the first opportunity to conceal it from our sight. At 9 o'clock we set off, and followed the creek down part of the way which we had come the day before. This we did purposely to fill our bottles with the water, and to get other things necessary as a proof of our having been to Western Port. Myself and Mr. Hume rode to the extreme point of land which separates the two branches, to take another view of this fine bay and harbour before we take our departure for home. I have already spoken much in its praise. Should I say much more, it may be thought I have said too much, I shall therefore leave the rest for those that may be sent to survey both it and the country. When that is done, I feel little fear of being contradicted in the account I have given of either. By 10 a.m. we began to retrace our steps, but kept nearer to the water than when we had come. By so doing we avoided the stones which we before passed through, and about the distance of fifteen miles we stopped for the night, beside Dickson's Creek. This creek comes from Mount Wollstonecraft. Round the edge of the salt water are numerous black swans and pelicans, and other sea birds. On the downs are numbers of emus, native companions, and Cape Barren geese. The emus run too fast to be caught by our dogs. We have not seen, since leaving the small river on this side of the Murrumbidgee, either the swamp or forest oak, nor the apple tree; but the black or white thorn grows close to the water's (sea) side on very rich soil. To the very top of Mount Wollstonecraft is fine green grass, and many parts that we have passed through to-day is fine young grass, notwithstanding the long drought.

We shot a white cockatoo this morning, which differs somewhat from those about Cumberland, both in their note, and in the shape of the beak. They are white outside, but red underneath to the skin. Last night we heard the roaring of the sea. I suppose at the entrance.

Sunday, 19th December.—A little before we set out this morning, say, ten minutes before eight, every man except Mr. Hume, heard what they thought was a cannon gun. It appeared to come from the bay, but the distance is very great, and I think too far to be heard from there, notwithstanding the wind came from that direction. Each man had a different conjecture, but each was satisfied of the reality of the thing, at the same time regarding it impossible to get near to where we supposed the vessel lay. Had we been sure that there was one, we could not have got to the point which separates Western Port from Port Phillip under three

days; and to have gone round to the eastward round that large
sheet of water (besides the rivers with which we must have expected to have fallen in to have got to the bay) would have been
a labour too great, under the present circumstances, to have
undertaken. Besides there was the chance of her not being there
when we arrived. We kept a little nearer the water to look if
there was anything to be seen sailing in the bay. We took notice
of two smokes on the south side which the natives had made as
signals to each other, after we started. There was now some
appearance of a change of weather, which we may expect at the
change of the moon, which will be to-morrow evening. We continued our course about N. 25 deg. W. till we arrived at the banks
of the Arndell, which was at some distance lower down than
where we crossed it before. Having recrossed it we kept a little
up till we came to good feed for our cattle. Here we stopped to
kill a bullock, which we found impossible to take any further.
Poor old " Captain" had been our leader the whole distance coming. From having to make a road for the others, besides carrying
his load, the great change of feed, and above all the cold weather,
which he felt very severely and which had struck to his limbs, he
became at last unable to walk. To leave him behind to be destroyed by the natives I thought bad policy. As for any chance
of his getting home by himself there was not the least, the distance
being too great. But there was a greater reason for killing him
ourselves, viz., the men had now been without meat one week, and
had had only one kangaroo for a fortnight before that; and their
allowance of flour, as I before mentioned, has been reduced, they
were becoming very weak. Under all circumstances I thought it
the most advisable plan to kill him and eat him ourselves than
to leave it for the natives to do for us, or him. The water of the
Arndell is fresh as far as we have been down, which perhaps will be
within the distance of five or six miles from the bay. It was
fortunate for the men that I killed the bullock, as there are not
more than two that have shoes to their feet. Therefore the skin
comes in for mocassins for them, which answer the place of
shoes.

Tuesday, 21st December.—Having retraced our steps to the
spot which gave us fresh hopes that we should accomplish our
object, I have only now to return thanks to Providence, not only
for enabling us to surmount every obstacle which presented itself
as well as gaining our point in arriving at the place we took our
departure for when leaving home for that purpose, but also that

we should have been so very fortunate as to find so delightful a country adjoining to where our journey terminated, with every possible advantage attached to it, and without that scrub and brush which we were led to expect at least within thirty miles of the sea coast (as we were given to understand would be the case). I say again, in expressing my gratitude, that nothing could have been more fortunate, and in addition to this there is all that fine country west of the Australian Alps to where we now are; and this is the only place where there can be any communication (that is to say, easy communication) without the trouble of crossing those troublesome mountains. But from this direction there will be no inconvenience attending a regular intercourse between the two countries.

Having spoken much in praise of the country now behind us, and which we shall lose sight of to-morrow, (I was going to say, perhaps for ever, but I hope that will not be the case,) I would wish, before I take my leave of it to say that I do not see any reason for making any alteration in the statement which I made when going. But, on the contrary, I think I might venture to make some addition, but as I presume it will not be long before it will be examined by abler and more competent judges, I shall say but little more on the subject. I hope when it is surveyed that the season will be the same as it is now. In that case I should not have much fear of being contradicted. I mention this because the change of season sometimes alters the appearance (for better or worse) of the country from what it was at the time when persons were taking a memorandum of it.

I was fearful that as my eyes were generally fixed (when approaching the end of our journey, in the direction where we should fall in with the sea) towards the front and seldom exceeding an angle of 45 deg. from the front on each side of me, I might have mis-stated some part and forgotten others. But now we are returning and I am so well satisfied with the country, my eyes are as much behind as they are in front, admiring the different spots which occasionally present themselves to view. I have only now to say that I think those persons who may come to settle here first should make choice of the Duke of York's downs, because it is better supplied with timber for uses about their farms, being so much nearer to the Jullian range and Australian Alps, which have the timber for building, as also the shelter from the cold S.W. and N.W. winds. Whether the soil is inferior to the other downs or not I am not able to say, but this I may venture to say, that it cannot be better. The great advantage this country will derive will be the communication with the interior, as also with the country east of the Alps, along the river Yar through the Gap. I gave it that name from the great resemblance of this country to the County of Norfolk, and the Yar the principal river in it.

X. LOCKYER'S EXPLORATION OF THE BRISBANE RIVER

[MAJOR EDMUND LOCKYER, late of the 57th Regiment of Foot, was despatched from Sydney in 1825 to explore the Brisbane River. The copy of his Journal from which the following extracts have been made was lent to the editor by his son, Sir Nicholas Lockyer.]

Sept. 1st.—Embarked on board the cutter Mermaid.

2nd.—At 5 a.m. sailed from Sydney. After a fine run anchored inside Nobby's Island, Hunter River.

6th.—Passed in between reef of rocks and flat island. Eighteen fathoms to eleven to the outer buoys of the Channel, leading into Morton Bay by Amity Point. Good anchorage inside and close under the shore of Amity Point. From this anchorage through the channel up to Peel's Island not less than four fathoms at high water. After rounding Peel's Island plenty of water for ships of any size which continues all the way up to Green Islands thence to the buoy on spit off the mouth of the Brisbane.

7th.—Weighed anchor and stood for the river, came to anchor at the buoy at end of spit. The navigation would be considerably facilitated by regular buoys of different colours placed to mark the sides of the channel. Learning from the master of the Mermaid that he did not think it prudent to take the cutter over the bar, I departed in my boat to the settlement up the river.

10th.—Several natives were seen on the side opposite the settlement. Capt. Bishop and Lieut. Miller informed me that they did not appear before in numbers. On this occasion I think there were upwards of thirty men, women and children. They seemed desirous to cross the river. I learnt on my return they had swam across higher up after my departure but could not be persuaded to approach the settlement nearer than two hundred yards, where they remained for a while and then made off.

At 5 p.m. landed on the right side of river going up, which we observed to be a brush with long grass, thinly wooded and rising in a gradual slope from the river. A very pretty situation where I halted for the night, which was very cold and a heavy dew falling. Mosquitoes innumerable and very troublesome, which we found to disperse by our smoking. The boat's sail made a good substitute for a tent, though it did not keep out the rain, which was very heavy.

11th.—The Wood on the banks Fig-tree Blue gum, Swamp oak, Ironbark. For the last half distance no Pines, here and there a solitary Cedar. On landing found spinach in abundance, also mint, parsley and poppy. Halted on left side of river, a sandstone rock forming a jetty.

12th.—The country as yesterday. Except the hills being high with fine downs thinly wooded, with very high grass of the cat species. Very few Pines to be seen. The river in some places very narrow then wide. Over the rapids rather shallow, obliged to track them over, to do which the men were forced to get out. Mr. Oxley had been thus far.

13th.—This day from the number of rapids and shoals, the getting of the boats up was a matter of great difficulty as the men were in the water for six hours. At 2.30 landed and camped for the night. Saw cedar trees, honeysuckle and swamp oak. On the high ground blue gum and ironbark. Fires of the natives; caught cod fish similar to that of Bathurst River.

14th.—8.30 proceeded up the river. The hills beautifully covered with Pine trees, the bank with swamp oak, honeysuckle, blue gum and ironbark. Saw some of the natives and ordered the boats to pull up where they stood. After much hesitation and the sight of a looking glass they came within a few yards. We gave them biscuit; showed them two sheep and also two of the soldiers with red hair, which was a matter of curiosity to them. They were naked, stout, clean skinned, well made people and showed no signs of hostility. From the short intercourse I had, I think they had not seen a European before. In the evening heavy rain; the sail completely drenched through. Passed a very uncomfortable night, the fires going out, much thunder and lightning.

15th.—About 7 rain ceased and the weather began to break. We soon got our clothes dry and embarked at 9 o'clock. The natives we saw yesterday again made their appearance. Saw an old man a cripple, also a little boy. Gave them fishing hooks and lines. At 2 p.m. I ordered a landing. Under a range of hills camped near a blue gum. I caused a broad arrow to be cut four feet from bottom. Country very good on both sides. Kangaroos in abundance extremely shy. The whole country appeared to be well timbered with tall pines. Walked several miles, found the grass very long and fatiguing to walk in. Rain fell.

16th.—At 9 a.m. departed. Landed at the spot where Mr. Gray the Pilot had stated he saw the white race. We made our huts for the night. The Pine hills which we had left in our rear presented only their tops, which proved we had ascended. This place was pointed out by Thomas Robinson one of the sailors who was with Mr. Gray, stated that he saw only two or three men running in the bush who appeared to be of a light color but he saw no bows nor arrows. N.B.—The natives are known on some occasions to whiten themselves with wood ashes.

17th.—At half past eight again set out. Much obstruction from dead trees lying across a narrow and winding part of the river, too numerous and large to attempt cutting a passage through them, consequently had to pull the boats over, taking every article out of them and in making a distance of a mile and a half they were unladen four times which occupied upwards of three hours, the stream running four knots and a half. Shot several wild ducks, also a yellow snake. On the left side going up and opposite our halting place a large stream joined the main river. The men caught several cod fish and eels, the former were particularly good. The country about this place was fine and the soil excellent. Ironbark and stones in abundance.

18th.—Landed at 4.30 p.m. From the number of falls and rapidity of the stream this proved laborious and the party were knocked up. Parroquetes in great variety, but similar to those seen in the country about Sydney.

19th.—Rain began to pour in torrents about 12, which compelled us to shelter at a remarkable spot under a high hill near its base about the size of a side box of a theatre, the abode of cats and dogs. Walked up the hill for one hour and half. It appeared to me to be not less than 1000 feet high. On reaching the summit we had a good view of the country. Mountainous to the W.N.W. To the S. and S.E. high land discernable. To the W.N.W. was a large flat country 30 or 40 miles finely wooded with blue and ironbark. The ironstone prevails, very rotten, good sand stone and fine soil fit for any cultivation. Rain the greater part of the night.

20th.—Weather cleared and we quitted this spot at 9 a.m. As I could not ascertain the direction the natives had taken we took the boats and proceeded up about a mile when two natives were seen and calling to us. We went on shore and after some difficulty induced them to have confidence to allow us to approach. They were a woman and a lad about 14. The former had an infant in arms. Gave them looking glasses, beads, and fish hooks. They appear surprised at seeing people opposite in color to themselves. It is certain that they had never seen white people before. They appeared to believe that the boats were living animals as I could not induce them to go near the boats. She shook her head and made signs as if she was afraid they would bite; several women and children were seen at a distance. Finding we could not induce them to approach we left our new acquaintances of friendly intentions. The woman in return for what I had given her held out a neat basket made of plaited straw, and a kangaroo skin. The former I took, but declined the latter as it was of value to them. As we proceeded up the river these poor people continued to wave and shout after us until out of sight. They were black and perfectly naked. We shot wild ducks. At 5 p.m. landed for the night. This place from the color of the soil was called Red Bank.

21st.—This morning at 7.30 I observed the water had risen a foot in less than an hour, and its discoloration indicating that a flood was coming down, no time was to be lost in getting the boats up this rapid into the next reach. We accordingly left.

The country on both banks of the river was fine with rich alluvial soil, and on both sides all the way up quite fit for the cultivation of wheat, barley, oats, maize, fruit, vegetables, grape, coffee, cotton, rice and sugar cane. Fine fish were caught.

24th.—Heavy rain during the night, river running with much noise in rushing over the rocks. At this place a considerable stream runs into the river from eastward. The weather proved so bad that I considered it advisable to remain where we were.

25th.—We attempted to go with the boats but found it impossible to make headway against the stream running at least eight or nine knots. We landed and had the ropes carried well up the bank as the river was rising fast. Opposite our camp was a range of mountains, the largest of which and the nearest was about 1500 ft. high. Having landed at about 1 o'clk we made an excursion into the country. There can be no doubt that the natives avoid us. From the marks of fires and empty huts and the number of trees barked, I should think them rather numerous in the neighbourhood.

26th.—We again attempted at 8 o'clk to proceed. The river we found had gone down 6 feet. Advanced about a mile but found it impossible to pull against the stream against a rapid, made arrangements for tracking the boats up by sending ashore and

I. D.   l the party passing the end of a rope to each other along the banks and all the party hauling one boat at a time against the stream, remaining myself to steer her clear of trees and stumps lying in the middle. We succeeded in doing so nearly half way up the rapid when the rope broke and the boat carried a distance down without coming into contact with anything, but by steering into an eddy I got the boat to the opposite shore. I found it useless to make further attempt up this rapid, which was upwards of a mile, and trying the stream with the log line found it running at the rate of nine knot, therefore considerable danger was to be apprehended. The loss of the boat and of the provisions would have placed me in an awkward situation. I directed everything to be landed, having fixed on a good spot under the mountain. I made arrangements to proceed by land for further exploring the river, leaving the Corporal in charge. I gave strict orders to the Corporal to be on his guard in the event of the approach of any number of natives, to prevent any violence being offered to them, and to behave towards them in a manner to convince them no hostility was intended. Everything being ready I set out at 12 o'clk accompanied by Mr. Dulhunty, private of the 40th, one sailor and two convicts, kept the river in view, found walking difficult in the long grass four or five feet high out of which started numbers of kangaroo of the large sort or forest kangaroo. Private Ward nearly trod on an immense snake 10 feet in length which was shot. It was of the diamond species and measured 7 inches round. We crossed three considerable beds of rivers running down from the mountain to the main river. The water in the streams was excellent. At 5 we halted for the night a quarter of a mile from the river bank. The night was cold and a number of emus which our fires had disturbed making an intolerable noise all night. From the number of trees newly barked as well of the skeleton of bark huts, we concluded that the natives must be numerous and not far off.

27th.—At 8 o'clk we again set out keeping the river in view. Nothing can possibly exceed the fine rich country we are now in. We continued till 12 o'clk. Here the bed of the river though broad was nearly dry, except a small stream passing through it and quite impossible for boats, and from the large number of streams running down the Brisbane Mountain I am induced to suppose that the river to be chiefly supplied by these streams as it certainly terminates here as a river, but I think it very probable that the large swamp into which the river at Bathurst loses itself, occasionally overflows and is the cause of tremendous floods, that at times take place in the Brisbane River. From the Brisbane Mountain looking to the west all a flat country behind a ridge of hills running North and South. These hills well wooded with Pine trees and with thick long grass making it dreadfully fatiguing to walk through it with our loads. In consequence of this, seeing the impossibility of making any progress by land, I determined to rejoin the boats, which we accomplished the same evening after having crossed the easternmost end of the Brisbane mountain at half past six p.m. myself and companions quite knocked up.

28th.—Much rain, directed the boats to be got ready to descend the river, as my instructions were to return if possible by the middle of October. At 10 we left the Brisbane mountain and before quitting I caused a tree to be barked and a broad arrow to be cut into it. Made rapid progress going at the rate of eight or nine knots, which was attended with considerable danger for the want of ropes to ease the boats down. The weather threatening I deemed it prudent to land, raining very hard with thunder and lightning as we had experienced these three days past. Made the distance 25 miles.

29th.—At 9 set out and continued going down the river until 3 o'clk. In passing down one of the falls the whale boat was caught by the stump of a tree and nearly upset, she was half full of water before she was clear. I also with the green boat struck a tree with great force, the jerk nearly threw me out of the boat being head and shoulders in the water, but was prevented from going further by one of the men holding me by the leg. Shot several duck. Smoke was seen in several directions around us. Saw a bird not unlike a goose but he was too quick to get a shot at him.

30th.—We again set out at 8, passed through several falls. Several fresh obstacles had taken place by the flood having taken away large trees from the banks. Arrived at the caves at 2 o'clk, heavy rain, shot a wild duck of a new species which proved good eating. I could not find any variety of rocks, they were either rotten iron stone or sandstone. Distance 14 miles.

2nd.—From the circumstance of having clothes wet and having a wish to examine the large branch which here joined from the southward I determined on haling at this spot. Took one of the boats and went up this branch three miles, found a large open country with scarcely any wood to impede cultivation on it, the trees chiefly blue gums. The natives had set fire to the long grass and the new grass was just above the ground appearing like a bowling green. The soil rich beyond idea, it would be well adapted for the cultivation of rice, sugar cane, cotton and coffee. Saw plenty of kangaroos and wild turkey. After traversing this fine piece of land which was six to seven thousand acres I returned to the camp.

3rd.—In passing through one of the reaches saw a native on the banks where Mr. Gray had stated he had seen white people. This man was sick and was indifferent to our presence. Landed at 3 and discovered some natives about a mile. Two men, a woman and three children. We made them presents. The woman could not be induced to look up but hid her face between her legs. As soon as we moved she on her legs and off like an arrow. The day's distance 22 miles.

4th.—Made rapid progress and arrived at the coal bed, filled a sack as a sample. There is fine coal just below. The whale boat struck a tree and knocked a hole in her bottom. Took everything out of her, hauled her up and in about two hours had her completely repaired. Made our distance this day 28 miles.

5th.—Passed down a fall with a remarkable bed of rocks in it. On going up the water was much lower, it was now nearly four feet higher and broke violently. We met several natives who were shy at first but soon became confident and were fine people. Distance 18 miles.

6th.—Arrived at the settlement at 11 o'clk, distance 20 miles, having been absent 27 days, the party being in good health and without meeting a single accident of any consequence. I am certain the distances are considerably underrated from a wish at the same time rather to underrate than otherwise. The obstructions in the river might be easily removed, the fine timber growing on its bank is fit for every purpose, particularly ship building. Moreton Bay is well calculated to become a place of trade when once settled.

8th.—Quitted the settlement to join the cutter at Moreton Bay for the purpose of returning to Sydney. It becoming dark on clearing the river we did not get on board till 11 p.m. as it was with great difficulty we discovered the cutter, which I should not have succeeded in doing, but for the discharging my fouling piece. We saw a light over a mile away.

9th.—Beat down to Peel's island. Landed and found it good soil and well wooded. On removing it from the surface found a good clay below. In the middle of the island is a lagoon of excellent fresh water. The island is from 12 to 15 miles in circumference and would be a very proper place to build a storehouse to deposit large stores from vessels that could not approach the settlement nearer than this. It would also feed cattle, and other stock.

10th.—Dropped down to Amity Point and anchored there with a strong sea-breeze from NE. Went on shore, a number of the natives being there, was much amused by their singing a song and pronouncing several English words most distinctly and by their instantly recognising James Finnegan, one of the three men who was wrecked there three years ago having been driven away to the Northward from Illawarra or the Five Islands by a gale of wind. These men were kindly treated and taken care of for nine months until discovered by Mr. Oxley. They appeared delighted at meeting Finnegan again and brought a supply of fish without expecting any return though I took care to give them fishhooks and several other things to show them we did not slight such good will. The stories told of their being cannibals are fabulous and absurd. They are a quiet inoffensive, good natured, lively set of people.

11th.—Quitted Moreton Bay at 9 p.m. with a land breeze leaving our friends the natives sitting on the shore at Amity Point watching us until lost from their view. The attachment of these people to their dogs is worthy of notice. I was very anxious to get one of the wild native breed of a black color, a very handsome puppy which one held in his arms. I offered a small axe for the animal, his companions urged him to take it and he was about to do so when he looked at his dog and the animal licked his face, which settled the business. I tried him afterwards with handkerchiefs of glaring colors but he would not part with his dog. I gave him however the axe and the handkerchief.

On Sunday 16th Oct. at 4 in the afternoon anchored in Sydney Cove and on Monday made my report to his Excellency the Governor.

XI. STURT'S DISCOVERY OF THE DARLING

[THE discovery of the Darling by Captain Charles Sturt in 1829 was one of the outstanding events in Australian exploration. It was followed by his even more important voyage down the Murray. Both expeditions are described by Sturt in his two volumes, *Two Expeditions into the Interior of Southern Australia*, published in London in 1834.]

The year 1826 was remarkable for the commencement of one of those fearful droughts to which we have reason to believe the climate of New South Wales is periodically subject. It continued during the two following years with unabated severity. The surface of the earth became so parched up that minor vegetation ceased upon it. Culinary herbs were raised with difficulty, and crops failed even in the most favourable situations. Settlers drove their flocks and herds to distant tracts for pasture and water, neither remaining for them in the located districts. The interior suffered equally with the coast, and men, at length, began to despond under so alarming a visitation. It almost appeared as if the Australian sky were never again to be traversed by a cloud.

But, however severe for the colony the seasons had proved, or were likely to prove, it was borne in mind at this critical moment, that the wet and swampy state of the interior had alone prevented Mr. Oxley from penetrating further into it, in 1818. Each successive report from Wellington Valley, the most distant settlement to the N.W., confirmed the news of the unusually dry state of the lowlands, and of the exhausted appearance of the streams falling into them. It was, consequently, hoped that an expedition, pursuing the line of the Macquarie, would have a greater chance of success than the late Surveyor General had; and that the difficulties he had to contend against would be found to be greatly diminished, if not altogether removed. The immediate fitting out of an expedition was therefore decided upon, for the express purpose of ascertaining the nature and extent of that basin into which the Macquarie was supposed to fall, and whether any connection had existed between it and

CHARLES STURT, AGED 73.

From a drawing by Koberwein, reproduced in " The Life of
Charles Sturt."

the streams falling westerly. As I had early taken a great interest in the geography of New South Wales, the Governor was pleased to appoint me to the command of this expedition.

In the month of September, 1828, I received his Excellency's commands to prepare for my journey; and by the commencement of November, had organized my party, and completed the necessary arrangements. On the 9th of that month, I waited on the Governor, at Paramatta, to receive his definitive instructions. As the establishments at Sydney had been unable to supply me with the necessary number of horses and oxen, instructions had been forwarded to Mr. Maxwell, the superintendent of Wellington Valley, to train a certain number for my use; and I was now directed to push for that settlement without loss of time. I returned to Sydney in the afternoon of the 9th, and on the 10th took leave of my brother officers, to commence a journey of very dubious issue; and, in company with my friend, Staff-surgeon M'Leod, who had obtained permission to accompany me to the limits of the colony, followed my men along the great western road. We moved leisurely over the level country, between the coast and the Nepean River, and availed ourselves of the kind hospitality of those of our friends whose property lay along that line of road, to secure more comfortable places of rest than the inns would have afforded. . . .

On the 17th of January, 1829, we encamped under New Year's Range, which is the first elevation in the interior of Eastern Australia to the westward of Mount Harris. Yet when at its base, I do not think that we had ascended above forty feet higher than the plains in the neighbourhood of that last mentioned eminence. There certainly is a partial rise of country, where the change of soil takes place from the alluvial deposits of the marshes, to the sandy loam so prevalent on the plains we had lately traversed; but I had to regret that I was unable to decide so interesting a question by other than bare conjecture.

Notwithstanding that Mr. Hume had already been on them, I encouraged hopes that a second survey of the country from the highest point of New Year's Range, would enable us to form some opinion of it, by which to direct our future movements; but I was disappointed.

The two wooded hills I had seen from Oxley's Table Land were visible from the range, bearing south; and other eminences bore by compass S.W. and W. by S.; but in every other direction the horizon was unbroken. To the westward, there appeared to be a valley of considerable extent, stretching N. and S., in which latter direction there was a long strip of cleared ground, that looked very like the sandy bed of a broad and rapid river. The bare possibility of the reality determined me to ascertain the inspection, whether my conjecture was right, and Mr. Hume accompanied me on this excursion. After we left the camp we crossed a part of the range, and travelled for some time through open forest land that would afford excellent grazing in most seasons. We passed some hollows, and noticed many huts that had been occupied near them; but the hollows were now quite dry, and the huts had been long deserted. After about ten miles' ride we reached a plain of white sand, from which New Year's Range was distinctly visible; and this no doubt was the spot that had attracted my attention. Pools of water continued on it, from which circumstance it would appear that the sand had a substratum of clay or marl. From this plain we proceeded southerly through acacia scrub, bounding gently undulating forest land, and at length ascended some small elevations that scarcely deserved the name of hills. They had fragments of quarts profusely scattered over them; and the soil, which was sandy, contained particles of mica.

The view from them was confused, nor did any fresh object meet our observation. We had, however, considerably neared the two wooded hills, and the elevations that from the range were to the S.W., now bore N.W. of us. We had wandered too far from the camp to admit of our returning to it to sleep; we therefore commenced a search for water, and having found some, we tethered our horses near it for the night, and should have been tolerably comfortable, had not the mosquitoes been so extremely troublesome. They defied the power of smoke, and annoyed me so much, that, hot as it was, I rolled myself in my boat cloak, and perspired in consequence to such a degree, that my clothes were wet through, and I had to stand at the fire in the morning to dry them. Mr. Hume, who could not bear such confinement, suffered the penalty, and was most unmercifully bitten.

We reached the camp about noon the following day, and learnt, to our vexation, that one of the men, Norman, had lost himself shortly after we started, and had not since been heard of. Dawber, my overseer, was out in search of him. I awaited his return, therefore, before I took any measures for the man's recovery; nor was I without hopes that Dawber would have found him, as it appeared he had taken one of the horses with him, and Dawber, by keeping his tracks, might eventually have overtaken him. He returned, however, about 3 p.m. unsuccessful, when Mr.

Hume and I mounted our horses, and proceeded in different directions in quest of him, but were equally disappointed.

We met at the creek in the dark, and returned to the camp together, when I ordered the cypresses on the range to be set on fire, and thus illuminated the country round for many miles. In the morning, however, as Norman had not made his appearance, we again started in search of the poor fellow, on whose account I was now most uneasy; for his horse, it appeared, had escaped him, and was found with the others at watering time.

I did not return to the camp until after sunset, more fatigued than I recollect ever having been before. I was, however, rejoiced on being informed that the object of my anxiety was safe in his tent; that he had caught sight of the hill the evening before, and that he had reached the camp shortly after I left it. He had been absent three nights and two days, and had not tasted water or food of any kind during that time.

To my enquiries he replied, that, being on horseback, he thought he could have overtaken a kangaroo, which passed him whilst waiting at the creek for the cattle, and that in the attempt, he lost himself. It would appear that he crossed the creek in the dark, and his horse escaped from him on the first night. He complained more of thirst than of hunger, although he had drunk at the watering-place to such an excess, on his return, as to make him vomit; but, though not a little exhausted, he had escaped better than I should have expected.

New Year's Range consists of a principal group of five hills, the loftiest of which does not measure 300 feet in height. It has lateral ridges, extending to the N.N.W. on the one hand, and bending in to the creek on the other. The former have a few cypresses, sterculia, and iron bark upon them; the latter are generally covered with brush, under box; the brush for the most part consisting of two distinct species of stenochylus, and a new acacia. The whole range is of quartz formation, small fragments of which are profusely scattered over the ridges, and are abundantly incrusted with oxide of iron. The soil in the neighbourhood of New Year's Range is a red loam, with a slight mixture of sand. An open forest country lies between it and the creek, and it is not at all deficient in pasture.

That a change of soil takes place to the westward of the creek, is obvious, from the change of vegetation, the most remarkable feature of which is the sudden check given to the further extension of the acacia pendula, which is not to be found beyond it, it being succeeded by another acacia of the same species and habits; neither do the plants of the chenopedia class exist in the immediate vicinity of the range.

As New Year's Creek was leading northerly, it had been determined to trace it down as long as it should keep that course, or one to the westward of it. We broke up the camp, therefore, under the range, on the evening of the 18th, and moved to the creek, about two miles north of the place at which we had before crossed it, with the intention of prosecuting our journey on the morrow. But both Mr. Hume and I were so fatigued that we were glad of an opportunity to rest, even for a single day. We remained stationary, therefore, on the 19th; nor was I without hope that the natives whom we had surprised in the woods, would have paid us a visit, since Mr. Hume had met them in his search for Norman, and they had promised not only to come to us, but to do all in their power to find the man, whose footsteps some of them had crossed. They did not, however, venture near us; and I rather attribute their having kept aloof, to the circumstance of Mr. Hume's having fired a shot, shortly after he left them, as a signal to Norman, in the event of his being within hearing of the report. They must have been alarmed at so unusual a sound; but I am sure nothing was further from Mr. Hume's intention than to intimidate them; his knowledge of their manners and customs, as well as his partiality to the natives, being equally remarkable. The circumstance is, however, a proof of the great caution that is necessary in communicating with them.

I have said that we remained stationary the day after we left the range, with a view to enjoy a little rest; it would, however, have been infinitely better if we had moved forward. Our camp was infested by the kangaroo fly, which settled upon us in thousands. They appeared to rise from the ground, and as fast as they were swept off were succeeded by fresh numbers. It was utterly impossible to avoid their persecution, penetrating as they did into the very tents.

The men were obliged to put handkerchiefs over their faces, and stockings upon their hands; but they bit through every thing. It was to no purpose that I myself shifted from place to place; they still followed, or were equally numerous everywhere. To add to our discomfort, the animals were driven almost to madness, and galloped to and fro in so furious a manner that I was apprehensive some of them would have been lost. I never experienced such a day of torment; and only when the sun set, did these little creatures cease from their attacks.

It will be supposed that we did not stay to subject ourselves to another trial; indeed it was with some degree of horror that the men saw the first light of morning streak the horizon. They got up immediately, and we moved down the creek, on a northerly course, without breakfasting as usual. We found that dense brushes of casuarina lined the creek on both sides, beyond which, to our left, there was open rising ground, on which eucalypti, cypresses, and the acacia longifolia, prevailed; whilst to the east, plains seemed to predominate.

Although we had left the immediate spot at which the kangaroo flies (cabarus) seemed to be collected, I did not expect that we should have got rid of them so completely as we did. None of them were seen during the day; a proof that they were entirely local. They were about half the size of a common house fly, had flat brown bodies, and their bite, although sharp and piercing, left no irritation after it.

About noon we stopped at the creek side to take some refreshment. The country bore an improved appearance around us, and the cattle found abundance of pasture. It was evident that the creek had been numerously frequented by the natives, although no recent traces of them could be found. It had a bed of coarse red granite, of the fragments of which the natives had constructed a weir for the purpose of taking fish. The appearance of this rock in so isolated a situation, is worthy the consideration of geologists.

The promise of improvement I have noticed, gradually disappeared as we proceeded on our day's journey, and we at length found ourselves once more among brushes, and on the edge of plains, over which the rhagodia prevailed. Nothing could exceed in dreariness the appearance of the tracks through which we journeyed, on this and the two following days. The creek on which we depended for a supply of water, gave such alarming indications of a total failure, that I at one time, had serious thoughts of abandoning my pursuit of it. We passed hollow after hollow that had successively dried up, although originally of considerable depth; and, when we at length found water, it was doubtful how far we could make use of it. Sometimes in boiling it left a sediment nearly equal to half its body; at other times it was so bitter as to be quite unpalatable. That on which we subsisted was scraped up from small puddles, heated by the sun's rays; and so uncertain were we of finding water at the end of the day's journey, that we were obliged to carry a supply on one of the bullocks. There was scarcely a living creature, even of the feathered race, to be seen to break the stillness of the forest. The native dogs alone wandered about, though they had scarcely strength to avoid us; and their melancholy howl, breaking in upon the ear at the dead of the night, only served to impress more fully on the mind the absolute loneliness of the desert.

It appeared, from their traces, that the natives had lingered on this ground, on which they had perhaps been born, as long as it continued to afford them a scanty though precarious subsistence; but that they had at length been forced from it. Neither fish nor muscles remained in the creek, nor emus nor kangaroos on the plains. How then could an European expect to find food in deserts through which the savage wandered in vain? There is no doubt of the fate that would have overtaken any one of the party who might have strayed away, and I was happy to find that Norman's narrow escape had made a due impression on the minds of his comrades.

We passed some considerable plains, lying to the eastward of the creek, on parts of which the grass, though growing in tufts, was of luxuriant growth. They were, however, more generally covered with salsola and rhagodia, and totally destitute of other vegetation, the soil upon them being a red sandy loam. The paths across the plains, which varied in breadth from three to eight miles, were numerous; but they had not been recently trodden. The creek continued to have a thick brush of casuarina and acacia near it, to the westward of which there was a rising open forest track; the timber upon it being chiefly box, cypress, and the acacia longifolia. It was most probably connected with New Year's Range, those elevations being about thirty miles distant. It terminated in some gentle hills which, though covered in places with acacia shrub, were sufficiently open to afford an extensive view. From their summit Oxley's Table Land, towards which we had been gradually working our way, was distinctly visible, distant about twenty miles, and bearing by compass W. by S. On descending from these hills, which were scattered over with fragments of slaty quartz, we traversed a box flat, apparently subject to overflow, having a barren sandy scrub to its left. I had desired the men to preserve a W.N.W. direction, on leaving them, supposing that that course would have kept them near the creek; but, on overtaking the party, I found that they had wandered completely away from it. The fact was, that the creek had taken a sudden bend to the eastward of N. and had thus thrown them out. It was with some difficulty that we regained it before sunset; and we were at length obliged to stop for the night at a small plain, about a quarter of a mile short of it, but we had the satisfaction of having excellent feed for the animals.

Fearful that New Year's Creek would take us too far to the eastward, and being anxious to keep westward as much as possible, it struck me that we could not, under existing circumstances, do better than make for Oxley's Table Land. Water, I knew, we should find in a swamp at it's base, and we might discover some more encouraging feature than I had observed on my hasty visit to it. We left the creek, therefore, on the 23d, and once more took up a westerly course. Passing through a generally open country, we stopped at noon to rest the animals; and afterwards got on an excellent grazing forest track, which continued to the brush, through another part of which I had penetrated to the marsh more to the south. While making our way through it, we came upon a small pond of water, and must have alarmed some natives, as there was a fresh made fire close to it. Our journey had been unusually long, and the cattle had felt the heat so much, that the moment they saw water they rushed into it; and, as this created some confusion, I thought it best to stop where we were for the night.

In the morning, Mr. Hume walked with me to the hill, a distance of about a mile. It is not high enough to deserve the name of a mountain, although a beautiful feature in the country, and showing well from any point of view. We ascended it with an anxiety that may well be imagined, but were wholly disappointed in our most sanguine expectations. Our chief object, in this second visit to Oxley's Table Land, had been to examine, more at leisure, the face of the country around it, and to discover, if possible, some fixed point on which to move.

If the rivers of the interior had already exhausted themselves, what had we to expect from a creek whose diminished appearance where we left it made us apprehend its speedy termination, and whose banks we traversed under constant apprehension? In any other country I should have followed such a water course, in hopes of its ultimately leading to some reservoir; but here I could encourage no such favourable anticipation.

The only new object that struck our sight was a remarkable and distant hill of conical shape, bearing by compass S. 10 E. To the southward and westward, in the direction of D'Urban's Group, a dense and apparently low brush extended; but to the N. and N.W., there was a regular alternation of wood and plain. I left Mr. Hume upon the hill, that he might the more readily notice any smoke made by the natives; and returned myself to the camp about one o'clock, to move the party to the swamp. Mr. Hume's perseverance was of little avail. The region he had been overlooking was, to all appearance, uninhabited, nor did a single fire indicate that there was even a solitary wanderer upon its surface.

Our situation, at this time, was extremely embarrassing, and the only circumstance on which we had to congratulate ourselves was, the improved condition of our men; for several of the cattle and horses were in a sad plight. The weather had been so extremely oppressive, that we had found it impossible to keep them free from eruptions. I proposed to Mr. Hume, therefore, to give them a few days' rest, and to make an excursion, with such of them as were serviceable, to D'Urban's Group. We were both of us unwilling to return to the creek, but we foresaw that a blind reliance upon fortune, in our next movements, might involve us in inextricable difficulty.

On the other hand, there was a very great risk in delay. It was more than probable, from the continued drought, that our retreat would be cut off from the want of water, or that we should only be enabled to effect our retreat with loss of most of the animals. The hope, however, of our intersecting some stream, or of falling upon a better country, prevailed over other considerations; and the excursion was, consequently, determined upon.

We left the camp on the 25th, accompanied by Hopkinson and the tinker; and, almost immediately after, entered an acacia scrub of the most sterile description, and one, through which it would have been impossible to have found a passage for the boat carriage. The soil was almost a pure sand, and the lower branches of the trees were decayed so generally as to give the whole an indescribable appearance of desolation. About mid-day, we crossed a light sandy plain, on which there were some dirty puddles of water. They were so shallow as to leave the backs of the frogs in them exposed, and they had, in consequence, been destroyed by solar heat, and were in a state of putrefaction. Our horses refused to drink, but it was evident that some natives must have partaken of this sickening beverage only a few hours before our arrival. Indeed, it was clear that a wandering family must have slept near this spot, as we observed a fresh made gunneah (or native hut), and their foot-prints were so fresh along the line we were pursuing, that we momentarily expected to have overtaken them. It was late in the evening when we got out of this brush into better and more open ground, where, in ordinary seasons we should, no doubt, have found abundance of water. But we now searched in vain for it, and were contented to be enabled to give our wearied animals better food than they had tasted for many days, the forest grass, though in tufts, being abundant.

We brought up for the night at the edge of a scrub, having travelled from thirty-two to thirty-five miles, judging the distance from the mountains still to be about twelve.

In the morning we started at an early hour, and immediately entered the brush, beneath which we had slept; pursuing a westerly course through it. After a short ride, we found ourselves upon a plain, that was crowded with flocks of cockatoos. Here we got a supply of water, such as it was—so mixed with slime as to hang in strings between the fingers; and, after a hasty breakfast, we proceeded on our journey, mostly through a barren sandy scrub that was a perfect burrow from the number of wombats in it, to within a mile of the hill group, where the country appeared like one continuous meadow to the very base of them. I never saw anything like the luxuriance of the grass on this tract of country, waving as it did higher than our horses' middles as we rode through it. We ascended the S.W. face of the mountain to an elevation of at least 800 feet above the level of the plain, and had some difficulty in scaling the masses of rock that opposed themselves to our progress. But on gaining the summit, we were amply repaid for our trouble. The view extended far and wide, but we were again disappointed in the main object that had induced us to undertake the journey. I took the following bearings by compass. Oxley's Table Land bore N. 40 E. distant forty-five miles; small and distant hill due E.; conical peak seen from Oxley's Table Land S. 60 E., very distant; long ridge of high land, S.E.; distant thirty-five miles; high land, S. 30 E., distant thirty miles; long range, S. 25 W.

To the westward, as a medium point, the horizon was unbroken, and the eye wandered over an apparently endless succession of wood and plain. A brighter green than usual marked the course of the mountain torrents in several places, but there was no glittering light among the trees, no smoke to betray a water hole, or to tell that a single inhabitant was traversing the extensive region we were overlooking. We were obliged to return to the plain on which we had breakfasted, and to sleep upon it.

D'Urban's Group is of compact sandstone formation. Its extreme length is from E.S.E. to W.N.W., and cannot be more than from seven to nine miles, whilst its breadth is from two to four. The central space forms a large basin, in which there are stinted pines and eucalyptus scrub, amid huge fragments of rocks. It rises like an island from the midst of the ocean, and as I looked upon it from the plains below, I could without any great stretch of the imagination, picture to myself that it really was such. Bold and precipitous, it only wanted the sea to lave its base; and I cannot but think that such must at no very remote period have been the case, and that the immense flat we had been traversing, is of comparatively recent formation.

We reached the camp on the 28th of the month, by nearly the same route; and were happy to find that, after the few days' rest they had enjoyed, there was a considerable improvement in the animals.

Our experience of the nature of the country to the southward, and the westward, was such as to deter us from risking anything, by taking such a direction as was most agreeable to our views. Nothing remained to us but to follow the creek, or to retreat; and as we could only be induced to adopt the last measure when every other expedient should have failed, we determined on pursuing our original plan, of tracing New Year's Creek as far as practicable.

Oxley's Table Land is situated in lat. 29° 57′ 30″, and in E. long. 145° 43′ 30″, the mean variation being 6.32 easterly. It consists of two hills that appear to have been rent asunder by some convulsion of nature, since the passage between them is narrow and their inner faces are equally perpendicular. The hill which I have named after the late Surveyor-general, is steep on all sides; but the other gradually declines from the south, and at length loses itself in a large plain that extends to the north. It is from four to five miles in length, and is picturesque in appearance, and lightly wooded. A few cypresses were growing on Oxley's Table Land; but it had, otherwise, very little timber upon its summit. Both hills are of sandstone formation, and there are some hollows upon the last that deserve particular notice. They have the appearance of having been formed by eddies of water, being deeper in the centre than at any other part, and contain fragments and slabs of sandstone of various size and breadth, without a particle of soil or of sand between them. It is to be observed that the edges of these slabs, which were perfect parallelograms, were unbroken, and that they were as clean as if they had only just been turned out of the hand of the mason. We counted thirteen of these hollows in one spot about twenty-five feet in diameter, but they are without doubt of periodical formation, since a single hollow was observed lower than the summit of the hill upon its south extremity, that had evidently long been exposed to the action of the atmosphere, and had a general coating of moss over it.

We left Oxley's Table Land on the morning of the 31st of January, pursuing a northern course through the brush and across a large plain, moving parallel to the smaller hill, and keeping it upon our left. The soil upon this plain differed in character from that on the plains to the eastward, and was much freer from sand. We stopped to dine at a spot, whence Oxley's Table Land bore by compass, S. by W., distant about twelve miles. Continuing our journey, at 2 p.m. we cleared the plain, and entered a tract covered with the polygonum junceum, on a soil evidently the deposit of floods. Box-trees were thinly scattered over it, and among the polygonum, the crested pigeons were numerous. These general appearances, together with a dip of country to the N.N.W., made us conclude that we were approaching the creek, and we accordingly intersected it on a N.N.E. course, at about three miles' distance from where we had dined. It had, however, undergone so complete a change, and had increased so much in size and in the height of its banks, that we were at a loss to recognize it. Still, with all these favourable symptoms, there was not a drop of water in it. But small shells lay in heaps in its bed, or were abundantly scattered over it; and we remarked that they differed from those on the plains of the Macquarie. A circumstance that surprised us much, was the re-appearance of the flooded-gum upon its banks, and that too of a large size. We had not seen any to the westward of the marshes, and we were, consequently, led to indulge in more sanguine expectation as to our ultimate success than we had ever ventured to do before.

The party crossed to the right bank of the creek, and then moved in a westerly direction along it in search of water. A brush extended to our right, and some broken stony ground, rather elevated, was visible, to which Mr. Hume rode; nor did he join me again until after I had halted the party for the night.

My search for water had been unsuccessful, and the sun had set, when I came upon a broad part of the creek that appeared very favourable for an encampment, as it was encompassed by high banks, and would afford the men a greater facility of

I. D.   m watching the cattle, that I knew would stray away if they could.

My anxiety for them led me to wander down the bed of the creek, when, to my joy, I found a pond of water within a hundred yards of the tents. It is impossible for me to describe the relief I felt at this success, or the gladness it spread among the men. Mr. Hume joined me at dusk, and informed me that he had made a circuit, and had struck upon the creek about three miles below us but that, in tracing it up, he had not found a drop of water until he came to the pond near which we had so providentially encamped. On the following morning, we held a westerly course over an open country for about eight miles and a half. The prevailing timber appeared to be a species of eucalypti, with rough bark, of small size, and evidently languishing from the want of moisture. The soil over which we travelled was far from bad, but there was a total absence of water upon it. At 6 p.m. Oxley's Table Land was distant from us about fifteen miles, bearing S. 20 E. by compass.

We had not touched upon the creek from the time we left it in the morning, having wandered from it in a northerly direction, along a native path that we intersected, and that seemed to have been recently trodden, since footsteps were fresh upon it. At sunset, we crossed a broad dry creek that puzzled us extremely, and were shortly afterwards obliged to stop for the night upon a plain beyond it. We had, during the afternoon, bent down to the S.W. in hopes that we should again have struck upon New Year's Creek; and, under an impression that we could not be far from it, Mr. Hume and I walked across the plain, to ascertain if it was sufficiently near to be of any service to us. We came upon a creek, but could not decide whether it was the one for which we had been searching, or another.

Its bed was so perfectly even that it was impossible to say to what point it flowed, more especially as all remains of debris had mouldered away. It was, however, extremely broad, and evidently, at times, held a furious torrent. In the centre of it, at one of the angles, we discovered a pole erected, and at first thought, from the manner in which it was propped up, that some unfortunate European must have placed it there as a mark to tell of his wanderings, but we afterwards concluded that it might be some superstitious rite of the natives, in consequence of the untowardness of the season, as it seemed almost inconceivable that an European could have wandered to such a distance from the located districts in safety.

The creek had flooded-gum growing upon its banks, and, on places apparently subject to flood, a number of tall straight saplings were observed by us. We returned to the camp, after a vain search for water, and were really at a loss what direction next to pursue. The men kept the cattle pretty well together, and, as we were not delayed by any preparations for breakfast, they were saddled and loaded at an early hour. The circumstance of there having been natives in the neighbourhood, of whom we had seen so few traces of late, assured me that water was at hand, but in what direction it was impossible to guess. As the path we had observed was leading northerly, we took up that course, and had not proceeded more than a mile upon it, when we suddenly found ourselves on the banks of a noble river. Such it might in truth be called, where water was scarcely to be found. The party drew up upon a bank that was from forty to forty-five feet above the level of the stream. The channel of the river was from seventy to eighty yards broad, and enclosed an unbroken sheet of water, evidently very deep, and literally covered with pelicans and other wild fowl. Our surprise and delight may better be imagined than described. Our difficulties seemed to be at an end, for here was a river that promised to reward all our exertions, and which appeared every moment to increase in importance to our imagination. Coming from the N.E., and flowing to the S.W., it had a capacity of channel that proved that we were as far from its source as from its termination. The paths of the natives on either side of it were like well trodden roads; and the trees that overhung it were of beautiful and gigantic growth.

Its banks were too precipitous to allow of our watering the cattle, but the men eagerly descended to quench their thirst, which a powerful sun had contributed to increase; nor shall I ever forget the cry of amazement that followed their doing so, or the looks of terror and disappointment with which they called out to inform me that the water was so salt as to be unfit to drink! This was, indeed, too true: on tasting it, I found it extremely salt, being apparently a mixture of sea and fresh water. Whence this arose, whether from local causes, or from a communication with some inland sea, I knew not, but the discovery was certainly a blow for which I was not prepared. Our hopes were annihilated at the moment of their apparent realization. The cup of joy was dashed out of our hands before we had time to raise it to our lips. Notwithstanding this disappointment, we proceeded down the river, and halted at about

five miles, being influenced by the goodness of the feed to provide for the cattle as well as circumstances would permit. They
would not drink of the river water, but stood covered in it for
many hours, having their noses alone exposed above the stream.
Their condition gave me great uneasiness. It was evident they
could not long hold out under their excessive thirst, and unless
we should procure some fresh water, it would be impossible for
us to continue our journey. On a closer examination, the river
appeared to me much below its ordinary level, and its current
was scarcely perceptible. We placed sticks to ascertain if there
was a rise or fall of tide, but could arrive at no satisfactory conclusion, although there was undoubtedly a current in it. Yet,
as I stood upon its banks at sunset, when not a breath of air
existed to break the stillness of the waters below me, and saw
their surface kept in constant agitation by the leaping of fish,
I doubted whether the river could supply itself so abundantly,
and the rather imagined, that it owed such abundance, which
the pelicans seemed to indicate was constant, to some mediterranean sea or other. Where, however, were the human inhabitants of this distant and singular region? The signs of a numerous
population were around us, but we had not seen even a solitary
wanderer. The water of the river was not, by any means, so
salt as that of the ocean, but its taste was precisely similar.
Could it be that its unnatural state had driven its inhabitants
from its banks?

One would have imagined that our perplexities would have
been sufficient for one day, but ere night closed, they increased
upon us, although our anxiety, with regard to the cattle, was
happily removed. Mr. Hume, with his usual perseverance,
walked out when the camp was formed; and, at a little distance
from it, ascended a ridge of pure sand, crowned with cypresses.
From this, he descended to the westward, and, at length, struck
upon the river, where a reef of rocks crossed its channel, and
formed a dry passage from one side to the other; but the bend,
which the river must have taken, appeared to him so singular,
that he doubted whether it was the same beside which we had
been travelling during the day. Curiosity led him to cross it,
when he found a small pond of fresh water on a tongue of land,
and, immediately afterwards, returned to acquaint me with the
welcome tidings. It was too late to move, but we had, at least,
the prospect of a comfortable breakfast in the morning.

In consequence of the doubts that hung upon Mr. Hume's
mind, as to the course of the river, we arranged that the animals

should precede us to the fresh water; and that we should keep close in upon the stream, to ascertain that point. After traversing a deep bight, we arrived nearly as soon as the party, at the appointed rendezvous. The rocks composing the channel of the river at the crossing place, were of indurated clay. In the course of an hour, the animals appearing quite refreshed, we proceeded on our journey, and at about four miles crossed New Year's Creek, at its junction with the salt river. We passed several parts of the main channel that were perfectly dry, and were altogether at a loss to account for the current we undoubtedly had observed in the river when we first came upon it. At mid-day D'Urban's Group bore S. 65 E. distant about 32 miles. We made a little westing in the afternoon. The river continued to maintain its character and appearance, its lofty banks, and its long still reaches: while, however, the blue-gum trees upon its banks were of magnificent size, the soil had but little vegetation upon it, although an alluvial deposit.

We passed over vast spaces covered with the polygonum junceum, that bore all the appearance of the flooded tracks in the neighbourhood of the marshes, and on which the travelling was equally distressing to the animals. Indeed, it had been sufficiently evident to us that the waters of this river were not always confined to its channel, capacious as it was, but that they inundated a belt of barren land, that varied in width from a quarter of a mile to a mile, when they were checked by an outer embankment that prevented them from spreading generally over the country, and upon the neighbouring plains. At our halting place, the cattle drank sparingly of the water, but it acted as a violent purgative both on them and the men who partook of it.

On the 5th, the river led us to the southward and westward. Early in the day, we passed a group of seventy huts, capable of holding from twelve to fifteen men each. They appeared to be permanent habitations, and all of them fronted the same point of the compass. In searching amongst them we observed two beautifully made nets, of about ninety yards in length. The one had much larger meshes than the other, and was, most probably, intended to take kangaroos; but the other was evidently a fishing net.

In one hut, the floor of which was swept with particular care, a number of white balls, as of pulverised shells or lime, had been deposited—the use of which we could not divine. A trench was formed round the hut to prevent the rain from running under it, and the whole was arranged with more than ordinary attention.

We had not proceeded very far when we came suddenly upon the tribe to which this village, as it might be called, belonged. In breaking through some brush to an open space that was bounded on one side by the river, we observed three or four natives, seated on a bank at a considerable distance from us; and directly in the line on which we were moving. The nature of the ground so completely favoured our approach, that they did not become aware of it until we were within a few yards of them, and had ascended a little ridge, which, we afterwards discovered, ended in an abrupt precipice upon the river, not more than thirty yards to our right. The crack of the drayman's whip was the first thing that aroused their attention. They gazed upon us for a moment, and then started up and assumed an attitude of horror and amazement; their terror apparently increasing upon them. We stood perfectly immoveable, until at length they gave a fearful yell, and darted out of sight.

Their cry brought about a dozen more natives from the river, whom we had not before observed, but who now ran after their comrades with surprising activity, and without once venturing to look behind them. As our position was a good one, we determined to remain upon it, until we should ascertain the number and disposition of the natives. We had not been long stationary, when we heard a crackling noise in the distance, and it soon became evident that the bush had been fired. It was, however, impossible that we could receive any injury on the narrow ridge upon which we stood, so that we waited very patiently to see the end of this affair.

In a short time the fire approached pretty near to us, and dense columns of smoke rose into the air over our heads. One of the natives, who had been on the bank, now came out of the bush, exactly from the spot into which he had retreated. He advanced a few paces towards us, and bending his body so that his hands rested on his knees, he fixed his gaze upon us for some time; but, seeing that we remained immoveable, he began to throw himself into the most extravagant attitudes, shaking his foot from time to time. When he found that all his violence had no effect, he turned his rear to us in a most laughable manner, and absolutely groaned in spirit when he found that this last insult failed of success.

He stood perplexed and not knowing what next to do, which gave Mr. Hume an opportunity to call out to him, and with considerable address he at length got the savage to approach close up to him; Mr. Hume himself having advanced a short distance from the animals in the first instance. As soon as I thought the savage had sufficiently recovered from his alarm, I went up to him with a tomahawk, the use of which he immediately guessed. We now observed that the natives who had fled from the river, had been employed in setting a net. They had placed it in a semicircle, with either end to the shore, and rude pieces of wood were attached to it to keep the upper part perpendicular. It was in fact a sein, only that the materials, with the exception of the net-work, were simpler and rougher than cork or lead, for which last, we afterwards discovered stones had been substituted.

We had on this occasion a remarkable instance of the docility of the natives of the interior, or of the power they have of subduing their apprehensions; manifesting the opposite extremes of fear and confidence. These men whom we had thus surprised, and who, no doubt, imagined that we were about to destroy them, having apparently never seen nor heard of white men before, must have taken us for something preternatural; yet from the extremity of fear that had prompted them to set their woods in flames, they in a brief space so completely subdued those fears as to approach the very beings who had so strongly excited their alarm. The savage who had been the principal actor in the scene, was an elderly man, rather descending to the vale of years than what might be strictly called aged. I know not how it was, but I regarded him with peculiar interest. Mr. Hume's manners had in a great measure contributed to allay his evident agitation; but, from the moment I approached him, I thought there was a shade of anxiety upon his brow, and an expression of sorrow over his features, the cause of which did not originate with us. I could see in a moment, that his bosom was full even to bursting, and he seemed to claim at once our sympathy and our protection, although we were ignorant of that which oppressed him. We had not long been seated together, when some of his tribe mustered sufficient courage to join him. Both Mr. Hume and I were desirous of seeing the net drawn, but the old man raised some objection, by pointing to the heavens and towards the sun. After a little more solicitation, however, he gave a whistle, and, four or five natives having obeyed the summons, he directed them to draw the net, but they were unfortunate, and our wish to ascertain the kind of fish contained in the river was disappointed. As his tribe gathered round him, the old chief threw a melancholy glance upon them, and endeavoured, as much as he could, to explain the cause of that

affliction which, as I had rightly judged, weighed heavily upon
him. It appeared, then, that a violent cutaneous disease raged
throughout the tribe, that was sweeping them off in great
numbers. He called several young men to Mr. Hume and myself,
who had been attacked by this singular malady. Nothing could
exceed the anxiety of his explanations, or the mild and soothing
tone in which he addressed his people, and it really pained me
that I could not assist him in his distress. We now discovered
the use to which the conical substance that had been deposited
with such unusual care in one of the huts, was applied. There
were few of the natives present who were not more or less
marked with it, and it was no doubt, indicative of mourning.

Some of the men, however, were painted with red and yellow
ochre, with which it was evident to me they had besmeared
themselves since our appearance, most likely in preparing for the
combat in which they fancied they would be engaged. We distributed such presents as we had to those around us, and when
we pursued our journey, the majority accompanied us, nor did
they wholly leave us until we had passed the place to which
their women had retired. They might have left us when they
pleased, for we intended them no harm; as it was, however,
they struck into the brushes to join their families, and we
pushed on to make up for lost time.

The travelling near the river had been so bad, not only in
consequence of the nature of the soil and brush, but from the
numerous gullies that had been formed by torrents, as they
poured into its channel after heavy rains and floods, that it was
thought advisable to keep at a greater distance from it. We
turned away, therefore, to the plains, and found them of much
firmer surface. They partook, however, of the same general
character as the plains we had traversed more to the eastward.
Their soil was a light sandy loam, and the same succulent plants
still continued to prevail upon them, which we have already
noticed as existing upon the other plains. Both emus and kangaroos were seen, though not in any considerable numbers, but
our dogs were not in a condition to run, and were all but killed
by the extreme heat of the weather. We had fallen on a small
pool of water shortly after we started in the morning, but we
could do no more than refresh ourselves and the animals at it.
In the afternoon, we again turned towards the river, and found
it unaltered. Its water was still salt, and from the increased
number of wild fowl and pelicans upon it, as well as from the
general flatness of the country, I certainly thought we were

rapidly approaching some inland sea. It was, however, uncertain how long we should be enabled to continue on the river. The animals were all of them extremely weak, and every day increased the probable difficulty of our return. There was not the least appearance of a break-up of the drought, the heavens were without a cloud, and the atmosphere was so clear that the outline of the moon could be distinctly seen, although she was far in her wane.

On the 6th, we journeyed again through a barren scrub, although on firmer ground, and passed numerous groups of huts. At about eight miles from our last encampment, we came upon the river, where its banks were of considerable height. In riding along them, Mr. Hume thought he observed a current running, and he called to inform me of the circumstance. On a closer examination, we discovered some springs in the very bed of the river, from which a considerable stream was gushing, and from the incrustation around them, we had no difficulty in guessing at their nature; in fact, they were brine springs, and I collected a quantity of salt from the brink of them.

After such a discovery, we could not hope to keep our position. No doubt the current we had observed on first reaching the river, was caused by springs that had either escaped our notice or were under water. Here was at length a local cause for its saltness that destroyed at once the anticipation and hope of our being near its termination, and, consequently, the ardour with which we should have pressed on to decide so interesting a point.

Our retreat would have been a measure of absolute necessity ere this, had we not found occasional supplies of fresh water, the last pond of which was now about eighteen miles behind us.

Whether we should again find any, was a doubtful question, and I hesitated to run the risk. The animals were already, from bad food, and from the effects of the river water, so weak, that they could scarcely carry their loads, and I was aware, if any of the bullocks once fell, he would never rise again. Under such circumstances, I thought it better to halt the party at the edge of the scrub, though the feed was poor, and the water not drinkable. Our situation required most serious consideration. It was necessary that we should move either backward or forward in the morning. Yet we could not adopt either measure with satisfaction to ourselves, under such unfavourable circumstances. I determined to relieve my own mind by getting the animals into a place of safety, as soon as possible; and, as the only effectual way of doing this was to retire upon the nearest fresh water, I resolved at once to do so. The party turned back on the morning of the 6th; nor do I think the cattle would ever have reached their destination had we not found a few buckets of rain water in the cleft of a rock, to refresh them. Thus it will appear that under our most trying circumstance, we received aid from Providence, and that the bounty of Heaven was extended towards us, when we had least reason to expect it.

Notwithstanding we had been thus forced to a partial retreat, both Mr. Hume and myself were unwilling to quit the pursuit of the river, in so unsatisfactory a manner. There was no difference in the appearance of the country to the westward of it; but a seeming interminable flat stretched away in that direction. A journey across it was not likely, therefore, to be attended with any favourable results, since it was improbable that any other leading feature was within our reach. I proposed, therefore, to take the most serviceable of the horses with me down the river, that, in the event of our finding fresh water, we might again push forward. Mr. Hume requesting to be permitted to accompany me, it was arranged that we should start on the 8th, thereby giving the animals a day's rest. We had not seen any natives since our parting with the chief horde; and as we were stationed at some little distance from the river, I hoped that they would not visit the camp during my absence. This was the only circumstance that gave me uneasiness, but the men had generally been behaving so well that I relied a great deal upon them.

About 3 p.m. on the 7th, Mr. Hume and I were occupied tracing the chart upon the ground. The day had been remarkably fine, not a cloud was there in the heavens, nor a breath of air to be felt. On a sudden we heard what seemed to be the report of a gun fired at the distance of between five and six miles. It was not the hollow sound of an earthly explosion, or the sharp cracking noise of falling timber, but in every way resembled a discharge of a heavy piece of ordnance. On this all were agreed, but no one was certain whence the sound proceeded. Both Mr. Hume and myself had been too attentive to our occupation to form a satisfactory opinion; but we both thought it came from the N.W. I sent one of the men immediately up a tree, but he could observe nothing unusual. The country around him appeared to be equally flat on all sides, and to be thickly wooded: whatever occasioned the report, it made a strong impression on all of us; and to this day, the singularity of such a sound, in such a situation, is a matter of mystery to me.

On the 8th, we commenced our journey down the river, accompanied by two men, and a pack-horse, carrying our provisions on one side and a bucket of water on the other. Keeping in general near the stream, but making occasional turns into the plains, we got to the brush from which the party had turned back, about 3 p.m. Passing through, we crossed a small plain, of better soil and vegetation than usual; but it soon gave place to the sandy loam of the interior; nor did we observe any material alteration, either in the country or the river, as we rode along. The flooded-gum trees on the banks of the latter, were of beautiful growth, but in the brushes dividing the plains, box and other eucalypti, with cypresses and many minor shrubs, prevailed. We slept on the river side, and calculated our distance from the camp at about twenty-six or twenty-eight miles.

The horses would not drink the river water, so that we were obliged to give them a pint each from our own supply. On the following morning we continued our journey. The country was generally open to the eastward, and we had fine views of D'Urban's Group, distant from twenty to twenty-five miles. About noon, turning towards the river to rest, both ourselves and the horses, we passed through brush land for about a mile and a half. When we came upon its banks, we found them composed of a red loam with sandy superficies. We had, in the course of the day, crossed several creeks, but in none of them could we find water, although their channels were of great depth.

The day had been extremely warm, and from shaking in the barrel our supply of water had diminished to a little more than a pint; it consequently became a matter of serious consideration, how far it would be prudent to proceed farther; for, however capable we were of bearing additional fatigue, it was evident our animals would soon fail, since they trembled exceedingly, and had the look of total exhaustion. We calculated that we were forty miles from the camp, in a S.W. direction, a fearful distance under our circumstances, since we could not hope to obtain relief for two days. Independently, however, of the state of the animals, our spirits were damped by the nature of the country, and the change which had taken place on the soil, upon which it was impossible that water could rest; while the general appearance of the interior shewed how much it had suffered from drought. On the other hand, although the waters of the river had become worse to the taste, the river itself had increased in size, and stretched away to the westward, with all the uniformity of a magnificent canal, and gave every promise of increasing importance; while the pelicans were in such numbers upon it as to be quite dazzling to the eye. Considering, however, that perseverance would only involve us in inextricable difficulties, and that it would also be useless to risk the horses, since we had gained a distance to which the bullocks could not have been brought, I intimated my intention of giving up the farther pursuit of the river, though it was with extreme reluctance that I did so.

As soon as we had bathed and finished our scanty meal, I took the bearings of D'Urban's Group, and found them to be S. 58 E. about thirty-three miles distant; and as we mounted our horses, I named the river the "Darling," as a lasting memorial of the respect I bear the governor.

I should be doing injustice to Mr. Hume and my men, if I did not express my conviction that they were extremely unwilling to yield to circumstances, and that, had I determined on continuing the journey, they would have followed me with cheerfulness, whatever the consequences might have been.

Whether the discoveries that have been made during this expedition, will ultimately prove of advantage to the colony of New South Wales, is a question that time alone can answer. We have in the meanwhile to regret that no beneficial consequences will immediately follow them. The further knowledge that has been gained of the interior is but as a gleam of sunshine over an extensive landscape. A stronger light has fallen upon the nearer ground, but the distant horizon is still enveloped in clouds. The veil has only as it were been withdrawn from the marshes of the Macquarie, to be spread over the channel of the Darling. Unsatisfactory, however, as the discoveries may as yet be considered in a commercial point of view, the objects for which the expedition had been fitted out were happily attained. The marsh it had been directed to examine, was traversed on every side, and the rivers it had been ordered to trace, were followed down to their terminations to a distance far beyond where they had ceased to exist as living streams. To many who may cast their eyes over the accompanying chart, the extent of newly discovered country may appear trifling; but when they are told, that there is not a mile of that ground that was not traversed over and over again, either by Mr. Hume or by myself, that we wandered over upwards of 600 miles more than the main body of the expedition, on difference occasions, in our constant and anxious search for water, and that we seldom dismounted from our horses, until long after sunset, they will acknowledge the difficulties with which we had to contend, and will make a generous allowance for them; for, however unsuccessful in some respects the expedition may have been, it accomplished as much, it is to be hoped, as under such trying circumstances could have been accomplished.

XII.—STURT'S DISCOVERY OF THE MURRAY

THE expedition of which we have just detailed the proceedings was so far satisfactory in its results, that it not only set at rest the hypothesis of the existence of an internal shoal sea in southern Australia, and ascertained the actual termination of the rivers it had been directed to trace, but also added very largely to our knowledge of the country considerably to the westward of former discoveries. And although no land had been traversed of a fertile description of sufficient extent to invite the settler, the fact of a large river such as the Darling lying at the back of our almost intertropical settlements, gave a fresh importance to the distant interior. It was evident that this river was the chief drain for carrying off the waters falling westerly from the eastern coast, and as its course indicated a decline of country diametrically opposite to that which had been calculated upon, it became an object of great importance to ascertain its further direction. Had not the saline quality of its waters been accounted for, by the known existence of brine springs in its bed, it would have been natural to have supposed that it communicated with some mediterranean sea; but, under existing circumstances, it remained to be proved whether this river held on a due south course, or whether it ultimately turned westerly, and ran into the heart of the interior. In order fully to determine this point, it would be necessary to regain its banks, so far below the parallel to which it had been traced as to leave no doubt of its identity; but it was difficult to fix upon a plan for approaching that central stream without suffering from the want of water, since it could hardly be expected that the Lachlan would afford such means, as it was reasonable to presume that its termination was very similar to that of the Macquarie. The attention of the government was, consequently, fixed upon the Morumbidgee, a river stated to be of considerable size and of impetuous current. Receiving its supplies from the lofty ranges behind Mount Dromedary, it promised to hold a longer course that those rivers which, depending on periodical rains alone for existence, had been found so soon to exhaust themselves.

The fitting out of another expedition was accordingly determined upon; and about the end of September 1829, I received the Governor's instructions to make the necessary preparations for a second descent into the interior, for the purpose of tracing the Morumbidgee, or such rivers as it might prove to be connected with, as far as practicable. In the event of failure in this object, it was hoped that an attempt to regain the banks of the Darling on a N.W. course from the point at which the expedition might be thwarted in its primary views, would not be unattended with success. Under any circumstances, however, by pursuing these measures, an important part of the colony would necessarily be traversed, of which the features were as yet altogether unknown.

It became my interest and my object to make the expedition as complete as possible, and, as far, as in me lay, to provide for every contingency: and as it appeared to me that, in all likelihood, we should in one stage or other of our journeys have to trust entirely to water conveyance, I determined on taking a whale-boat, whose dimensions and strength should in some measure be proportioned to the service required. I likewise constructed a small still for the distillation of water, in the event of our finding the water of the Darling salt, when we should reach its banks.

From our camp, the Morumbidgee held a direct westerly course for about three miles. The hills under which we had encamped, rose so close upon our right as to leave little space between them and the river. At the distance of three miles, however, they suddenly terminated, and the river changed its direction to the S.W., while a chain of ponds extended to the westward, and separated the alluvial flats from a somewhat more elevated plain before us. We kept these ponds upon our left for some time, but, as they ultimately followed the bend of the river, we left them. The blacks led us on a W. by S. course to the base of a small range two or three miles distant, near which there was a deep lagoon. It was evident they here expected to have found some other natives. Being disappointed, however, they turned in towards the river again, but we stopped short of it on the side of a serpentine sheet of water, an apparent continuation of the chain of ponds we have left behind us, forming a kind of ditch round the S.W. extremity of the range, parallel to which we had continued to travel. This range, which had been gradually decreasing in height from the lagoon, above which it rose perpendicularly, might almost be said to terminate here. We fell in with two or three natives before we halted, but the evident want of population in so fine a country, and on so noble a river, surprised me extremely. We saw several red kangaroos in the course of the day, and succeeded in killing one. It certainly is a beautiful animal, ranging the wilds in native freedom. The female and the kid are of a light mouse-colour. Wild turkeys abound on this part of the Morumbidgee, but with the exception of a few terns, which are found hovering over the lagoons, no new birds had as yet been procured; and the only plant that enriched our collection was an unknown metrosideros. In crossing the extremity of the range, the wheels of the dray sunk deep into a yielding and coarse sandy soil, of decomposed granite, on which forest-grass prevailed in tufts, which, being far apart, made the ground uneven, and caused the animals to trip. We rose at one time sufficiently high to obtain an extensive view, and had our opinions confirmed as to the level nature of the country we were so rapidly approaching. From the N. to the W.S.W. the eye wandered over a wooded and unbroken interior, if I except a solitary double hill that rose in the midst of it, bearing S. 82° W. distant 12 miles, and another singular elevation that bore S. 32° W. called by the natives, Kengal. The appearance to the E.S.E. was still that of a mountainous country, while from the N.E., the hills gradually decrease in height, until lost in the darkness of surrounding objects to the northward. We did not travel this day more than 13 miles on a W. by N. course. The Morumbidgee, where we struck it, by its increased size, kept alive our anticipations of its ultimately leading us to some important point. The partial rains that had fallen while we were on its upper branch, had swollen it considerably, and it now rolled along a vast body of water at the rate of three miles an hour, preserving a medium width of 150 feet; its banks retaining a height far above the usual level of the stream. A traveller who had never before descended into the interior of New Holland, would have spurned the idea of such a river terminating in marshes; but with the experience of the former journey, strong as hope was within my breast, I still feared it might lose itself in the vast flat upon which we could scarcely be said to have yet entered. The country was indeed taking up more and more every day the features of the N.W. interior. Cypresses were observed upon the minor ridges, and the soil near the river, although still rich, and certainly more extensive than above, was occasionally mixed with sand, and scattered over with the claws of crayfish and shells, indicating its greater liability to be flooded; nor indeed could I entertain a doubt that the river had laid a great part of the levels around us under water long after it found that channel in which nature intended ultimately to confine it. We killed another fine red kangaroo in the early part of the day, in galloping after which I got a heavy fall.

The two blacks who had been with us so long, and who had not only exerted themselves to assist us, but had contributed in no small degree to our amusement, though they had, from M'Leay's liberality, tasted all the dainties with which we had provided ourselves, from sugar to concentrated cayenne, intimated that they could no longer accompany the party. They had probably got to the extremity of their beat, and dared not venture any further. They left us with evident regret, receiving, on their departure, several valuable presents, in the shape of tomahawks, etc. The last thing they did was to point out the way to us, and to promise to join us on our return, although they evidently little anticipated ever seeing us again.

In pursuing our journey, we entered a forest, consisting of box-trees, casuarinae, and cypresses, on a light sandy soil, in which both horses and bullocks sunk so deep that their labour was greatly increased, more especially as the weather had become much warmer. At noon I altered my course from N.W. by W. to W.N.W., and reached the Morumbidgee at 3 in the afternoon. The flats bordering it were extensive and rich, and, being partially mixed with sand, were more fitted for agricultural purposes than the stiffer and purer soil amidst the mountains; but the interior beyond them was far from being of corresponding quality. We crossed several plains on which vegetation was scanty, probably owing to the hardness of the soil, which was a stiff loamy clay, and which must check the growth of plants, by preventing the roots from striking freely into it. The river where we stopped for the night appeared to have risen considerably, and the fish were rolling about on the surface of the water with a noise like porpoises. No elevations were visible, so that I had not an opportunity of continuing the chain of survey with the points I had previously taken.

We started on the 26th November, on a course somewhat to the N.W., and traversed plains of the same wearisome description as those I have already described. The wheels of the drays sank up to their axle-trees, and the horses above their fetlocks at every step. The fields of polygonum spread on every side of us like a dark sea, and the only green object within range of our vision was the river line of trees. In several instances, the force

I. D.

of both teams was put to one ɑ ray, to extricate it from the bed into which it had sunk, and the labour was considerably increased from the nature of the weather. The wind was blowing as if through a furnace, from the N.N.E., and the dust was flying in clouds, so as to render it almost suffocating to remain exposed to it. This was the only occasion upon which we felt the hot winds in the interior. We were, about noon, endeavouring to gain a point of a wood at which I expected to come upon the river again, but it was impossible for the teams to reach it without assistance. I therefore sent M'Leay forward, with orders to unload the pack animals as soon as he should make the river, and send them back to help the teams. He had scarcely been separated from me 20 minutes, when one of the men came galloping back to inform me that no river was to be found— that the country beyond the wood was covered with reeds as far as the eye could reach, and that Mr. M'Leay had sent him back for instructions. This intelligence stunned me for a moment or two, and I am sure its effect upon the men was very great. They had unexpectedly arrived at a part of the interior similar to one they had held in dread, and conjured up a thousand difficulties and privations. I desired the man to recal Mr. M'Leay; and, after gaining the wood, moved outside of it at right angles to my former course, and reached the river, after a day of severe toil and exposure, at half-past five. The country, indeed, bore every resemblance to that around the marshes of the Macquarie, but I was too weary to make any further effort: indeed it was too late for me to undertake any thing until the morning.

The circumstances in which were we so unexpectedly placed, occupied my mind so fully that I could not sleep; and I awaited the return of light with the utmost anxiety. If we were indeed on the outskirts of marshes similar to those I had on a former occasion found so much difficulty in examining, I foresaw that in endeavouring to move round them I should recede from water, and place the expedition in jeopardy, probably, without gaining any determinate point, as it would be necessary for me to advance slowly and with caution. Our provisions, however, being calculated to last only to a certain period, I was equally reluctant to delay our operations. My course was, therefore, to be regulated by the appearance of the country and of the river, which I purposed examining with the earliest dawn. If the latter should be found to run into a region of reeds, a boat would be necessary to enable me to ascertain its direction; but, if ultimately it should be discovered to exhaust itself, we should have to strike into the interior on a N.W. course, in search of the Darling. I could not think of putting the whale-boat together in our then state of uncertainty, and it struck me that a smaller one could sooner be prepared for the purposes for which I should require it. These considerations, together with the view I had taken of the measures I might at last be forced into, determined me, on rising, to order Clayton to fell a suitable tree, and to prepare a saw-pit. The labour was of no consideration, and even if eventually the boat should not be wanted, no injury would arise, and it was better to take time by the forelock. Having marked a tree preparatory to leaving the camp, M'Leay and I started at an early hour on an excursion of deeper interest than any we had as yet undertaken; to examine the reeds, not only for the purpose of ascertaining their extent, if possible, but also to guide us in our future measures. We rode for some miles along the river side, but observed in it no signs, either of increase or of exhaustion. Its waters, though turbid, were deep, and its current still rapid. Its banks, too, were lofty, and showed no evidence of decreasing in height, so as to occasion an overflow of them, as had been the case with the Macquarie. We got among vast bodies of reeds, but the plains of the interior were visible beyond them. We were evidently in a hollow, and the decline of country was plainly to the southward of west. Every thing tended to strengthen my conviction that we were still far from the termination of the river. The character it had borne throughout, and its appearance now so far to the westward, gave me the most lively hopes that it would make good its way through the vast level into which it fell, and that its termination would accord with its promise. Besides I daily anticipated its junction with some stream of equal, if not of greater magnitude from the S.E. I was aware that my resolves must be instant, decisive, and immediately acted upon, as on firmness and promptitude at this crisis the success of the expedition depended. About noon I checked my horse, and rather to the surprise of my companion, intimated to him my intention of returning to the camp. He naturally asked what I purposed doing. I told him it appeared to me more than probable that the Morumbidgee would hold good its course to some fixed point, now that it had reached a meridian beyond the known rivers of the interior. It was certain, from the denseness of the reeds, and the breadth of the belts, that the teams could not be brought any farther, and that, taking every thing into consideration, I had resolved on a bold

and desperate measure, that of building the whale-boat, and
sending home the drays. Our appearance in camp so suddenly,
surprised the men not more than the orders I gave. They all
thought I had struck on some remarkable change of country,
and were anxious to know my ultimate views. It was not my
intention, however, immediately to satisfy their curiosity. I had
to study their characters as long as I could, in order to select
those best qualified to accompany me on the desperate adventure
for which I was preparing.

The attention of both M'Leay and myself, was turned to the
hasty building of the whale-boat. A shed was erected and every
necessary preparation made, and although Clayton had the keel
of the small boat already laid down, and some planks prepared,
she was abandoned for the present, and, after four days more of
arduous labour, the whale-boat was painted and in the water.
From her dimensions, it appeared to me impossible that she
would hold all our provisions and stores, for her after-part had
been fitted up as an armoury, which took away considerably
from her capacity of stowage. The small boat would still, therefore, be necessary, and she was accordingly re-laid, for half the
dimensions of the large boat, and in three days was alongside
her consort in the river. Thus, in seven days we had put together
a boat, twenty-seven feet in length, had felled a tree from the
forest, with which we had built a second of half the size, had
painted both, and had them at a temporary wharf ready for
loading. Such would not have been the case had not our hearts
been in the work, as the weather was close and sultry, and we
found it a task of extreme labour. In the intervals between the
hours of work, I prepared my despatches for the Governor, and
when they were closed, it only remained for me to select six
hands, the number I intended should accompany me down the
river, and to load the boats, ere we should once more proceed
in the further obedience of our instructions.

It was impossible that I could do without Clayton, whose
perseverance and industry had mainly contributed to the building of the boats; of the other prisoners, I chose Mulholland and
Macnamee; leaving the rest in charge of Robert Harris, whose
steady conduct had merited my approbation. My servant,
Harris, Hopkinson, and Fraser, of course, made up the crews.
The boats were loaded in the evening of Jan. 6th, as it had been
necessary to give the paint a little time to dry. On the 4th, I
had sent Clayton and Mulholland to the nearest cypress range
for a mast and spar, and on the evening of that day some blacks

had visited us; but they sat on the bank of the river, preserving a most determined silence; and, at length, left us abruptly, and apparently in great ill humour. In the disposition of the loads, I placed all the flour, the tea, and tobacco, in the whale-boat. The meat-casks, still, and carpenters' tools, were put into the small boat.

As soon as the different arrangements were completed, I collected the men, and told off those who were to accompany me. I then gave the rest over in charge to Harris, and, in adverting to their regular conduct hitherto, trusted they would be equally careful while under his orders. I then directed the last remaining sheep to be equally divided among us; and it was determined that, for fear of accidents, Harris should remain stationary for a week, at the expiration of which time, he would be at liberty to proceed to Goulburn Plains, there to receive his instructions from Sydney; while the boats were to proceed at an early hour of the morning down the river,—whether ever to return again being a point of the greatest uncertainty.

The camp was a scene of bustle and confusion long before daylight. The men whom I had selected to accompany me were in high spirits, and so eager to commence their labours that they had been unable to sleep, but busied themselves from the earliest dawn in packing up their various articles of clothing, etc. We were prevented from taking our departure so early as I had intended, by rain that fell about six. At a little after seven, however, the weather cleared up, the morning mists blew over our heads, and the sun struck upon us with his usual fervour. As soon as the minor things were stowed away, we bade adieu to Harris and his party; and, shortly after, embarked on the bosom of that stream along the banks of which we had journeyed for so many miles.

Notwithstanding that we only used two oars, our progress down the river was rapid. Hopkinson had arranged the loads so well, that all the party could sit at their ease, and Fraser was posted in the bow of the boat, with gun in hand, to fire at any new bird or beast that we might surprise in our silent progress. The little boat, which I shall henceforward call the skiff, was fastened by a painter to our stern.

As the reader will have collected from what has already fallen under his notice, the country near the depot was extensively covered with reeds, beyond which vast plains of polygonum stretched away. From the bed of the river we could not observe the change that took place in it as we passed along, so that we found it necessary to land, from time to time, for the purpose of noting down its general appearance. At about fifteen miles from the depot, we came upon a large creek-junction from the N.E., which I did not doubt to be the one, M'Leay and I had crossed on the 25th of December. It was much larger than the creek of the Macquarie, and was capable of holding a very great body of water, although evidently too small to contain all that occasionally rushed from its source. I laid it down as the supposed junction of the Lachlan, since I could not, against the corroborating facts in my possession, doubt its originating in the marshes of that river. Should this, eventually, prove to be the case, the similar termination of the two streams traced by Mr. Oxley will be a singular feature in the geography of the interior.

We were just about to land, to prepare our dinner, when two emus swam across the river a-head of us. This was an additional inducement for us to land, but we were unfortunately too slow, and the birds escaped us. We had pushed in to the right bank, and found on ascending it, that the reeds with which it had hitherto been lined, had partially ceased. A large plain, similar to those over which we had wandered prior to our gaining the flooded region, stretched away to a considerable distance behind us, and was backed by cypresses and brush. The soil of the plain was a red sandy loam, covered sparingly with salsolae and shrubs; thus indicating that the country still preserved its barren character, and that it is the same from north to south. Among the shrubs we found a tomb that appeared to have been recently constructed. No mound had been raised over the body, but an oval hollow shed occupied the centre of the burial place, that was lined with reeds and bound together with strong network. Round this, the usual walks were cut, and the recent traces of women's feet were visible upon them, but we saw no natives, although, from the number and size of the paths that led from the river, in various directions across the plain, I was led to conclude, that, at certain seasons, it is hereabouts numerously frequented. Fraser gathered some rushes similar to those used by the natives of the Darling in the fabrication of their nets, and as they had not before been observed, we judged them, of course, to be a sign of our near approach to that river.

As soon as we had taken a hasty dinner, we again embarked, and pursued our journey. I had hoped, from the appearance of the country to the north of us, although that to the south gave little indication of any change, that we should soon clear the reeds; but at somewhat less than a mile they closed in upon the river, and our frequent examination of the neighbourhood on either side of it only tended to confirm the fact, that we were passing through a country subject to great and extensive inundation. We pulled up at half-past five, and could scarcely find space enough to pitch our tents.

The Morumbidgee kept a decidedly westerly course during the day. Its channel was not so tortuous as we expected to have found it, nor did it offer any obstruction to the passage of the boats. Its banks kept a general height of eight feet, five of which were of alluvial soil, and both its depth and its current were considerable. We calculated having proceeded from 28 to 30 miles, though, perhaps, not more than half that distance in a direct line. No rain fell during the day, but we experienced some heavy squalls from the E.S.E.

The second day of our journey from the depot was marked by an accident that had well nigh obliged us to abandon the further pursuit of the river, by depriving us of part of our means of carrying it into effect. We had proceeded, as usual, at an early hour in the morning, and not long after we started, fell in with the blacks who had visited us last, and who were now in much better humour than upon that occasion. As they had their women with them, we pushed in to the bank, and distributed some presents, after which we dropped quietly down the river. Its general depth had been such as to offer few obstructions to our progress, but about an hour after we left the natives, the skiff struck upon a sunken log, and immediately filling, went down in about twelve feet of water. The length of the painter prevented any strain upon the whale-boat, but the consequence of so serious an accident at once flashed upon our minds. That we should suffer considerably, we could not doubt, but our object was to get the skiff up with the least possible delay, to prevent the fresh water from mixing with the brine, in the casks of meat. Some short time, however, necessarily elapsed before we could effect this, and when at last the skiff was hauled ashore, we found that we were too late to prevent the mischief that we had anticipated. All the things had been fastened in the boat, but either from the shock, or the force of the current, one of the pork casks, the head of the still, and the greater part of the carpenter's tools, had been thrown out of her. As the success of the expedition might probably depend upon the complete state of the still, I determined to use every effort for its recovery; but I was truly at a loss how to find it; for the waters of the river were extremely turbid. In this dilemma, the blacks would have been of the most essential service, but they were far behind us, so that we had to depend on our own exertions alone. I directed the whale-boat to be moored over the place where the accident had happened, and then used the oars on either side of her, to feel along the bottom of the river, in hopes that by these means we should strike upon the articles we had lost. However unlikely such a measure was to prove successful, we recovered in the course of the afternoon, every thing but the still-head, and a cask of paint. Whenever the oar struck against the substance that appeared, by its sound or feel to belong to us, it was immediately pushed into the sand, and the upper end of the oar being held by two men, another descended by it to the bottom of the river, remaining under water as long as he could, to ascertain what was immediately within arm's length of him. This work was, as may be imagined, most laborious, and the men at length became much exhausted. They would not, however, give up the search for the still-head, more especially after M'Leay, in diving, had descended upon it. Had he, by ascertaining his position, left it to us to heave it up, our labours would soon have ended; but, in his anxiety for its recovery, he tried to bring it up, when finding it too heavy, he let it go, and the current again swept it away.

At sunset, we were obliged to relinquish our task, the men complaining of violent head-aches, which the nature of the day increased. Thinking our own efforts would be unavailing, I directed two of the men to go up the river for the blacks, at daylight in the morning, and set the reeds on fire to attract their notice. The day had been cloudy and sultry in the afternoon, the clouds collecting in the N.E.; we heard the distant thunder, and expected to have been deluged with rain. None, however, fell, although we were anxious for moisture to change the oppressive state of the atmosphere. The fire I had kindled raged behind us, and threw dense columns of smoke into the sky, that cast over the landscape a shade of the most dismal gloom. We were not in a humour to admire the picturesque, but soon betook ourselves to rest, and after such a day of labour as that we had undergone, I dispensed with the night-guard.

In the morning we resumed our search for the still-head, which Hopkinson at length fortunately struck with his oar. It had been swept considerably below the place at which M'Leay had dived, or we should most probably have found it sooner. With its recovery, all our fatigues were at once forgotten, and I

ordered the breakfast to be got ready preparatory to our reload-
ing the skiff. Fraser and Mulholland, who had left the camp at
daylight, had not yet returned. I was sitting in the tent, when
Macnamee came to inform me that one of the frying-pans was
missing, which had been in use the evening previous, for that he
himself had placed it on the stump of a tree, and he therefore
supposed a native dog had run away with it. Soon after this,
another loss was reported to me, and it was at last discovered
that an extensive robbery had been committed upon us during
the night, and that, in addition to the frying-pan, three cut-
lasses, and five tomahawks, with the pea of the steelyards, had
been carried away. I was extremely surprised at this instance of
daring in the natives, and determined, if possible, to punish it.
About ten, Fraser and Mulholland returned with two blacks.
Fraser told me he saw several natives on our side of the river,
as he was returning, to whom those who were with him spoke,
and I felt convinced from their manner and hesitation, that
they were aware of the trick that had been played upon us.
However, as Fraser had promised them a tomahawk to induce
them to accompany him, I fulfilled the promise.

Leaving this unlucky spot, we made good about sixteen miles
during the afternoon. The river maintained its breadth and
depth nor were the reeds continuous upon its banks. We passed
several plains that were considerably elevated above the alluvial
deposits, and the general appearance of the country induced me
strongly to hope that we should shortly get out of the region of
reeds, or the great flooded concavity on which we had fixed our
depot; but the sameness of vegetation, and the seemingly diminutive size of the timber in the distance, argued against any
change for the better in the soil of the interior. Having taken
the precaution of shortening the painter of the skiff, we found
less difficulty in steering her clear of obstacles, and made rapid
progress down the Morumbidgee during the first cool and refreshing hours of the morning. The channel of the river became
somewhat less contracted, but still retained sufficient depth for
larger boats than ours, and preserved a general westerly course.
Although no decline of country was visible to the eye, the current in places ran very strong. It is impossible for me to convey
to the reader's mind an idea of the nature of the country through
which we passed. On this day the favourable appearances,
noticed yesterday, ceased almost as soon as we embarked. On
the 10th, reeds lined the banks of the river on both sides, without any break, and waved like gloomy streamers over its turbid

waters; while the trees stood leafless and sapless in the midst of them. Wherever we landed, the same view presented itself— a waving expanse of reeds, and a country as flat as it is possible to imagine one. The eye could seldom penetrate beyond three quarters of a mile, and the labour of walking through the reeds was immense; but within our observation all was green and cheerless. The morning had been extremely cold, with a thick haze at E.S.E. About 2 p.m. it came on to rain heavily, so that we did not stir after that hour.

I had remarked that the Morumbidgee was not, from the depot downwards, so broad or so fine a river as it certainly is at the foot of the mountain ranges, where it gains the level country. The observations of the last two days had impressed upon my mind an idea that it was rapidly falling off, and I began to dread that it would finally terminate in one of those fatal marshes in which the Macquarie and the Lachlan exhaust themselves. My hope of a more favourable issue was considerably damped by the general appearance of the surrounding country; and from the circumstance of our not having as yet passed a single tributary. As we proceeded down the river, its channel gradually contracted, and immense trees that had been swept down it by floods, rendered the navigation dangerous and intricate. Its waters became so turbid, that it was impossible to see objects in it, notwithstanding the utmost diligence on the part of the men.

About noon, we fell in with a large tribe of natives, but had great difficulty in bringing them to visit us. If they had *heard* of white men, we were evidently the first they had ever *seen*. They approached us in the most cautious manner, and were unable to subdue their fears as long as they remained with us. Collectively, these people could not have amounted to less than one hundred and twenty in number.

As we pushed off from the bank, after having staid with them about half an hour, the whale-boat struck with such vilence on a sunken log, that she immediately leaked on her starboard side. Fortunately she was going slowly at the time, or she would most probably have received some more serious injury. One of the men was employed during the remainder of the afternoon in bailing her out, and we stopped sooner than we should otherwise have done, in order to ascertain the extent of damage, and to repair it. The reeds terminated on both sides of the river some time before we pulled up, and the country round the camp was more elevated than usual, and bore the appearance of open forest pasture land, the timber upon it being a dwarf species of box, and the soil a light tenacious earth.

About a mile below our encampment of the 12th, we at length came upon a considerable creek-junction from the S.E. Below it, the river increased both in breadth and depth; its banks were lofty and perpendicular, and even the lowest levels were but partially covered with reeds. We met with fewer obstructions in consequence, and pursued our journey with restored confidence. Towards evening a great change also took place in the aspect of the country, which no longer bore general marks of inundation. The level of the interior was broken by a small hill to the right of the stream, but the view from its summit rather damped than encouraged my hopes of any improvement. The country was covered with wood and brush, and the line of the horizon was unbroken by the least swell. We were on an apparently boundless flat, without any fixed point on which to direct our movements, nor was there a single object for the eye to rest upon, beyond the dark and gloomy wood that surrounded us on every side.

Soon after passing this hill, the whale-boat struck upon a line of sunken rocks, but fortunately escaped without injury. Mulholland, who was standing in the bow, was thrown out of her, head foremost, and got a good soaking, but soon recovered himself. The composition of the rock was iron-stone, and it is the first formation that occurs westward of the dividing range. We noticed a few cypresses in the distance, but the general timber was dwarf-box, or flooded-gum, and a few of the acacia longa scattered at great distances. In verifying our position by some lunars, we found ourselves in 142° 46′ 30″ of east long., and in lat. 35° 25′ 15″ S., the mean variation of the compass being 4° 10″ E., it appearing that we were decreasing the variation as we proceeded westward.

On the 13th, we passed the first running stream that joins the Morumbidgee, in a course of more than 340 miles. It came from the S.E., and made a visible impression on the river at the junction, although in tracing it up, it appeared to be insignificant in itself. The circumstance of these tributaries all occurring on the left, evidence the level nature of the country to the north. In the afternoon, we passed a dry creek also from the S.E., which must at times throw a vast supply of water into the river, since for many miles below, the latter preserved a breadth of 200 feet, and averaged from 12 to 20 feet in depth, with banks of from 15 to 18 feet in height. Yet, notwithstanding its general equality of depth, several rapids occurred, down which the boats were hurried with great velocity. The body of water in the river continued undiminished, notwithstanding its increased breadth of channel; for which reason I should imagine that it is fed by springs, independently of other supplies. Some few cypresses were again observed, and the character of the distant country resembled, in every particular, that of the interior between the Macquarie and the Darling. The general appearance of the Morumbidgee, from the moment of our starting on the 13th, to a late hour in the afternoon, had been such as to encourage my hopes of ultimate success in tracing it down; but about three o'clock we came to one of those unaccountable and mortifying changes which had already so frequently excited my apprehension. Its channel again suddenly contracted, and became almost blocked up with huge trees, that must have found their way into it down the creeks or junctions we had lately passed. The rapidity of the current increasing at the same time, rendered the navigation perplexing and dangerous. We passed reach after reach, presenting the same difficulties, and were at length obliged to pull up at 5 p.m., having a scene of confusion and danger before us that I did not dare to encounter with the evening's light; for I had not only observed that the men's eyesight failed them as the sun descended, and that they mistook shadows for objects under water, and vice-versa, but the channel had become so narrow that, although the banks were not of increased height, we were involved in comparative darkness, under a close arch of trees, and a danger was hardly seen ere we were hurried past it, almost without the possibility of avoiding it. The reach at the head of which we stopped, was crowded with the trunks of trees, the branches of which crossed each other in every direction, nor could I hope, after a minute examination of the channel, to succeed in taking the boats safely down so intricate a passage.

We rose in the morning with feelings of apprehension, and uncertainty; and, indeed, with great doubts on our minds whether we were not thus early destined to witness the wreck, and the defeat of the expedition. The men got slowly and cautiously into the boat, and placed themselves so as to leave no part of her undefended. Hopkinson stood at the bow, ready with poles to turn her head from anything upon which she might be drifting. Thus prepared, we allowed her to go with the stream. By extreme care and attention on the part of the men we passed this formidable barrier. Hopkinson in particular exerted himself, and more than once leapt from the boat upon apparently rotten logs of wood, that I should not have judged capable of bearing his weight, the more effectually to save the boat. It might have been imagined that where such a quantity of timber had accumulated, a clearer channel would have been found below, but such was not the case. In every reach we had to encounter fresh difficulties. In some places huge trees lay athwart the stream, under whose arched branches we were obliged to pass; but, generally speaking, they had been carried, roots foremost, by the current, and, therefore, presented so many points to receive us, that, at the rate at which we were going, had we struck full upon any one of them, it would have gone through and through the boat. About noon we stopped to repair, or rather to take down the remains of our awning, which had been torn away; and to breathe a moment from the state of apprehension and anxiety in which our minds had been kept during the morning. About one we again started. The men looked anxiously out a-head; for the singular change in the river had impressed on them an idea, that we were approaching its termination, or near some adventure. On a sudden, the river took a general southern direction, but, in its tortuous course, swept round to every point of the compass with the greatest irregularity. We were carried at a fearful rate down its gloomy and contracted banks, and, in such a moment of excitement, had little time to pay attention to the country through which we were passing. It was, however, observed, that chalybeate-springs were numerous close to the water's edge. At 3 p.m., Hopkinson called out that we were approaching a junction, and in less than a minute afterwards, we were hurried into a broad and noble river.

It is impossible for me to describe the effect of so instantaneous a change of circumstances upon us. The boats were allowed to drift along at pleasure, and such was the force with which we had been shot out of the Morumbidgee, that we were carried nearly to the bank opposite its embouchure, whilst we continued to gaze in silent astonishment on the capacious channel we had entered; and when we looked for that by which we had been led into it, we could hardly believe that the insignificant gap that presented itself to us was, indeed, the termination of the beautiful and noble stream, whose course we had thus successfully followed. I can only compare the relief we experienced to that which the seaman feels on weathering the rock upon which he expected his vessel would have struck—to the calm which succeeds moments of feverish anxiety, when the dread of danger is succeeded by the certainty of escape.

To myself personally, the discovery of this river was a circumstance of a particularly gratifying nature, since it not only confirmed the justness of my opinion as to the ultimate fate of the Morumbidgee, and bore me out in the apparently rash and hasty step I had taken at the depot, but assured me of ultimate success in the duty I had to perform. We had got on the high road, as it were, either to the south coast, or to some important outlet; and the appearance of the river itself was such as to justify our most sanguine expectations. I could not doubt its being the great channel of the streams from the S.E. angle of the island. Mr. Hume had mentioned to me that he crossed three very considerable streams, when employed with Mr. Hovell in 1823 in penetrating towards Port Phillips, to which the names of the Goulburn, the Hume, and the Ovens, had been given; and as I was 300 miles from the track these gentlemen had pursued, I considered it more than probable that those rivers must already have formed a junction above me, more especially when I reflected that the convexity of the mountains to the S.E. would necessarily direct the waters falling inwards from them to a common centre.

We entered the new river at right angles, and, as I have remarked, at the point of junction the channel of the Morumbidgee had narrowed so as to bear all the appearance of an ordinary creek. In breadth it did not exceed fifty feet, and if, instead of having passed down it, I had been making my way up the principal streams, I should little have dreamt that so dark and gloomy an outlet concealed a river that would lead me to the haunts of civilized man, and whose fountains rose amidst snow-clad mountains. Such, however, is the characteristic of the streams falling to the westward of the coast ranges. Descending into a low and level interior, and depending on their immediate springs for existence, they fall off, as they increase their distance from the base of the mountains in which they rise, and in their lower branches give little results of the promise they had previously made.

The opinion I have expressed, and which is founded on my personal experience, that the rivers crossed by Messrs. Hovell and Hume had already united above me, was strengthened by the capacity of the stream we had just discovered. It had a medium width of 350 feet, with a depth of from twelve to twenty. Its reaches were from half to three-quarters of a mile in length, and the views upon it were splendid. Of course, as the Morumbidgee entered it from the north, its first reach must have been E. and W., and it was so, as nearly as possible; but it took us a little to the southward of the latter point, in a distance of about eight miles that we pulled down it in the course of the afternoon. We then landed and pitched our tents for the night. Its transparent waters were running over a sandy bed at the rate of two-and-a-half knots an hour, and its banks, although averaging eighteen feet in height, were evidently subject to floods.

We had not seen any natives since falling in with the last tribe on the Morumbidgee. A cessation had, therefore, taken place in our communication with them, in re-establishing which I anticipated considerable difficulty. It appeared singular that we should not have fallen in with any for several successive days, more especially at the junction of the two rivers, as in similar situations they generally have an establishment. In examining the country back from the stream, I did not observe any large paths, but it was evident that fires had made extensive ravages in the neighbourhood, so that the country was, perhaps, only temporarily deserted. Macnamee, who had wandered a little from the tents, declared that he had seen about a dozen natives round a fire, from whom (if he really did see them) he very precipitately fled, but I was inclined to discredit his story, because in our journey on the following day, we did not see even a casual wanderer.

The river maintained its character, and raised our hopes to the highest pitch. Its breadth varied from 150 to 200 yards; and only in one place, where a reef of iron-stone stretched nearly across from the left bank, so as to contract the channel near the right and to form a considerable rapid, was there any apparent obstruction to our navigation. I was sorry, however, to remark that the breadth of alluvial soil between its outer and inner banks was very inconsiderable, and that the upper levels were poor and sandy. Blue-gum generally occupied the former, while the usual productions of the plains still predominated upon the latter, and shewed that the distant interior had not yet undergone any favourable change. We experienced strong breezes from the north, but the range of the thermometer was high, and the weather rather oppressive than otherwise. On the night of the 16th, we had a strong wind from the N.W., but it moderated with day-light, and shifted to the E.N.E., and the day was favourable and cool. Our progress was in every way satisfactory, and if any change had taken place in the river, it was that the banks had increased in height, in many places to thirty feet, the soil being a red loam, and the surface much above the reach of floods. The bank opposite to the one that was so elevated, was proportionably low, and, in general, not only heavily timbered, but covered with reeds, and backed by a chain of ponds at the base of the outer embankment.

About 4 p.m., some natives were observed running by the river side behind us, but on our turning the boat's head towards the shore, they ran away. It was evident that they had no idea what we were, and, from their timidity, feeling assured that it would be impossible to bring them to a parley, we continued onwards till our usual hour of stopping, when we pitched our tents on the left bank for the night, it being the one opposite to that on which the natives had appeared. We conjectured that their curiosity would lead them to follow us, which they very shortly did; for we had scarcely made ourselves comfortable when we heard their wild notes through the woods as they advanced towards the river; and their breaking into view with their spears and shields, and painted and prepared as they were for battle, was extremely fine. They stood threatening us, and making a great noise, for a considerable time, but, finding that we took no notice of them, they, at length, became quiet. I then walked to some little distance from the party, and taking a branch in my hand, as a sign of peace, beckoned them to swim to our side of the river, which, after some time, two or three of them did. But they approached me with great caution, hesitating at every step. They soon, however, gained confidence, and were ultimately joined by all the males of their tribe. I gave the *first* who swam the river a tomahawk (making this a rule in order to encourage them) with which he was highly delighted. I shortly afterwards placed them all in a row and fired a gun before them: they were quite unprepared for such an explosion, and after standing stupified and motionless for a moment or two, they simultaneously took to their heels, to our great amusement. I succeeded, however, in calling them back, and they regained their confidence so much, that sixteen of them remained with us all night, but the greater number retired at sunset.

On the following morning, they accompanied us down the river, where we fell in with their tribe, who were stationed on an elevated bank a short distance below—to the number of eighty-three men, women, and children. Their appearance was extremely picturesque and singular. They wanted us to land, but

STURT'S DISCOVERIES, 1828-9 AND 1829-30.
From "The Life of Charles Sturt."

time was too precious for such delays. Some of the boldest of the natives swam round and round the boat so as to impede the use of the oars, and the women on the bank evinced their astonishment by mingled yells and cries. They entreated us, by signs, to remain with them, but, as I foresaw a compliance. on this occasion would hereafter be attended with inconvenience, I thought it better to proceed on our journey, and the natives soon ceased their importunities, and, indeed, did not follow or molest us.

The river improved upon us at every mile. Its reaches were of noble breadth, and splendid appearance. Its current was stronger, and it was fed by numerous springs. Rocks, however, were more frequent in its bed, and in two places almost formed a barrier across the channel, leaving but a narrow space for the boats to go down. We passed several elevations of from 70 to 90 feet in height, at the base of which the stream swept along. The soil of these elevations was a mixture of clay (marl) and sand, upon coarse sandstone. Their appearance and the manner in which they had been acted upon by water, was singular, and afforded a proof of the violence of the rains in this part of the interior. From the highest of these, I observed that the country to the S.E. was gently undulated, and so far changed in character from that through which we had been travelling; still, however, it was covered with a low scrub, and was barren and unpromising.

About noon of the 18th, we surprised two women at the waterside, who immediately retreated into the brush. Shortly after, four men shewed themselves, and followed us for a short distance, but hid themselves upon our landing. The country still appeared undulated to the S.E.; the soil was sandy, and cypresses more abundant than any other tree. We passed several extensive sand-banks in the river, of unusual size and solidity, an evident proof of the sandy nature of the interior generally. The vast accumulations of sand at the junctions of every creek were particularly remarkable. The timber on the alluvial flats was not by any means so large as we had hitherto observed it; nor were the flats themselves so extensive as they are on the Morumbidgee and the Macquarie. Notwithstanding the aspect of the country which I have described, no *positive* change has as yet taken place in the general feature of the interior. The river continued to flow in a direction somewhat to the northward of west, through a country that underwent no perceptible alteration. Its waters, confined to their immediate bed, swept along considerably

I. D.   *o* below the level of its inner banks; and the spaces between them and the outer ones, though generally covered with reeds, seemed not recently to have been flooded; while, on the other hand, they had, in many places, from successive depositions, risen to a height far above the reach of inundation. Still, however, the more remote interior maintained its sandy and sterile character, and stretched away, in alternate plain and wood, to a distance far beyond the limits of our examination.

About the 21st, a very evident change took place in it. The banks of the river suddenly acquired a perpendicular and water-worn appearance. Their summits were perfectly level, and no longer confined by a secondary embankment, but preserved an uniform equality of surface back from the stream. These banks, although so abrupt, were not so high as the upper levels, or secondary embankments. They indicated a deep alluvial deposit, and yet, being high above the reach of any ordinary flood, were covered with grass, under an open box forest, into which a moderately dense scrub occasionally penetrated. We had fallen into a concavity similar to those of the marshes, but successive depositions had almost filled it, and no longer subject to inundation, it had lost all the character of those flooded tracts. The kind of country I have been describing, lay rather to the right than to the left of the river at this place, the latter continuing low and swampy, as if the country to the south of the river were still subject to inundation. As the expedition proceeded, the left bank gradually assumed the appearance of the right; both looked water-worn and perpendicular, and though not more than from nine to ten feet in height, their summits were per-fectly level in receding, and bore diminutive box-timber, with widely-scattered vegetation. Not a single elevation had, as yet, broken the dark and gloomy monotony of the interior; but as our observations were limited to a short distance from the river, our surmises on the nature of the distant country were necessarily involved in some uncertainty.

On the 19th, as we were about to conclude our journey for the day, we saw a large body of natives before us. On approach-ing them, they shewed every disposition for combat, and ran along the bank with spears in rests, as if only waiting for an opportunity to throw them at us. They were upon the right, and as the river was broad enough to enable me to steer wide of them, I did not care much for their threats; but upon another party appearing upon the left bank, I thought it high time to disperse one or the other of them, as the channel was not wide enough to enable me to keep clear of danger, if assailed by both, as I might be while keeping amid the channel. I found, however, that they did not know how to use the advantage they possessed, as the two divisions formed a junction; those on the left swimming over to the stronger body upon the right bank. This, fortunately, prevented the necessity of any hostile measure on my part, and we were suffered to proceed unmolested, for the present. The whole then followed us without any symptom of fear, but making a dreadful shouting, and beating their spears and shields together, by way of intimidation. It is but justice to my men to say that in this critical situation they evinced the greatest coolness, though it was impossible for any one to witness such a scene with indifference. As I did not intend to fatigue the men by continuing to pull farther than we were in the habit of doing, we landed at our usual time on the left bank, and while the people were pitching the tents, I walked down the bank with M'Leay, to treat with these desperadoes in the best way we could, across the water, a measure to which my men shewed great reluctance, declaring that if during our absence the natives approached them, they would undoubtedly fire upon them. I assured them it was not my intention to go out of their sight. We took our guns with us, but determined not to use them until the last extremity, both from a reluctance to shed blood and with a view to our future security. I held a long pantomimical dialogue with them, across the water, and held out the olive branch in token of amity. They at length laid aside their spears, and a long consultation took place among them, which ended in two or three wading into the river, contrary, as it appeared, to the earnest remonstrances of the majority, who, finding their entreaties had no effect, wept aloud, and followed them with a determination, I am sure, of sharing their fate, whatever it might have been. As soon as they landed, M'Leay and I retired to a little distance from the bank, and sat down; that being the usual way among the natives of the interior, to invite to an interview. When they saw us act thus, they approached, and sat down by us, but without looking up, from a kind of diffidence peculiar to them, and which exists even among the nearest relatives, as I have already had occasion to observe. As they gained confidence, however, they shewed an excessive curiosity, and stared at us in the most earnest manner. We now led them to the camp, and I gave, as was my custom, the first who had approached, a tomahawk; and to the others, some pieces of iron hoop. Those who had crossed the river amounted to about thirty-five in number. At sunset, the majority of them left us; but three old men remained at the fire-side all night. I observed that few of them had either lost their front teeth or lacerated their bodies, as the more westerly tribes do. The most loathsome diseases prevailed among them. Several were disabled by leprosy, or some similar disorder, and two or three had entirely lost their sight. They are, undoubtedly, a brave and a confiding people, and are by no means wanting in natural affection. In person, they resemble the mountain tribes. They had the thick lip, the sunken eye, the extended nostril, and long beards, and both smooth and curly hair are common among them. Their lower extremities appear to bear no proportion to their bust in point of muscle strength; but the facility with which they ascend trees of the largest growth, and the activity with which they move upon all occasions, together with their singularly erect stature, argue that such appearance is entirely deceptive.

The old men slept very soundly by the fire, and were the last to get up in the morning. M'Leay's extreme good humour had made a most favourable impression upon them, and I can picture him, even now, joining in their wild song. Whether it was from his entering so readily into their mirth, or from anything peculiar that struck them, the impression upon the whole of us was, that they took him to have been originally a black, in consequence of which they gave him the name of Rundi. Certain it is, they pressed him to shew his side, and asked if he had not received a wound there—evidently as if the original Rundi had met with a violent death from a spear-wound in that place. The whole tribe, amounting in number to upwards of 150, assembled to see us take our departure. Four of them accompanied us, among whom there was one remarkable for personal strength and stature.—The 21st passed without our falling in with any new tribe, and the night of the 22nd, saw us still wandering in that lonely desert together. There was something unusual in our going through such an extent of country without meeting another tribe, but our companions appeared to be perfectly aware of the absence of inhabitants, as they never left our side.

Although the banks of the river had been of general equality of height, sandy elevations still occasionally formed a part of them, and their summits were considerably higher than the alluvial flats.

It was upon the crest of one of these steep and lofty banks, that on the morning of the 22nd, the natives who were a-head of the boat, suddenly stopped to watch our proceedings down a foaming rapid that ran beneath. We were not aware of the danger to which we were approaching, until we turned an angle of the river, and found ourselves too near to retreat. In such a moment, without knowing what was before them, the coolness of the men was strikingly exemplified. No one even spoke after they became aware that silence was necessary. The natives (probably anticipating misfortune) stood leaning upon their spears upon the lofty bank above us. Desiring the men not to move from their seats, I stood up to survey the channel, and to steer the boat to that part of it which was least impeded by rocks. I was obliged to decide upon a hasty survey, as we were already at the head of the rapid. It appeared to me that there were two passages, the one down the centre of the river, the other immediately under its right bank. A considerable rock stood directly in our way to the latter, so that I had no alternative but to descend the former. About forty yards below the rock, I noticed that a line of rocks occupied the space between the two channels, whilst a reef, projecting from the left bank, made the central passage distinctly visible, and the rapidity of the current proportionably great. I entertained hopes that the passage was clear, and that we should shoot down it without interruption; but in this I was disappointed. The boat struck with the fore-part of her keel on a sunken rock, and, swinging round as it were on a pivot, presented her bow to the rapid, while the skiff floated away into the strength of it. We had every reason to anticipate the loss of our whale-boat, whose build was so light, that had her side struck the rock, instead of her keel, she would have been laid open from stem to stern. As it was, however, she remained fixed in her position, and it only remained for us to get her off the best way we could. I saw that this could only be done by sending two of the men with a rope to the upper rock, and getting the boat, by that means, into the still water, between that and the lower one. We should then have time to examine the channels, and to decide as to that down which it would be safest to proceed. My only fear was, that the loss of the weight of the two men would lighten the boat so much, that she would be precipitated down the rapid without my having any command over her; but it happened otherwise. We succeeded in getting her into the still water, and ultimately took her down the channel under the right bank, without her sustaining any injury. A few miles below this rapid the river took a singular bend, and we found, after pulling several miles, that we were within a stone's throw of a part of the stream we had already sailed down.

The four natives joined us in the camp, and assisted the men at their various occupations. The consequence was, that they were treated with more than ordinary kindness; and Fraser, for his part, in order to gratify these favoured guests, made great havoc among the feathered race. He returned after a short ramble with a variety of game, among which were a crow, a kite, and a laughing jackass (alcedo gigantea), a species of king's-fisher, a singular bird, found in every part of Australia. Its cry, which resembles a chorus of wild spirits, is apt to startle the traveller who may be in jeopardy, as if laughing and mocking at his misfortune. It is a harmless bird, and I seldom allowed them to be destroyed, as they were sure to rouse us with the earliest dawn. To this list of Fraser's spoils, a duck and a tough old cockatoo must be added. The whole of these our friends threw on the fire without the delay of plucking, and snatched them from that consuming element ere they were well singed, and devoured them with uncommon relish.

We pitched our tents upon a flat of good and tenacious soil. A brush, in which there was a new species of melaleuca, backed it, in the thickest part of which we found a deserted native village. The spot was evidently chosen for shelter. The huts were large and long, all facing the same point of the compass, and in every way resembling the huts occupied by the natives of the Darling. Large flocks of whistling ducks, and other wild fowl, flew over our heads to the N.W., as if making their way to some large or favourite waters. My observations placed us in lat. 34° 8' 15" south, and in east long. 141° 9' 42" or nearly so; and I was at a loss to conceive what direction the river would ultimately take. We were considerably to the N.W. of the point at which we had entered it, and in referring to the chart, it appeared, that if the Darling had kept a S.W. course from where the last expedition left its banks, we ought ere this to have struck upon it, or have arrived at its junction with the stream on which we were journeying.

The natives, in attempting to answer my interrogatories, only perplexed me more and more. They evidently wished to explain something, by placing a number of sticks across each other as a kind of diagram of the country. It was, however, impossible to arrive at their meaning. They undoubtedly pointed to the westward, or rather to the south of that point, as the future course of the river; but there was something more that they were anxious to explain, which I could not comprehend. The poor fellows seemed quite disappointed, and endeavoured to beat it into Fraser's head with as little success. I then desired Macnamee to get up into a tree. From the upper branches of it he said he could see hills; but his account of their appearance was such that I doubted his story: nevertheless it might have been correct. He certainly called our attention to a large fire, as if the country to the N.W. was in flames, so that it appeared we were approaching the haunts of the natives at last.

It happened that Fraser and Harris were for guard, and they sat up laughing and talking with the natives long after we retired to rest. Fraser, to beguile the hours, proposed shaving his sable companions, and performed that operation with admirable dexterity upon their chief, to his great delight. I got up at an early hour, and found to my surprise that the whole of them had deserted us. Harris told me they had risen from the fire about an hour before, and had crossed the river. I was a little angry, but supposed they were aware that we were near some tribe, and had gone on a-head to prepare and collect them.

After breakfast, we proceeded onwards as usual. The river had increased so much in width that, the wind being fair, I hoisted sail for the first time, to save the strength of my men as much as possible. Our progress was consequently rapid. We passed through a country that, from the nature of its soil and other circumstances, appeared to be intersected by creeks and lagoons. Vast flights of wild fowl passed over us, but always at a considerable elevation, while, on the other hand, the paucity of ducks on the river excited our surprise. Latterly, the trees upon the river, and in its neighbourhood, had been a tortuous kind of box. The flooded-gum grew in groups on the spaces subject to inundation, but not on the levels above the influence of any ordinary rise of the stream. Still they were much smaller than they were observed to be in the higher branches of the river. We had proceeded about nine miles, when we were surprised by the appearance in view, at the termination of a reach, of a long line of magnificent trees of green and dense foliage. As we sailed down the reach, we observed a vast concourse of natives under them, and, on a nearer approach, we not only heard their war-song, if it might so be called, but remarked that they were painted and armed, as they generally are, prior to their engaging in deadly conflict. Notwithstanding these outward signs of hostility, fancying that our four friends were with them, I continued to steer directly in for the bank on which they were collected. I found, however, when it was almost too late to turn into the succeeding reach to our left, that an attempt to land would only be attended with loss of life. The natives seemed determined to resist it. We approached so near that they held their spears quivering in their grasp ready to hurl. They were painted in various ways. Some who had marked their ribs, and thighs, and faces with a white pigment, looked like skeletons, others were daubed over with red and yellow ochre, and their bodies shone with the grease with which they had besmeared themselves. A dead silence prevailed among the front ranks, but those in the background, as well as the women, who carried supplies of darts, and who appeared to have had a bucket of whitewash capsized over their heads, were extremely clamorous. As I did not wish a conflict with these people, I lowered my sail, and putting the helm to starboard, we passed quietly down the stream in mid channel. Disappointed in their anticipations, the natives ran along the bank of the river, endeavouring to secure an aim at us; but, unable to throw with certainty, in consequence of the onward motion of the boat, they flung themselves into the most extravagant attitudes, and worked themselves into a state of frenzy by loud and vehement shouting.

It was with considerable apprehension that I observed the river to be shoaling fast, more especially as a huge sand-bank, a little below us, and on the same side on which the natives had gathered, projected nearly a third-way across the channel. To this sand-bank they ran with tumultuous uproar, and covered it over in a dense mass. Some of the chiefs advanced to the water to be nearer their victims, and turned from time to time to direct their followers. With every pacific disposition, and an extreme reluctance to take away life, I foresaw that it would be impossible any longer to avoid an engagement yet with such fearful numbers against us, I was doubtful of the result. The spectacle we had witnessed had been one of the most appalling kind, and sufficient to shake the firmness of most men; but at that trying moment my little band preserved their temper coolness, and if any thing could be gleaned from their countenances, it was that they had determined on an obstinate resistance. I now explained to them that their only chance of escape depended, or would depend, on their firmness. I desired that after the first volley had been fired, M'Leay and three of the men, would attend to the defence of the boat with bayonets only, while I, Hopkinson, and Harris, would keep up the fire as being more used to it. I ordered, however, that no shot was to be fired until after I had discharged both my barrels. I then delivered their arms to the men, which had as yet been kept in the place appropriated for them, and at the same time some rounds of loose cartridge. The men assured me they would follow my instructions, and thus prepared, having already lowered the sail, we drifted onwards with the current. As we neared the sand-bank, I stood up and made signs to the natives to desist; but without success. I took up my gun, therefore, and cocking it, had already brought it down to a level. A few seconds more would have closed the life of the nearest of the savages. The distance was too trifling for me to doubt the fatal effects of the discharge; for I was determined to take deadly aim, in hopes that the fall of one man might save the lives of many. But at the very moment, when my hand was on the trigger, and my eye was along the barrel, my purpose was checked by M'Leay, who called to me that another party of blacks had made their appearance upon the left bank of the river. Turning round, I observed four men at the top of their speed. The foremost of them as soon as he got a-head of the boat, threw himself from a considerable height into the water. He struggled across the channel to the sand-bank, and in an incredibly short space of time stood in front of the savage, against whom my aim had been directed. Seizing him by the throat, he pushed him backwards, and forcing all who were in the water upon the bank, he trod its margin with a vehemence and an agitation that were exceedingly striking. At one moment pointing to the boat, at another shaking his clenched hand in the faces of the most forward, and stamping with passion on the sand; his voice, that was at first distinct and clear, was lost in hoarse murmurs. Two of the four natives remained on the left bank of the river, but the third followed his leader, (who proved to be the remarkable savage I have previously noticed) to the scene of action. The reader will imagine our feelings on this occasion: it is impossible to describe them. We were so wholly lost in interest at the scene that was passing, that the boat was allowed to drift at pleasure. For my own part I was overwhelmed with astonishment, and in truth stunned and confused; so singular, so unexpected, and so strikingly providential, had been our escape.

We were again roused to action by the boat suddenly striking upon a shoal, which reached from one side of the river to the other. To jump out and push her into deeper water was but the work of a moment with the men, and it was just as she floated again that our attention was withdrawn to a new and beautiful stream, coming apparently from the north. The great body of the natives having posted themselves on the narrow tongue of land formed by the two rivers, the bold savage who has so unhesitatingly interfered on our account, was still in hot dispute with them, and I really feared his generous warmth would have brought down upon him the vengence of the tribes. I hesitated, therefore, whether or not to go to his assistance. It appeared, however, both to M'Leay and myself, that the tone of the natives had moderated, and the old and young men having listened to the remonstrances of our friend, the middle-aged warriors were alone holding out against him. A party of about seventy blacks were upon the right bank of the newly discovered river, and I thought that by landing among them, we should make a diversion in favour of our late guest; and in this I succeeded. If even they had still meditated violence, they would have to swim a good broad junction, and that, probably, would cool them, or we at least should have the advantage of position. I therefore, ran the boat ashore, and landed with M'Leay amidst the smaller party of natives, wholly unarmed, and having directed the men to keep at a little distance from the bank. Fortunately, what I anticipated was brought about by the stratagem to which I had had recourse. The blacks no sooner observed that we had landed, than curiosity took place of anger. All wrangling ceased, and they came swimming over to us like a parcel of seals. Thus, in less than a quarter of an hour from the moment when it appeared that all human intervention was at an end, and we were on the point of commencing a bloody fray, which, independently of its own disastrous consequences, would have blasted the success of the expedition, we were peacefully surrounded by the hundreds who had so lately threatened us with destruction; nor was it until after we had returned to the boat, and had surveyed the multitude upon the sloping bank above us, that we became fully aware of the extent of our danger, and of the almost miraculous intervention of Providence in our favour. There could not have been less than six hundred natives upon that blackened sward. But this was not the only occasion upon which the merciful superintendance of that Providence to which we had humbly committed ourselves, was strikingly manifested. If these pages fail to convey entertainment or information, sufficient may at least be gleaned from them to furnish matter for serious reflection; but to those who have been placed in situations of danger where human ingenuity availed them not, and where human foresight was baffled, I feel persuaded that these remarks are unnecessary.

It was my first care to call for our friend, and to express to him, as well as I could, how much we stood indebted to him, at the same time that I made him a suitable present; but to the chiefs of the tribes, I positively refused all gifts, notwithstanding their earnest solicitations. We next prepared to examine the new river, and turning the boat's head towards it, endeavoured to pull up the stream. Our larboard oars touched the right bank, and the current was too strong for us to conquer it with a pair only; we were, therefore, obliged to put a second upon her, a movement that excited the astonishment and admiration of the natives. One old woman seemed in absolute extacy, to whom M'Leay threw an old tin kettle, in recompense for the amusement she afforded us.

As soon as we got above the entrance of the new river, we found easier pulling, and proceeded up it for some miles, accompanied by the once more noisy multitude. The river preserved a breadth of one hundred yards, and a depth of rather more than twelve feet. Its banks were sloping and grassy, and were overhung by trees of magnificent size. Indeed, its appearance was so different from the water-worn banks of the sister stream, that the men exclaimed, on entering it, that we had got into an English river. Its appearance certainly almost justified the expression; for the greenness of its banks was as new to us as the size of its timber. Its waters, though sweet, were turbid, and had a taste of vegetable decay, as well as a slight tinge of green. Our progress was watched by the natives with evident anxiety. They kept abreast of us, and talked incessantly. At length, however, our course was checked by a net that stretched right across the stream. I say *checked*, because it would have been unfair to have passed over it with the chance of disappointing the numbers who apparently depended on it for subsistence that day. The moment was one of intense interest to me. As the men rested upon their oars, awaiting my further orders, a crowd of thoughts rushed upon me. The various conjectures I had formed of the course and importance of the Darling passed across my mind. Were they indeed realized? An irresistible conviction impressed me that we were now sailing on the bosom of that very stream from whose banks I had been twice forced to retire. I directed the Union Jack to be hoisted, and giving way to our satisfaction, we all stood up in the boat, and

gave three distinct cheers. It was an English feeling, an ebulli-
tion, an overflow, which I am ready to admit that our circumstances and situation will alone excuse. The eye of every native
had been fixed upon that noble flag, at all times a beautiful
object, and to them a novel one, as it waved over us in the heart
of a desert. They had, until that moment been particularly
loquacious, but the sight of that flag and the sound of our voices
hushed the tumult, and while they were still lost in astonishment,
the boat's head was speedily turned, the sail was sheeted home,
both wind and current were in our favour, and we vanished from
them with a rapidity that surprised even ourselves, and which
precluded every hope of the most adventurous among them to
keep up with us.

Arrived once more at the junction of the two rivers, and unmolested in our occupations, we had leisure to examine it more
closely. Not having as yet given a name to our first discovery,
when we re-entered its capacious channel on this occasion, I laid
it down as the Murray River, in compliment to the distinguished
officer, Sir George Murray, who then presided over the colonial
department, not only in compliance with the known wishes
of his Excellency General Darling, but also in accordance with
my own feelings as a soldier.

The new river, whether the Darling or an additional discovery,
meets its more southern rival on a N. by E. course; the latter,
running W.S.W. at the confluence, the angle formed by the two
rivers, is, therefore, so small that both may be considered to
preserve their proper course, and neither can be said to be
tributary to the other. At their junction, the Murray spreads
its waters over the broad and sandy shore, upon which our boat
grounded, while its more impetuous neighbour flows through
the deep but narrow channel it has worked out for itself, under
the right bank. The strength of their currents must have been
nearly equal, since there was as distinct a line between their
respective waters, to a considerable distance below the junction,
as if a thin board alone separated them. The one half the channel
contained the turbid waters of the northern stream, the other
still preserved their original transparency.

The banks of the Murray did not undergo any immediate
change as we proceeded. We noticed that the country had, at
some time, been subject to extensive inundation, and was, beyond
doubt, of alluvial formation. We passed the mouths of several
large creeks that came from the north and N.W., and the country
in those directions seemed to be much intersected by water-

courses; while to the south it was extremely low. Having descended several minor rapids, I greatly regretted that we had no barometer to ascertain the actual dip of the interior. I computed, however, that we were not more than from eighty to ninety feet above the level of the sea. We found the channel of the Murray much encumbered with timber, and noticed some banks of sand that were of unusual size, and equalled the largest accumulations of it on the sea shore, both in extent and solidity.

We would gladly have fired into the flights of wild fowl that winged their way over us, for we, about this time, began to feel the consequences of the disaster that befel us in the Morumbidgee. The fresh water having got mixed with the brine in the meat casks, the greater part of our salt provisions had got spoiled, so that we were obliged to be extremely economical in the expenditure of what remained, as we knew not to what straits we might be driven. It will naturally be asked why we did not procure fish? The answer is easy. The men had caught many in the Morumbidgee, and on our first navigation of the Murray, but whether it was that they had disagreed with them, or that their appetites were palled, or that they were too fatigued after the labour of the day to set the lines, they did not appear to care about them. The only fish we could take was the common rod or perch; and, without sauce or butter, it is insipid enough. We occasionally exchanged pieces of iron-hoop for two other kinds of fish, the one a bream, the other a barbel, with the natives, and the eagerness with which they met our advances to barter, is a strong proof of their natural disposition towards this first step in civilization.

As they threw off all reserve when accompanying us as ambassadors, we had frequent opportunities of observing their habits. The facility, for instance, with which they procured fish was really surprising. They would slip, feet foremost, into the water as they walked along the bank of the river, as if they had accidentally done so, but, in reality, to avoid the splash they would necessarily have made if they had plunged in head foremost. As surely as they then disappeared under the surface of the water, so surely would they re-appear with a fish writhing upon the point of their short spears. The very otter scarcely exceeds them in power over the finny race, and so true is the aim of these savages, even under water, that all the fish we procured from them were pierced either close behind the lateral fin, or in the very centre of the head. It is certain, from their indifference to them, that the natives seldom eat fish when they can get anything else. Indeed they seemed more anxious to take the small turtle, which, sunning themselves on the trunks or logs of trees over the water, were, nevertheless, extremely on their guard. A gentle splash alone indicated to us that any thing had dropped into the water, but the quick eyes and ears of our guides immediately detected what had occasioned it, and they seldom failed to take the poor little animal that had so vainly trusted to its own watchfulness for security. It appeared that the natives did not, from choice, frequent the Murray; it was evident, therefore, that they had other and better means of subsistence away from it, and it struck me, at the time, that the river we had just passed watered a better country than any through which the Murray had been found to flow.

We encamped rather earlier than usual upon the left bank of the river, near a broad creek; for as the skiff had been a great drag upon us, I determined on breaking it up, since there was no probability that we should ever require the still, which alone remained in her. We, consequently, burnt the former, to secure her nails and iron work, and I set Clayton about cutting the copper of the latter into the shape of crescents, in order to present them to the natives. Some large huts were observed on the side on the creek, a little above the camp, the whole of which faced the N.E. This arrangement had previously been noticed by us, so that I was led to infer that the severest weather comes for the opposite quarter in this part of the interior. I had not the least idea, at the time, however, that we should, ere we reached the termination of our journey, experience the effects of the S.W. winds.

We must have fallen considerably during the day from the level of our morning's position, for we passed down many reaches where the decline of country gave an increased velocity to the current of the river.

I had feared, not only in consequence of the unceremonious manner in which we had left them, but, because I had, in some measure, rejected the advances of their chiefs, that none of the natives would follow us, and I regretted the circumstance on account of my men, as well as the trouble we should necessarily have in conciliating the next tribe. We had not, however, been long encamped, when seven blacks joined us. I think they would have passed on if we had not called to them. As it was, they remained with us but for a short time. We treated them very kindly, but they were evidently under constraint, and were, no doubt, glad when they found we did not object to their departing.

I have stated, that I felt sati fied in my own mind, that the beautiful stream we had passed was no other than the river Darling of my former journey. The bare assertion, however, is not sufficient to satisfy the mind of the reader, upon a point of such importance, more especially when it is considered how remarkable a change the Darling must have undergone, if this were indeed a continuation of it. I am free to confess that it required an effort to convince myself, but after due consideration, I see no reason to alter the opinion I formed at a moment of peculiar embarrassment. Yet it by no means follows that I shall convince others, although I am myself convinced. The question is one of curious speculation, and the consideration of it will lead us to an interesting conjecture, as to the probable nature of the distant interior, between the two points. It will be remembered that I was obliged to relinquish my pursuit of the Darling, in east long. 144° 48′ 30″ in lat. 30° 17′ 30″ south. I place the junction of the Murray and the new river, in long. 140° 56′ east, and in south lat. 34° 3′. I must remark, however, that the lunars I took on this last occasion, were not satisfactory, and that there is, probably, an error, though not a material one, in the calculation. Before I measure the distance between the above points, or make any remarks on the results of my own observations, I would impress the following facts upon the reader's mind.

I found and left the Darling in a complete state of exhaustion. As a river it had ceased to flow; the only supply it received was from brine springs, which, without imparting a current, rendered its waters saline and useless, and lastly, the fish in it were different from those inhabiting the other known rivers of the interior. It is true, I did not procure a perfect specimen of one, but we satisfactorily ascertained that they were different, inasmuch as they had large and strong scales, whereas the fish in the western waters have smooth skins. On the other hand, the waters of the new river were sweet, although turbid; it had a rapid current in it; and its fish were of the ordinary kind. In the above particulars, therefore, they differed as much as they could well differ. Yet there were some strong points of resemblance in the appearance of the rivers themselves, which were more evident to me than I can hope to make them to the reader. Both were shaded by trees of the same magnificent dimensions; and the same kind of huts were erected on the banks of each, inhabited by the same description, or race, of people, whose weapons, whose implements, and whose nets corresponded in most respects.

It now appeared that the Murray had taken a permanent southerly course; indeed, it might strictly be said that it ran away to the south. As we proceeded down it, the valley expanded to the width of two miles; the alluvial flats became proportionately larger; and a small lake generally occupied their centre. They were extensively covered with reeds and grass, for which reason, notwithstanding that they were little elevated above the level of the stream, I do not think they are subject to overflow. Parts of them may be laid under water, but certainly not the whole. The rains at the head of the Murray, and its tributaries, must be unusually severe to prolong their effects to this distant region, and the flats bordering it appear, by successive depositions, to have only just gained a height above the further influence of the floods. Should this prove to be the case, the valley may be decidedly laid down as a most desirable spot, whether we regard the richness of its soil, its rock formation, its locality or the extreme facility of water communication along it. It must not, however, be forgotten or concealed, that the summits of the cliffs by which the valley is enclosed, have not a corresponding soil. On the contrary, many of the productions common to the plains of the interior still existed upon them, and they were decidedly barren; but as we measured the reaches of the river, the cliffs ceased, and gave place to undulating hills, that were very different in appearance from the country we had previously noted down. It would have been impossible for the most tasteful individual to have laid out pleasure ground to more advantage, than Nature had done in planting and disposing the various groups of trees along the spine, and upon the sides of the elevations that confined the river, and bounded the low ground that intervened between it and their base. Still, however, the soil upon these elevations was sandy, and coarse, but the large oat-grass was abundant upon them, which yielded pasture at least as good as that in the broken country between Underaliga and Morumbidgee.

We had now gained a distance of at least sixty miles from that angle of the Murray at which it reaches its extreme west. The general aspect of the country to our right was beautiful, and several valleys branched away into the interior upon that side which had a most promising appearance, and seemed to abound with kangaroos, as the traces of them were numerous, and the dogs succeeded in killing one, which, to our great mortification, we could not find.

While, however, the country to the westward had so much to

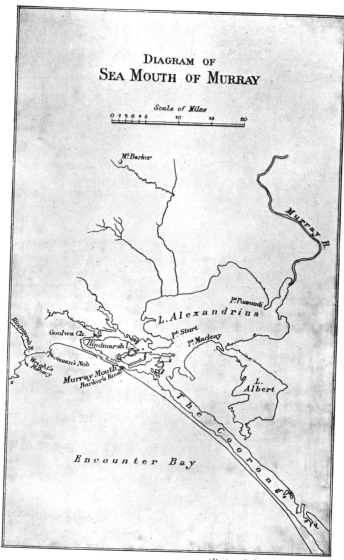

DIAGRAM OF
SEA MOUTH OF MURRAY

Scale of Miles
0 1 2 8 4 5   10   15   20

M.̇Barker

Murray R.

P.̇Pomundi

L. Alexandrina

Pt Sturt

Goolwa Ch.

Hindmarsh R.

Lindmarsh I.

Pt Macleay

Jenman's Nob

Wright's Fishery

Murray Mouth
Barker's Knoll

L. Albert

The Coorong &c

Encounter Bay

Pt 4.

(By permission of John Murray.)

STURT'S DIAGRAM OF SEA MOUTH OF THE MURRAY.
From " The Life of Charles Sturt."

recommend it, the hills to our left became extremely bare. It was evident that the right was the sheltered side of the valley. The few trees on the opposite side bent over to the N.E., as if under the influence of some prevailing wind.

We experienced at this time a succession of gales from the S.W., against which we, on several occasions, found it useless to contend: the waves on the river being heavy and short; and the boat, driving her prow into them, sent the spray over us and soon wet us through. Indeed, it is difficult for the reader to imagine the heavy swell that rolled up the river, which had increased in breadth to the third of a mile, and in the length of its reaches to eight or ten. I was satisfied that we were not only navigating this river at a particularly stormy, perhaps *the* stormy, season; but also, that the influence of the S.W. wind is felt even as far in the interior as to the supposed Darling; in consequence of the uniform build of the huts, and the circumstance of their not only facing the N.E., but also being almost invariably erected under the lee of some bush.

The weather, under the influence of the wind we experienced, was cool and pleasant, although the thermometer stood at a medium height of 86°; but we found it very distressing to pull against the heavy breezes that swept up the valley, and bent the reeds so as almost to make them kiss the stream.

We communicated on the 6th and 7th with several large tribes of natives, whose manners were on the whole quiet and inoffensive. They distinctly informed us, that we were fast approaching the sea, and, from what I could understand, we were nearer to it than the coast line of Encounter Bay made us. We had placed sticks to ascertain if there was any rise or fall of tide, but the troubled state of the river prevented our experiments from being satisfactory. By selecting a place, however, that was sheltered from the effects of the wind, we ascertained that there was an apparent rise of about eight inches.

It blew a heavy gale during the whole of the 7th; and we laboured in vain at the oar. The gusts that swept the bosom of the water, and the swell they caused, turned the boat from her course, and prevented us from making an inch of way. The men were quite exhausted, and, as they had conducted themselves so well, and had been so patient, I felt myself obliged to grant them every indulgence consistent with our safety. However precarious our situation, it would have been vain, with our exhausted strength, to have contended against the elements. We, therefore, pulled in to the left bank of the river, and

I. D.   *p* pitched our tents on a little rising ground beyond the reeds that lined it.

I had been suffering very much from tooth-ache for the last three or four days, and this day felt the most violent pain from the wind. I was not, therefore, sorry to get under even the poor shelter our tents afforded. M'Leay, observing that I was in considerable pain, undertook to wind up the chronometer; but, not understanding or knowing the instrument, he unfortunately broke the spring. I shall not forget the anxiety he expressed, and the regret he felt on the occasion; nor do I think M'Leay recovered the shock this unlucky accident gave him for two or three days, or until the novelty of other scenes drove it from his recollection.

We landed close to the haunt of a small tribe of natives, who came to us with the most perfect confidence, and assisted the men in their occupations. They were cleaner and more healthy than any tribe we had seen; and were extremely cheerful, although reserved in some respects. As a mark of more than usual cleanliness, the women had mats of oval shape, upon which they sat, made, apparently, of rushes. There was a young girl among them of a most cheerful disposition. She was about eighteen, was well made, and really pretty. This girl was married to an elderly man who had broken his leg, which having united in a bent shape, the limb was almost useless. I really believe the girl thought we could cure her husband, from her importunate manner to us. I regretted that I could do nothing for the man, but to shew that I was not inattentive to her entreaties, I gave him a pair of trowsers, and desired Fraser to put them upon him; but the poor fellow cut so awkward an appearance in them, that his wife became quite distressed, and Fraser was obliged speedily to disencumber him from them again.

We could not gain any satisfactory information, as to the termination of the river, from these people. It was evident that some change was at hand; but what it was we could not ascertain.

On the morning of the 9th, we left our fair friend and her lame husband, and proceeded down the river. The wind had moderated, although it still blew fresh. We ascended every height as we went along, but could not see any new feature in the country. Our view to the eastward was very confined; to the westward the interior was low and dark, and was backed in the distance by lofty ranges parallel to which we had been running for some days. The right bank of the valley was beautifully undulated, but the left was bleak and bare. The valley was a breadth of from three to four miles, and the flats were more extensive under the former than under the latter. They were scarcely two feet above the level of the water, and were densely covered with reeds. As there was no mark upon the reeds to indicate the height to which the floods rose, I cannot think that these flats are ever wholly laid under water; if they are, it cannot be to any depth: at all events a few small drains would effectually prevent inundation.

The soil upon the hills continued to be much mixed with sand, and the prevailing trees were cypress and box. Among the minor shrubs and grass, many common to the east coasts were noticed; and although the bold cliffs had ceased, the basis of the country still continued of the fossil formation. At a turn of the stream hereabouts, however, a solitary rock of coarse red granite rose above the waters, and formed an island in its centre; but only in this one place was it visible. The rock was composed principally of quartz and feldspar.

A little below it, we found a large tribe anxiously awaiting our arrival. They crowded to the margin of the river with great eagerness, and evinced more surprise at our appearance than any tribe we had seen during the journey; but we left them very soon, notwithstanding that they importuned us much to stay.

After pulling a mile or two, we found a clear horizon before us to the south. The hills still continued upon our left, but we could not see any elevation over the expanse of reeds to our right. The river inclined to the left, and swept the base of the hills that still continued on that side. I consequently landed once more to survey the country.

I still retained a strong impression on my mind that some change was at hand, and on this occasion, I was not disappointed; but the view was one for which I was not altogether prepared. We had, at length, arrived at the termination of the Murray. Immediately below me was a beautiful lake, which appeared to be a fitting reservoir for the noble stream that had led us to it; and which was now ruffled by the breeze that swept over it. The ranges were more distinctly visible, stretching from south to north, and were certainly distant forty miles. They had a regular unbroken outline; declining gradually to the south, but terminating abruptly at a lofty mountain northerly. I had no doubt on my mind of this being the Mount Lofty of Captain Flinders; or that the range was that immediately to the eastward of St. Vincent's Gulf. Since the accident to the chronometer, we had not made any westing, so that we knew our position as nearly as possible. Between us and the ranges a beautiful promontory shot into the lake, being a continuation of the right bank of the Murray. Over this promontory the waters stretched to the base of the ranges, and formed an extensive bay. To the N.W. the country was exceedingly low, but distant peaks were just visible over it. To the S.W. a bold headland shewed itself; beyond which, to the westward, there was a clear and open sea visible, through a strait formed by this headland and a point projecting from the opposite shore. To the E. and S.E. the country was low, excepting the left shore of the lake, which was backed by some minor elevations, crowned with cypresses. Even while gazing on this fine scene, I could not but regret that the Murray had thus terminated; for I immediately foresaw that, in all probability, we should be disappointed in finding any practicable communication between the lake and the ocean, as it was evident that the former was not much influenced by tides. The wind had again increased; it still blew fresh from the S.W., and a heavy sea was rolling direct into the mouth of the river. I hoped, notwithstanding, that we should have been enabled to make sail, for which reason we entered the lake about 2 p.m. The natives had kindled a large fire on a distant point between us and the further head-land, and to gain this point our efforts were now directed. The waves were, however, too strong, and we were obliged to make for the eastern shore, until such time as the weather should moderate. We pitched our tents on a low track of land that stretched away seemingly for many miles directly behind us to the eastward. It was of the richest soil, being a black vegetable deposit, and although now high above the influence, the lake had, it was evident, once formed a part of its bed. The appearance of the country altogether encouraged M'Leay and myself to walk out, in order to examine it from some hills a little to the S.E. of the camp. From them we observed that the flat extended over about fifty miles, and was bounded by the elevations that continued easterly from the left bank of the Murray to the north, and by a line of rising-ground to the south. The whole was lightly wooded, and covered with grass. The season must have been unusually dry, judging from the general appearance of the vegetation, and from the circumstance of the lagoons in the interior being wholly exhausted.

Thirty-three days had now passed over our heads since we left the depot upon the Morumbidgee, twenty-six of which had been passed upon the Murray. We had, at length, arrived at the grand reservoir of those waters whose course and fate had previously been involved in such obscurity. It remained for us to ascertain whether the extensive sheet of water upon whose bosom we had embarked, had any practicable communication with the ocean, and whether the country in the neighbourhood of the coast corresponded with that immediately behind our camp, or kept up its sandy and sterile character to the very verge of the sea. As I have already said, my hopes on the first of these points were considerably damped, but I could not help anticipating a favourable change in the latter, since its features had so entirely changed.

The greatest difficulty against which we had at present to contend was the wind; and I dreaded the exertion it would call for, to make head against it; or the men were so much reduced that I felt convinced they were inadequate to any violent or prolonged effort. It still blew fresh at 8 p.m., but at that time it began to moderate. It may be imagined that I listened to its subdued gusts with extreme anxiety. It did not wholly abate until after 2 a.m., when it gradually declined, and about 3 a light breeze sprung up from the N.E.

We had again placed sticks to ascertain with more precision the rise of tide, and found it to be the same as in the river. In the stillness of the night too we thought we heard the roaring of the sea, but I was myself uncertain upon the point, as the wind might have caused the sound.

From the top of the hill from which we had obtained our first view of the lake, I observed the waves breaking upon the distant head-land, and enveloping the cliff in spray; so that, independent of the clearness of the horizon beyond it, I was further led to conclude that there existed a great expanse of water to the S.W.; and, as that had been the direction taken by the river, I thought it probable that by steering at once to the S.W. down the lake, I should hit the outlet. I, consequently, resolved to gain the southern extremity of the lake, as that at which it was natural to expect a communication with the ocean would be found.

At 4 we had a moderate breeze, and it promised to strengthen; we lost no time therefore in embarking, and with a flowing sheet stretched over to the W.S.W., and ran along the promontory formed by the right bank of the Murray. We passed close under its extreme point at nine. The hills had gradually declined, and we found the point to be a flat, elevated about thirty feet above

the lake. It was separated from the promontory by a small
channel that was choaked up with reeds, so that it is more
than probable that the point is insulated at certain periods;
whilst in its stratification it resembled the first cliffs I have
described that were passed below the Darling. It is a remarkable
fact in the geology of the Murray, that such should be the case;
and that the formation at each extremity of the great bank or
bed of fossils should be the same. Thus far, the waters of the
lake had continued sweet; but on filling a can when we were
abreast of this point, it was found that they were quite unpalate-
able, to say the least of them. The transition from fresh to salt
water was almost immediate, and it was fortunate we made the
discovery in sufficient time to prevent our losing ground. But,
as it was, we filled our casks, and stood on, without for a moment
altering our course.

It is difficult to give a just description of our passage across
the lake. The boisterous weather we had had seemed to have
blown over. A cool and refreshing breeze was carrying us on at
between four and five knots an hour, and the heavens above us
were without a cloud. It almost appeared as if nature had
resisted us in order to try our perseverance, and that she had
yielded in pity to our efforts. The men, relieved for a time from
the oar, stretched themselves at their length in the boat, and
commented on the scenery around them, or ventured their
opinions as to that which was before them. Up to this moment
their conduct had been most exemplary; not a murmur had
escaped from them, and they filled the water-casks with the
utmost cheerfulness, even whilst tasting the disagreeable beverage they would most probably have to subsist on for the next
three or four days.

As soon as we had well opened the point, we had a full view
of the splendid bay that, commencing at the western-most of the
central points, swept in a beautiful curve under the ranges. No
land was visible to the W.N.W. or to the S.S.W.: in both these
quarters the lake was as open as the ocean. It appeared, therefore, that the land intermediate was an island. To the north
the country was extremely low, and as we increased our distance
from it we lost sight of it altogether. At noon we were nearly
abreast of the eastern head-land, or in the centre of the strait
to which I have alluded. At this time there was an open sea
from W.N.W. to N. by E. A meridian altitude gave our latitude
35° 25'. The land to our left was bold and precipitous; that to
the right was low and wooded; and there was evidently a con-

siderable space between the shores of the lake and the base of the ranges. The country to the eastward was hidden from us by the line of cliffs, beyond which, from E.S.E. to W.S.W. there was an open sea. We had kept the lead going from the first, and I was surprised at the extreme shallowness of the lake in every part, as we never had six feet upon the line. Its bottom was one of black mud, and weeds of enormous length were floating on its surface, detached by the late gales, and which, from the shallowness of the lake, got constantly entangled with our rudder.

We tried to land on the eastern point, but found the water too shallow, and were obliged to try the western shore. In passing close under the head, we observed several natives upon it, who kindled a large fire as soon as they saw they were noticed, which was answered from every point; for, in less than ten minutes afterwards, we counted no fewer than fourteen different fires, the greater number of which were on the side of the ranges.

As we were standing across from one shore to the other, our attention was drawn to a most singular object. It started suddenly up, as above the waters to the south, and strikingly resembled an isolated castle. Behind it, a dense column of smoke rose into the sky, and the effect was most remarkable. On a nearer approach, the phantom disappeared, and a clear and open sea again presented itself to our view. The fact was, that the refractive power upon the coast had elevated the sand hillocks above their true position, since we satisfactorily ascertained that they alone separated the lake from the ocean, and that they alone could have produced the semblance we noticed. It is a singular fact, that this very hillock was the one which Capt. Barker ascended whilst carrying on the survey of the south coast, and immediately previous to his tragical death.

It was not without difficulty that we succeeded in landing on the western shore; but we did, at length, succeed, and prepared our dinners. The shore was low, but above the reach of all floods; the soil was rich, and superficially sandy. It was covered with high grasses, and abounded in kangaroos; within the space of a few yards we found five or six, but they were immediately lost to us and to the dogs in the luxuriance of the vegetation amidst which they were feeding.

As soon as we had finished our meal, we once more embarked, and stood along the shore to the S.W., but the lake was so shoal, that I was every moment apprehensive we should ground. I ran across, therefore, to the south, towards a low flat that had just appeared above the line of the horizon, in hope that, in sounding, we should have found the channel, but there either was none, or else it was so narrow that we passed over it between the heaves of the lead. At this time, the western shore was quite distinct, and the scenery was beautiful.

The flat we were approaching was a mud-flat, and, from its appearance, the tide was certainly at the ebb. We observed some cradles, or wicker frames, placed far below high water-mark, that were each guarded by two natives, who threatened us violently as we approached. In running along the land, the stench from them plainly indicated what they were which these poor creatures were so anxiously watching.

We steered a S.W. course, towards some low and wooded hills, passing a rocky island, and found that we had struck the mouth of a channel running to the W.S.W. It was about half-a-mile wide, was bounded to the right by some open flat ground, and to the left by a line of hills of about sixty or seventy feet in elevation, partly open and partly covered with beefwood.

Upon the first of these hills, we observed a large body of natives, who set up the most terrific yells as we approached. They were fully equipped for battle, and, as we neared the shore, came down to meet us with the most violent threats. I wished much to communicate with them, and, not without hopes of quieting them, stood right in with the intention of landing. I observed, however, that if I did so, I should have to protect myself. I hauled a little off, and endeavoured, by holding up a branch and a tomahawk, to gain their confidence, but they were not to be won over by any shew of pacification. An elderly man walked close to the water's edge unarmed, and, evidently, directed the others. He was followed by seven or eight of the most daring, who crept into the reeds, with their spears shipped to throw at us. I, therefore, took up my gun to return their salute. It then appeared that they were perfectly aware of the weapon I carried, for the moment they saw it, they dashed out of their hiding place and retreated to the main body; but the old man, after saying something to them, walked steadily on, and I, on my part, laid my firelock down again.

It was now near sunset; and one of the most lovely evenings I had ever seen. The sun's radiance was yet upon the mountains, but all lower objects were in shade. The banks of the channel, with the trees and the rocks, were reflected in the tranquil waters, whose surface was unruffled save by the thousands of wild fowl that rose before us, and made a noise as of a multitude clapping hands, in their clumsy efforts to rise from the waters. Not one of them allowed us to get within shot.

We proceeded about a mile below the hill on which the natives were posted; some few still following us with violent threats. We landed, however, on a flat, bounded all round by the continuation of the hills. It was an admirable position, for, in the centre of it, we could not be taken by surprise, and, on the other hand, we gave the natives an opportunity of communicating with us if they would. The full moon rose as we were forming the camp, and, notwithstanding our vicinity to so noisy a host, the silence of death was around us, or the stillness of the night was only broken by the roar of the ocean, now too near to be mistaken for wind, or by the silvery and melancholy note of the black swans as they passed over us, to seek for food, no doubt, among the slimy weeds at the head of the lake. We had been quite delighted with the beauty of the channel, which was rather more than half-a-mile in width. Numberless mounds, that seemed to invite civilised man to erect his dwelling upon them, presented themselves to our view. The country round them was open, yet ornamentally wooded, and rocks and trees hung or drooped over the waters.

We had in one day gained a position I once feared it would have cost us infinite labour to have measured. Indeed, had we been obliged to pull across the lake, unless during a calm, I am convinced the men would have been wholly exhausted. We had to thank a kind Providence that such was not the case, since it had extended its mercy to us at so critical a moment. We had indeed need of all the little strength we had remaining, and could ill have thrown it away on such an effort as this would have required. I calculated that we could not have run less than forty-five miles during the day, a distance that, together with the eight miles we had advanced the evening previously, would give the length of the lake at fifty-three miles.

We had approached to within twelve miles of the ranges, but had not gained their southern extremity. From the camp, Mount Barker bore nearly north. The ranges appeared to run north and south to our position, and then to bend away to the S.S.W., gradually declining to that point, which I doubted not terminated in Cape Jervis. The natives kept aloof during the night, nor did the dogs by a single growl intimate that any had ventured to approach us. The sound of the surf came gratefully to our ears, for it told us we were near the goal for which we had so anxiously pushed, and we all of us promised ourselves a view of the boundless ocean on the morrow.

As the morning dawned, we saw that the natives had thrown an out-post of sixteen men across the channel, who were watching our motions, but none shewed themselves on the hills behind us, or on any part of the south shore. We embarked as soon as we had breakfasted. A fresh breeze was blowing from the N.E. which took us rapidly down the channel, and our prospects appeared to be as cheering as the day, for just as we were about to push from the shore, a seal rose close to the boat, which we all regarded as a favourable omen. We were, however, shortly stopped by shoals; it was in vain that we beat across the channel from one side to the other; it was a continued shoal, and the deepest water appeared to be under the left bank. The tide, however, had fallen, and exposed broad flats, over which it was hopeless, under existing circumstances, to haul the boat. We again landed on the south side of the channel, patiently to await the high water.

M'Leay, myself, and Fraser, ascended the hills, and went to the opposite side to ascertain the course of the channel, for immediately above us it turned south round the hills. We there found that we were on a narrow tongue of land. The channel was immediately below us, and continued to the E.S.E. as far as we could trace it. The hills we were upon, were the sandy hills that always bound a coast that is low, and were covered with banksias, casuarina, and the grass-tree.

To the south of the channel there was a flat, backed by a range of sand-hummocks, that were covered with low shrubs; and beyond them the sea was distinctly visible. We could not have been more than two and a half miles from the beach where we stood.

Notwithstanding the sandy nature of the soil, the fossil formation again shewed itself, not only on these hills, but also on the rocks that were in the channel.

A little before high water we again embarked. A seal had been observed playing about, and we augured well from such an omen. The blacks had been watching us from the opposite shore, and as soon as we moved, rose to keep abreast of us. With all our efforts we could not avoid the shoals. We walked up to our knees in mud and water, to find the least variation in the depth of the water so as to facilitate our exertions, but it was to no purpose. We were ultimately obliged to drag the boat over the flats; there were some of them a quarter of a mile in breadth, knee-deep in mud; but at length got her into deep water again. The turn of the channel was now before us, and we had a good run for about four or five miles. We had completed the bend, and the channel now stretched to the E.S.E. At about nine miles from us there was a bright sand-hill visible, near which the channel seemed to turn again to the south; and I doubted not that it terminated there. It was to no purpose, however, that we tried to gain it. Shoals again closed in upon us on every side. We dragged the boat over several, and at last got amongst quicksands. I, therefore, directed our efforts to hauling the boat over to the south side of the channel, as that on which we could most satisfactorily ascertain our position. After great labour we succeeded, and, as evening had closed in, lost no time in pitching the tents.

While the men were thus employed, I took Fraser with me, and, accompanied by M'Leay, crossed the sand-hummocks behind us, and descended to the sea-shore. I found that we had struck the south coast deep in the bight of Encounter Bay. We had no time for examination, but returned immediately to the camp, as I intended to give the men an opportunity to go to the beach. They accordingly went and bathed, and returned not only highly delighted at this little act of good nature on my part, but loaded with cockles, a bed of which they had managed to find among the sand. Clayton had tied one end of his shirt up, and brought a bag full, and amused himself with boiling cockles all night long.

If I had previously any hopes of being enabled ultimately to push the boat over the flats that were before us, a view of the channel at low water convinced me of the impracticability of any further attempt. The water was so low that every shoal was exposed, and many stretched directly from one side of the channel to the other; and, but for the treacherous nature of the sand-banks, it would not have been difficult to have walked over dry footed to the opposite side of it. The channel stretched away to the E.S.E., to a distance of seven or eight miles, when it appeared to turn south under a small sand-hill, upon which the rays of the sun fell, as it was sinking behind us.

There was an innumerable flock of wild-fowl arranged in rows along the sides of the pools left by the tide, and we were again amused by the singular effect of the refraction upon them, and the grotesque and distorted forms they exhibited. Swans, pelicans, ducks, and geese, were mingled together, and, according to their distance from us, presented different appearances.

Some were exceedingly tall and thin, others were unnaturally broad. Some appeared reversed, or as if they were standing on their heads, and the slightest motion, particularly the flapping of their wings, produced a most ridiculous effect. No doubt, the situation and the state of the atmosphere were favourable to the effect I have described. The day had been fine, the evening was beautiful,—but it was the rarefaction of the air immediately playing on the ground, and not the haze of sunset that caused what I have noticed. It is distinct from mirage, although it is difficult to point out the difference. The one, however, distorts, the other conceals objects, and gives them a false distance. The one is clear, the other is cloudy. The one raises objects above their true position, the other does not. The one plays about, the other is steady; but I cannot hope to give a proper idea either of mirage or refraction so satisfactorily as I could wish. Many travellers have dwelt upon their effects, particularly upon those of the former, but few have attempted to account for them.

Our situation was one of peculiar excitement and interest. To our right the thunder of the heavy surf, that almost shook the ground beneath us, broke with increasing roar upon our ears; to our left the voice of the natives echoed through the brush, and the size of their fires at the extremity of the channel, seemed to indicate the alarm our appearance had occasioned.

XIII.—MITCHELL'S EXPLORATION OF AUSTRALIA FELIX

[MAJOR T. L. MITCHELL left Sydney in March 1836, with instructions to survey the Darling, previously discovered by Sturt, trace the course of that river till it formed its junction with the Murray, and examine the territory on the left bank of the Murray. The following narrative, taken from Mitchell's *Three Expeditions into the Interior of Eastern Australia*, describes his journey through western Victoria, which he called Australia Felix.]

June 29, 1836.—The party moved forward in the direction of Mount Hope, and leaving it on the left, we continued towards Pyramid Hill, where we encamped at about three-quarters of a mile from its base. We were under no restraint now in selecting a camp, from any scarcity of water or grass; for all hollows in the plains contained some water, and grass grew everywhere. The strips of wood which diversified the country as seen from the hills, generally enclosed a depression with polygonum bushes, but without any marks of having had any water in them, although, in very wet seasons, some probably lodges there, as in so many canals, and this indeed seemed to me to be a country where canals would answer well, not so much perhaps for inland navigation, as for the better distribution of water over a fertile country, enclosed as this is by copious rivers.

June 30.—Having seen the party on the way, and directed it to proceed on a bearing of 215° from N., I ascended the rocky pyramidic hill, which I found arose to the height of 300 feet above the plain. Its apex consisted of a single block of granite, and the view was exceedingly beautiful over the surrounding plains, shining fresh and green in the light of a fine morning. The scene was different from anything I had ever before witnessed, either in New South Wales or elsewhere. A land so inviting, and still without inhabitants! As I stood, the first European intruder on the sublime solitude of these verdant plains, as yet untouched by flocks or herds, I felt conscious of being the harbinger of mighty changes, and that our steps would soon be followed by the men and the animals for which it seemed to have been prepared. A

189

haziness in the air prevented me, however, from perceiving clearly
the distant horizon from that summit, but I saw and intersected
those mountains to the southward, which I had observed from
Mount Hope.

The progress of the party was still visible from that hill, pur-
·suing their course over the distant plains, like a solitary line of
ants. I overtook it when a good many miles on; and we encamped
after travelling upwards of fourteen miles, in one uninterrupted,
straight line. Our camp was chosen on the skirts of a forest of box,
having a plain on the east covered with rich grass, and where we
found some small pools of rain water.

July 1.—Proceeding still on the bearing followed yesterday, we
reached at three miles from our camp, a fine chain of ponds. They
were deep, full of water, and surrounded by strong yarra trees.
Passing them, we met a small scrub of casuarinae, which we
avoided; and we next entered on a fine plain, in which the anthistiria or oatgrass appeared. This is the same grass which grows
on the most fertile parts of the counties of Argyle and Murray,
and is, I believe, the best Australian grass for cattle; it is also one
of the surest indications of a good soil and dry situation. Beyond
the plain, the line of noble yarra trees, which I had observed from
Mount Hope, gave almost certain promise of a river; and at 6½
miles our journey was terminated by a deep running stream. The
banks were steep, and about twenty feet high, but covered thickly
with grass to the edge of the water. The yarra trees grew by
the brink of the stream, and not on the top of the bank. The
water had a brown appearance as if it came from melted snow,
but from the equality of depth (about nine feet) and other circumstances, I was of opinion that it was a permanent running
stream. The current ran at the rate of four chains in 122 seconds,
or near 1½ miles per hour; thus it would appear, from what we had
seen, that there is much uniformity in the velocity of the rivers,
and consequently in the general inclination of the surface. The
banks of this little river were, however, very different in some
respects from any we had previously seen, being everywhere
covered thickly with grass. No fallen timber impeded its course,
nor was there any indication in the banks, that the course was
ever in the least degree affected by such obstructions. It was so
narrow, that I anticipated little difficulty in making a bridge by
felling some of the overhanging trees. Finding a large one already
fallen across the stream, where the slopes of the banks could be
most readily made passable, we lost no time in felling another,
which broke against the opposite bank and sunk into the water.

No other large trees grew near, but the banks were, at that place, so favourable for the passage of the waggons, that I determined to take advantage of the large fallen tree; and to construct a bridge by bringing others of smaller dimensions to it, not unmindful of the useful suggestions of Sir Howard Douglas, respecting temporary bridges.

July 2.—Late in the evening of this day we completed a bridge formed of short but strong sleepers, laid diagonally to the fallen tree, which constituted its main support, and the whole was covered with earth from cuttings made in the banks to render it accessible to the carts. At length every thing was ready for crossing, and we had thus a prospect of being able to advance beyond the river, into that unknown but promising land of hill and dale.

July 3.—This morning our bridge was no longer to be seen, the river having risen so much during the night, that it was four feet under water. Yet no rain had fallen for five days previous, and we could account for this unexpected flood only by supposing that the powerful shining of the sun, during the last two days, had melted the snow near the sources of the stream. At noon, the water had risen fourteen feet. A whispering sound, much resembling wind among the trees, now arose from it, and, however inconvenient to us, the novelty of a sudden rise in the river was quite refreshing, accustomed as we had been so long, to wander in the beds of rivers and to seek in vain for water. Our little bridge continued to be passable even when covered with four feet of water, but as it had no parapets, we could not prevent some of the bullocks from going over the side, on attempting to cross, when it was thus covered. The river still continuing to rise, we were compelled at last to launch the boats, and by this means, we effected the passage of the whole party and equipment before sunset; the boats having been also again mounted on the carriage the same evening. The carts and boat-carriage were drawn through the bed of the river by means of the drag-chains, which reached from the carriage on one side, to a strong team of bullocks on the other. This was a very busy day for the whole party—black and white; I cannot fairly say savage and civilised, for in most of our difficulties by flood and field, the intelligence and skill of our sable friends made the "white-fellows" appear rather stupid. They could read traces on the earth, climb trees, or dive into the water, better than the ablest of us. In tracing lost cattle, speaking to "the wild natives," hunting, or diving, Piper was the most accomplished man in the camp. In person he was the tallest, and in authority he was allowed to consider himself almost next to me, the better to secure his best exertions. When Mr. Stapylton first arrived, Piper came to my tent and observed that "That fellow had two coats," no doubt meaning that I ought to give one of them to him! The men he despised, and he would only act by my orders. This day, he rendered us much useful assistance in the water; for instance, when a cart stuck in the bottom of the river, the rope by which it was to be drawn through having broken, Piper, by diving, attached a heavy chain to it, thereby enabling the party to draw it out with the teams.

At this place the widow, being far beyond her own country, was inclined to go back; and although I intended to put her on a more direct and safe way home after we should pass the heads of the Murrumbidgee on our return, I could not detain her longer than she wished. Her child, to whom she appeared devotedly attached, was fast recovering the use of its broken limb; and the mother seemed uneasy under an apprehension, that I wanted to deprive her of this child. I certainly had always wished to take back with me to Sydney an aboriginal child, with the intention of ascertaining, what might be the effect of education upon one of that race. This little savage, who at first would prefer a snake or lizard to a piece of bread, had become so far civilised at length, as to prefer bread; and it began to cry bitterly on leaving us. The mother, however, thought nothing of swimming, even at that season, across the broad waters of the "Millewa," as she should be obliged to do, pushing the child before her, floating on a piece of bark.

July 4.—At the distance of about a mile to the southward, a line of trees marked the course of another channel, which, containing only a few ponds, we crossed without difficulty. Beyond it, we traversed a plain five miles in extent, and backed by low, grassy hills, composed of grey gneiss. The most accessible interval between these hills still appeared to be in the direction I had chosen at Mount Hope, as leading to the lowest opening of a range, still more distant: I, therefore, continued on that bearing, having the highest of those hills to our left, at the distance of five or six miles. On entering the wood skirting the wide plain, our curiosity was rather disappointed at finding, instead of rare things, the blackbutted gum and casuarinae, trees common in the colony. The woolly gum also grew here, a tree much resembling the box in the bark on its trunk, although that on the branches, unlike the box, is smooth and shining. In this wood we recognised the rosella parrot, and various plants, so common near Sydney; but not before seen by us in the interior.

At ten miles, we travelled over undulating ground, for the first time, since we left the banks of the Lachlan; and we crossed a chain of ponds watering a beautiful and extensive valley, covered with a luxuriant crop of the anthistiria grass. Kangaroos were now to be seen on all sides, and we finally encamped on a deeper chain of ponds, probably the chief channel of the waters of that valley. A ridge of open forest-hills appearing before us, I rode to the top of one of the highest summits, while the men pitched the tents; and from it, I perceived a hilly country, through whose intricacies I, at that time, saw no way, and beyond it, a lofty mountain-range arose in the south-west. To venture into such a region with wheel-carriages, seemed rather hazardous, when I recollected the coast ranges of the colony; and I determined to examine it further, before I decided, whether we should penetrate these fastnesses, or travel westward round them, thus to ascertain their extent in that direction, and that of the good land watered by them.

July 5.—I proceeded with several men mounted, towards the lofty hill to the eastward of our route, the highest of those I had intersected from Mount Hope and the Pyramid-hill, its aboriginal name, as I afterwards learnt, being Barrabungale. Nearly the whole of our way was over granite rocks. We had just reached a naked mass, near the principal summit, when the clouds, which had been lowering for some time, began to descend on the plains to the northward, and soon closing over the whole horizon, compelled me to return, without having had an opportunity of observing more than the westward. This was, however, a fact of considerable importance with respect to our further progress; for I could enter that mountain-region with less hesitation, as I knew, that I could leave it, if necessary, and proceed westward by following down any of the vallies which declined in that direction.

July 6.—The morning being rainy, I could learn nothing more by ascending Barrabungale as I intended; but I rode into the country to the southward, in order to examine it in the direction, in which I thought it most desirable to lead the party. After passing over several well-watered, grassy flats or vallies, each bounded by open forest-hills, we crossed at six miles from the camp, a range, the summit of which was covered by a low scrub, but it did not much impede our way. Beyond this range, we again found open forest land, and we saw extensive flats still more open to our right, in which direction all the waters seemed to fall. At length, after travelling about twelve miles, we came upon a deep

I. D.

q

chain of ponds, winding through a flat thickly covered with
anthistiria, and resembling a field of ripe grain. Smoke arose in
all directions from an extensive camp of natives; but, although I
cooyed and saw them at a distance, they continued to crouch behind trees, and would not approach. I did not disturb them
further, but returned with the intention of leading the party
there the next day, when I hoped to see more of these natives.
An abundance of a beautiful white or pale yellow-flowered, her-
baceous plant, reminding me of the violets of Europe, to which it
was nearly allied, grew on the sides of hills.

In the evening, the widow returned with her child on her back.
She stated, that after we left our late encampment, a numerous
tribe arrived on the opposite bank of the river, and seeing the
fires on her side, called out very angrily, as Piper translated her
tale, "Murry coola," (very angry); inquiring, who had made those
fires; and that, receiving no reply, (for she was afraid, and had hid
herself,) they danced a corrobory in a furious style, during which
she and the child crept away, and had passed two nights without
fire and in the rain. Piper seemed angry at her return, but I took
particular care, that she should be treated with as much kindness
as before. She was a woman of good sense, and had been with us
long enough to feel secure under our protection, even from the
wrath of Piper, as displayed on this occasion; and I discovered,
that her attempted return home had been suggested by Piper's
gin, who probably anticipated a greater share of food, after the
widow's departure.

July 7.—The party moved to the creek, where I had before
seen the natives; and Piper found at their fires an old woman and
several boys. They said, pointing far to the south-east, doubtless
to Port Phillip, that a station of white-fellows was there, and that
they had been themselves to the sea, which was not very distant.
The old woman spoke with expressive gestures, of a part of the
coast, she called "Cadong," where the waves raged; and of a river,
she named Woollamaee, running into it. It appeared that the
rest of the tribe were at that time in search of opossums; but she
promised, that when they returned in the evening or next day,
some of them should visit our camp.

July 8.—This morning, Piper prevailed on an old man, with his
gins and some boys, to come to us. The former pointed towards
"Cadong," in the direction of 232° from N. and in reply to my
queries, through Piper, said it was not "Geelong " (Port Phillip),
but a water like it; and that no white men had ever been there.
On mentioning lake Alexandrina, by its native name Keyinga, he

said, that it was a place filled sometimes with rain (*i.e.* river-)
water, and not like "Cadong" which was salt water. He described
the whole country before us as abounding in good water and
excellent grass; and he said, that in the direction I was pursuing,
there was no impediment between me and the sea-coast. Piper's
countenance brightened up with the good news this man gave
him; assuring me that we should "find water all about; no more
want water." In return for all this intelligence, I presented the
old man with an iron tomahawk, which he placed under him as
he sate; and he continued to address me with great volubility for
some time. I was told by Piper, that he was merely saying "how
glad he was," and enumerating (apparently with a sort of poetic
fervour) the various uses to which he could apply the axe I had
given him. I left these natives with the impression on my mind,
that they were quiet, well-disposed people.

Proceeding a little west of south-west, we intersected this
creek (Tarray) three times, leaving it finally flowing southward,
and to our left, into that of Dyoonboors, which it joined, at a mile
and a half from where we had been encamped. At three miles,
having crossed a low ridge of forest land, we entered a fine valley,
backed on the west by romantic, forest hills, and watered by some
purling brooks, which united in the woods on the east. The flat
itself had a few stately trees upon it, and seemed quite ready to
receive the plough; while some round hillocks, on the north, were
so smooth and grassy, that the men said they looked as if they
had already been depastured by sheep. From an extremity of the
clear ridge, I obtained an extensive view of the mountain chain to
the south-east; and I intersected most of its summits. The whole
seemed smooth (*i.e.* not rocky), grassy, and thinly timbered.
Crossing the lower or outer extremity of this forest ridge, we entered another fine valley watered by a creek which we passed at
six miles from the commencement of the day's journey. This
little channel was grassy to the water's edge, and its banks were
firm and about eight feet high; the course being eastward. In the
valley I saw the Banksia for the first time, since we left the Lachlan. A calamifolia, or needle-leaved wattle, occurred also in considerable quantity. After crossing two more brooks and some
flats of fine land, with grassy forest-hills on our right, we reached
the crest of a forest-range, which afforded an extensive view over
the country beyond it. The surface seemed to be low for some
distance, but then to rise gradually towards some rocky points,
over which were partially seen the summits of a higher range,
still further southward. The descent to the low country, was easy

for our carts; and we found there, a beautifully green and level flat, bounded on the south by a little river, flowing westward. The banks of this stream consisted of rounded acclivities, and were covered with excellent grass. The bed was 18 or 20 feet below the level of the adjacent flats, and from its resemblance in some respects to the little stream in England, I named it the Loddon. We encamped on its bank in latitude 36° 36' 49" S., longitude 143° 35' 30" E.

July 9.—By continuing the same line of route, we crossed several minor rivulets, all flowing through open grassy vales, bounded by finely undulating hills. At about three miles, we came to a deep chain of ponds, the banks being steep and covered with grass. Keeping a tributary to that channel on our left, we passed some low hills of quartz; and a little beyond them, we crossed poor hills of the same rock, bearing an open box-forest. After travelling through a little scrub, we descended on one of the most beautiful spots I ever saw:—The turf, the woods, and the banks of the little stream which murmured through the vale, had so much the appearance of a well kept park, that I felt loth to injure its surface by the passage of our cart wheels. Proceeding for a mile and a half along the rivulet, and through a valley wholly of the same description, we at length encamped on a flat of rich earth (nearly quite black), and where the anthistiria grew in greater luxuriance than I had ever before witnessed in Australian grasses. The earth indeed seemed to surpass in richness, any that I had seen in New South Wales; and I was even tempted to bring away a specimen of it. Our dogs killed three kangaroos, and this good fortune was most timely, as I had that very morning, thought it advisable to reduce the allowance of rations.

July 10.—Tracing upwards the rivulet of the vale we left this morning, we passed over much excellent grassy land watered by it, the channel containing some very deep ponds, surrounded by the white barked eucalyptus. A hill on its bank, consisted of a conglomerate in which the ferruginous matter predominated over the embedded fragments of quartz. The ground beyond was hilly, and we at length ascended a ridge, apparently an extremity of a higher range. On these hills grew the varieties of eucalypti known in the colony, such as iron-bark, blue-gum, and stringy-bark. The lower grounds were so wet and soft, and the water-courses in them so numerous, that I was desirous to follow a ridge as long as it would take us in the direction, in which we were proceeding; and this range answered well for the purpose.

Its crest consisted of ferruginous sandstone much inclined, the strike extending north-north-west. I found the opposite side much more precipitous, and that it overlooked a much lower country. In seeking a favourable line of descent for the carts, I climbed a still higher forest-hill on the left, which consisted chiefly of quartz-rock. I not only recognised from that hill, some lofty points to the eastward, and obtained angles on them, but I also perceived very rugged summits of a range at a great distance in the south-west. Having selected among the various hills and dales before me, that line of route which seemed the best, and having taken its bearing, I returned to conduct the carts by a pass along one side of that hill, having found it, in a very practicable state for wheel carriages. At three miles beyond the pass, we crossed a deep creek running westward, which I named the Avoca, and we encamped on an excellent piece of land beyond it. This day, we had even better fortune in our field sports than on the one before, for besides three kangaroos, we killed two emus, one of which was a female and esteemed a great prize, for I had discovered, that the eggs, found in the ovarium, were a great luxury in the bush; and afforded us a light and palatable breakfast for several days.

July 11.—At the end of two miles on this day's journey, we crossed a deep stream running westward. The height of its banks above the water was twelve feet, and they were covered with a rich sward. The land along the margins of the stream was as good as that we were now accustomed to see everywhere around us, so that it was no longer necessary to note the goodness or beauty of any place in particular. At four miles, we passed over a forest-hill composed of mica-slate, and after crossing another good valley at six miles, I saw before us, on gaining a low forest ridge, other grassy hills of still greater height, connected by a rock, that cost us less trouble to ascend than I expected. It was in the vallies now, that we met most difficulty; the earth having become so soft and wet, that the carts could be got through some places only by the tedious process of dragging each successively, with the united strength of several teams.

From a high forest-hill, about a mile east of our route, I first obtained a complete view of a noble range of mountains, rising in the south to a stupendous height, and presenting as bold and picturesque an outline as ever painter imagined. The highest and most eastern summit was hid in the clouds, although the evening was serene. It bore W. of S. 26° 54′; and the western extremity, which consisted of a remarkably round hill, bore 16° 30′ S. of W.

Having descended from the range by an easy slope to the southward, we passed through a beautiful valley, in which we crossed,
at a mile and a quarter from the hills, a fine stream flowing also
westward; and in other respects similar to those we had already
met. I named it Avon water, and we encamped on its left bank.

July 12.—At two miles and a half from the spot, where we had
slept, we crossed another stream flowing west-north-west, which
I named the Smallburn. Beyond it, the ground was good and
grassy, but at this season very soft, so that the draught was most
laborious for the cattle. At seven miles, we crossed a wet flat with
ponds of water standing on it, and beyond we entered on a clay
soil, altogether different from any hitherto passed on this side the
Yarrayne. About eight miles from our camp, we reached a fine
running brook with grassy banks, its course being to the north-
west. The bed consisted of red-sand and gravel, and the banks
were about fourteen feet high, presenting fine swelling slopes
covered with turf. On this stream, which I named the Doscasas,
I halted, as it was doubtful whether some of the carts could be
brought even so far before night; the ground having proved soft
and rotten to such a degree, especially on the slopes of low hills,
that in some cases the united strength of three teams had been
scarcely sufficient to draw them through. It was night before the
last cart arrived, and two bullocks had been left behind, in an
exhausted state.

July 13.—We had at length discovered a country ready for the
immediate reception of civilised man; and destined perhaps to become eventually a portion of a great empire. Unencumbered by
too much wood, it yet possessed enough for all purposes; its soil
was exuberant, and its climate temperate; it was bounded on
three sides by the ocean; and it was traversed by mighty rivers,
and watered by streams innumerable. Of this Eden I was the
first European to explore its mountains and streams—to behold
its scenery—to investigate its geological character—and, by my
survey, to develope those natural advantages, certain to become, at
no distant date, of vast importance to a new people. The lofty
mountain range, which I had seen on the 11th, was now before us,
but still distant between thirty and forty miles; and as the cattle
required rest, I determined on an excursion to its lofty eastern
summit. Such a height was sure to command a view of the
country between these mountains and the sea, in the direction of
Lady Julia Percy's Isles; and of that region between the range
and those less connected forest-hills, I had seen to the eastward.

When I first discovered these mountains, I perceived that the land immediately to the eastward of them, was very low, and that if I found it necessary, I might conduct the party in that direction to the coast. I was, however, more desirous to level my theodolite on that summit first, and thus obtain valuable materials for the construction of an accurate map of the whole country around it. I accordingly left the party encamped, and proceeded towards the mountain, accompanied by six men on horseback; having previously instructed Mr. Stapylton to employ the men, during my absence, in forming a way down the bank, and a good ford across the stream, in order that there might be no impediment to the immediate advance of the party, on my return.

Pursuing the bearing of 193°, we crossed, at three miles from the camp, a deep creek, similar to that on which it was placed; and the first adventure of the morning occurred here. The fordable place was so narrow, that the horse of one of the party plunged into the deep water with its rider, who, while the animal was swimming, incautiously pulled the bridle, and of course overturned it, so that they parted company in the water, the horse reaching one bank, the rider the other. The latter, who was my botanical collector, Richardson, took his soaking on a cold frosty morning so philosophically, talking to his comrades as he made his way to the bank, partly swimming, partly floating on two huge portfolios, that I gave his name to the creek, the better to reconcile him to his wet jacket. We entered soon after, upon one of the finest tracts of grassy forest land, we had ever seen. The whole country recently crossed was good, but this was far better, having several broad and deep ponds, or small lakes in the woods, and all full of the clearest water. At eight miles, I perceived a forest-hill on my left (or to the eastward), and the country before us was so open, sloping and green, that I felt certain, we were approaching a river; and we soon came upon one, which was full, flowing, and thirty feet wide, being broader than the Yarrayne, but not so uniformly deep. Unlike the latter river, reeds grew about its margin in some places, and its banks, though grassy and fifteen feet high, were neither so steep as those of the Yarrayne, nor so closely shut together. We swam our horses across, but our progress had scarcely commenced again on the other side, when it was impeded by another similar stream or channel. In this we managed, with Piper's assistance, to find a ford, but at less than a quarter of a mile, we met a third channel, more resembling the first in the height of its banks and velocity of the current, and also from its flowing amongst bushes. This we likewise forded, and immediately after we ascended a piece of rising ground, which convinced me, that we had at length crossed all the branches of that remarkable river. It is probable we came upon it where it received the waters of tributaries, and some of these channels might be such.

We next fell in with some undulating ground, different in many respects from any, that we had traversed during the morning. The soil was poor and sandy; and the stunted trees and shrubs of the Blue mountains grew upon it, instead of the novelties we expected at such a great distance from home. We also recognised the birds, common about Sydney. On reaching the higher part of this ground (at nine miles), I again saw the mountain, which then bore 196°. The intervening ground seemed to consist of a low ridge rather heavily wooded, its crest presenting a line as level as the ocean. At eleven miles, I suppose we were upon the dividing ground between the sea-coast country and that of the interior, and on what appeared to be the only connection between the forest mountains to the eastward, and the lofty mass then before us. We found upon this neck, huge trees of iron-bark and stringy-bark; some fine forest-hills appeared to the eastward, and distant only a few miles. At the end of sixteen, eighteen, nineteen, twenty-one, and twenty-three miles, we crossed small rivers, all flowing westward, and the third over sandstone. After passing the last or fifth stream, we halted on a very fine, open, dry and grassy flat. We found a large fallen tree, which we set on fire, and passed the night, a very mild one, most comfortably, on the ground beside it, with the intention of renewing our journey at daylight in the morning.

July 14.—On leaving our bivouac we crossed some hills of trap-rock which were lightly wooded, and covered with the finest grass, in great abundance. The scenery around them, the excellent quality of the soil, the abundance of water and verdure, contrasted strangely with the circumstance of their lying waste and unoccupied. It was evident that the reign of solitude in these beautiful vales was near a close; a reflection which, in my mind, often sweetened the toils and inconveniences of travelling through such houseless regions. At the foot of the last hill, and about a mile on our way, we crossed a chain of deep ponds running to the south-west. Beyond them was a plain of the very finest open forest-land, on which we travelled seven miles; and then came upon a river with broad deep reaches of very clear water, and flowing towards the north-west. We easily found a ford, and on proceeding, entered upon a tract of white sand, where banksia and casuarinae were the chief trees. There was also some good grass, but it grew rather thinly upon it. The next water we crossed was a small mountain-torrent, hurrying along to the eastward in a deep and rocky channel, overhung with bushes. Being now close under the mountain, we dismounted, and sent our horses back, for the sake of food, to the bank of the last mentioned river. The first part of our ascent, on foot, was extremely steep and laborious, although it was along the most favourable feature I could find. Above it, the impediments likely to obstruct our further ascent, were two high and perpendicular rocky cliffs; but I had observed before ascending, those crevices and intervals between rocks, where we might most easily effect an ascent; and through these we accordingly penetrated without much difficulty. The upper precipice consisted of cliffs, about 140 feet in perpendicular height. Fortunately the ablest of the men with me, was a house carpenter, and, being accustomed to climb roofs, he managed to get up, and then assist the rest. Having gained the top of this second precipice, we found winter and desolation under drizzling clouds, which afforded but partial and transient glimpses of the world below. The surface at the summit of the cliffs was broad, and consisted of large blocks of sandstone, separated by wide fissures, full of dwarf bushes of banksia and casuarinae. These rocks were inclined but slightly towards the north-west, and the bushes being also wet and curiously encrusted with heavy icicles, it was by no means a pleasant part of our journey to travel nearly half a mile upwards, either on the slippery rock or between fissures among wet bushes. At length however we reached the highest point, and found that it consisted of naked sandstone. The top block was encrusted with icicles; and had become hoary under the beating of innumerable storms. At the very summit I found a small heath-like, bushy Leucopogon, from six inches to a foot high. It was in flower, although covered with ice. Also a variety of *Leucopogon villosus*, with rather less hair than usual, and another species of the same genus, probably new. Near the highest parts of the plateau, I found a new species of eucalyptus with short broad viscid leaves, and rough-warted branches. All around us was hidden in mist. It was now within half an hour of sunset, but the ascent had cost so much trouble, and the country, this summit commanded, was so interesting to us, that I was unwilling to descend without trying, whether it might not be clear of clouds at sunset. We had not come prepared in any way to pass the night on such a wild and desolate spot, for we had neither clothing, nor food, nor was there any shelter; but I was willing to suffer any privations, for the attainment of the object of our ascent. One man, Richardson, an old traveller, had most wisely brought his day's provisions in his haversack, and these I divided equally among five. No rocks could be found near the summit, to shelter us from the piercing wind and sleet. The thermometer stood at 29°, and we strove to make a fire to protect us from the piercing cold; but the green twigs, encrusted with icicles, could not by our united efforts be blown into a flame sufficient to warm us. There was abundance of good wood at the foot of the cliffs—huge trees of iron-bark, stringy-bark, and blue gum; but had we descended, a second ascent might have appeared too laborious, on a mere chance of finding the summit clear; so we remained above. The men managed to manufacture some tea in a tin pot, and into the water as it boiled, I plunged a thermometer, which rose to exactly 95° of the centigrade scale. We got through that night of misery as well as might have been expected under the circumstances, and we succeeded in keeping the fire alive, although while twigs were blown into red heat at one end, icicles remained at the other, even within a few inches of the flame. In order to maintain it through the night, we divided, at eleven o'clock, the stock of branches which had been gathered before dark, into eight parcels; this being the number of hours we were destined to sit shivering there; and as each bundle was laid on the dying embers, we had the pleasure at least of knowing, that it was an hour nearer daylight. I coiled myself round the fire in all the usual attitudes of the blacks, but in vain; to get warm was quite impossible, although I did once feel something like comfort, when one of the men gave me for a seat, a flat stone on which the fire had been blown for some hours. Partial cessations in the fall of sleet were also cheering occasionally; but the appearance of stars, two hours before daylight, promised to reward our enterprise, and inspired me with hope.

July 15.—At six o'clock, the sky became clear, the clouds had indeed left the mountain, and as soon as it was day, I mounted the frozen rock. In the dawn, however, all lower objects were blended in one grey shade, like the dead colouring of a picture. I could distinguish only a pool of water, apparently near the foot of the mountain. This water, I afterwards found to be a lake eight miles distant, and in my map I have named it Lake Lonsdale, in honour of the Commandant then, or soon after, appointed to Port Phillip. I hastily levelled my theodolite, but the scene, although sublime enough for the theme of a poet, was not at all suited to the more common-place objects of a surveyor. The sun rose amid red and stormy clouds, and vast masses of a white vapour concealed from view both sea and land, save where a few isolated hills were dimly visible. Towards the interior, the horizon was clear, and during a short interval, I took what angles I could obtain. To the westward, the view of the mountain ranges was truly grand. Southward, or towards the sea, I could at intervals perceive plains clear of timber, and that the country was level, a circumstance of great importance to us; for I was apprehensive that between these mountains and the coast, it might be broken by mountain gullies, as it is in the settled colony and all along the Eastern coast. If such had proved to be the case, the carts could not have been taken there; and I must have altered the plan of my intended route. Before I could observe the angles so desirable, clouds again enveloped the mountain, and I was compelled to quit its summit without completing the work. The wind blew keenly, the thermometer stood as low as 27° and in the morning the rocks were more thickly encrusted with ice. The difficulty of our descent under such circumstances was, therefore, increased, but no impediment could have arrested us then, the lower regions having so many attractive charms for such cold and hungry beings. That night on the summit materially injured the health of two of my best men, and who had been with me on all three of my expeditions. Muirhead was seized with ague, and Woods with a pulmonary complaint; and although both recovered in a few weeks, they were never so strong afterwards. We found upon the mountain, besides those already mentioned, various interesting plants, which we had seen nowhere else. Amongst them a most beautiful downy-leaved Epacris, with large, curved, purple flowers, allied to E. *grandiflora*, but much handsomer. A most remarkable species of Phebalium with holly-like leaves and bright red flowers, resembling those of a Boronia. It was related to P. *phylicifolium*, but quite distinct. A new Cryptandra remarkable for its downy leaves. A beautiful species of Baeckea, with downy leaves, and rose-coloured flowers, resembling those of the dwarf almond. A new Pultenaea allied to P. *biloba*, but more hairy, and with the flowers half concealed among the leaves. A new species of Bossiaea which had the appearance of a Rosemary bush, and differed from all the published kinds in having linear pungent leaves. A beautiful, new, and very distinct species of Genetyllis, possessing altogether the habit of a Cape Diosma, the heath-like branches being terminated by clusters of bright pink and white flowers. Several species of Grevillea, particularly a remarkable kind, with leaves like those of an European holly, but downy; another fine new species, with leaves like those of an European oak; and a third with brownish red flowers and hoary leaves, varying from an erect straight-branched bush, to a diffuse entangled shrub; lastly a new Leucopogon, besides that found on the summit as already mentioned.

In adding this noble range of mountains to my map, I felt some difficulty in deciding on a name. To give appellations that may become current in the mouths of future generations, has often been a perplexing subject with me, whether they have been required to distinguish new counties, towns, or villages, or such great natural features of the earth as mountains and rivers. I have always gladly adopted aboriginal names, and in the absence of these, I have endeavoured to find some good reason for the application of others, considering descriptive names the best, such being in general the character of those used by the natives of this and other countries. Names of individuals seem eligible enough, when at all connected with the history of the discovery, or that of the nation by whom it was made. The capes on the coast, I was then approaching, were chiefly distinguished with the names of naval heroes; and as such capes were but subordinate points of the primitive range, I ventured to connect this summit with the name of the sovereign in whose reign the extensive, valuable, and interesting region below was first explored; and, I confess, it was not without some pride, as a Briton, that I, "more majorum," gave the name of the Grampians, to these extreme summits of the southern hemisphere.

We reached the banks of the little river, where the horses awaited us, in three hours, the distance being eight miles from the summit of Mount William. There, we found a large fire, and under a wide spreading casuarina, during a delightful interval of about twenty minutes, I enjoyed the pleasures of eating, sleeping, resting, and warming myself, almost all at the same time. To all who would know how to enjoy most intensely a good fire, shelter, sunshine and the dry soft turf, I would recommend, by way of whet, a winter night on a lofty mountain, without fire, amidst frost-covered rocks and clouds of sleet. I shall long remember the pleasure of those moments of repose, which I enjoyed on my arrival in the warm valley, after such a night. We could afford no longer delay, however, having brought provisions only for one day with us, whereas this was the morning of the third of our absence from the camp. Retracing our steps, we reached the little river only at eight in the evening, and as I hoped to find a ford in it at daylight, we lay down on its bank for the night.

July 16.—I slept on a snug bit of turf, within two feet of the stream; so that the welcome murmur of its rippling waters, assisted my dreams of undiscovered rivers. As soon as morning dawned, I succeeded in finding a ford on that branch across which we swam our horses on the 13th. We thus met with less cause of delay, and reached the camp at an early hour, with excellent appetites for breakfast.

Two natives had visited the party during my absence; and had slept by the fires. They had been at cattle-stations, and could say "milk." They consequently approached our camp boldly, and during the night shewed much restlessness, endeavouring to decoy the gins away with them. But the widow gave the alarm and, very properly handed over these insidious wooers to the especial surveillance of the man on duty. Notwithstanding they were vigilantly watched, they contrived to steal a tomahawk, and went off leaving their wooden shovels at our camp, saying they should return. I had now several men on the sick-list, but under the treatment of Drysdale, our medical attendant, they speedily recovered.

July 17.—The ground on the sides of the low hills was still so soft, (and in this respect, I had found the country we had lately crossed, even worse than that previously traversed by the carts,) that the only prospect which remained to us of being able to continue the journey, was by proceeding, over the plains, extending along the interior side of the Grampians of the South. The soil of such plains consisted chiefly of clay, and we had recently found, that it bore the wheels of the waggons much better during the winter season, than the thin and loose soil on the sides of hills; apparently, because this lay on rock, or a substratum so tenacious as to support the water in, or just under, the surface. The wheels, and also the feet of the cattle, sunk at once to this rocky subsoil whatever its depth, and up came the water, so that on level parts, our track resembled a ditch of mud and water, and on slopes it formed a current of water, and a drain from the sides of the hills. I had observed the plains during my reconnaissance of the interior from the side of Mount William, and I now directed our course towards them. We crossed without difficulty the little river, by the passage Mr. Stapylton had prepared during my absence; and after travelling about four miles, first west and then north-west, we came upon an extensive plain. The soil consisted of good strong clay on which the cattle travelled very well, and it was covered with the best kind of grass. On reaching it I resumed my former course, which was nearly west-south-west, towards Mount Zero, a name I applied to a remarkable cone, at

the western extremity of the chain of mountains. After travelling
2½ miles over the plain, we again reached the banks of Richardson's creek, and forded it after some delay and considerable difficulty, on account of the softness of the bottom. We next entered
on a tract of grassy, forest land, the trees being chiefly box and
casuarinae. At 2½ miles beyond Richardson's creek we crossed a
small run of water, flowing west-north-west, apparently towards
it. After passing over similar ground for some miles further, and
having had another plain on our right, we at length encamped
near a large serpentine pond or lake, which was broad, deep, and
bordered with lofty gum-trees.

July 18.—We continued for five miles along good firm ground,
on which there was an open forest of box and gum-trees; and part
of the bold outline of the Grampians appeared to our left. At
9 miles we fell in with a flowing stream, the water being deep and
nearly as high as the banks. I did not doubt, that this was the
channel of the waters from the north-side of these mountains,
and, I was convinced, that it contained the water of all the
streams we had crossed on our way to Mount William, with the
exception of Richardson's creek, already crossed by the party,
where it was flowing to the north-west. The richness of the soil,
and the verdure near the river, as well as the natural beauty
of the scenery, could scarcely be surpassed in any country. The
banks were in some places open and grassy, and shaded by lofty
yarra trees, in others mimosa-bushes nodded over the eddying
stream.

Continuing along the right bank in a north-west direction, we
travelled two miles on a grassy plain; and we then turned towards
the river, encamping on its banks, in latitude 36° 46' 30" S.,
longitude 142° 39' 25" E. Magnetic variation 5° 21' 45" E.

Some natives being heard on the opposite bank, Piper advanced towards them as cautiously as possible ; but he could not
prevail on them to come over, although he ascertained, that the
name of the river was the "Wimmera."

July 19.—On examining the Wimmera with Piper's assistance,
I found that it was fordable in some places ; but, in order to
effect a passage with greater facility, we took over several of the
loads in one of the boats. Thus, the whole party had gained,
what I considered to be the left bank, by ten A.M. On proceeding,
I perceived some yarra trees before me, which grew, as we soon
discovered, beside a smaller branch, the bottom of which was
soft. We had however the good fortune to pass the carts across
this branch also. At a quarter of a mile further, we came upon

another flowing stream, apparently very deep, and having steep but grassy banks. The passage of this, occupied the party nearly two hours, one of the carts having sunk up to the axle in a soft bank or channel island. While the men were releasing the cart, I rode forward and found a fourth channel, deep, wide, and full to the brim. In vain did Tally-ho (trumpeter, master of the horse, etc. to the party) dash his horse into the stream in search of a bottom; though at last, one broad, favourable place was found, where the whole party forded, at a depth of not more than 2½ feet. Beyond these channels another similar one still obstructed our progress; but this we also successfully forded, and at length we found rising ground before us, consisting of an open plain which extended to the base of the mountains. On its skirt, we pitched our tents, at a distance of not quite one mile and a half from our last camp; a short journey certainly, but the passage of the five branches of the Wimmera was, nevertheless, a good day's work. I had frequently observed in the Australian rivers, an uniformity of character throughout the whole course of each, and the peculiarities of this important stream were equally remarkable, it being obviously the same, we had crossed in three similar channels, when on our way to Mount William, twenty miles above this point. The shrubs on the banks at the two places were also similar.

July 20.—While Mr. Stapylton conducted the party across the plains in a west-south-west direction, I proceeded towards Mount Zero, the most western extremity of the mountain range, and distant from our camp 8½ miles. I found this hill consisted also of highly micacious sandstone; the whole being inclined towards the north-west. Having planted my theodolite on the summit, I intersected various higher points to the eastward, and also a very remote, isolated hill, on the low country, far to the northward, which I had also seen from Mount William, and from several stations on our route. Several specimens of shrubs and flowers, that had not been previously seen by us, were gathered on the sides of this rocky hill. Among them, was a very singular, hairy Acacia, covered with a profusion of the most brilliant yellow flowers. In some respects it resembled A. *lanigera*, but it proved upon examination to be undescribed. An isolated mass appeared to the westward, having near its base a most remarkable rock resembling a mitre. Beyond this, the distant horizon was not *quite* so level as the plains of the interior usually are; and, as far as I could see northward with a good telescope, I perceived open forest-land and various fine sheets of water. I observed with great satisfaction, that the Grampians, terminated to the westward, on a comparatively low country. This was an important object of attention to me then, as it comprised all that intervened between us and the southern coast; in which direction, I perceived only one or two groups of conical hills. I resolved, however, before turning southwards, to extend our journey to the isolated mass already mentioned, which I afterwards named Mount Arapiles. After descending from Mount Zero, I proceeded towards the track of the carts, and found that the plains, unlike any hitherto seen, undulated so much, that in one place, I could perceive only the tops of trees in the hollows. On these plains, I found small nodules of highly ferruginous sandstone, apparently similar to that which occurs near Jervis Bay and in other places, along the eastern coast. Reaching at length a low green ridge of black soil very different from that of the plains, I found it formed the eastern bank of another of those remarkable circular lakes, of which I had seen so many near the Murray. The bed of this hollow consisted of rich black earth, and was thirty-two feet below the level of the adjacent plain. It seemed nearly circular ; the diameter being about three-quarters of a mile. One peculiarity in this lake was a double bank on the eastern side, consisting first of a concentric break or slope from the plain, the soil not being clay as usual, but a dry red sand; and then arose the green bank of black earth, leaving a concentric fosse or hollow between. A belt of yarra trees grew around the edge of this singular hollow, which was so dry and firm, that the carts, in the track of which I was riding, had traversed it without difficulty. I learnt from Mr. Stapylton, on reaching the camp, that the party had previously passed near two other lakes, the largest containing salt water; and in the neighbourhood of these, he had also remarked a great change of soil; so that what with the verdure upon it, the undulating surface, and clumps of casuarinae on light soil, or lofty yarra trees growing in black soil, that part of the country looked tolerably well.

July 21.—At a quarter of a mile from the camp, we crossed a running stream, which also contained deep, and apparently permanent pools. Several pine or callitris trees grew near its banks, being the first we had seen for some time. I named this mountain stream the Mackenzie. Beyond it, were grassy, undulating plains, with clumps of casuarinae, and box trees (eucalypti). At three miles and a half, we crossed another chain of ponds, and at four miles, we came to a deep stream, running with considerable rapidity, over a bed of sandstone rock. It was overhung with mimosa-bushes; and it was not until after considerable search, that I could find a convenient place for fording it. This I named the Norton. Good grassy hills arose beyond, and after crossing them, we found an undulating country and sandy soil, where there were shallow lagoons and but little grass. At nine miles, I was aware, from the sloping of the ground, of the vicinity of a river; and we soon came once more upon the Wimmera, flowing in one deep channel nearly as broad as the Murrumbidgee, but in no other respect at all similar. The banks of this newly dis-covered river were not water-worn, but characterised by verdant slopes, the borders being fringed with bushes of mimosa. The country was indeed fine adjacent to the Wimmera, and at the point where we came to it, the river was joined by a running creek from the south, which we crossed, and at two miles and a quarter further, we encamped on a spot overlooking a reedy lagoon, from which some long slopes, descended towards the river, distant from our camp about half a mile. When we thus again intersected the Wimmera, I was travelling due west, partly with a view to ascertain its ultimate course. The isolated hill lay before me, and it was now to be ascertained, whether the course of the stream was to the south or north of it. The appearance of the country from Mount Zero certainly afforded no prospect of our falling in with the river where we did, but at this camp, Burnett having climbed to the top of a high tree, thought he could trace the course to the southward of the hill before us, which bore nearly west. This prospect accorded with my wishes, and I hoped to trace it to the coast, without deviating too far to the westward of my intended route.

July 22.—A small stream from the south crossed our way, when we had proceeded about half a mile. At six miles and a half, we met with another; and three miles beyond it, I per-ceived a change in the appearance of the country. We had been for some time travelling through forest land, which now opened into grassy and level plains, variegated with belts and clumps of lofty trees, giving to the whole the appearance of a park. We had now the hilly mass of Mount Arapiles on our right, or north of us, but to my surprise there was no river flowing between us and those heights, as I had reason to suppose from what had been seen from the tree by Burnett. Turning towards the north-west, therefore, and at last northward, we finally encamped on a spot to the westward of the hill, after a journey of sixteen miles. Much of the ground near this hill was so soft, that one of the carts could not be brought in before midnight, although assisted by

I. D.

r

several teams, sent back from the camp. We were now encamped on a dark coloured soil, from which arose the same peculiar smell, that I had remarked at Cudjàllagong (Regent's Lake of Oxley). What had become of the Wimmera, I could scarcely imagine, but anxious to ascertain its course, I hastened before sunset, to a western extremity of the hill; but instead of the river, of which I could see no trace, I beheld the sun setting over numerous lakes; the nearest, two miles and a half to the northward, being apparently six miles in circumference. It seemed to be nearly circular, and a group of low grassy hills formed a concentric curve around the eastern margin, and from the total absence of any reeds, trees, or smoke of natives, it was too obvious that the water was salt. From the spot where I then stood, I counted twelve such lakes, most of them appearing to have a crescent-shaped mound or bank on the eastern side. This certainly was a remarkable portion of the earth's surface, and rather resembled that of the moon as seen through a telescope. The eastern and principal summit of the hill was at some distance; and I returned to the camp, in hopes of being able to discover from that point, in the morning, some indication of the further course of the Wimmera.

July 23.—Having ascended the highest summit, I counted from that height, twenty-seven circular lakes, two of the largest being about seven miles to the north-east, the direction in which I expected to see the river. Beyond these, however, I observed an extensive woody valley, whence much smoke arose, marking, to all appearance, the course of the Wimmera, which must have taken a turn in that direction, not far below the junction of the last creek crossed by the party. Beyond that supposed bed of the Wimmera, the country appeared to be undulated, open, and grassy; and it was probably covered with lakes similar to those on this side, for I had observed from Mount Zero, patches of water in that direction. From this summit, I had a good view of the Grampians of the South, and discovering that a lofty range extended from them southward, I named it the Victoria range, having also recognised and intersected Mount William, distant 53½ miles. I could see no high land to the westward, and the hill on which I stood seemed to divide the singular lacustrine country, from that where the character of the surface was fluviatile. Mount Arapiles is a feature which may always be easily recognised, both by its isolated position, and by its small companion the Mitre Rock, situated mid-way between it and the lake to the northward, which I named Mitre Lake after the little hill, its

neighbour. Like the mountains in the east, Mount Arapiles consists of sandstone passing into quartz, the whole apparently
an altered sandstone, the structure being in one part almost
destroyed; in others perfectly distinct, and containing pebbles
of quartz. At the western extremity, this rock occurs in
columns, resembling, at a distance, those of basalt. On the
steep slopes grew pines, casuarinae, and a variety of shrubs,
among which we found a fine new species of Baeckea, forming
a handsome evergreen bush, the ends of whose graceful
branches were closely covered with small white delicate flowers.
This mass occupies about two square miles, its highest summit
being elevated above Mitre Lake 726 feet. I ascended this hill
on the anniversary of the battle of Salamanca, and hence the
name.

July 24.—While Mr. Stapylton rode northward in search of the
Wimmera, I proceeded to examine and survey some of these
remarkable lakes. On the margin of one of them, bearing 55½° W.
of N. from our camp, a green hill of rather singular shape rose to
a considerable height, above the surrounding country. I found
the water in the lake beside it, shallow and quite salt. The basin
was nearly circular, though partially filled with firm level earth,
which was water-worn at the brink, its surface being about three
feet higher than the water. This was surrounded by a narrow
beach of soft white mud or clay, in which we found no change,
on digging to the depth of several feet. The green hill was
the highest of several semicircular ridges. There was a remarkable analogy in the form and position of all these hills; the
form being usually that of a curve, concentric with the lake, and
the position invariably on the eastern or north eastern shores, a
peculiarity I had previously observed, not only in the lakes near
the banks of the Murray, but also in others on the Murrumbidgee
and Lachlan, where the ridge consisted of red sand. The country
on the western shore of these lakes is, on the contrary, low and
wooded like the surrounding country. In such hills concretions
of indurated marl frequently occur, but the earth they consist of
is sometimes light coloured, in other cases very dark, like the soil
from trap-rock, and the ridges beside the lakes on the Murrumbidgee, consisted of red sand. The water of Mitre lake was also
salt, but there were numbers of ducks and black swans upon it.
The western shore was low, and the soil where it had been thrown
up, in the roots of fallen trees, was nearly as white as chalk. A
gray rather fine quartzose sand occurred in some places; and
along the water's edge a very minute shell had been cast up in

considerable quantities by the waves. The hills to the eastward of this lake were arranged in a crescent around the basin, but this being composed of a number of hills almost separate from each other, had a less regular or uncommon appearance, although they were, apparently, the remains of a curve equally as symmetrical as the others. The basin of this lake was very extensive, but partly filled, on the side next the low hills, by a level tract of dry land, covered with a brown bush (Salicornia arbuscula of Brown); and the concentric curves in which it grew, as if closing on the lake, seemed to record its progressive diminution. The breadth of this healthy-looking flat, between the water and the crescent of low hills, was nearly half a mile. A small rill of fresh water oozed into the lake from the sides of Mount Arapiles. The bed of this watercourse was soft and boggy near the lake, so that I could cross only by going up its channel much nearer to the hill, and at a point where some rocks protruded and prevented our horses from sinking.

Mr. Stapylton, in his search for the Wimmera, rode about six miles to the northward without reaching the river, although he saw the valley, through which he thought it flowed ; and where the river seemed likely to resume a course to the southward of west. Upon the whole, I think that the estuary of the Wimmera will most probably be found either between Cape Bernouilli and Cape Jaffa, or at some of the sandy inlets laid down by Captain Flinders to the northward of the first of these capes. The country which Mr. Stapylton crossed, assumed the barren character of the lower parts of the Murray. He actually passed through a low scrub of the eucalyptus dumosa ; but I have no doubt that the country on the immediate banks of the Wimmera continues good, whatever its course may be, even to the sea-coast. At all events, I here abandoned the pursuit of that river, and determined to turn towards the south-west, that we might ascertain what streams fell in that direction, from the Grampians ; and also the nature of the country between these mountains and the shores of the Southern Ocean.

July 25.—Proceeding accordingly about south-west, we crossed at less than a mile from our camp, the dry bed of a circular lake. The ground on the eastern shore was full of wombat holes, which had been made in a stratum of compact tuff, about a foot in thickness. The tuff was irregularly cavernous; and it was loose, calcareous or friable in the lower part, where the wombats had made their burrows. On the opposite margin of this dry lake, the

surface was covered with concretions of indurated marl; and the
burrows of the wombat were even more numerous there than in
the other bank; the stratum of compact tuff occurring also, and
being three feet in thickness. At 2½ miles, we came upon the
shores of Red lake, which I so named from the colour of a weed
growing upon its margin. The lake was nearly a mile in length
and half a mile broad; the water was so slightly brackish, that
reeds grew upon the borders, which were frequented by many
swans and ducks. A very symmetrical bank overlooked the
eastern shore, the ground on the westward being low and wooded,
with the ordinary trees of the country. We next crossed a flat of
dry white sand, on which banksia grew thickly; and then we
reached some low white sand-hills, on which were stunted iron-
bark trees (eucalypti). In the higher part of those hills, we crossed
a small dry hollow or lake which had also its bank on the eastern
side. At the end of 5½ miles, we passed two small lakes of fresh
water, about half a mile to the right, and soon after, another
about the same distance to the left. On completing seven miles,
we crossed a low ridge of white sand, on which grew stunted trees
of stringy-bark, and black butted gum-trees (both belonging to
the genus eucalyptus). Beyond this we crossed a country, in
which wet, reedy swamps of fresh water, white sand-hills, and
fine flats of good forest-land, occurred alternately. Towards the
end of our day's journey, the barren sand-hills seemed to prevail,
but at length we descended from them rather suddenly to a
smooth firm plain, clothed with the finest grass, and, on the edge
of this, we pitched our tents for the night.

July 26.—We proceeded through a thick fog, and found the
plain studded with clumps of casuarinae. About a mile from the
camp, we came upon an extensive swamp or lake, full of grass
and rushes. Turning this, by the left, we crossed some more good
country, and then reached the banks of an extensive lagoon, also
full of green rushes and water. The western bank was high, and
consisted of rich grassy land, very open; a small stream of water
fell into the lake on the north-west side, and another on the
south-east. It was surrounded by lofty gum-trees, and had a
wood on the south and east. We met with sand-hills and stunted
timber beyond. They enclosed a long grassy flat covered with
water, stretching away to the south-east. We next entered on a
fine flat of forest-land, bounded by a low ridge, with callitris
pyramidalis, or pine trees. From this, I perceived a circular lake a
little to our right, and on riding to it, I found the water salt and
of a very white colour. No trees grew on the margin, and the

surrounding scene was so dreary, that it resembled a mountain-tarn. Two solitary ducks were upon it, apparently of a species new to us, but this I could not ascertain, having had only my rifle with me, and the cap missing fire, I lost even that chance of killing them. The bed of the lake also consisted of a very white marl. A high semi-circular bank swept round the eastern shore; that opposite, or towards the west, being low and swampy. On that side, I saw two natives at a distance, making the best of their way to the southward. We had this day noticed some of their huts, which were of a very different construction from those of the aborigines, in general, being large, circular, and made of straight rods meeting at an upright pole in the centre; the outside had been first covered with bark and grass, and then entirely coated over with clay. The fire appeared to have been made nearly in the centre; and a hole at the top had been left as a chimney. The place seemed to have been in use for years, as a casual habitation. In this hut, the natives had left various articles, such as jagged spears, some of them set with flints; and an article of their manufacture which we had not before seen, namely, bags of the gins, very neatly wrought, apparently made of a tough small rush. Two of these also resembled reticules, and contained balls of resin, flints for the spearheads, etc. The iron bolt of a boat was likewise found in one of these huts. The natives invariably fled at our approach; a circumstance to be regretted, perhaps, on account of the nomenclature of my map; but other-wise their flight was preferable to the noisy familiarity of the natives of the Darling, perplexing us between their brands of defiance, and treacherous invitations to dance. Indeed the two regions were as different in character as the manners of their respective inhabitants. Instead of salsolaceous deserts and mesembryanthemum, we now found a variety of every thing most interesting in a newly discovered country. Every day we passed over land, which, for natural fertility and beauty, could scarcely be surpassed; over streams of unfailing abundance and plains covered with the richest pasturage. Stately trees and majestic mountains adorned the ever-varying scenery of this region, the most southern of all Australia, and the best. Beyond the White Lake, which may be the distinguishing name of the last-mentioned, we passed over several tracts of open forest-land, separated by dry sand-hills, and at length encamped on a rich flat. The cattle were very much fatigued from the heaviness of the draught, owing to the extreme softness of the surface, especially on the more open forest-lands; and one bullock-driver

remained behind with a cart, until we could send back a team by
moonlight to his assistance.

July 27.—The cart which had fallen behind came in about
three o'clock in the morning. The natives had soon been heard
about the solitary driver, and four of them came up to him and
demanded tomahawks; but, being an old bushranger, he, on their
approach, laid out all his cartridges one by one before him on a
tarpaulin, with his pistol and carabine, ready for action; but,
fortunately, his visitors did not proceed to extremities. The
morning was very foggy, and as this weather did not admit of
my choosing a good line of route, and as the surface of the
country was so soft, that it was imperatively necessary to look
well before us, I halted. I could thus at least bring up my maps
and journals, and rest the jaded cattle after so much long-continued daily toil in travelling through the mud. I directed Mr.
Stapylton to ride in the direction of 30° W. of S. (my intended
route), and ascertain whether we were approaching any river.
The country we were in, being still lacustrine, I hoped to find
the surface more favourable for travelling upon, where it was
drained by rivers; for on that amongst the salt lakes, although the
land was very good in point of fertility, there was evidently a
deficiency of slope, and consequently much more water retained
in the soil. Still the ground presented undulations, being rarely
quite level like the plains, except indeed in the beds of swamps.
Recent experience had taught us to avoid the very level parts,
and to seek any kind of rising ground. The hills we occasionally
fell in with consisted of white sand, and at first looked like connected ridges, where we might find streams; but we ascertained
that they always parted without enclosing any channels, and left
us in the mud. The sand itself still consisted of the same rock
(decomposed), which appeared to be so generally spread over
the country then between us and the eastern shores of New
Holland. Mr. Stapylton did not return this evening, a circumstance which very much alarmed me, as he had taken only one
man with him, and was to have come back before sunset.

July 28.—Supposing that Mr. Stapylton had gone past our
camp, in returning, the afternoon having been very rainy, I this
morning sent out two parties, the one to proceed east, the other
west, in search of his track, which, if found by either, was to be
followed until he was overtaken. Mr. Stapylton returned, however, before mid-day, having ridden twenty miles in the direction
pointed out, without having seen any river. He had passed a
number of circular lakes, similar to those already described; the

seventh and most remote having appeared the largest. Just then, as he turned his horse, he perceived that the land beyond became higher, indicating a change of country. The party, which had gone eastward, heard our signal shot on Mr. Stapylton's arrival, and returned, having also seen four similar lakes; but the party sent westward did not reach the camp until some hours after the other. They had unfortunately come upon some huts of the natives, where one of them remained, and who, refusing to listen to Piper's explanations, was about to hurl his spear at Pickering, when this man, at Piper's desire, immediately fired his carabine and wounded the native in the arm. I regretted this unlucky collision exceedingly, and blamed Pickering for having been so precipitate; but his defence was, that Piper told him unless he fired, he would be instantly speared.

July 29.—We endeavoured to proceed to-day in a direction more to the eastward, than the route of Mr. Stapylton, in the hope of finding firmer ground than he had seen, by following that which was highest and sandy. But even in this way we could not accomplish five miles and a half, although the last of the carts did not arrive at the spot, where we were at length compelled to re-encamp, until long after it became dark. The wheels sank up to the axles, and the cattle, from wallowing in the mud, had become so weak as to be scarcely able to go forward when unyoked, much less to draw the laden carts. I had with difficulty found a spot of firm ground where we could encamp, but during that evening, I had reconnoitred a more favourable looking line, which I meant to try in the morning.

Soon after we commenced this day's journey, while I was watching in some anxiety the passage of a soft hollow by the carts, a man was sent back by the chaining party to inform me, that a number of natives had come before them, pointing their spears. On going forward, I found they had retired, having probably, with their usual quickness of perception, observed the messenger sent back, and guessed his errand. But their conduct, as I then explained it to the men, was quite reasonable on this occasion. One (I was told), had spoke very loud and fast, pointing west towards where the man had been fired at the day before, and then touching his shoulder, in allusion to the wound, he finally poised his spear at Blanchard, as if in just resentment.

While awaiting the slow progress of the carts through the mud, I found a most curious new genus allied to Correa, with the habit of C. speciosa, and with long tubular four-petaled, green flowers. It had been previously observed by Mr. Cunningham, who called it Sida correoides; it was, however, not a Sida, nor even a Malvaceous plant, but a new form of Australasian Rutacear, differing from Correa in having the petals each rolled round a pair of stamens, in his quadripartite conical calyx, and in there being constantly two seeds in each cell of the fruit.

July 30.—By pursuing a course towards the base of the friendly mountains, I hoped that we should at length intercept some stream, channel or valley, where we might find a drier soil, and so escape, if possible, from the region of lakes. We could but follow such a course, however, only as far as the ground permitted, and after travelling over the hardest that we could this day find for a mile and a half, I discovered a spacious lake on the left, bounded on the east by some fine-looking green hills. These separated it from a plain where I found the ground firm, and also from several smaller lakes to the right of my intended route. I accordingly proceeded along the ground between them, and I found that it bore the wheels much better than any, we had recently crossed. The lakes were, however, still precisely similar in character to those of which we had already seen so many. The water in them was rather too brackish to be fit for use, and the ridges were all still on the eastern shores. From the highest of these ridges, the pinnacled summits of the Victoria range presented an outline of the grandest character. The noble coronet of rocks was indeed a cheering object to us, after having been so long half immersed in mud. We had passed between the lakes, and were proceeding as lightly as we could across the plain, when down went the wheel of a cart, sinking to the axle, and the usual noise of flogging (cruelty which I had repeatedly forbidden), and a consequent delay of several hours, followed. In the meantime, I rode to some grassy hills on the right, and found behind them on the south-west, another extensive lake, on which I saw a great number of ducks. Its bed consisted of dark-coloured mud, and the water was also salt. The green hills before mentioned, were curiously broken and scooped out into small cavities, much resembling those on Green-hill Lake, near Mount Arapiles. The plain rose gradually towards the east, to some scrubby ground nearly as high as these hills, and in a fall beyond this scrub, I found at length, to my great delight, a small hollow sloping to the south-east, and a little water running in it. Following it down, I almost immediately perceived a ravine before me, and at a mile and a quarter from the first fall of the ground, I crossed a chain of fine ponds, in a valley where we finally encamped on a fine stream, flowing to the south-west over granite rocks. Thus suddenly were we at length relieved, from all the difficulties of travelling in mud. We had solid granite beneath us; and instead of a level horizon, the finely rounded points of ground, presented by the sides of a valley thinly wooded and thickly covered with grass. This transition from all that we sought to avoid, to all we could desire in the character of the country, was so agreeable, that I can record that evening as one of the happiest of my life. Here too the doctor reported, that no men remained on the sick-list, and thus we were in all respects prepared for going forward, and making up for so much time lost.

July 31.—We now moved merrily over hill and dale, but were soon, however, brought to a full stop by a fine river flowing, at the point where we met it, nearly south-west. The banks of this stream were thickly overhung with bushes of the mimosa, which were festooned in a very picturesque manner with the wild vine. The river was everywhere deep and full, and as no ford could be found we prepared to cross it with the boats. But such a passage required at least a day, and when I saw the boats afloat, I was tempted to consider, whether I might not explore the further course of this river in them, and give the cattle some rest. It was likely, I imagined, soon to join another, where we might meet with less obstruction. During the day every thing was got across save the empty carts and the boat-carriage, our camp being thus established on the left bank. One bullock was unfortunately drowned in attempting to swim across, having got entangled in the branches of a sunken tree; which, notwithstanding a careful search, previously made in the bottom of the stream, had not been discovered.

The river was here, on an average, 120 feet wide, and 12 feet deep. Granite protruded in some places, but in general the bold features of the valley through which this stream flowed, were beautifully smooth and swelling; they were not much wooded, but on the contrary almost clear of timber, and accessible every-where. The features were bold and round, but only so inclined, that it was just possible to ride in any direction without obstruction; a quality of which those who have been shut up among the rocky gullies of New South Wales, must know well the value. I named this river the Glenelg, after the Right Hon. the Secretary of State for the Colonies, according to the usual custom.

Aug. 1.—The first part of this day was taken up in dragging the carts and boat-carriage through the river. At one P.M. I embarked in the boats, taking in them a fortnight's provisions, and leaving Mr. Stapylton in a strong position, with nine men, the stores and the cattle. We proceeded for two miles without encountering much obstruction, but we found on going further, that the river ran in several channels, all of these being overgrown with bushes, so that it was not without great difficulty, that we could penetrate about a mile farther by the time it had become nearly quite dark. It was no easy matter, to push through the opposing branches even to reach the bank. Many similar branches had been cut during this day's navigation; Woods, Palmer, and most of the other men, having been more in the water than in the boats during the last mile. Every article having been at length got to land, we encamped on the side of a steep hill for the night, and I made up my mind to resume our land journey next day, unless I saw the river more favourable a-head. By the banks of the Glenelg, we found a stiff furze-like bush, with small purple flowers, spiny branches, and short stiff spiny leaves. It proved to be a new Daviesia allied to D. colletioides. Bossiaea cordifolia, a hairy shrub, with beautiful purple and yellow flowers, was common.

Aug. 2.—There was a noble reach, a quarter of a mile below the point to which we had brought the boats, and it was terminated by a rocky fall, which we had heard during the night. Beyond that point, the river turned southward, and this being the direction of our intended journey, I perceived that we could more conveniently and in less time pursue its course by land. The country on its banks was, as far as I could see, the finest imaginable, either for sheep and cattle or for cultivation. A little rill then murmured through each ravine,

> " Whose scattered streams from granite basins burst,
> Leap into life, and sparkling woo your thirst."

But it was in returning along a winding ridge towards the camp, that I was most struck with the beauty and substantial value of the country on the banks of this river. It seemed, that the land was everywhere alike good, alike beautiful; all parts were verdant, whether on the finely varied hills or in the equally romantic vales, which seemed to open in endless succession on both banks of the river. No time was lost this morning in raising the boats out of the water; and having proceeded myself to the camp at an early hour, and led the carts round, and the carriage to take up the boats, the whole party was once more in movement by eleven o'clock. As far as I had yet traced the course of the river, it appeared to flow towards the west-south-west, and it was thus doubtful, at that stage of our progress, whether the estuary might not be to the westward of Cape Northumberland; whereas my chief inducement in looking for a river on this side of the Grampians, was the promising situation afforded by the great bay to the eastward of that cape, for some harbour or estuary, and this being more likely, considering the position of the mountains. I had little doubt that under such circumstances, some river would be found to enter the sea there; and having left the Wimmera flowing westward, and crossed as I imagined the highest ground, that could extend from the mountain range to Cape Bernouilli, I expected to meet at length with rivers falling southward. The ultimate course of the Glenelg, could only be ascertained by following it down, and to do this by land was not easy; first, because it was joined by many small tributaries flowing through deep valleys, and from all points of the compass; and secondly, because the general horizon was so level, that no point commanding any extensive view over the country could be found. Thus, while our main object was to pursue the river, we were obliged to grope our way round the heads of ravines often very remote from it, but which were very perplexing from their similarity to the ravine in which the main stream flowed. A more bountiful distribution of the waters, for the supply of a numerous population, could not be imagined, nor a soil better adapted for cultivation. We this day crossed various small rivulets or chains of ponds, each watering a grassy vale, sheltered by fine swelling hills. The whole country consisted of open forest land, on which grew a few gum-trees (or eucalypti), with banksia, and, occasionally, a few casuarinae.

Aug. 3.—The ponds where we had encamped, were large and deep, and I endeavoured to ascertain whether the cod-perch (Gristes Peelii) inhabited these waters. Neither this fine fish, nor either of the two others found in the streams flowing towards the interior from the eastern coast range, have ever been seen in the rivers which reach the eastern shores; and I had now ascertained, that all the waters in which we had procured the fish in question belonged to the extensive basin of the Murray. We were at length on channels evidently distinct, both from those leading to the eastern coast, and those belonging to the basin of the Murray. The beds of the rivers flowing to the east coast are chiefly rocky, containing much sand but very little mud, consequently no reeds grow on their banks, nor is the freshwater muscle found in them, as in rivers on the interior side, which in general flow over a muddy bed, and are not unfrequently distinguished by reedy banks. Judging therefore from the nature of the soil of this southern region, the fishes peculiar to the Murray might be looked for in the rivers of the south, rather than those fishes known in the rivers falling eastward.   It was important to ascertain at least, what point of the coast separated the rivers containing different kinds of fish.   In these ponds we caught only some very small fry, and the question could not be satisfactorily determined, although the natives declared that none of them were the spawn of cod-perch.

It was no easy matter now to ascertain in what direction the waters of the valley ran, but by the tendency of the hollows on each side, they appeared to decline, in general, to the left or northward. In proceeding on our route, the heads of other similar ravines rendered our course very intricate: to have been shut in between any such ravine and the river must have been rather embarrassing, and seemed then almost inevitable. We had the good fortune however to avoid this; and at length, keeping along dry ground, a beautiful scene appeared on the left, in an open valley about two miles in width, where the hills sloped gradually to the confluence of two streams, brimful of water, which shone through some highly ornamental wood.   Both streams came from vallies of a similar character; and beyond them I saw hills of the finest forms, all clothed with grass to their summits, and many entirely clear of timber. A bronze-winged pigeon flew up just as I discovered the stream, and as this bird had not been before seen by us on that side of the mountains, I named the waters "Pigeon" ponds. We descended to that part of the valley which lay in our proposed course, and found that some of these ponds rather deserved to be styled lakes. The soil was everywhere black and rich.

Aug. 4.—Proceeding over ground of a similar character, we crossed several fine streams, some flowing in shallow channels over rocks, others in deep ravines. The ground on the higher parts was, however, still so soft as to yield to the wheels, and very much impeded the progress of the party, especially at one place, where an extensive lake, full of reeds or rushes, appeared to the right. The drays sunk to the axles, the whole of the soil in our way having become so liquid, that it rolled in waves around the struggling bullocks. The passage of some of the streams could not be accomplished, until we had filled up the bed with large logs, covered them with boughs, and strewed over the whole, the earth cut away from the steep banks. Under such circumstances, I considered six miles a good day's journey, and, indeed, too much for the cattle. I halted for the night, with a small advanced party only, on a fine little stream running over a rocky bed; while the main body was compelled to remain with the carts several miles behind, having broken, in the efforts made to extricate the carts and boat-carriage, many of the chains, and also a shaft. The small river I had reached, ran in a bed of little width, but was withal so deep, that it seemed scarcely passable without a bridge. At the junction, however, of a similar one, some rocks, favourably situated, enabled us to effect a passage by bedding logs between them, and covering the whole with branches and earth, leaving room for the water to pass between.

Aug. 5.—A halt was this day unavoidable, but the necessity was the less to be regretted, as the weather was very unfavourable. Indeed, we had scarcely seen one fine day for some weeks. Mr. Stapylton set out to trace the rivulet downwards, and returned in the evening, after having reached its junction with the Glenelg, at the distance of nine miles in a north-west direction. The course of the river, thus determined to that junction, appeared to be more to the westward than I had previously expected, and I begun again to think its estuary might still be to the westward of Cape Northumberland, and this prospect induced me to alter our course. The carts having come up about one P.M., the black-smith was set to work, and wrought throughout the night to repair all the claw-chains. While other men were employed at the log-bridge, some natives were heard coming along the most southern of the two streams; whereupon Piper went towards them as usual, and found they were females, with children; but from the moment they discovered us, until they were fairly out of hearing, their shrieks were so loud and incessant, that it seemed, for once, our presence in that country had been unknown to the surrounding natives, a proof perhaps of the smallness of their numbers. In the evening, other natives (men), were heard approaching along the creek, and we at first supposed they had come to that place, as their rendezvous, to meet the gins and their families, whom we had unwillingly scared; but Mr. Stapylton, during his ride home along one side of the ravine, had observed four natives very intent on following the outward track of his horses' hoofs on the other; and these were doubtless the same men guided by his tracks to our camp. They could not be brought to a parley, however, although Piper and Burnett at first invited them towards the camp, and when they set off, pursued them across the opposite ridge. On the bank of this little stream, I found a charming species of Tetratheca, with large rich purple flowers, and slender stems growing in close tufts about a foot high. It was

perhaps the most beautiful plant we met with during the ex
pedition.

Aug. 6.—The passage of the rivulet, which I named the Chet-
wynd, after Stapylton, who had explored it at considerable risk,
was effected with ease by the temporary bridge, and we proceeded,
soon crossing by similar means two other running streams, probably tributaries to this. When we had travelled four miles we
came to a swamp, where a considerable current of water was flowing into it through some ponds; the margin of this running water
being broad, flat, and grassy, and having also lofty gum-trees (white
bark eucalypti) growing on it. Unfortunately, it was so soft and
rotten, as the men described it, that all the wheels sunk to the
axles, and although in such cases it was usual to apply the combined force of several teams to draw each vehicle through in turn,
we found that the cattle could have no firm footing to enable
them to pull. It was night before we could, with the strength of
all the teams united by long chains and yoked to each vehicle
successively, bring the whole through, the broad wheels of each
cart actually ploughing to the depth of the axle in soft earth; the
labour of the cattle may therefore be imagined. We encamped on
a small barren plain much resembling a heath, and just beyond
the swamp which had proved so formidable an impediment.

Aug. 7.—Our progress this day was still less than that made
during the preceding one, for it did not much exceed a mile. To
that distance we had proceeded tolerably well, having crossed two
small running brooks, and all appeared favourable before us.
But a broad piece of rising ground, which being sandy with
banksia and casuarinae trees on it, I had considered firm, proved
so very soft, that even my own horse went down with me and
wallowed in the mud. There was no way of avoiding this spot, at
least without delay, and I ordered the men immediately to
encamp; being determined to go forward with a party on horse
back, and ascertain the position of some point where the ground
was more favourable, and then to adopt such a mode of extricat
ing the carts and proceeding thither, as circumstances permitted.
I took with me provisions for three days, that I might explore the
country, if necessary, to the coast. I had not proceeded above five
miles southward, when I perceived before me a ridge in bluey
distance, rather an unusual object in that close country. We soon
after emerged from the wood, and found that we were on a kind
of table-land, and approaching a deep ravine coming from our
right, and terminating on a very fine looking open country below,
watered by a winding river. We descended by a bold feature to the

bottom of the ravine, and found there a foaming little river hurrying downwards over rocks. After fording this stream, we ascended a very steep but grassy mountain-side, and on reaching a brow of high land, what a noble prospect appeared! a river winding amongst meadows, that were fully a mile broad, and green as an emerald. Above them rose swelling hills of fantastic shapes, but all smooth and thickly covered with rich verdure. Behind these were higher hills, all having grass on their sides and trees on their summits, and extending east and west, throughout the landscape, as far as I could see. I hastened to ascertain the course of the river, by riding about two miles along an entirely open grassy ridge, and then found again the Glenelg, flowing eastward, towards an apparently much lower country. All our difficulties seemed thus already at an end, for we had here good firm ground clear of timber, on which we could gallop once more. The river was making for the most promising bay on the coast (for I saw that it turned southward some miles below the hill on which I stood,) through a country far surpassing in beauty and richness any part hitherto discovered. I hastened back to my men in the mud, and arrived before sunset with the good news, having found most of the intervening country fit for travelling upon. Thus the muddy hill which had before seemed insurmountable, led to the immediate discovery of the true course of the river, and prevented me from continuing my route into the great angle of its course over unfavourable ground, instead of thus reaching it so much sooner by a much less deviation from the course I wished to pursue. I now hoped to extricate the carts in the morning, and henceforward to accomplish journeys of considerable length.

Aug. 8.—It was in vain that I reconnoitered the environs of the hill of mud for some portion of surface harder than the rest; and we could only extricate ourselves by floundering through it. Patches of clay occurred, but they led only to places, where the surface under the pressure of the cattle was immediately converted into white and liquid mud. It was necessary to take the loads from the carts, and carry them by hand half a mile; and then to remove the empty vehicles by the same means. After all this had been accomplished, the boat-carriage, (a four-wheeled waggon,) still remained immoveably fixed up to the axle-tree in mud, in a situation where the block and tackle used in hoisting out the boats could not be applied. Much time was lost in our attempts to draw it through, by joining all the chains we possessed, and applying the united strength of all the bullocks; but even this was at length accomplished after the sun had set;

THE RIVER DARLING, 1838.
From a drawing by Major T. L. Mitchell.

the wheels, four inches broad, actually cutting through to the full depth of the spokes. On the eastern side of the hill the ground descended into a ravine, where it was grassy and firm enough; and it was a great relief to us all to feel thus at liberty, even by sunset, to start next morning towards the beautiful country, which we now knew lay before us.

Aug. 9.—Once more in a state of forward movement, we crossed green hills and running brooks, until, when we had travelled nearly six miles from Muddy Camp, and had crossed six fine streams or burns, we met with a more formidable impediment in the seventh. The sides of this ravine were so uncommonly steep, that our new difficulty was how to move the vehicles down to the bank of the stream. In one place, where a narrow point of ground projected across, a passage seemed just possible; and after we had made it better with spades, we attempted to take a light cart over. The acclivity was still, however, rather too much, and over went the cart, carrying the shaft bullock with it, and depositing all my instruments, etc. under it in the bed of the stream. With travellers on roads, this might have been thought a serious accident, but in our case, we were prepared for joltings, and nothing was in the least degree injured; neither was the animal hurt, and we ascertained by the experiment, dangerous though it was, that still more was necessary to be done for the passage of the heavy carts and boats, which were still some way behind; and I encamped on the bank beyond, that the men might set about this work. No time was lost in filling up the hollow with all the dead trees that lay about, and what others we could cut for the purpose; and thus, before sunset, the three carts and one waggon were got across. The rocks in the bed of this stream, consisted of grey gneiss, and on the hills beyond it, I found nodules of highly ferruginous sandstone.

Aug. 10.—By means of a block and tackle attached to a large tree, the remaining carts and the boat-carriage were safely lowered to the bed of the stream. To draw them up the opposite bank was practicable only by uniting the strength of several teams, yet this too was effected successfully, and the whole party were enabled to go forward in the morning. At a mile and a half from the camp, a scene was displayed to our view, which gladdened every heart. An open grassy country, extending as far as we could see—hills round and smooth as a carpet—meadows broad, and either green as an emerald, or of a rich golden colour, from the abundance, as we soon afterwards found, of a little ranunculus-like flower. Down into that delightful vale, our vehicles trundled

I. D.   s over a gentle slope, the earth being covered with a thick matted turf, apparently superior to anything of the kind, previously seen. That extensive valley was enlivened by a winding stream, the waters of which glittered through trees fringing each bank. As we went on our way rejoicing, I perceived at length two figures at a distance, who at first either did not see, or did not mind us. They proved to be a gin with a little boy, and as soon as the female saw us, she began to run. I presently overtook her, and with a few words I knew, prevailed on her to stop, until the two gins of our party could come up; for I had long been at a loss for the names of localities. This woman was not so much alarmed as might have been expected; and I was glad to find that she and the gins perfectly understood each other. The difference in the costume on the banks of the Wando, immediately attracted the notice of the females from the Lachlan. The bag usually carried by gins, was neatly wove in basket-work, and composed of a wiry kind of rush. She of Wando carried this bag fastened to her back, having under it two circular mats of the same material, and beneath all, a kangaroo cloak, so that her back at least was sufficiently clothed, although she wore no dress in front. The boy was supported between the mats and the cloak; and his pleased and youthful face, he being a very fine specimen of the native race, presented a striking contrast to the miserable looks of his whining mother. In the large bag, she carried some pieces of fire-wood, and a few roots, apparently of Tao, which she had just been digging from the earth. Such was the only visible inhabitant of this splendid valley, resembling a nobleman's park on a gigantic scale. She stated that the main river was called " Temiangandgeen," a name unfortunately too long to be introduced into maps. We also obtained the gratifying intelligence, that the whole country to the eastward was similar to these delightful vales; and that, in the same directon, as Piper translated her statement, " there was no more sticking in mud." A favourable change in the weather accompanied our fortunate transition, from the land of watery soil and dark woody ravines, to an open country. The day was beautiful; and the balmy air was sweetened with a perfume resembling hay, which arose from the thick and matted herbs and grass. Proceeding along the valley, the stream on our left vanished at an isolated, rocky hill; but, on closer examination, I found the apparent barrier cleft in two, and that the water passed through, roaring over rocks. This was rather a singular feature in an open valley, where the ground on each side of it, was almost as low as the rocky bed of the stream itself. The hill was composed of granular felspar, in a state of decomposition; the surrounding country consisting chiefly of very fine grained sandstone. It is not so easy to suppose that the river could ever have watered the valley in its present state, and forced its way since, through that isolated hill of hard rock; as to believe that the rock, now isolated, originally contained a chasm, and afforded once the lowest channel for the water, before the valley, now so open, had been scooped out on each side, by gradual decomposition. Another rivulet approached this hill, flowing under its eastern side, and joining the Wando just below. According to my plan of following down the main river, it was necessary to cross both these tributaries. In the open part of the valley, the channels of these streams were deep, and the banks soft; but at the base of the hill of Kinganyu (for such was its name,) we found rock enough, and having effected a passage there of both streams that afternoon, we encamped, after travelling about three miles further, on the banks of the Glenelg once more. Our route lay straight across an open grassy valley, at the foot of swelling hills of the same description. Each of these vallies presented peculiar and very romantic features, but I could not decide which looked most beautiful. All contained excellent soil and grass, surpassing in quality any I had seen in the present colony of New South Wales. The chase of the emu and kangaroo, which were both numerous, afforded us excellent sport on these fine downs. When about to cross the Wando, I took my leave of the native woman before mentioned, that she might not have the trouble of fording the river, and I presented her with a tomahawk, of which our females explained to her the use—although she seemed still at a loss to conceive the meaning of a present. The use of the little hatchet would be well enough known, however, to her tribe, so leaving her to return to it, and assuring her at the same time of our friendly disposition towards the natives, we proceeded.

The left bank of the principal stream was very bold, where we reached it on this occasion, but still open, and covered with rich turf. The right bank was woody, and this was generally its character at the other points where we had seen the Glenelg. It was flowing with considerable rapidity, amongst the same kind of bushes we had met with above, but they did not appear so likely here to obstruct the passage of boats.

On the plains, we found a singular acacia, the leaves being covered with a clammy exudation resembling honey-dew. It differed from A. graveolens in its much more rigid habit, shorter and broader leaves, and much shorter peduncles.

Aug. 11.   Passing along the bank of the river, under the steep grassy hills, which consisted of very fine-grained, calcareous sandstone, we began, two miles on, to ascend these heights; as well to avoid a place where they closed precipitously on the Glenelg, as to gain a point, from which I hoped to command an extensive view of its further course, and so cut off some of the windings. From that point, or rather on riding through the woods to some distance beyond it, I perceived that the river was joined by another, coming from the south-east, through an open country of the finest character. Below their junction, the principal river disappeared on passing through a woody range, and turned towards the south-west. Nothing could be seen beyond that crest, which seemed a very predominant feature, bounding the fine valley of the Wannon on the south. By turning round the eastern brow of the high ground on which we then were, we gained a long ridge of smooth grassy land, leading, by an easy descent, from this height to the junction of the rivers. This high ground was thickly wooded with stringy-bark trees, of large dimensions, and a few other eucalypti, together with banksia and casuarinae. The soil there was soft and sandy, and the substratum contained masses of iron-stone. The shrubs upon the whole reminded me of those in the wooded parts of the sand hills on the shores of Port Jackson. Smoke arose from the various parts of the distant country before us; and we perceived one native running at prodigious speed across the plain below. On reaching the banks of the Wannon, we found it a deep flowing stream, about half as large as the river itself. We succeeded in finding a ford, and crossed, after cutting away some bushes and levelling the banks. Beyond the Wannon, we travelled 2¾ miles over a portion of very fine country, and encamped in a little vale in the bosom of a woody range, the western side of which overhung the river at the distance of two miles.

Aug. 12.—A fine clear morning gave full effect to the beauty of the country which I now saw to the eastward, from a hill near our camp. The summit of the Victoria range crowned the distant landscape; and the whole of the intervening territory appeared to consist of green hills, partially wooded. We crossed a mountain-stream by filling up its bed with logs, and as we ascended the slopes beyond, we found the country grassy, until we reached the high and wooded crest. Lofty stringy-bark trees and other timber grew there on a white sandy soil; but we found among the bushes, abundance of the anthistiria or kangaroo grass.

After travelling some miles beyond this crest, we at length

found the ground sloping to the southward; and some swampy hollows with reeds in them, obliged us to turn to the right, or south-west, as the water in these depressed parts falling eastward, or to the left, shewed that we were not so very near the river, on the right, which I was endeavouring to follow. We were delayed in several of these hollows by the sinking of the carts and boat-carriage. We next traversed an extensive moor or heath, on which the ground was firm, and a little way beyond it, some rising ground bounded our view. On ascending this highest feature which I named the Rifle range, I found it commanded an extensive view over a low and woody country. One peaked hill alone appeared on the otherwise level horizon, and this bore 68° W. of S. I supposed this to be Mount Gambier, near Cape Northumberland, which, according to my survey, ought to have appeared in that direction at a distance of forty-five miles. I expected to find the river on reaching the lower country beyond this range; but, instead of the Glenelg and the rich country on its banks, we entered on extensive moors of the most sterile description. They were, however, firm enough for travelling upon, the surface being very level, and the soil a whitish sand. These open wastes were interrupted, in some parts, by clumps of stringy-bark forest, which entirely concealed from view the extent of this kind of country. Swamps full of water, and containing reeds of a dark yellow colour, at length became numerous; and, although I succeeded in pursuing a course clear of these obstacles, we were obliged to encamp at twilight, without having any immediate prospect of a better country before us. There was, however, abundance of grass in these wet swamps, and our carts passed over one, quite covered with water, without sinking. Our camp was marked out on a low hill of white sand, on which grew mahogany and stringy-bark trees of large dimensions. The range from which we had descended, now appeared continuous as far as we could see eastward. Much smoke arose from this lower country when we entered upon it, and after sunset, the incessant calls of a native were heard near our camp, as if he had lost some comrade. I sent up a rocket, that he might be convinced, we had not arrived by stealth, as the tribes do, when they insidiously make war on each other, but he only reiterated his calls the more.

Aug. 13.—At day-break, the cries of the native were renewed. I then made Piper cooy to him, whereupon he became silent, and I heard him no more, the natives of that country being, as Piper expressed it, " still very wild." This morning we were on the march as soon as the sun rose, all being very anxious to see the river again, and a better country. At two miles, we passed along a sandy ridge between two extensive swamps; but at a mile and a half farther, I found at length a small hollow and water running in it, a feature which convinced me at once, that the river could not be very distant. In the bank there was a thin stratum of shelly limestone, bearing a resemblance to some of the oolitic limestones of England; and in the bed were irregular concretions of iron-stone, containing grains of quartz, some of the concretions having externally a glazed appearance, arising from a thin coating of compact brown hœmatite. *Casuarinae* and *banksia* growing on grassy slopes, were the next marks of a different country from that of the swamps, and at less than a mile from this point, we came upon the river. Its banks had a different character from that which they presented above, but they were still fine. The river now flowed in a narrow valley, the bed being about 70 feet below the common level of the swampy flats. At sharp bends, the banks consisted of cliffs of a soft limestone, composed, in part, of comminuted fragments of corallines, the interstices being rarely filled up; the rock contained also a few specimens of Foraminifera, most probably of recent species. In the narrow valley all was flourishing and green, attesting the rich luxuriance of the alluvial soil. The *mimosa* trees predominated, but still the bushes of leptospermum darkened the stream, which was deep, rapid, and muddy, its breadth being about 40 yards, and the bed consisting of a friable or soft calcareous sandstone. In accompanying it in its course downward, we met with less difficulty than I had expected, but I perceived that the barren swampy land, or, more frequently, the stringy-bark forests, approached the higher banks on both sides the river. The few ravines falling in our way, were only the drains from swamps close at hand, and they were easily crossed by the party, at the fall of the ground, where we found rocky strata. After tracing the river more than four miles, we encamped on an elevated point overlooking a flat of good grass, so necessary for the cattle.

Aug. 14.—Some of the bullocks were missing, and we were compelled to wait an hour or two, while parties went in search of them; one party being guided by Piper, the other by the two Tommies. I availed myself of the leisure afforded by this delay, to measure the breadth, depth, and velocity of the river, which were respectively as follows:—

Average breadth 35 yards.
Mean depth 17 feet.

Velocity of the current 1,863 yards per hour; the general course, as far as we had traced this portion being nearly S.E.

When most of the cattle had been brought in, we proceeded, and in endeavouring to keep along the highest ground between the swamps, I unavoidably left the river at some distance on our right, a circumstance I considered of less consequence, as the ground appeared to be falling on my left towards some tributary; and at four miles, we came upon a small river flowing rapidly, in a valley nearly as deep and wide as the main stream. The country on its immediate bank looked better than that last found on the main stream. Limestone rock appeared in the bank opposite, and at the foot of some cliffs we found fossil oyster-shells. Mr. Stapylton traced this stream to its junction with the river, about two miles lower down.

Aug. 15.—Two bullocks were still missing, and I had recourse to compulsory measures with Piper and the man who lost them, in order to find them again; I declared that unless they were found, Piper should have no provisions for a week; and I condemned the man who lost them to be kept every second night on watch, during the remainder of the journey. The passage of the little river (which I named the Stokes, in memory of a brother officer, who fell at Bajadoz,) was not to be easily accomplished, owing to the depth and softness of the alluvial soil, through which it flowed. One place passable on horseback was found after long search, by Mr. Stapylton and myself. Out of the bed of the stream at that part, we drew some dead trees, and after two hours of great exertion, the passage of the boat-carriage and carts was effected, the latter sinking deeper in the water than they ever had done in any river which we had previously forded. We found the country beyond very intricate, being so intersected with swamps, draining off in all directions, and so divided by stringy-bark forests, that it was next to impossible to avoid the soft swampy ground, or reach the river bank again. We headed one deep ravine falling towards it, and had indeed travelled in the desired direction, about four miles further on dry ground, but only by winding about as the swamps permitted, when, at length, the ground appeared to slope towards the river, being also covered with the fine grass and the kind of trees which usually grew near it. But this ground, notwithstanding its firm appearance, proved to be as soft, as that of Mount Mud; and it spread at length around us on all sides, except that from which we had approached it by so circuitous a route. We had no alternative but to cross this bad ground, and after finding out, by careful examination, the narrowest part, we prepared to pass to the nearest firm ground beyond, an undertaking infinitely more difficult and laborious to us, than the passage of the broadest river. One of the carts was with much labour taken across, and being anxious to know the actual situation of the river, I rode southward into the wood, taking with me the chain or measuring men, and leaving the rest of the people at work in the mud. I found much of the ground equally soft as I proceeded, but all consisted of excellent open forest-land, covered with good grass. I found there a woolly Correa, profusely covered with pink, bell shaped blossoms, and small round rufous leaves; and the beautiful Kennedya prostrata was climbing among the bushes, and rendering them brilliant with its rich crimson flowers. At length I approached a ravine on the left, which I at first took for that of the river; but I soon perceived through the trees on my right, a still greater opening, and there I at last found the valley of the Glenelg. In the ravine to the left ran another small stream, rather larger than that crossed yesterday. We reached the bank of this at 2¾ miles from the place where we left the party, and at about half a mile above its junction with the main stream. The high ground between the two streams terminated in a round, grassy promontory, overlooking one of the finest flats imaginable. I determined to endeavour once more, to explore the river's course with the boats; provided we should succeed in transporting them over the mud to this spot; and I returned with this intention to the muddy scene, where I had left the men. It was quite dark before I found it again, and then they had succeeded in getting through only the three light carts. I did not despair of accomplishing the passage, at least in the course of time; but I was indeed impatient for daylight, that I might carefully examine with that view, all parts of the country between our camp and the place where I intended to launch the boats into the Glenelg again.

Aug. 15.—This morning it rained heavily, and there was a balmy and refreshing mildness in the air, probably owing to the vicinity of the sea. It occurred to me, that as the ground appeared to slope towards the south-east, we might reach some hollow on that side leading to the little river, we discovered yesterday; and that such a hollow would afford the best chance of escape from the soft flats, which now impeded us, since the drainage they afforded to the immediate banks, was likely to leave them at least firm enough to be travelled upon. On this principle alone, I understood why the ground, on the banks of the stream seen yesterday, was so firm; and I therefore hoped that the head of any ravine, found near our camp, would lead by a dry though perhaps circuitous route, first to the tributary, and next, by its bank, to the point already mentioned, where it joined the Glenelg. I accordingly instructed Mr. Stapylton to examine the ground in the direction proposed, while I superintended the exertions of the party to drag the boat-carriage through the mud. We finally succeeded in this last effort, and just as I stood watching with joy the ascent of the carriage to the firm ground beyond, Mr. Stapylton came to me with the intelligence, that he had found the head of a ravine, and firm ground on its bank, in the direction where he had been. One bad place alone intervened between our present position and the firm ground at the head of the ravine, but this, Mr. Stapylton said, was very bad indeed. By 10 A.M. everything was got across the first swamp, the loads of all the carts having been carried by the men. To the new difficulty mentioned by Mr. Stapylton, I therefore led them next, and we soon accomplished the passage of the light carts; after which I proceeded, leaving to Mr. Stapylton the management of the rest, having first brought the boat-carriage within reach of the firm ground opposite, by means of blocks and tackle attached to trees, and drawn by five bullocks. On going forward with the carts, I was guided altogether by the course of the ravine or gully, keeping along the fall of the ground, and so avoiding the softer soil above. Thus we proceeded successfully, for although another ravine came in our way, I managed to travel round its head, near which I found a place where we crossed the small water-course it contained, by filling up the chasm with logs. On passing this, we entered the stringy-bark forest, which I had traversed on the day previous; and I at length recognised through the trees, the hill from which I had seen the junction of the streams. A tremendous hail-storm met us in the face, just as we descended to encamp in the valley, near the bank of the river, but this troubled us but little, while we were up to the waist in the thickest crop of grass, growing on the richest black soil, I had ever seen. Mr. Staplyton and Burnett came up in the evening with the intelligence, that the whole party had effected a safe passage across the swampy ground; but that the wheels of the boat-carriage and some of the carts had sunk deep in the earth, where I had previously crossed on horseback followed by the light carts without leaving any impression, and that consequently they had made but little progress beyond the swamp.

Aug. 17.—I sent Burnett back with some spare bullocks to assist the people in bringing on the carts and the boat-carriage, a man having been despatched from them early to inform me, that the carriage had again stuck fast. Piper drew my attention to the sound of a distant waterfall, which, he said, he had heard all night, and wished now to go down the river to look at. I directed him to do so, and to examine the river also still further if he could, that he might bring back information as to how the boats might get down the stream. On his return in the afternoon, he stated, that the river was joined just below, by several large streams from the left, and by one still larger from the right, which falling on rocks, made the noise he had heard, during the night: also, that on climbing a high tree he had seen the river very large "like the Murray," adding that it was excellent for boats. All this news only made me the more impatient to embark in them, while they were still afar on the muddy hills. The whole day passed without any tidings of their approach, and another night had closed over us, before I heard the distant calls of the bullock-drivers; but I had the satisfaction soon after of seeing the whole party and equipment again united on the banks of this promising stream. The barometer was rising, the spring was advancing, and the approaching warmth might be expected to harden the ground. The cattle would be refreshed by a week's rest in the midst of the rich pasture around us, while our labours to all appearance were on the eve of being crowned by the discovery of some harbour, which might serve as a port to one of the finest regions upon earth. At all events, if we could no longer travel on land, we had at length arrived with two boats within reach of the sea, and this alone was a pleasing reflection after the delays we had lately experienced.

Aug. 18.—An uncommonly fine morning succeeded a clear frosty night. The boats were hoisted out to be launched once more on the bosom of the newly discovered Glenelg; and they were loaded with what the party going with them might require for ten days. I left with Mr. Stapylton instructions, that the men under his charge should move up to, and occupy the round point of the hill, a position which I named Fort O'Hare, in memory of a truly brave soldier, my commanding officer, who fell at Badajoz in leading the forlorn hope of the Light Division to the storm. At twelve o'clock, I embarked on the river with sixteen men, in two boats, leaving eight with Mr. Stapylton in the depot. We met with many dead trees for the first mile or two, but none of these either prevented or delayed our passage; and the river then widened into fine reaches wholly clear of timber, so that the passage further down was quite uninterrupted. The scenery on the banks was pleasing and various; at some points picturesque limestone cliffs overhung the river, and cascades flowed out of caverns hung with stalactites; at others, the shores were festooned with green dripping shrubs and creepers, or terminated in a smooth grassy bank sloping to the water's edge. But none of the banks consisted of water-worn earth; they were in general low and grassy, bounding the alluvial flats, that lay between the higher points of land. Within the first three or four miles from Fort O'Hare, two tributaries joined the main stream from the right or westward, and one from the left or eastward; one of the former ending in a noisy cascade at the junction. The river soon opened to a uniform width of sixty yards, its waters being everywhere smooth and unruffled, and the current scarcely perceptible. Ducks were always to be seen in the reaches before us, and very frequently the ornithorynchus paradoxus, an animal which had not, I believe, been hitherto seen so near the sea. After rowing about sixteen miles we landed on the left bank, near a cascade falling from under a limestone cliff, and there we encamped for the night. The sun was setting in a cloudless sky, while I eagerly ascended the highest cliffs in hopes of obtaining a sight of the coast, but nothing was visible beyond a gently undulating woody country, some swamps alone appearing in it to the westward. The land about the cliffs of limestone, was tolerably good and grassy, but towards the end of this day's pull, forests of the stringy-bark sort of eucalyptus, having in them trees of large dimensions, closed on the river. We endeavoured, but in vain, to catch fish, and whether the waters contained the cod-perch (Gristes Peelii) or not, remained a question. Our position and our prospects were now extremely interesting, and throughout the night, I was impatient for the light of the next day.

Aug. 19.—I arose at three in order to determine the latitude more exactly, by the altitude of various stars then approaching the meridian. These were Aries and Menkar; while the two feet of the Centaur, both fine circum-polar stars, were so steadily reflected in the placid stream, that I obtained by that means, the altitude of both below the pole. It was most essential to the accuracy of my survey of the river, that I should determine the latitude as frequently and exactly as possible. The sun afterwards rose in a cloudless sky, and I ascertained the breadth of the river, by means of a micrometer telescope, to be exactly 70 yards. We continued our interesting voyage, and found the river of very uniform width, and that its depth increased.

The current was slower but still perceptible, although we found

the water had ebbed six inches during the night, an indication
that it was already influenced by the tide, although it tasted
perfectly fresh. At a place where I observed the sun's meridian
altitude, I found the breadth on measurement to be 71 yards,
and the depth, on sounding, 4½, 3½, and 3 fathoms. The direction
of the course had there, however, changed. To the camp of last
night it had been remarkably straight towards south-south-east,
although full of turnings, being what may be termed "straight
serpentine," and I had accordingly expected to find the estuary
at Portland Bay, in which case it was likely to be sheltered sufficiently by Cape Nelson to form a harbour. Now, however, the
general course was nearly west, and it preserved the same general
direction without much winding, during the progress we made
throughout the day. I had therefore every reason to suppose,
that it would thus terminate in the wide bay between Cape
Northumberland and Cape Bridgewater. The scenery on the long
reaches was in many places very fine, from the picturesque
character of the limestone-rock, and the tints and outline of the
trees, shrubs, and creepers upon the banks. In some places
stalactitic-grottoes, covered with red and yellow creepers, overhung or enclosed cascades; at other points, casuarinae and
banksia were festooned with creeping vines, whose hues of warm
green or brown were relieved by the grey cliffs of more remote
reaches, as they successively opened before us. Black swans being
numerous, we shot several; and found some eggs, which we
thought a luxury, among the bulrushes at the water's edge. But
we had left, as it seemed, all the good grassy land behind us; for
the stringy-bark and a species of Xanthorhaea (grass tree), grew
to the water's edge, both where the soil looked black and rich,
and where it possessed that red colour which distinguishes the
best soil in the vicinity of limestone rock. One or two small
tributaries joined the river, the principal one coming from the
left bank, at that point or angle, where the great change takes
place in its course. When the sun was near setting, we put ashore
on this bank, and from a tree on the highest part of the country
behind it, we now once again saw Mount Gambier, bearing 57° W.
of N. Here the water was slightly brackish but still very good for
use; the saltness being most perceptible when the water was used
for tea. The river had increased considerably both in width and
depth; for here the measured breadth was 101 yards, and the mean
depth, five fathoms. It was, upon the whole, considering the
permanent fulness of its stream, the character of its banks, and
uniformity of width and depth, the finest body of fresh water I

of granular felspar, in a state of decomposition; the surrounding country consisting chiefly of very fine grained sandstone. It is not so easy to suppose that the river could ever have watered the valley in its present state, and forced its way since, through that isolated hill of hard rock; as to believe that the rock, now isolated, originally contained a chasm, and afforded once the lowest channel for the water, before the valley, now so open, had been scooped out on each side, by gradual decomposition. Another rivulet approached this hill, flowing under its eastern side, and joining the Wando just below. According to my plan of following down the main river, it was necessary to cross both these tributaries. In the open part of the valley, the channels of these streams were deep, and the banks soft; but at the base of the hill of Kinganyu (for such was its name,) we found rock enough, and having effected a passage there of both streams that afternoon, we encamped, after travelling about three miles further, on the banks of the Glenelg once more. Our route lay straight across an open grassy valley, at the foot of swelling hills of the same description. Each of these vallies presented peculiar and very romantic features, but I could not decide which looked most beautiful. All contained excellent soil and grass, surpassing in quality any I had seen in the present colony of New South Wales. The chase of the emu and kangaroo, which were both numerous, afforded us excellent sport on these fine downs. When about to cross the Wando, I took my leave of the native woman before mentioned, that she might not have the trouble of fording the river, and I presented her with a tomahawk, of which our females explained to her the use—although she seemed still at a loss to conceive the meaning of a present. The use of the little hatchet would be well enough known, however, to her tribe, so leaving her to return to it, and assuring her at the same time of our friendly disposition towards the natives, we proceeded.

The left bank of the principal stream was very bold, where we reached it on this occasion, but still open, and covered with rich turf. The right bank was woody, and this was generally its character at the other points where we had seen the Glenelg. It was flowing with considerable rapidity, amongst the same kind of bushes we had met with above, but they did not appear so likely here to obstruct the passage of boats.

On the plains, we found a singular acacia, the leaves being covered with a clammy exudation resembling honey-dew. It differed from A. graveolens in its much more rigid habit, shorter and broader leaves, and much shorter peduncles.

fine river and the two basins, was choked merely by the sand thrown up by the sea. The river was four fathoms deep, the water being nearly fresh enough for use, within sight of the shore. Unfortunately, perhaps, for navigation, there is but little tide on that coast; the greatest rise in the lower part of the river (judging by the floating weeds,) did not exceed a foot. I was too intent on the completion of my survey, to indulge much in contemplating the welcome sight of old ocean; but when a plank was picked up by the men on that desolate shore, and we found the initials, I.W.B., and the year 1832, carved on wood which had probably grown in old England, the sea really seemed like home to us. Although it was low water, a boat might easily have been got out, and it is probable that in certain states of the tide and sand, small craft might get in; but I, nevertheless, consider the mouth of this river quite unavailable as a harbour. Near the beach were holes, dug apparently by the natives, in which we found the water perfectly sweet. The hills sheltering the most eastern of the two basins, were well wooded, as were also those behind. The line of sand-hills on the beach seemed to rise into forest hills, at about five miles further eastward, and all those in the west, to within a short distance of the coast, were equally woody. The day was squally, with rain; nevertheless, during an interval of sunshine, I obtained the sun's meridian altitude, making the latitude 38° 2′ 58″ S. I also completed, by two P.M., my survey of the mouth of the river and adjacent country; and we then again embarked to return a few miles up the river, and encamp where wood and water were at hand. On re-entering the river from the sea, I presented the men with a bottle of whiskey, with which it was formally named the Glenelg, after the present Secretary of State for the Colonies, according to my previous intention.

Aug. 21.—We had encamped in a rather remarkable hollow on the right bank, at the extreme western bend of the river. There was no modern indication, that water either lodged in or ran through that ravine, although the channel resembled in width the bed of some considerable tributary; the rock presenting a section of cliffs on each side, and the bottom being broad, but consisting of black earth only, in which grew trees of *eucalyptus*. I found, on following it some way up, that it led to a low tract of country, which I regretted much I could not then examine further. I found shells embedded in limestone, varying considerably in its hardness, being sometimes very friable, and the surface, in some places, presenting innumerable fragments of corallines, with pectens, spatangi, echini, ostrea, and foraminifera. In the opposite bank of the river, I found several thin strata of compact chert, containing probably fragments of corallines, not only on the surface, but imbedded in the limestone. In pulling up the river this morning, we observed a cavern or opening in the side of the limestone rock, and having ascended to it by means of a rope, we entered with lights. It proved to be only a large fissure, and after penetrating about 150 yards under ground, we met with red earth, apparently fallen from the surface. We found, at the mouth of the fissure, some fine specimens of shells, coral, and other marine productions, embedded in several thin strata of a coarser structure, under one of very compact limestone, upwards of 20 feet thick. While the people in the boat awaited us there, a fish was taken by Muirhead, who had also caught the first fish in the river Darling. That of the Glenelg was a salt-water fish, known at Sydney by the name of Snapper.

The weather was more moderate today, although still showery; and the scenery, as we proceeded upwards, was very picturesque, and full of variety. At sunset, we encamped about a mile and a half short of our camp of the 18th, and just as the trees were groaning under a heavy squall, which obliged us to land on the first spot where sufficient room was left in the thick woods, for our tents. This spot happened to be on a steep bit of bank; and, in the evening, I was called in haste to a new danger. The wind had suddenly changed, and blew with great fury, filling my tent with sparks from a large fire which burnt before it. I had placed in it, according to usual custom, our stock of ammunition packed in a keg; and, notwithstanding these precautions, its preservation now, between the two elements of fire and water, was rather doubtful. We contrived, however, to avert the danger, and were no more disturbed during the night, except by the storm.

Aug. 22.—The squally weather continued until noon, when sunbeams again adorned the river-scenery. We met with no impediment in the current, until within about six miles of the depot-camp, when dead trees in the channel began again to appear; but we passed them all without hindrance, and reached Fort O'Hare at two o'clock, where we found all well. Mr. Stapylton had set Vulcan to repair the broken chains, etc.—a ford had been cleared across the stream, from the north east, which I named the Crawford; and the cattle being refreshed, we were once more in trim to continue the land journey. The height of the water in the river had undergone no change during our absence, and was probably about its usual level there, although I observed abundant marks of flood in the branches of trees, where dry floated matter remained at the height of fifteen feet above the water, as it stood then. The rock about this position consisted of limestone, apparently similar to that seen on its banks higher up. It possessed a stalactitic aspect, by the infiltration of calcareous matter, and, in crevices below, I found a reddish stalagmite containing grains of sand. Large petrified oyster shells, lay loosely about the bank above these cliffs. No natives had approached the depot during our absence, and we had indeed reason to believe that the adjacent country contained but few inhabitants. During the afternoon, I laid down my survey of the estuary of the Glenelg, and completed, by 10 p.m. not only my plan of it, but that of the river also. I found a considerable difference between the result of my survey and the Admiralty charts, not only in the longitude, but also in the relative position of the two capes with respect to Mount Gambier, a solitary hill easily recognised.

Aug. 23.—Having at length disposed of the course of the Glenelg, my next object was to cross and examine the high ground which enclosed its basin on the east, supplying those tributaries which the river received from its left bank, and evidently extending from the Grampians to Cape Bridgewater. I had named this the Rifle range, in crossing that branch of it extending north-westward, when I ascertained its characteristics to be lofty woods and swamps; but its ramifications in other directions, and how it was connected backwards with the mountains, still remained to be discovered; and from what I did know of this range, I apprehended considerable difficulty in getting over it with our heavy carriages, at such a season. That we might, if possible, escape the bogs, I devoted the day to an extensive reconnoissance of the country before us; my guide in this case being the river Crawford, which, flowing in deep ravines, was likely to afford (so long as its general course continued to be nearly parallel to our route), one means at least of avoiding those soft swampy flats, which could not possibly impede us, so long as the side of such a ravine as that of the river was within reach. I had the good fortune to find that the range in general was firm under the hoof, and its direction precisely such as I wished. Extensive swamps occasionally appeared on my right; but I had on the left the deep ravines of the Crawford, and I travelled across the highest slopes of the ground. Having thus found good sound turf, for twelve miles in the direction in which I wished to take the carriages, I returned on descending from a trap-range, where the rock consisted of granular felspar and hornblende with crystals of glassy felspar. On this hill the soil was exceedingly rich, and the grass green and

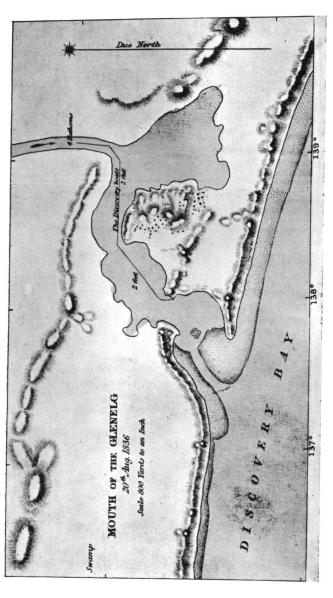

MOUTH OF THE GLENELG.

Discovered by Mitchell in 1836. From " 'Three Expeditions into the Interior of Eastern Australia, 1839.' "

luxuriant. I obtained thence a most useful bearing on Mount Gambier, and saw also some heights to the eastward, beyond the Rifle range. The timber grew to an enormous size on the ranges which I traversed this day; it consisted chiefly of that useful species of eucalpytus, known as "stringy-bark." Some of the trees we measured were 13 feet and one as much as 14½ feet in circumference, and 80 feet was no uncommon height. The fallen timber was of such magnitude as to present a new impediment to our progress, for we had not previously met with such an obstruction on any journey.

Aug. 24.—The carriages were taken across the Crawford without much delay, considering its depth and the softness of the banks. The carts sank at least five feet in the water, yet nothing was damaged, for we had taken care to pack the flour and other perishable articles on the tops of the loads. We succeeded in crossing the rivulets at the heads of several ravines, by filling up their channels with logs; and thus, after crossing the last of these, and ascending the steep bank beyond it, we encamped, after a journey of seven miles. The weather had been stormy on both days, since I crossed the Crawford, a circumstance very much against our progress. Near this camp, we found a new Correa, resembling C. virens, but having distinctly cordate toothed leaves, with less down on their under side, and a much shorter calyx.

Aug. 25.—In our progress eastward, we were still governed by the line of the Crawford; and the tortuous direction of the ravines connected with it, required constant attention, while the very variable character of the swamps at the head of them was still more perplexing. We succeeded in finding a passage between all, this day also, and on again crossing a small mountain torrent by filling up the chasm with dead timber, we encamped after another journey of seven miles. On our left to the northward, lay a deep valley, in which we found a broad sheet of water covered with ducks, the banks being soft and overgrown with reeds. A considerable stream flowed westward from this lake through a narrow part of the valley, so that I concluded we were still on the principal branch of the Crawford. Trees of large dimensions were abundant, and the fallen timber impeded our progress even more, than any unusual softness of the earth.

Aug. 26.—After proceeding several miles without lett or hindrance, having successfully crossed some swampy rivulets, all flowing to the left amidst thick scrubs, we at length arrived at a water-course in which my horse went down, and which filled a very wide swampy bed, enclosed by a thick growth of young mimosa trees, through which it was necessary to cut a passage wide enough for the carts. The scrub—having been thus cleared to the extent of about 100 yards with much labour, I found only then, unfortunately, that although the roots grew very closely, and that water flowed over the surface, the earth was withal so soft, that I could at every point, with ease, push a stick five feet down, without reaching any firm bottom. The loose cattle were driven in, an experiment which until then we had tried with success, in doubtful places—but they with difficulty got across this, for one of them sank and could not be extricated without considerable delay. While the men were busily employed there, I rode to the head of the swamp, which extended about a mile to the southward. On this swampy plain I at length succeeded in finding, with Mr. Stapylton's assistance, a line of route likely to bear the carts, and we passed safely in that direction, not one carriage having gone down. While on this swampy surface, we distinctly heard the breakers of the sea, apparently at no great distance to the south-west, and I was convinced that the head of this swamp was about the highest ground immediately adjacent to Discovery Bay. On travelling a mile and a half further, we reached a small rivulet, the first we had crossed flowing to the south. Beyond it the country appeared open and good, consisting of what is termed forest-land, with casuarinae and banksia growing upon it. We had at length reached the highest parts of the range, and were about to descend into the country beyond it. We continued to travel a considerable distance further than the rivulet flowing to the south. Crossing others running northward or to the left, and leaving also on the same side a swamp, we finally came to a higher range clothed with trees of gigantic size, attesting the strength and depth of the soil, and here enormous old trunks obstructed our passage, covering the surface so as to form an impediment almost as great to us as the swampy ground had been; but this large timber so near the coast, was an important feature in that country. Piper having climbed to the top of one of these trees, perceived some fine green hills to the south-east, saying they were very near us, and that the sea was visible beyond them. It was late in the afternoon, when I reluctantly changed my intended route, which had been until then eastward, to proceed in the direction recommended by Piper, or to the south-east, and so to follow down a valley, instead of my proposed route, which had been along a favourable range. I had still less reason to be satisfied with the change when, after pushing my horse through thick scrubs and bogs until twilight, and looking in vain for a passage for the carts, I encountered at length bushes so thickly set, and bogs so soft, that any further progress in that direction was out of the question ; and thus on the evening when I hoped to have entered a better sort of country, after so success- ful a passage of the range, we encamped where but little grass could be found for the cattle, our tents being not only under lofty trees, but amongst thick bushes and bogs during very rainy weather.

Aug. 27.—I was so anxious to get into open ground again, that as soon as daylight permitted, I carefully examined the environs of our camp, and I found that we occupied a broad flat, where the drainage from the hills met and spread among bushes; so that at one time, I almost despaired of extricating the party otherwise than by returning to the hill at which I had first altered my route. The track we made, had been, however, so much cut up by our wheels, that I preferred the chance of finding a passage northward, which, of course, was also less out of our way. We reached an extremity of the hill, (the nearest to us on that side,) with much less difficulty than I had reason to apprehend; and keeping along that feature, we soon regained a range, which led us east-north-east. By proceeding in this direction, however, we could not avoid the passage of a valley where the water was not confined to any channel, but spread and lodged on a wide tract of very soft ground, also covered with mimosa bushes, and a thick growth of young saplings of eucalyptus. The light carts and the first heavy cart got over this soft ground or bog, but the others, and the boat carriage, sank up to the axles, so that we were obliged to halt after having proceeded about five miles only. This was near a fine forest-hill, consisting of trap-rock in a state of decomposition, but apparently similar to that of the trap range I had ascended on the 23rd of August; and from a tree there, Burnett thought he saw the sea to the north-east, and even to the northward of a remarkable conical hill. The discovery of the sea in that direction, was so different from the situation of the shore as laid down on the maps, that I began to hope an inlet might exist there as yet undiscovered—the " Cadong " perhaps, of the native woman, "where white men had never been." I had now proceeded far enough to the eastward, to be able to examine the coast about Portland Bay, and extend my survey to the capes in its neighbourhood, the better to ascertain their longitude. I therefore determined to make an excursion in that direction, and thus afford time not only for the extrication of the heavy carts still remaining in the mud, but also for the repose of the cattle after their labours.

Aug. 28.—By the survey proposed, I hoped to extend my map of the country sufficiently in that direction to be at liberty, on my return to the party, to pursue a route directly homeward; not doubting that at a short distance to the northward of our camp, we should again enter the beautiful open country, which, when seen from the mouth of the Wannon, seemed to extend as far as could be seen to the eastward. In our ride to the south, we reached, at four miles from the boggy ground, a fine green hill consisting of trap-rock, and connected with a ridge of the same description, which extended about two miles further to the southward. There we found it to terminate abruptly in a lofty brow quite clear of timber, and commanding an extensive view to the east and south, over a much lower country. This hill had a very remarkable feature—a deep chasm, separating it from the ridge behind, the sides being so steep, as to present a section of the trap-rock, which consisted principally of compact felspar. The hill, which I named Mount Eckersley, was covered, as well as the ridge to which it belonged, with a luxuriant crop of anthistirium, or kangaroo grass. Unfortunately the weather was squally, but by awaiting the intervals between clouds on the horizon, I obtained angles, at length, on nearly all the distant hills, the waters of Portland Bay just appearing in the south over an intervening woody ridge. From this hill I recognised a very conspicuous, flat-topped hill to the northward, which had been previously included in a series of angles observed on the 12th instant from the valley of the Wannon, and which I now named Mount Napier. Portland Bay was distant about fifteen miles, but the intervening country seemed so low, and swamps, entirely clear of timber, appeared in so many places, that I could scarcely hope to get through it—knowing it to contain all the water from those boggy vallies where our progress had been already so much impeded. Smoke arose from various parts of the lower country— a proof that at least some dry land was there. We were provided with horses only, and, therefore, desperately determined to flounder through or even to swim if necessary, we thrust them down the hill. On its side we met an emu which stood and stared, apparently fearless, as if the strange quadrupeds had withdrawn its keen eye from the more familiar enemies who bestrode them. In the lower country we saw also a kangaroo, an animal that seldom frequents marshy lands. I was agreeably surprised to find also, on descending, that the rich grass extended among the trees across the lower country; and I was still more pleased on coming to a fine running stream, at about three miles from the hill, and after crossing a tract of land of the richest description. Reeds grew thickly amongst the long grass, and the ground appeared to be of a different character from any that I had previously seen. This seemed to be just such land as would produce wheat during the driest seasons, and never become sour even in the wettest, such as this season undoubtedly was. The timber was thin and light, and with a fine deep stream flowing through it, the tract which at first sight from Mount Eckersley, I had considered so sterile and wet, proved to be one likely, at no distant day, to smile under luxuriant crops of grain. We found the river (which I named the Fitzroy) fordable, although deep at the place where we first came upon it. Shady trees of the mimosa kind grew along the banks, and the earth was now good and firm on both sides. We heard the natives as we approached this stream, and cooyed to them; but our calls had only the effect, as appeared from the retiring sound of their voices, of making them run faster away. Continuing our ride southward, we entered at two miles beyond the Fitzroy, a forest of the stringy-bark eucalyptus; and, although the anthistirium still grew in hollows, I saw swampy open flats before us, which I endeavoured to avoid, sometimes by passing between them, and, finally, by turning to a woody range on the left. I ascended this range as night came on, in hopes of finding grass for our horses; but there the mimosa and xanthorhaea alone prevailed—the latter being a sure indication of sterility, and scanty vegetation. We found naked ground higher up, consisting of deep lagoons and swamps, amongst which I was satisfied with my success, in passing through in such a direction, as enabled me to regain, in a dark and stormy night, the shelter of the woods on the side of the range. But I sought in vain for the grass, so abundant elsewhere on this day's ride, and we were at length under the necessity of halting for the night, where but little food could be found for our horses, and under lofty trees that creaked and groaned to the blast.

Aug. 29.—The groaning trees had afforded us shelter, without letting fall even a single branch upon our heads, but the morning was squally and unfavourable for the objects of the excursion, and we had still to ride some way, before I could commence operations. Proceeding along the skirts of the woody ridge on the left in order to avoid swamps, we at length saw through the trees, the blue waters of the sea, and heard the roar of the waves. My intended way towards the deepest part of the bay, and the hills beyond it, did not lead directly to the shore, and I continued to pursue a course through the woods, having the shore on our left. We thus met a deep and rapid little river, exactly resembling the Fitzroy, and coming also from the westward. Tracing this a short distance upwards, we came to a place set with a sort of trellice work of bushes by the natives, for the purpose, no doubt, of catching fish. Here we found the stream fordable, though deep; a brownish granular limestone appearing in the bank. We crossed, and then continuing through a thick wood, we came out at length on the shore of Portland Bay, at about four miles beyond the little river. Straight before us lay "Laurence's Island," or rather, islands, there being two small islets of rock in that situation; and, some way to the eastward, I perceived a much larger island, which I concluded was one of "Lady Julia Percy's Isles." At a quarter of a mile back from the beach, broad broom-topped casuarinae were the only trees we could see; these grew on long ridges, parallel to the beach, resembling those long breakers, which, aided by winds, had probably thrown such ridges up. They were abundantly covered with excellent grass; and, as it wanted about an hour of noon, I halted that the cattle might feed, while I took some angles, and endeavoured to obtain the sun's altitude during the intervals between heavy squalls; some of which were accompanied by hail and thunder. On reaching the sea shore at this beach, I turned to observe the face of "Tommy Came-last," one of my followers, who being a native from the interior, had never before seen the sea. I could not discover in the face of this young savage, even on his first view of the ocean, any expression of surprise; on the contrary, the placid and comprehensive gaze he cast over it, seemed fully to embrace the grand expanse then for the first time opened to him. I was much more astonished, when he soon after came to tell me of the fresh tracks of cattle, that he had found on the shore, and the shoe marks of a white man. He also brought me portions of tobacco-pipes, and a glass bottle without a neck. That whaling vessels occasionally touched there, I was aware, as was indeed obvious from the carcases and bones of whales on the beach; but how cattle could have been brought there, I did not understand. Proceeding round the bay with the intention of examining the head of an inlet and continuing along shore as far as Cape Bridgewater, I was struck with the resemblance to houses that some supposed grey rocks under the grassy cliffs presented;

and while I directed my glass towards them, my servant Brown said he saw a brig at anchor; a fact of which I was soon convinced, and also that the grey rocks were in reality wooden houses. The most northern part of the shore of this bay was comparatively low, but the western consisted of bold cliffs rising to the height of 180 feet.

We ascended these cliffs near the wooden houses, which proved to be some deserted sheds of the whalers. One shot was heard as we drew near them, and another on our ascending the rocks. I then became somewhat apprehensive that the parties might either be, or suppose us to be, bushrangers, and to prevent if possible some such awkward mistake, I ordered a man to fire a gun and the bugle to be sounded; but on reaching the higher ground, we discovered not only a beaten path, but the track of two carts, and while we were following the latter, a man came towards us from the face of the cliffs. He informed me in answer to my questions, that the vessel at anchor was the "Elizabeth of Launceston"; and that just round the point there was a considerable farming establishment, belonging to Messrs. Henty, who were then at the house. It then occurred to me, that I might there procure a small additional supply of provisions, especially of flour, as my men were on very reduced rations. I, therefore, approached the house, and was kindly received and entertained by the Messrs. Henty, who as I learnt had been established there during upwards of two years. It was very obvious indeed from the magnitude and extent of the buildings, and the substantial fencing erected, that both time and labour had been expended in their construction. A good garden stocked with abundance of vegetables, already smiled on Portland Bay; the soil was very rich on the overhanging cliffs, and the potatoes and turnips produced there, surpassed in magnitude and quality any I had ever seen elsewhere. I learnt that the bay was much resorted to by vessels engaged in the whale fishery, and that upwards of 700 tons of oil had been shipped that season. I was likewise, informed that only a few days before my arrival, five vessels lay at anchor together in that bay, and that a communication was regularly kept up with Van Diemen's Land by means of vessels from Launceston. Messrs. Henty were importing sheep and cattle as fast as vessels could be found to bring them over, and the numerous whalers touching at or fishing on the coast, were found to be good customers for farm produce and whatever else could be spared from the establishment.

Portland Bay is well sheltered from all winds except the east-south-east, and the anchorage is so good that a vessel is said to have rode out a gale even from this quarter. The part of the western shore where the land is highest, shelters a small bay, which might be made a tolerable harbour by means of two piers or quays, erected on reefs of a kind of rock apparently very favourable for the purpose, namely amygdaloidal trap in rounded boulders. The present anchorage in four fathoms is on the outside of these reefs, and the water in this little bay is in general smooth enough for the landing of boats. A fine stream falls into the bay there, and the situation seems altogether a most eligible one for the site of a town. The rock is trap, consisting principally of felspar; and the soil is excellent, as was amply testified by the luxuriant vegetation in Mr. Henty's garden.

Aug. 30.—I proceeded with the theodolite to a height near Cape Nelson, and from it I intersected that cape and also Cape Bridgewater, Cape Sir William Grant, the islands to the eastward, etc. I here recognised also the high hill, which appeared within these capes when first seen from the westward. It formed the most elevated part of the Rifle range at its termination on the coast, and I was informed by Mr. Henty, that there was a fine lake at its base. I named the Hill Mount Kincaid, after my old and esteemed friend of Peninsular recollections. Returning to the party at Portland Bay, where I had left my sextant, I then obtained a good observation on the sun's meridian altitude. I was accommodated with a small supply of flour by Messrs. Henty, who having been themselves on short allowance, were awaiting the arrival of a vessel then due two weeks. They also supplied us with as many vegetables, as the men could carry away on their horses. Just as I was about to leave the place, a "whale" was announced, and instantly three boats, well manned, were seen cutting through the water, a harpooneer standing up at the stern of each with oar in hand, and assisting the rowers by a forward movement at each stroke. It was not the least interesting scene in these my Australian travels, thus to witness from a verandah on a beautiful afternoon at Portland Bay, the humours of the whale fishery, and all those wondrous perils of harpooners and whale boats of which I had delighted to read as scenes of "the stormy north." The object of the present pursuit was "a hunchback," and being likely to occupy the boats for some time, I proceeded homewards. I understood it frequently happened, that several parties of fishermen, left by different whaling vessels, would engage in the pursuit of the same whale, and that in the struggle for possession, the whale would occasionally escape from them all and run ashore, in which case it is of little value to whalers, as the removal, etc. would be too tedious, and they in such cases carry away part of the head matter only. The natives never approach these whalers, nor had they ever shewn themselves to the white people of Portland Bay; but as they have taken to eat the cast-away whales, it is their custom to send up a column of smoke when a whale appears in the bay, and the fishers understand the signal. This affords an instance of the sagacity of the natives, for they must have reflected, that by thus giving timely notice, a greater number will become competitors for the whale, and that consequently there will be a better chance of the whale running ashore, in which case a share must fall finally to them. The fishers whom I saw were fine able fellows; and with their large ships and courageous struggles with the whales, they must seem terrible men of the sea to the natives. The neat trim of their boats, set up on stanchions on the beach, looked well, with oars and in perfect readiness to dash at a moment's notice, into the "angry surge." Upon the whole, what with the perils they undergo, and their incessant labour in boiling the oil, these men do not earn too cheaply the profits derived from that kind of speculation. I saw on the shore the wreck of a fine boat, which had been cut in two by a single stroke of the tail of a whale. The men were about to cast their net into the sea to procure a supply of fish for us, when the whale suddenly engaged all hands.

We returned along the shore of the bay, intersecting at its estuary, the mouth of the little river last crossed, and which, at the request of Mr. Henty, I have named the Surry. This river enters Portland Bay in latitude 38° 15' 43" S.; longitude (by my survey) 141° 58' E. We encamped on the rich grassy land just beyond, and I occupied for the night, a snug old hut of the natives.

Aug. 31.—Early this morning Richardson caught a fine bream, and I had indeed been informed by Messrs. Henty that these streams abound with this fish. On ascending the highest point of the hill, immediately behind the estuary of the Surry, and which I named Mount Clay, I found it consisted of good forest-land, and that its ramifications extended over as much as three miles. Beyond it, we descended into the valley of the Fitzroy, and at noon I ascertained the latitude, where we had before forded it, to be 38° 8' 51" S. The river had risen in the interim a foot and a half, so that we were obliged to carry the flour across, on the heads of the men, wading up to the neck.

When we reached the summit of Mount Eckersley, the horizon being clear, I completed my series of angles on points visible from that station, by observing the " Julian Island " and Mount Abrupt, two of great importance in my survey, which were hidden from our sight by the squally weather, when I was last on this hill. We reached the camp about sunset, and found all right there, the carts having been drawn out of the bogs; all the claw chains repaired by the blacksmith; our hatchets resteeled; and two new shafts made for the heavy carts. Piper had, during our absence, killed abundance of kangaroos, and I now rejoiced at his success, on account of the aboriginal portion of our party, for whose stomachs, being of savage capacity, quantity was a more important consideration than quality in the article of food, and we were then living on a very reduced scale of rations. On my return from such excursions, the widow and her child frequently gave notice of our approach, long before we reached the camp; their quick ears seemed sensible of the sound of horses' feet at an astonishing distance, for in no other way, could the men account for the notice which Turandurey and her child, seated at their own fire, were always the first to give, of my return, sometimes long before our appearance at the camp. Piper was usually the first to meet me, and assure me of the safety of the party, as if he had taken care of it during my absence; and I encouraged his sense of responsibility, by giving him credit for the security they had enjoyed. A serene evening, lovely in itself, looked doubly beautiful then, as our hopes of getting home were inseparable from fine weather, for on this chance our final escape from the mud and bogs seemed very much to depend. The barometer, however, indicated rather doubtfully.

Sept. 1.—Heavy rain and fog detained us in the same camp this morning, and I availed myself of the day for the purpose of laying down my recent survey. The results satisfied me, that the coast-line on the engraved map was very defective, and indeed the indentations extended so much deeper into the land, that I still entertained hopes of finding some important inlet to the eastward, analogous to that remarkable break of the mountain-chain at Mount William.

Sept. 2.—We travelled as much in a north-east direction as the ground permitted, but although I should most willingly have followed the connecting features whatever their directions, I could not avoid the passage of various swamps or boggy soft hollows, in which the carts, and more especially the boat-carriage, notwithstanding the greatest exertions on the part of the men, again sank up to the axles. I had proceeded with the light carts and one heavy cart nearly nine miles, while the boat-carriage fell at least six miles behind me, the other heavy carts having also been retarded, from the necessity for yoking additional teams to the cattle drawing the boats. The weather was still unsettled, and the continued rains had at length made the surface so soft, that even to ride over it was in many places difficult. I had reached some fine forest land on the bank of a running stream, where the features were bolder, and I hoped to arrive soon at the good country near the head of the Wannon. I encamped without much hope that the remainder of the party could join us that night, and they, in fact, did remain six miles behind. I had never been more puzzled in my travels, than I was with respect to the nature of the country before us then. Mount Napier bore 74° E. of N. distant about 16 miles. The little rivulet was flowing northward, and yet we had not reached the interior side of that elevated though swampy ground, dividing the fine vallies we had seen further westward, from the country sloping towards the sea.

Sept. 3.—This morning we had steady rain, accompanied as usual by a north-west wind; I remarked also that at any rise of the barometer after such rain, the wind changed to the south-east in situations near the coast, or to the north-east when we were more inland. I sent back the cattle, we had brought forward to this camp, to assist those behind, and in the meanwhile, Mr. Stapylton took a ride along the ridge on which we were encamped, in order to ascertain its direction. Towards evening Burnett returned from the carts with the intelligence, that the boat-carriage could not be got out of the swamps, and that after the men had succeeded in raising it with levers, and had drawn it some way, it had again sunk, and thus delayed the carts, but that the latter were at length coming on, two men having been left behind with the boat-carriage. Mr. Stapylton returned in the afternoon, having ascertained that a swamp of upwards of a mile in breadth, and extending north and south as far as he could see, lay straight before us, and he had concluded, that the rivulet upon which we were then encamped, turned into it. Under such circumstances, we could not hope to be able to travel much further with the boats, nor even indeed with the carts, unless we found ground with a firmer surface in the country before us. Ere we could reach the nearest habitations of civilised men, we had yet to traverse 400 miles of a country intersected by the highest mountains, and watered by the largest rivers, known in New Holland.

Sept. 4.—Although the boats and their carriage had been of late a great hindrance to us, I was very unwilling to abandon such useful appendages to an exploring party, having already drawn them overland nearly 3000 miles. A promising part of the coast might still be explored, large rivers were to be crossed, and we had already found boats useful on such occasions. One, however, might answer these temporary purposes, since, for the main object, the exploration of inland seas, they could not possibly be wanted. We had two, and the outer one, which was both larger and heavier than the inner, had been shaken so much when suspended without the thwarts, that she was almost unserviceable in the water, and very leaky, as we had lately found in exploring the Glenelg. She had, in fact, all along served as a case for the inner boat, which could thus be kept distended by the thwarts, and was consequently in excellent repair, and in every respect the best. I determined therefore to abandon the outer boat, and shorten the carriage, so that the fore and hind wheels would be brought two feet nearer each other. I expected from this arrangement, that instead of boats retarding the party, this one might thus be drawn in advance with the light carts. Having directed the alteration to be made during my intended absence, I set out for Mount Napier, and soon found the broad swamp before me. After riding up an arm of it to the left, for a mile and a half, I found it passable, and having crossed, we proceeded towards the hill by a rather circuitous route, but over a fine tract of country, although then very soft under our horses' feet. We next reached a deeper ravine, where the land on each side was more open, and also firmer, while a small rivulet flowing through it amongst bushes, was easily crossed, and we ascended some fine rising ground beyond it. Rich flats then extended before us, and we arrived at an open grassy valley, where a beautiful little stream, resembling a river in miniature, was flowing rapidly. Two very substantial huts shewed that even the natives had been attracted by the beauty of the spot, and as the day was showery, I wished to return, if possible, to pass the night there, for I began to learn that such huts, with a good fire before them, made very comfortable quarters in bad weather. We had heard voices in the woods several times this day, but their inhabitants seemed as timid as kangaroos, and not more likely to come near us. The blue mass of Mount Napier was visible occasionally through the trees, but I found as we proceeded, that we were not so near it as I had supposed, for at three miles beyond the little stream, we came upon one of greater magnitude, a river flowing southward, with open grassy banks in which two

kinds of trap-rock appeared. The edge of a thin layer of the
lowest, a nearly decomposed trap, projected over the stream;
the other lay in rounded blocks, in the face of the hill above, and
appeared to be decomposed amygdaloid, principally felspar.
The river ran through a valley where the forest land was remarkably open, being sprinkled with only a few trees as in a park, and
this stream appeared to fall into the head of the extensive swamp
already mentioned. About a mile beyond the river, (which I
named the Shaw,) we came upon the extremities of Mount
Napier, for at least so I considered some rough sharp-pointed
fragments of rock laying about in heaps, which we found it very
difficult and tedious to ride over; indeed so sharp-edged and
large were these rocks on the slopes of the terraces they formed,
that we were often obliged to dismount and lead our horses.
In these fragments I recognised the cellular character of the rocks
I had noticed in the bed of the Shaw. The rock here might have
been taken for decomposed amygdaloid, but having found the
vestiges of an old crater in the summit of the hill, I was induced
to consider it an ancient lava. The reefs at Portland Bay consist of the same rock in rounded nodules, a more compact trap-
rock consisting principally of felspar lying above them, as was
observable in the section of the coast. In some of the fragments
on Mount Napier, these cells or pores were several inches in
diameter, and, unlike amygdaloidal rocks, all were quite empty.
The surface consisted wholly of this stone, without any intermediate soil to soften its asperity under the feet of our horses,
and yet it was covered with a wood of eucalyptus and mimosa,
growing there as on the open forest land, between which and this
stony region the chief difference consisted in the ruggedness of
surface, this being broken, as already stated, into irregular
terraces, where loose stones lay in irregular heaps and hollows,
most resembling old stone quarries. We travelled over three
miles of this rough surface, before we reached the base of the cone.
On the sides of it we found some soft red earth mixed with
fragments of lava, and on reaching the summit, I found myself
on the narrow edge of a circular crater, composed wholly of lava
and scoriae. Trees and bushes grew luxuriantly everywhere,
except where the sharp rocks shot up almost perpendicularly.
The igneous character of these was so obvious, that one of the
men thrust his hand into a chasm to ascertain whether it was
warm. The discovery of an extinct volcano gave additional
interest to Mount Napier, but it was by no means a better station
for the theodolite on that account; on the contrary, it was the

worst possible, for as the trees grew on the edge of the crater,
no one station could be found to afford a view of the horizon,
until the whole circumference was cleared of the trees, and this
was too great a work for us at that visit. Mount William and the
Grampian range presented a noble outline of the northward.
The sun had set, before I could recognise distant points in the
highly interesting country, to be seen from this remarkable hill.
The weather was also unfavourable, and I descended to pass the
night at its base, in hopes that the next morning might be clear.

On reaching the spot where I had left the horses, I found that
our native friend, Tommy Came-last, could discover no water
in any of the numerous hollows around the hill, and though the
superabundance of this element had caused the chief impediment to our progress through the country at that time, we were
obliged to pass a night most uncomfortably from the total want
of it, at the base of Mount Napier. The spongy looking rocks
were, however, dry enough to sleep upon, a quality of which the
soil in general had been rather deficient, as most of us felt in our
muscles. I perceived a remarkable uniformity in the size of the
trees, very few of which were dead or fallen. From this circumstance, together with the deficiency of the soil and the sharp edge
of the rock generally, some might conclude, that the volcano had
been in activity at no very remote period.

Sept. 5.—A thick fog hung upon the mountain until half-past
10 A.M., and when I ascended an extremity, I could see nothing
of the distance. I had however ascertained the nature of the
country thus far, this having been the object of my visit, and as I
had resolved from what I had seen, to pass to the northward at
no great distance from this hill, I returned with less reluctance,
in hopes that I might have it in my power yet to revisit it, during
more favourable weather. The day was squally with several
very heavy showers, the wind being from the south-west. We
saw two natives at a fire, when we were returning, and our
friend Tommy readily advanced towards them, but they immediately set up such loud and incessant cries, that I called to him to
come away. After a ride of twenty-six miles across swamps and
many muddy hollows, we reached, soon after sunset, the camp,
which I had directed to be moved back, to near where the boats
lay. I found that these had been drawn out of the swamp, and
one only brought forward as I wished to this camp, and where I
found all the carts once more ranged together. The alteration
of the boat-carriage required a little more time, and I accordingly determined to halt one day, that we might also have our

horses shod, several shoes having come off on the rough rocks near Mount Napier.

Sept. 6.—This day I requested Mr. Stapylton to examine the country in a north-west direction. Some of the swamps crossed by me yesterday had appeared to fall westward, and I wished to ascertain the situation and character of the ground dividing them from those discharging their waters eastward or towards the sea, as it was only by keeping on that dividing ground, that I could hope to avoid them. Mr. Stapylton proceeded nine miles north-west, crossing many swampy flats, and at length a small rivulet, all falling westward. Beyond the rivulet, he got upon some good hills connected with higher land. Our best line of route homewards, was in a north-east direction, or at right angles to the route of Mr. Stapylton. The great swamp already mentioned, being the channel and recipient of the Shaw, was somewhat in my way, and my object now was, to trace out the dividing ground as we proceeded, so as to avoid the swamps on both sides. By sunset, the single boat was mounted in the short-ened carriage, the whole being now so manageable and light, that the boat could be lifted out by hand, without block and tackle; and when on the carriage, she could be drawn with ease wherever the light carts could pass. Thus we got rid of that heavy clog on our progress over soft ground, "the boats," by reserving but one; and we left the larger, keel upwards, at the swamp which had occasioned so much delay.

Sept. 7.—Having chosen for a general line of route, the bearing most likely to avoid the swamps, according to the knowledge I had gained of the country, I proceeded as these and the soft ground permitted, and had the singular, and indeed, unexpected good fortune to come upon my horse's track from Mount Napier, without having even seen the large swamp. The boat-carriage now travelled with the light carts, and we at length reached the first running stream at a short distance below where I had pre-viously crossed it. The bottom was boggy, and the water flowed in two channels, the ground between them being very soft. The whole party crossed it, with the exception of two carts, which did not arrive, and we encamped on the bank beyond, after a journey of about eight miles. Near this stream, we found a pretty new species of Dillwynia, with plain yellow flowers, clustered on a long stalk at the end of the branches, and with curiously hairy heath-like leaves. It resembles D. peduncularis, but proved, on examination, to be distinct. At this spot, we found a very small bower of twigs, only large enough to contain a child ; the floor was hollowed out, and filled with dry leaves and feathers; and the ground around had been cut smooth, several boughs having been also bent over it, so as to be fixed in the ground at both ends. The whole seemed connected with some mystic ceremony of the aborigines, but which the male natives, who were with us, could not explain. The gins, however, on being questioned, said it was usual to prepare such a bower for the reception of a new-born child. Kangaroos were more numerous in this part of the country, than in any other that we had traversed. I counted twenty-three in one flock, which passed before me, as I stood silently by a tree. Two of the men counted fifty-seven in another flock, and it was not unusual for them to approach our camp, as if from curiosity, on which occasions two or three were occasionally caught by our dogs.

Sept. 8.—The remainder of the heavy carts not having come up, I left the two with us, to await their arrival, that the men might assist the drivers with their teams, in crossing this stream. On proceeding then with the light carts only, I crossed several soft bad places, and one or two fine little rivulets, encamping at last where we again fell in with my horse's track, on an open space, about eight miles from Mount Napier. During the day's journey, we traversed some fine, open, forest hills near the banks of rivulets. We generally found the south-eastern slope of such heights very indistinct, and the ground soft, boggy, and covered with banksias. The rock in such places consisted of the same cellular trap, so common on this side of the Grampians. Our camp lay between two swamps, for no better ground appeared on any side. I hoped, however, to obtain a more general knowledge of the surrounding country from Mount Napier, during clear weather, and thus to discover some way by which we might make our escape to the northward. The carts did not overtake us this day, and I determined, when they should arrive, to overhaul them, and throw away every article of weight, not absolutely required for the rest of the journey.

Sept. 9.—Once more I set out for Mount Napier, followed by a party of men with axes to clear its summit, at least sufficiently for the purpose of taking angles with the theodolite. The night had been clear, and the morning was fine, but as soon as I had ascended the hill, rain-clouds gathered in the south-west, and obscured the horizon on all sides; I could only see some points at intervals, but I took as many as I could, after the men had cleared a station for the theodolite. I perceived two very extensive lakes in the low country between Mount Napier and the south-eastern portion of the Grampian range, which terminated in the hill, that I had previously named Mount Abrupt. Between the largest of these waters (called by me Lake Linlithgow,) and the mountains, there appeared an extensive tract of open grassy land. To the eastward, at the distance of twelve miles, I perceived a solitary hill, somewhat resembling Mount Napier, and named it Mount Rouse; but a haze still concealed the more distant country. On reaching the camp, where we arrived in the dark, I found that the carts had not, even then, returned; but as the barometer promised better weather, I did not much regret their non-arrival, as the delay would afford me another chance of having a clear day on Mount Napier.

Sept. 10.—I again proceeded to the hill, and obtained, at length, a clear and extensive view from it in all directions. In the north, the Grampian range, on all sides grand, presented a new and striking outline on this. Far in the west, I could recognise in slight breaks, on a low horizon, some features of the valley of Nangeela (Glenelg). Eastward, the summits of a range, I thought of naming the Australian Pyrenees, were just visible over a woody horizon; and to the south-east were several detached hills, and some elevated ridges of forest-land, apparently near the coast. One isolated hill, resembling a haystack, was very remarkable on the sea-shore. This I named Mount Hotspur, being the only elevation near Lady Julia Percy's Isle, (not Isles, as laid down on the charts, for there is but one, now called by whalers the Julian Island). To the southward, I could just distinguish the Laurence Islands, but a haze upon the coast prevented me from seeing that of Lady Julia Percy. Smoke arose from many parts of the lower country, and shewed that the inhabitants were very generally scattered over its surface. We could now look on such fires with indifference, so harmless were these natives, compared with those on the Darling, and the smoke now ascended in equal abundance from the furthest verge of the horizon. It was impossible to discover the sources of streams, or the direction of any ranges visible in the surrounding country; but upon the whole, I concluded that the only practicable route for us homewards, at that time, would be through the forests, and by passing as near as possible to the base of Mount Abrupt, the south-eastern extremity of the Grampians. Several forest-hills stood above the extensive level country, extending from our camp to Mount Abrupt; but I could trace no connection between these hills, and was rather apprehensive that a soft and swampy country intervened. I had this day leisure to examine the

I. D. *u*

crater on this hill more particularly, and found its breadth to be 446 feet; its average depth 80 feet. The cellular rocks and lava stood nearly perpendicular around one portion of it; but there was a gap towards the west-north-west, on which side the crater was open almost to its greatest depth. Several deep tongues of land descended from it to the west and north-west, forming the base of the hill, and had somewhat of the regularity of water-worn features. No marks of decomposition appeared in the fragments projecting from the highest points, however much exposed. On the contrary, all the stringy twisted marks of fusion were as sharp and fresh, as if the lava had but recently cooled. One species of moss very much resembled the Orchilla, and I thought it not improbable that this valuable weed might be found here, as it occurs on similar rocks at Teneriffe. Just as I reached the highest summit this morning, a bronze-wing pigeon arose from it; a circumstance rather remarkable, considering that this was the only bird of that species seen on this side the mountains, besides the one we saw in Pigeon Ponds, on the 3rd of August. On returning to the camp, I found that the carts had arrived soon after my departure in the morning; but the men had the misfortune to lose two bullocks in crossing the swampy stream where we had been previously encamped. One was suffocated in the mud, and the other having lain down in it, could not be made to rise. By observing the stars α and β Centauri, I ascertained the magnetic variation to be $3°\ 2'\ 45''$ E., and by the sun's altitude, observed this day at Mount Napier, I found the latitude of that hill to be $37°\ 52'\ 29''$ S.

Sept. 11.—In order to lighten the carts as much as possible, I caused the pack-saddles to be placed on the spare bullocks, and various articles carried upon them; thus lightening, to less than eight hundred weight each, the loads of two of the heavy carts, which had narrow wheels and sunk most in the ground. The old cover of the boat-carriage was also laid aside, and in its place, some tarpaulins, which had previously added to the loads, were laid across our remaining boat. A heavy jack used to raise cart wheels, was also left at this camp, and some iron bars, that had been taken from the boat-carriage when it was shortened. Thus lightened, we proceeded once more into the fields of mud, taking a northerly direction. For several miles, we encountered worse ground than we had ever crossed before, yet the carts came over it; but broad swamps still lay before us. Despairing at length of being able to avoid them, I impatiently galloped my horse into one, and the carts followed, thanks to my impatience for once, for I do not think that I could otherwise have discovered that a swamp so uninviting could possibly have borne my horse, and still less the carts. After this I ventured to pursue a less circuitous route. About that time a yellow flower in the grass caught my eye, and remembering that we had seen none of these golden flowers since we left the beautiful valley of the Wannon, I ventured to hope, that we were at length approaching the good country at the head of that stream. Such was my anxious wish, when I perceived through the trees a glimpse of an open grassy country, and immediately entered a fine clear valley with a lively little stream flowing westward through it, and which I named the Grange. This was indeed one of the heads of the Wannon, and we had at length reached the good country. The contrast between it and that from which we had emerged, was obvious to all; even to the natives, who for the first time, painted themselves in the evening, and danced a spirited corrobory on the occasion. This day, Piper had seen two of the native inhabitants, and had endeavoured to persaude them to come to me, but all to no purpose, until at length, enraged at the unreasonable timidity of one of them, he threw his tomahawk at him, and nearly hit him as he edged off, an act of which, as I told him, in the strongest terms, I very much disapproved.

Sept. 12.—The course of the little stream being to the northward, I proceeded along its right bank this morning, until it turned to the north-west; but we soon after came to another to which the former seemed to be but a tributary. Its course was almost due west, and the valley in which it flowed, was deep and boldly escarped. The stream thundered along with considerable rapidity over a rocky bottom, consisting of the same sort of trap or ancient lava. I had little doubt, that this was the principal head of the Wannon, a river crossed by us on the 11th of August. Meeting, next, an important branch falling into it from the south-east, and being obliged to cross this, we effected the passage, even with the carts, although the horses were nearly swimming. We proceeded next along a continuous ridge of fine firm ground covered with excellent grass, and soon after, we saw before us a smaller stream flowing through a broad grassy vale, and having crossed it also, without difficulty, we encamped in one of the valleys beyond, where this tributary appeared to originate. A finer country could scarcely be imagined; enormous trees of the mimosa or wattle, of which the bark is so valuable, grew almost every where; and several new varieties of Caladenia were found to-day. The blue, yellow, pink, and brown coloured were all observed on these flowery plains. The sublime peaks of the Grampians began to appear above the trees to the northward, and two lower hills of trap-rock arose, one to the southwest, the other north-west of our camp. That to the northward, I named Mount Bainbrigge, the other on the south, Mount Pierrepoint.

Sept. 13.—We broke up our camp early this morning, and on reaching the highest ground we discovered a large lake on our left; it was nearly circular, about half a mile in circumference, and surrounded by high firm banks, from which there was no visible outlet; I named it Lake Nivelle. At a few miles beyond this lake, the cheering sight of an open country extending to the horizon, first appeared through the trees; and we soon entered on these fine downs where the gently undulating surface was firm under our horses' feet, and thickly clothed with excellent grass. The cart-wheels trundled merrily along, so that twelve miles were accomplished soon after mid-day, and we encamped near the extreme southern point of the Grampians, which I named Mount Sturgeon. The weather was very wet, but this troubled us the less, as we had not known a day without rain for several months.

Sept. 14.—I was most anxious to ascend Mount Abrupt, the first peak to the northwards of Mount Sturgeon, that I might close my survey of these mountains, and also reconnoitre the country before us. This morning, clouds hung upon the mountains, however, and I could scarcely indulge a hope that the weather would be favourable for the proposed survey; nevertheless I bent my steps towards the mountains, having first set the carpenter to work to make an additional width of felloe to the narrow wheels of one of the carts, that it might pass with less difficulty over soft ground. We soon came to a deep stream flowing not from, but apparently towards the mountains; its general course being westward. It was so deep that our horses could scarcely ford it without swimming. Reeds grew about, and the bottom was soft, although two kinds of rock appeared in its banks. On the right was trap, on the left the ferruginous sandstone of which all these mountains consist. We soon entered on the barren and sandy but firm ground at their base, which, with its peculiar trees and shrubs, appeared so different from the grassy plains. The banksia, the casuarina, and the hardy xanthorhaea, reminded us of former toils on the opposite side of these ranges. The weather turned out better than I had expected, and from the summit of Mount Abrupt I beheld a truly sublime scene; the whole of the mountains, quite clear of clouds, the grand outline of the more distant masses blended with the sky, and forming a blue and purple background for the numerous peaks of the range on which I stood, which consisted of sharp cones and perpendicular cliffs foreshortened, so as to form one grand feature only of the extensive landscape, though composing a crescent nearly 30 miles in extent; this range being but a branch from the still more lofty masses of Mount William, which crowned the whole. Towards the coast, there was less haze than usual, for I could distinguish Lady Julia Percy's Isle, which I had looked for in vain from Mount Napier, a point twenty-four miles nearer to it. Here I could also trace the course of the stream we had crossed that morning, from its sources under the eastern base of the mountains to a group of lower hills twenty-seven miles distant to the westward; which hills, named by me Dundas group, formed a most useful point in my trigonometrical survey. Several extensive lakes appeared in the lowest parts adjacent; but what interested me most, after I had intersected the various summits, was the appearance of the country to the eastward, through which we were to find our way home. There I saw a vast extent of open downs, and could trace their undulations to where they joined a range of mountains, which, judging by their out-lines, appeared to be of easy access. Our straightest way home-wards passed just under a bluff head about fifty miles distant, and so far I could easily perceive a most favourable line of route, by avoiding several large reedy lakes. Between that open country and these lakes on one side, and the coast on the other, a low woody ridge extended eastward; and, by first gaining that, I hoped we should reach the open ground, in a direction which should enable us to leave all the lakes on our left.

The largest pieces of water, I could see, were Lake Linlithgow and its companion in the open grassy plains between the range and Mount Napier, as previously discovered from that hill. Several small and very picturesque lakes, then as smooth as mirrors, adorned the valley immediately to the westward of the hill, I was upon. They were fringed with luxuriant shrubs, so that it was really painful to me to hurry, as I was then compelled to do, past spots like these, involving in their unexplored recesses so much of novelty amidst the most romantic scenery. The rock consisted of a finely grained sandstone as in other parts of that mass. The Grampians of the south consist of three ranges, covering a surface which extends latitudinally 54 miles, and longitudinally 20 miles. The extreme eastern and highest summit is Mount William, in height 4,500 feet above the sea. The northern point is Mount Zero, in latitude 36° 52′ 35″ S., and the southern point is Mount Sturgeon, in latitude 37° 38′ 00″. I here again recognised the outline of the most northern and elevated range extending from Mount William to Mount Zero, but it was not so steep on the southern as on the northern side. From this hill two other ranges branch off to the south; the western being marked Victoria range on the map, the eastern, the Serra, from its serrated appearance; the broken outlines they present being highly ornamental to the fine country around. On the northern slopes of the range, are some forests of fine timber, but, in general, the higher summits are bare and rocky. The chief source of the Glenelg, is between the Victoria range and the most northern, whence it soon sinks into a deep glen or ravine, receiving numberless tributaries from other dells, intersecting the adjacent country. A considerable branch of the Glenelg, named by the natives the "Wannon," has its sources in the eastern and southern rivulets from these mountains. The waters falling northward, enter the "Wimmera," a different river, whose estuary has not yet been explored. Returning towards the camp, on approaching the stream, we met with one of the most strikingly beautiful species of the common genus Pultenaea; its narrow heath-like leaves were so closely covered with soft silky hairs as to have quite a silvery appearance, and the branches were loaded with the heads of yellow and brown flowers now fully open. It formed a new species of the "Proliferous" section, allied to Pultenaea stipularis.

Sept. 15.—Pursuing an easterly course in order to avoid the Wannon, we again found the ground so soft and boggy that it was impossible to proceed; and after advancing with incredible labour (under which one of the poor bullocks fell to rise no more), barely four miles, I ordered the tents to be again set up, but almost in despair, for having performed during the previous days several good journeys with perfect freedom from this species of impediment, and having seen no indication of any change in the surface, I had assured the men on descending from the mountains, that the country before us was favourable. We were nevertheless compelled to halt again at this part by the breaking of the iron axle of one of the carts, for it was necessary to endeavour to repair it, before we could proceed. The highest part of the woody ridge, between us and the plains, bore according to my map due east, being distant 14 miles.

I gave that bearing to Mr. Stapylton, who rode forward with Burnett to ascertain how far we were from firmer ground, while

I continued in my tent occupied with the map of the mountains. It was dark before Mr. Stapylton returned and brought the pleasing tidings, that the soft ground extended only to three or four miles from the camp, and that from beyond that distance to the forest hills, he had found the ground tolerably firm.

Sept. 16.—The country which proved so soft was nevertheless stony, and trap-rock projected from every higher portion; yet such rocky eminences being unconnected, each was surrounded by softer ground. I was resolved to make the very most of them; but an iron axle having been broken in our struggles with the mud, the smith required more time to repair it, and I therefore determined to proceed with but half the equipment drawn by all the bullocks, leaving Burnett and the remaining portion of the party and equipment to come on next day by the same means, as soon as the cattle could be sent back. Having previously examined the ground, and carefully traced out the hardest parts, connecting these rocky features, I led the way with the carts, and got through the first part of the journey much better than any of us had expected. After passing over four miles of soft boggy ground, we came to a small running stream, the surface beyond it rising to a somewhat steep ascent. On reaching that side, I found myself on a good, firm ridge, along which I continued for some time until we reached a swampy lagoon, the banks of which were very firm and good. Leaving this on our right, we at length saw the darkly wooded hills of the ridge before mentioned; and having travelled eleven miles, we encamped near a small lagoon, on a spot, where there was excellent grass; but it was still necessary to send back the poor cattle with their drivers that evening, to where the other party still remained encamped.

Sept. 17.—This day the rest of the party came up, but the cattle seemed quite exhausted. They had at length become so weak, from the continued heavy dragging through mud, that it was obvious they could not proceed much further until after they had enjoyed at least some weeks of repose. But our provisions did not admit of this delay, as the time had arrived, when I ought to have been at Sydney, although still so far from it. After mature deliberation, we hit upon a plan, which might, as I thought, enable us to escape. The arrangement proposed was, that I should go forward with some of the freshest of the cattle drawing the light carts and boat, with a month's provisions, and taking with me as many men as would enable me to leave with those who should remain, provisions for two months. That the cattle should rest at the present camp two weeks and then proceed, while I, by

travelling so far before them with so light a party, could send
back a supply of provisions, and also the boat, to meet this second
party following in my track, on the banks of the Murray. Thus I
could reach Sydney some weeks sooner, and also carry on my
survey much more conveniently; the cattle, which had been sinking almost daily, would be thus refreshed sufficiently to be able
to travel, and the chance of the whole party suffering from
famine would be much diminished. Such was the outline of the
plan, which our position and necessities suggested.

Sept. 18.—This day was passed, in making preparations for
setting out tomorrow with the light party, as proposed. The
catalogue of the objects of natural history, collected during the
journey, included several birds and animals not hitherto mentioned in this Journal. Amongst the most remarkable of these
was the pig-footed animal, found on June 16. It measured about
ten inches in length, had no tail, and the fore feet resembled
those of a pig. There was also the rat, which climbs trees like the
opossum; the flat-tailed rat from the scrubs of the Darling, where
it builds an enormous nest of branches and boughs, so interlaced as to be proof against any attacks of the native dog. The
unique specimen from the reedy country on the Murray of a
very singular animal much resembling the jerboa or desert rat
of Persia; also a rat-eared bat from the Lachlan. We had several
new birds, but the most admired of our ornithological discoveries,
was a white-winged superb warbler, from the junction of the
Darling and the Murray, all the plumage not white, being of a
bright blue colour; but of this we had obtained only one specimen. I had not many opportunities of figuring the birds from
life, so very desirable in ornithological subjects. The eye of the
eagle and the rich crest of the cockatoo of the desert, could not
be preserved, in dead specimens, and were too fine to be omitted
among the sketches, I endeavoured to snatch from nature. Our
herbarium had suffered from the continued wet weather, especially
in fording deep rivers; and this was the more to be regretted, as it
contained many remarkable specimens. The seeds and bulbous
roots, comprising varieties of Calostemma, Caladenia and
Anguillaria, besides a number of large liliaceous bulbs, were
however preserved in a very good state.

The camp in which Mr. Stapylton's party was to remain two
weeks, was in as favourable a place for refreshing the cattle as
could be found. The ground undulated, and was thickly clothed
with fresh verdure; a grassy swamp also, such as cattle delight in,
extended northward into a lake of fresh water, which I named

Lake Repose. The peaks of the Serra Range, and especially Mount Abrupt, were landmarks which secured the men from even the possibility of losing their way in looking after the cattle.

Of the natives in our party, it was arranged amongst themselves that Tommy Came-first, and the widow, who most required a rest, having sore feet, should remain with Mr. Stapylton, and that Piper and Tommy Came-last should accompany me.

Sept. 19.—When about to set out I observed that the widow " Turandurey," who was to remain with Mr. Stapylton's party and the carts, was marked with white round the eyes (the natives' fashion of mourning), and that the face of her child Ballandella was whitened also. This poor woman, who had cheerfully carried the child on her back, when we offered to carry both on the carts, and who was as careful and affectionate as any mother could be, had at length determined to entrust to me the care of this infant. I was gratified with such a proof of the mother's confidence in us, but I should have been less willing to take charge of her child, had I not been aware of the wretched state of slavery to which the native females are doomed. I felt additional interest in this poor child, from the circumstance of her having suffered so much by the accident, that befel her while with our party, and which had not prevented her from now preferring our mode of living so much, that I believe the mother at length despaired of being ever able to initiate her thoroughly in the mysteries of killing and eating snakes, lizards, rats, and similar food. The widow had been long enough with us to be sensible, how much more her sex was respected by civilised men than savages, and, as I conceived, it was with such sentiments that she committed her child to my charge, under the immediate care, however, of Piper's gin.

For several miles, we met with soft ground at the low connecting parts of hills, but we at length gained the woody ridge, so likely, as I had hoped, to favour our progress. Its turnings were intricate, but by one or two rivulets falling to my left, and then by others falling to the right, I learnt how to keep on the intermediate ground, until, at length, after a journey of nine miles, we emerged from the woods on a firm open surface, and an extensive prospect was seen before us. Leaving the party to encamp, I rode to a round forest-hill some miles to the eastward, and obtained a comprehensive view of the Grampians, and also of the country to the northward, which now appeared to be chiefly open; and I had little doubt that we should find it more favourable for travelling upon. Eastward of the forest-hill, the ground

sank into a deep valley which turned round to the south-east,
after receiving the drainage from some hollows in the open
country north of it. This ravine received also the waters from
the woody ridge now south of us, where the numerous deep
vallies were irrigated by streams arising in swamps; the whole
probably forming the head of some more important streams flowing to the coast, and which I here named the river Hopkins. This
eminence, which I distinguished as Mount Stavely, consisted,
apparently of decomposed clay-stone or felspar, having a tendency to divide naturally into regular prisms. A very beautiful
and singular looking shrub appeared on the hills we crossed this
day, and also on the open ground, where indeed it was most
abundant. It was a species of acacia, the leaves adhering edgeways to thorny branches; many of these shrubs were in blossom,
the flowers being yellow, and as large and round as marbles, and
those growing very thickly, they gave to the branches, the appearance of garlands of festoons, the effect altogether being extremely
graceful and singular. We found also a beautiful new species of
acacia, looking like a broad-leaved variety of A. armata. The
branches were singularly protected by short spiny forks, which
proved to be the hardened permanent stipules. With this occurred
another species with hard stiff scymetar-shaped leaves and a
profusion of balls of browner yellow flowers, which had been
previously observed (on June 22) in a more vigorous condition.
By observations from this hill I made the height of Mount
William about 4,500 feet above the sea.

Sept. 20.—Our wheels now rolled lightly over fine grassy
downs, and our faces were turned towards distant home. Before
us arose a low, thinly-wooded hill, which at first bounded our
view towards the north, and afterwards proved to be the feature,
connecting the low woody ridge near our last camp with the hills
still further to the northward. On reaching the summit, I perceived, that a considerable extent of open country intervened,
being watered in the lower parts by several lakes. Descending
northward along an offset of the same hills which had led us in
that direction, and which I now named Mount Nicholson, I
observed that the lakes occurred at intervals in a valley apparently falling from the westward in which no stream appeared,
although it was shut in by well escarped rocky banks. We
encamped, after a journey of ten miles, at a point where another
valley from the north joined the above, and I was somewhat
surprised to find after encamping, that the water in the adjacent
lakes was extremely salt. No connection existed by means of any
channel between them, although they formed together a chain of

lagoons in the bed of a deep and well defined valley. On the contrary, the soil was particularly solid and firm between them, and the margin of the most eastern of these lakes, was separated by a high bank from the bed of another valley, where a running stream of pure water flowed over a broad and swampy bed fifteen feet higher than the adjacent valley containing the stagnant salt lakes. The rocks enclosing these singular vallies was basalt, and from these peculiarities, considered with reference to the ancient volcano and the dip of the mountain strata to the north-west, it was evident that some upheaving or subsidence had materially altered the levels of the original surface.

I could find no brine-springs in or about these lakes, and as it was evident, that a stream had once washed the bed of the ravine now occupied by them, I may leave the solution of the problem to geologists. As we proceeded over the open ground, before we reached the spot where we finally encamped, several natives appeared at a great distance in a valley eastward of Mount Nicholson, and Piper went towards them supported by Brown, whom I sent after him on horseback. They proved to be three or four gins only, but Piper continued to pursue them to the top of a hill, when a number of men armed with spears suddenly started from behind trees, and were running furiously towards Piper, when Brown rode up. On presenting his pistol they came to a full stop, thereby showing that they had some idea of firearms, although they refused to answer Piper's questions or to remain longer. In the evening, four of them approaching our camp, Piper went forward with Burnett to meet them. They advanced to the tents apparently without fear, and I obtained from them the names of various localities. On being questioned respecting Cadong, they told us, that all these waters ran into it, and pointed to the south-east, saying that I should by-and-bye see it. When I found we could obtain no more information, I presented the most intelligent of them with a tomahawk, on which they went slowly away, repeatedly turning round towards us and saying something, which, according to Piper, had reference to their tribe coming again and dancing a corrobory, a proposal these savage tribes often make, and which the traveller who knows them well, will think it better to discourage. These men carried a singular kind of malga, of a construction different from any Piper had ever seen. The malga is a weapon usually made in the form of fig. 2,* but that with which these natives were provided somewhat resembled a pick-axe with one half broken off, being made so as to be thickest at the angle. The blow of

* Sketch omitted.

such a formidable weapon could not be easily parried, from the uncertainty whether it would be aimed with the thick heavy corner or the sharp point. All the weapons of this singular race are peculiar, and this one was not the least remarkable. At dusk, while Woods was looking after the cattle near the camp, he surprised a native concealed behind a small bush, who did not make his escape until Woods was within two yards of him. How many more had been about we could not ascertain, but next morning we found near the spot, one of the bags usually carried by gins, and containing the following samples of their daily food: three snakes, three rats, about 2 lbs. of small fish, like white bait; cray fish; and a quantity of the small root of the cichoraceous plant tao, usually found growing on the plains with a bright yellow flower. There were also in the bag, various bodkins and colouring stones, and two mogos or stone hatchets. It seemed that our civility had as usual inspired these savages with a desire to beat our brains out while asleep, and we were thankful that in effecting their cowardly designs, they had been once more unsuccessful.

Sept. 21.—Early in the morning, a tribe of about forty were seen advancing toward our camp, preceded by the four men who had been previously there. Having determined, that they should not approach us again, I made Piper advance to them, and inquire what they wanted last night behind the bush, pointing at the same time to the spot. They returned no answer to this question, but continued to come forward, until I ordered a burning bush to be waved at them, and when they came to a stand without answering Piper's question, I ordered a party of our men to charge them, whereupon they all scampered off. We saw them upon our encamping ground after we had proceeded about two miles, but they did not attempt to follow us. Whether they would find a letter which I had buried there for Mr. Stapylton or not, we could only hope to discover after that gentleman's return to the colony. It was understood between us, that where a cross was cut in the turf where my tent had stood, he would find a note under the centre of the cross. This I buried, by merely pushing a stick into the earth, and dropping into the hole thus made, the note twisted up like a cigar. The letter was written chiefly to caution him about these natives. Basalt appeared in the sides of the ravine, which contained the salt-lakes, and, in equal abundance, and of the same quality, in that which enclosed the living stream, where it lay in blocks forming small cliffs. Finding, at length, a favourable place for crossing this stream, we traversed the ravine, and resumed our direct course towards the southern extremity of a distant range, named Mammala by the natives; the bluff head previously seen from Mount Abrupt. We now travelled over a country quite open, slightly undulating, and well covered with grass. To the westward the noble outline of the Grampians terminated a view extending over vast plains, fringed with forests and embellished with lakes. To the northward appeared other more accessible looking hills, some being slightly wooded, some green and quite clear to their summits, long grassy vales and ridges intervening: while to the eastward, the open plain extended as far as the eye could reach. Our way lay between distant ranges, which, in that direction, mingled with the clouds. Thus I had both the low country, which was without timber, and the well wooded hills, within reach, and might choose either for our route, according to the state of the ground, weather, etc. Certainly a land more favourable for colonisation could not be found. Flocks might be turned out upon its hills, or the plough at once set to work in the plains. No primeval forests required to be first rooted out, although there was enough of wood for all purposes of utility, and as much also for embellishment as even a painter could wish. One feature peculiar to that country appeared on these open downs: it consisted of hollows, which being usually surrounded by a line of "yarra" gum trees, or white bark eucalyptus, seemed at a distance to contain lakes, but instead of water, I found only blocks of vesicular trap, consisting apparently of granular felspar, and hornblende rock also appeared in the banks enclosing them. Some of these hollows were of a winding character, as if they were the remains of ancient watercourses; but if ever currents flowed there, the surface must have undergone considerable alteration since, for the downs where these hollows appeared, were elevated at least 900 feet above the sea, and surrounded on all sides by lower ground. There was an appearance of moisture among the rocks, in some of these depressions; and whether, by digging a few feet, permanent wells might be made, may be a question worth attention when colonisation extends to that country. We found on other parts of this open ground, large blocks composed of irregular concretions of ironstone, covered with a thin coating of compact brown hœmatite. The purple-ringed *Anguillaria dioica*, first seen on Pyramid Hill, again appeared here; and in many places the ground was quite yellow with the flowers of the cichoraceous plant Tao, whose root, small as it is, constitutes the food of the native women and children. The cattle are very fond of the leaves of this plant, and seemed to thrive upon it. We also found a new bulbine with a delicate yellow flower, being perfectly distinct from both the species described by Brown. The genial warmth of spring had begun to shew its influence on these plants, and also brought the snakes from their holes, for on this day in particular, it was ascertained that twenty-two had been killed by the party. These were all of that species, not venomous I believe, which the natives eat. We encamped near a small clump of trees, for the sake of fire-wood.

Sept. 22.—This day's journey lay chiefly across the open downs, with wooded hills occasionally to the left. On the southward, these downs extended to the horizon; and several isolated hills at great distances, apparently of trap, presented an outline like the volcanic Mount Napier. All the various small rivulets we traversed in our line of route, seemed to flow in that direction. Having crossed three of these, we encamped on the right bank of the fourth. The hills on our left were of granite, and as different as possible in appearance from the mountains to the westward, which were all of red sandstone. In the afternoon there was a thunder storm, but the sky became again perfectly serene in the evening.

Sept. 23.—This morning a thick fog hung over us; but having well reconnoitred the country beyond, I knew that I might travel in a straight line, over open ground, for several miles. When the fog arose, some finely wooded hills appeared on our right; but after advancing seven miles on good firm earth, we again came upon very soft ground, which obliged us to turn, and wind, and pick our way, wherever the surface seemed most likely to bear us. The fog was succeeded by a fine warm day, and as we proceeded, we saw two gins and their children, at work separately, on a swampy meadow; and, quick as the sight of these natives is, we had travelled long within view, before they observed us. They were spread over the field much in the manner in which emus and kangaroos feed on plains, and we observed them digging in the ground for roots. All carried bags, and when Piper went towards them, they ran with great speed across the vast open plains to the southward. This day we perceived the fresh track of several bullocks, a very extraordinary circumstance in that situation. The beautiful yellow-wreathed acacia was not to be seen after we quitted the open country. The ground was becoming almost hopelessly soft, when we reached a small run of water from the hills, and by keeping along its bank, we had the good fortune to reach an extremity of the range, where the solid granite was as welcome to our feet, as a dry beach is to shipwrecked seamen.

We had at length arrived under Mammala, the bluff hill which had been my land-mark, from the time I left Mr. Stapylton. I found this was the southern extremity of a lofty range, which I lost no time in ascending, after I had fixed on a spot for the camp. It consisted of huge blocks of granite, and was crowned with such lofty timber, that I could only catch occasional peeps of the surrounding country; nevertheless, I obtained, by moving about among the trees with my pocket sextant, almost all the angles I wanted; and I thus connected the survey of the region I was leaving, with that I was about to enter. My first view over this eastern country was extensive, and when I at length descended to a projecting rock, I found the prospect extremely promising, the land being variegated with open plains and strips of forest, and studded with smooth green hills, of the most beautiful forms. In the extreme distance, a range, much resembling that on which I stood, declined at its southern extremity, in the same manner as this did, and thus left me a passage precisely in the most direct line of route homewards. The carts had still, however, to cross the range at which we had arrived, and which, as I perceived here, not only extended southward, but also broke into bold ravines on the eastern side, being connected with some noble hills, or rather mountains, all grassy to their summits, thinly wooded, and consisting wholly of granite. They resembled very much some hills of the lower Pyrenees, in Spain, only that they were more grassy and less acclivitous, and I named this hill Mount Cole. To the southward, the sea-haze dimmed the hori zon: but I perceived the eastern margin of a large piece of water bearing south-south-east, and which I supposed might be Cadong. It was sheltered on the south-east by elevated ground apparently very distant, but no high range appeared between us and that inlet of the sea. On the contrary, the heights extending southward from this summit being connected with the highest and most southern hills visible from it, seemed to be the only high land or separation of the waters falling north and south. With such a country before us, I bade adieu to swamps, and returned well pleased to the camp, being guided to it only by the gushing torrent, for I had remained on the hill as long as daylight lasted.

Sept. 24.—The morning was rainy, and our way having to be traced up the ravines and round the hills, was very tortuous for the first three miles. We then reached the dividing part of the range, and descended immediately after into vallies of a less intricate character. Having passed over the swampy bed of a rivulet flowing southward, and having also crossed several fine bold ridges with good streams between them, we at length encamped near a round hill, which, being clear on the summit, was therefore a favourable station for the theodolite. This hill also consisted of granite, and commanded an open and extensive view over the country to the eastward.

Sept. 25.—One bold range of forest land appeared before us, and after crossing it, we passed over several rivulets falling northward, then over a ridge of trapean conglomerate with embedded quartz pebbles, and descended into a valley of the finest description. Grassy hills clear of timber appeared beyond a stream also flowing northward. These hills consisted of old vesicular lava. We next entered a forest of very large trees of iron bark eucalyptus, and we finally encamped in a grassy valley in the midst of this forest.

Sept. 26.—We first crossed more hills of the trapean conglomerate, on which grew iron-bark eucalypti, and box. The rock consisted of a base of compact felspar, with embedded grains of quartz, giving to some parts the character of conglomerate, and there were also embedded crystals of common felspar. By diverging a little to the right, we entered upon an open tract of the most favourable aspect, stretching away to the south-west among similar hills, until they were lost in the extreme distance. The whole surface was green as an emerald, and on our right for some miles ran a fine rivulet between steep grassy banks, and over a bed of trap-rock. At length, this stream was joined by two others coming through similar grassy vallies from the south; and, when we approached two lofty, smooth, round hills, green to their summits, the united streams flowed in an open dell, which our carts rolled through without meeting any impediment. I ascended the most western of these hills, as it was a point which I had observed from various distant stations, and I enjoyed such a charming view eastward from the summit, as can but seldom fall to the lot of the explorers of new countries. The surface presented the forms of pristine beauty, clothed in the hues of spring; and the shining verdure of these smooth and symmetrical hills, was relieved by the darker hues of the wood with which they were interlaced; which exhibited every variety of tint, from a dark brown in the fore-ground, to a light blue in extreme distance. The hills consisted entirely of lava, and I named them, from their peculiar shape, the Mammeloid hills, and the station on which I stood, Mount Greenock. In travelling through this Eden, no road was necessary, nor any ingenuity in conducting wheel-carriages, wherever we chose. The beautiful little terrestrial orchidaceous plants, Caladenia dilatata and Diuris aurea, were already in full bloom; and we also found on the plains this day, a most curious little bush resembling a heath in foliage, but with solitary polypetalous flowers resembling those of Sollya. When we had completed fourteen miles, we encamped on the edge of an open plain and near a small rivulet, the opposite bank consisting of grassy forest land.

Sept. 27.—I was surprised to hear the voice of a Scotch-woman in the camp, this morning. The peculiar accent and rapid utterance could not be mistaken, as I thought, and I called to inquire who the stranger was, when I ascertained that it was only Tommy Came-last, who was imitating a Scotch female, who, as I then learnt, was at Portland Bay, and had been very kind to Tommy. The imitation was ridiculously true, through all the modulations of that peculiar accent, although, strange to say, without the pronunciation of a single intelligible word. The talent of the aborigines for imitation seems a peculiar trait in their character. I was informed that the widow could also amuse the men occasionally—by enacting their leader, taking angles, drawing from nature, etc.

While the party went forward over the open plains with Mr. Stapylton, I ascended a smooth round hill, distant about a mile to the southward of our camp, from which I could with ease continue my survey, by means of hills on all sides, the highest of them being to the southward. I could trace the rivulets flowing northward, into one or two principal channels, near several masses of mountain; these channels and ranges being probably connected with those crossed by us on our route from the Murray. In these bare hills, and on the open grassy plains, old vesicular lava abounded; small loose elongated fragments lay on the round hills, having a red scorified appearance, and being also so cellular, as to be nearly as light as pumice. We this day crossed several fine running streams, and forests of box and blue-gum growing on ridges of trapean conglomerate. At length, we entered on a very level and extensive flat, exceedingly green, and resembling an English park. It was bounded on the east by a small river flowing to the northwest, (probably the Loddon,) and abrupt but grassy slopes arose beyond its right bank. After crossing this stream, we encamped, having travelled nearly fifteen miles in one straight line, bearing $60\frac{1}{2}°$ east of north. This tract was rather of a different character from that of the fine country of which we had previously seen so much, and we saw for the first time, the

I. D.   x

Discaria Australia, a remarkable green leafless spiny bush, and resembling in a most striking manner the Colletias of Chili. Sheltered on every side by woods or higher ground, the spring seemed more advanced there than elsewhere, and our hard wrought cattle well deserved to be the first to browse on that verdant plain. The stream, in its course downwards, vanished amongst grassy hills to water a country apparently of the most interesting and valuable character.

Sept. 28.—The steep banks beyond the river consisted of clay-slate, having under it a conglomerate, containing fragments of quartz cemented by compact hœmatite. The day was hot, and we killed several large snakes of the species eaten by the natives. I observed that our guides looked at the colour of the belly, when in any doubt about the sort they preferred; these were white bellied; whereas the belly of a very fierce one with a large head, of which Piper and the others seemed much afraid, was yellow. On cutting this snake open, two young quails were found within; one of them not being quite dead. The country we crossed during the early part of the day, was at least as fine as that we had left. We passed alternately through strips of forest and over open flats well watered—the streams flowing southward; and at nine miles we crossed a large stream also flowing in that direction: all these being evidently tributaries to that on which we had been encamped. Beyond the greater stream, where we last crossed it, the country presented more of the mountain character, but good strong grass grew among the trees, which consisted of box and lofty blue-gum. After making out upwards of eleven miles, we encamped in a valley where water lodged in holes, and where we found also abundance of grass. We were fast approaching those summits which had guided me in my route from Mount Cole, then more than fifty miles behind us. Like that mountain these heights also belonged to a lofty range, and, like it, were beside a very low part of it, through which I hoped to effect a passage. Leaving the party to encamp, I proceeded forward in search of the hill I had so long seen before me, and I found that the hills immediately beyond our camp were part of the dividing range, and broken into deep ravines on the eastern side. Pursuing the connection between them and the still higher summits on the north-east, I came at length upon an open valley enclosed by hills very lightly wooded. This change was evidently owing to a difference in the rock, which was a fine grained granite, whereas the hills we had recently crossed, belonged chiefly to the volcanic class of rocks, with the exception of the range I had

traversed that evening in my way from the camp, which consisted
of ferruginous sandstone. With the change of rock, a difference
was also obvious in the shape of the hills, the quantity and quality
of the water, and the character of the trees. The hills presented
a bold sweeping outline, and were no longer broken by sharp-
edged strata, but crowned with large round masses of rock.
Running water was gushing from every hollow in much greater
abundance than elsewhere; and, lastly, the timber, which on the
other ranges, consisted chiefly of iron-bark and stringy-bark, now
presented the shining bark of the blue-gum or yarra, and the grey
hue of the box. The anthistiria australia, a grass which seems to
delight in a granitic soil, also appeared in great abundance, and
we also found the aromatic tea, Tasmania aromatica, which
represents in New Holland, the Winter's bark of the southern
extremity of South America. The leaves and bark of this tree
have a hot biting cinnamon-like taste, on which account it is
vulgarly called the pepper-tree. I could ride with ease to the
summit of the friendly hill, that I had seen from afar, and found
it but thinly wooded, so that I could take my angles around the
horizon without difficulty. Again reminded by the similar
aspect this region presented, of the lower Pyrenees and the pass
of Orbaicetta, I named the summit Mount Byng. A country fully
as promising as the fine region we had left, was embraced in my
view from that point. I perceived long patches of open plains,
interspersed with forest hills and low woody ranges, among which
I could trace out a good line of route for another fifty miles homewards. The highest of the mountains lay to the south, and evidently belonged to the coast range, if it might be so called; and on
that side, a lofty mass arose above the rest, and promised a view
towards the sea; that height being distant from the hill on which
I stood, about thirty miles. A broad chain of woody hills connected the coast range with Mount Byng, and I could trace the
general course of several important streams through the country
to the east of it. Northward, I saw a little of the interior plains,
and the points where the various ranges terminated upon them.
The sun was setting, when I left Mount Byng, but I depended on
one of our natives, Tommy-Came-last, who was then with me,
for finding our way to the camp; and who, on such occasions,
could trace my steps backwards, with wonderful facility by day
or night.

Sept. 29.—The range before us was certainly rather formidable
for the passage of carts, but home lay beyond it, while delay and
famine were synonymous terms with us at that time. By fol-

lowing up the valley in which we had encamped, I found, early on this morning, an easy way through which the carts might gain the lowest part of the range. Having conducted them to this point without any other inconvenience besides the overturning of one cart (from bad driving), we descended along the hollow of a ravine, after making it passable by throwing some rocks into the narrow part near its head. The ravine at length opened, as I had expected, into a grassy valley, with a fine rivulet flowing through it, and from this valley we debouched into the still more open granitic country at the foot of Mount Byng. The pass, thus auspiciously discovered and opened, over a neck apparently the very lowest of the whole range, I named Expedition-pass, confident that such a line of communication between the southern coast and Sydney, must, in the course of time, become a very considerable thoroughfare. The change of soil, however, introduced us to the old difficulty from which we had been happily relieved for some time, for we came once more upon rotten and boggy ground. We met with this unexpected impediment in an open-looking flat, near a rivulet I was about to cross, when I found the surface so extremely soft and yielding, that from the extreme resistance, a bolt of the boat-carriage gave way, a circumstance which obliged us immediately to encamp, although we had travelled only four miles.

Sept. 30.—Compelled thus to await the repair of the boat-carriage, I determined to make an excursion to the lofty mountain mass, which appeared about thirty miles to the southward, in order that I might connect my survey with Port Phillip, which I hoped to see thence. The horses were not found as soon as they were required, but when we at last got upon their backs, we were therefore less disposed to spare them. We crossed some soft hollows during the first few miles, and then arrived on the banks of a small and deep river with reeds on its borders, and containing many broad and deep reaches. It was full, and flowed, but not rapidly, towards the north-east, and it was not until we had continued along the left bank of this stream for a considerable way upwards, that we found a rapid, where we could cross without swimming. The left bank was of bold acclivity, but grassy and clear of timber, being very level on the summit; and I found it consisted of trap-rock of the same vesicular character, which I had observed in so many other parts of this southern region. Beyond the river (which I then named the Barnard), we first encountered a hilly country from which we emerged rather unexpectedly; for, after crossing a small rivulet flowing in a deep and grassy dell, where trap-rock again appeared, and ascending the opposite slope, we found that the summit consisted of an open level country of the finest description. It was covered with the best kind of grass, and the immediate object of our ride, the mountain, was now visible beyond these rich plains. Some fine forest-hills arose in various directions to the right and left, and indeed I never saw a more pleasing or promising portion of territory. The rich open ground, across which we rode, was not without slight undulations; and when we had traversed about four miles of it, we came quite unawares to a full and flowing stream, nearly on a level with its grassy banks; the bottom being so sound, that we forded it without the least difficulty. Emus were very numerous on the downs, and their curiosity brought them to stare at our horses, apparently unconscious of the presence of the biped on their backs, whom both birds and beasts seem instinctly to avoid. In one flock, I counted twenty-nine emus, and so near did they come to us, that having no rifle with me, I was tempted to discharge even my pistol at one, although without effect. Kangaroos were equally numerous. Having proceeded three miles beyond the stream, we came to another, flowing to the westward between some very deep ponds, and it was probably a tributary to the first. At twenty-two miles from the camp, on descending from some finely undulating open ground, we arrived at a stream flowing westward, which I judged to be also a branch of that we had first crossed. Its bed consisted of granitic rocks, and on the left bank I found trap. We had this stream afterwards in sight on our left until, at two miles further, we again crossed it and entered a wood of eucalyptus, being then only five miles distant from the mountain, and we subsequently found, that this wood extended to its base. The effects of some violent hurricane from the north were visible under every tree, the earth being covered with broken branches, some of which were more than a foot in diameter; the withering leaves remained upon them, and I remarked that no whole trees had been blown down, although almost all had lost their principal limbs, and not a few had been reduced to bare poles. The havoc which the storm had made, gave an unusual aspect to the whole of the forest land, so universally was it covered with withering branches. Whether this region is subject to frequent visitations of a like nature, I could not of course then ascertain; but I perceived that many of the trees had lost some of their top limbs at a much earlier period, in a similar manner. Neither had this been but a partial tempest, for to the very base of the mountain the same effects were visible. The trees on its side were of a much grander character than those in the forest, and consisted principally of black-butt and blue-gum eucalypti, measuring from six to eight feet in diameter. The rock was syenite, so weathered as to resemble sandstone. I ascended without having been obliged to alight from my horse, and I found that the summit was very spacious, being covered towards the south with tree-ferns, and the musk-plant grew in great luxuriance. I saw also many other plants found at the Illawarra, on the eastern coast of the colony of New South Wales. The summit was full of wombat holes, and, unlike that side by which I had ascended, it was covered with the dead trunks of enormous trees in all stages of decay. I had two important objects in view in ascending this hill; one being to determine its position trigonometrically, as a point likely to be seen from the country to which I was going, where it might be useful to me in fixing other points; the other being to obtain a view of Port Phillip, and thus to connect my survey with that harbour. But the tree-fern, musk-plant, brush, and lofty timber, together shut us up for a long time from any prospect of the low country to the southward, and it was not until I had nearly exhausted a fine sunny afternoon in wandering round the broad summit, that I could distinguish and recognise some of the hills to the westward; and when I at length obtained a glimpse of the country towards the coast, the features of the earth could scarcely be distinguished from the sky or sea, although one dark point looked more like a cape than a cloud, and seemed to remain steady. With my glass, I perceived that water lay inside of that cape, and that low plains extended northward from the water. I next discovered a hilly point outside of the cape or towards the sea; and on descending the hill to where the trees grew less thickly, I obtained an uninterrupted view of the whole piece of water. As the sun went down, the distant horizon became clearer towards the coast, and I intersected at length the two capes; also one at the head of the bay, and several detached hills. I perceived distinctly the course of the Exe and Arundell rivers, and a line of mangrove trees along the low shore. In short, I at length recognised Port Phillip and the intervening country around it, at a distance afterwards ascertained to be upwards of fifty miles from Indented Head, which proved to be the first cape I had seen; that outside being Point Nepean, on the east side of the entrance to this bay. At that vast distance, I could trace no signs of life about this harbour. No stockyards, cattle, or even smoke, although at the highest northern point of the bay, I saw a mass of white objects which might have been either tents or vessels. I perceived a white speck, which I took for breakers or white sand, on the projecting point of the north-eastern shore. On that day nine years exactly, I first beheld the heads of Port Jackson, a rather singular coincidence. Thus the mountain on which I stood, became an important point in my survey, and I gave it the name of Mount Macedon, with reference to that of Port Phillip. It had been long dark before I reached the base of the mountain, and picked out a dry bit of turf, on which to lie down for the night.

XIV. STURT'S JOURNEY INTO CENTRAL AUSTRALIA

[STURT'S *Narrative of an Expedition into Central Australia* was published in two volumes, London, 1849. His object in the expedition described in these pages was to reach the centre of the continent, and he expressed his keen regret at having been compelled to turn back after having so nearly achieved success.]

In May, 1844, Captain Grey, Governor of South Australia, received a private letter from Lord Stanley, referring to a despatch his Lordship had already written to him, to authorise the fitting out of an expedition to proceed under my command into the interior. This despatch, however, did not come to hand until the end of June, but on the receipt of it Captain Grey empowered me to organise an expedition, on the modified plan on which Lord Stanley had determined. . . .

I decided on our final departure from Adelaide on the 15th of August; for having received my instructions I should then have nothing further to detain me. That day, therefore, was fixed upon as the day on which we should start to overtake the party on its road to Moorundi. The sun rose bright and clear over my home on the morning of that day. It was indeed a morning such as is only known in a southern climate; but I had to bid adieu to my wife and family, and could but feebly enter into the harmony of Nature, as everything seemed joyous around me. . . .

We reached the Darling [on September 24th] at half-past five, as the sun's almost level beams were illuminating the flats, and every blade of grass and every reed appeared of that light and brilliant green which they assume when held up to the light. The change from barrenness and sterility to richness and verdure was sudden and striking, and nothing certainly could have been more cheering or cheerful than our first camp on the Darling River. The scene itself was very pretty. Beautiful and drooping trees shaded its banks, and the grass in its channel was green to the water's edge. Evening's mildest radiance seemed to linger on a scene so fair, and there was a mellow haze in the distance that softened every object. The cattle and horses were up to their flanks in grass and young reeds, and plants indicative of a better soil, such as the sowthistle, the mallow, peppermint, and indigofera were growing in profusion around us. Close to our tents there was a large and hollow gum-tree, in which a new fishing net had been deposited, but where the owner intended to use it was a puzzle to us, for it was impossible that any fish could remain in the shallow and muddy waters of the Darling; which was at its lowest ebb, and the current was so feeble that I doubted if it really flowed at all. Whether the natives anticipated the flood which shortly afterwards swelled it I cannot say, although I am led to believe they did, either from habit or experience. . . .

We commenced our journey up the Darling at nine o'clock, on a course somewhat to the eastward of north. We passed flat after flat of the most vivid green, ornamented by clumps of trees, sufficiently apart to give a most picturesque finish to the landscape. Trees of denser foliage and deeper shade drooped over the river, forming long dark avenues, and the banks of the river, grassed to the water, had the appearance of having been made so by art.

We halted, after a journey of fourteen miles, on a flat little inferior to that we had left, and again turned the cattle out to feed on the luxuriant herbage around them.

The Darling must have been in the state in which we found it for a great length of time, and I am led to infer, from the very grassy nature of its bed, that it seldom contains water to any depth, or length of time, since in such case the grass would be killed. Its flats, like those of the Murray, are backed by lagoons, but they had long been dry, and the trees growing round them were either dead or dying. . . .

The position we had taken up was a very favourable one, since, being on the right or northern bank of the creek, we were, by the flooding of the lake, cut off from the Darling natives. I now therefore determined on making an excursion into the interior to the N.W., to examine the ranges seen by Mr. Poole, and to ascertain if, as he supposed, there was a body of water to the westward of them. . . .

The principal object I had in view during the excursion I was then employed upon, was if possible to find a proper position to which the party might move; for I foresaw that my absence would be frequent and uncertain, and although my men were very well disposed towards the natives, I was anxious to prevent the chance of collision or misunderstanding. I had now found such a position, for on examining the water-hole I felt satisfied that it might be depended upon for ten days or a fortnight, whilst the grass in its neighbourhood although dry was abundant. Wishing, however, to penetrate the ranges by the gap through which the creek issued from them, I still thought it advisable to prosecute my intended journey up it. Accordingly on the 24th we mounted our horses and rode towards the hills. A little above where we had slept we passed a small junction from the westward, and at 7 miles entered the gap, the Coonbaralba, on the bearing of which we had run across the plains, being on our right. We had already passed several small water-holes, but at the entrance of the gap passed some larger ones in which the water was brackish, and these had the appearance of being permanent. Topar had shewn much indignation at our going on, and constantly remonstrated with us as we were riding along; however, we saw two young native dogs about a third grown, after which he bounded with incredible swiftness, but when they saw him they started off also. It was soon evident, that both were doomed to destruction, his speed being greater than that of the young brutes, for he rapidly gained upon them. The moment he got within reach of the hindmost he threw a stick which he had seized while running, with unerring precision, and striking it full in the ribs stretched it on the ground. As he passed the animal he gave it a blow on the head with another stick, and bounding on after the other was soon out of sight. All we knew further of the chase was, that before we reached the spot where his first prize lay, he was returning to us with its companion. As soon as he had secured his prey he sat down to take out their entrails, a point in which the natives are very particular. He was careful in securing the little fat they had about the kidneys, with which he rubbed his body all over, and having finished this operation he filled their insides with grass and secured them with skewers. This done he put them on the cart, and we proceeded up the pass, at the head of which we arrived sooner than I expected. We then found ourselves at the commencement of a large plain. The hills we had ascended the day before trended to the north, and there was a small detached range running perpendicular to them on our right. To the south there were different points, apparently the terminations of parallel ranges, and westward an unbroken line of hills. The creek seemed to trend to the S.W., and in that direction I determined to follow it, but Topar earnestly entreated us not to do so. He was in great consternation; said here was no water, and promised that if we would follow him he would shew us water in which we could swim. On this condition I turned as he desired, and keeping along the western base of the main or front range, took up a course somewhat obtuse to that by which I had crossed the plains of Cawndilla. The productions on the ground were of a salsolaceous kind, although it was so much elevated above the plains, but amongst them there was not any mesembryanthemum. At about three miles we passed a very remarkable and perfectly isolated hill, of about 150 feet in height. It ran longitudinally from south to north for about 350 yards, and was bare of trees or shrubs, with the exception of one or two casuarinas. The basis of this hill was a slaty ferruginous rock, and protruding above the ground along the spine of the hill there was a line of the finest hepatic iron ore I ever saw; it laid in blocks of various sizes, and of many tons weight piled one upon the other, without a particle of earth either on their faces or between them. Nothing indeed could exceed the clean appearance of these huge masses. On ascending this hill and seating myself on the top of one of them to take bearings, I found that the compass deviated 37° from the north point, nor could I place any dependance on the angles I here took.

At about nine miles the main range turned to the N.N.E., and Topar accordingly keeping near its base changed his course, and at five miles more led us into a pass in some respects similar to that by which we had entered the range. It was however less confined and more open. Steep hills, with rocks in slabs protruding from many parts, flanked it to the south, whilst on its northern side perpendicular rocks, varying in height from 15 to 20 feet, over which the hills rose almost as perpendicularly more than 200 feet higher, were to be seen. Close under these was the stony bed of a mountain torrent, but it was also evident that the whole pass, about 160 yards broad, was sometimes covered by floods. Down this gully Topar now led us, and at a short distance, crossing over to its northern side, he stopped at a little green puddle of water that was not more than three inches deep. Its surface was covered with slime and filth, and our horses altogether rejected it. Some natives had recently been at the place, but none were there when we arrived. I was exceedingly provoked at Topar's treachery, and have always been at a loss to account for it. At the time, both Mr. Browne and myself attributed it to the machinations of our friend Nadbuck; but his alarm at invading the hilly country was too genuine to have been counterfeited. It might have been that Nadbuck and

Toonda expected that they would benefit more by our presents and provisions than if we left them for the interior, and therefore tried by every means to deter us from going; they certainly had long conversations with Topar before he left the camp to accompany us. Still I may do injustice to them in this respect. However, whether this was the case or not, we had to suffer from Topar's misconduct. I turned out of the pass, and stopped a little beyond it, in a more sheltered situation. Here Topar coolly cooked his dogs, and wholly demolished one of them and part of the other. In wandering about the gorge of the glen, Mr. Browne found a native well, but there was no water in it.

Our camp at Cawndilla now bore S.S.E. from us, distant 70 odd miles, and having determined on moving the party, I resolved to make the best of my way back to it. On the following morning, therefore, we again entered the pass, but as it trended too much to the eastward, I crossed a small range and descended at once upon the plains leading to the camp. At about 17 miles from the hills, Topar led us to a broad sheet of water that must have been left by the recent rains. It was still tolerably full, and water may perhaps be found here when there is none in more likely places in the hills. This spot Topar called Wancookaroo; it was unfortunately in a hollow from whence we could take no bearings to fix its precise position.

We halted at sunset on the top of a small eminence, from which the hills Mr. Poole had ascended bore E.N.E., and the hill at the pass N.W. We were suddenly roused from our slumbers a little before daylight by a squall of wind that carried away every light thing about us, hats, caps, etc., all went together, and bushes of atriplex also went bounding along like so many footballs. The wind became piercing cold, and all comfort was gone. As morning dawned the wind increased, and as the sun rose it settled into a steady gale. We were here about forty miles from Cawndilla, nor do I remember having ever suffered so severely from cold even in Canada. The wind fairly blew through and through us, and Topar shivered so under it that Morgan gave him a coat to put on. As we seldom put our horses out of a walk, we did not reach the tents until late in the afternoon, but I never was more rejoiced to creep under shelter than on this occasion. . . .

Fully satisfied then that the greatest obstacle to the progress of the Expedition would be the want of water, and that it would only be by long and laborious search that we should succeed in gaining the interior, I determined on taking as much as I could on my proposed journey, and with a view to gaining more time for examining the country, I had a tank constructed, which I purposed to send a day or two in advance.

The little pond of which I have spoken at the head of the pass, had near it a beautiful clump of acacias of a species entirely new to us. It was a pretty graceful tree, and threw a deep shade on the ground; but with the exception of these and a few gumtrees the vicinity was clear and open. Our position in the creek on the contrary was close and confined. Heavy gusts of wind were constantly sweeping the valley, and filling the air with sand, and the flies were so numerous and troublesome that they were a preventative to all work. I determined, therefore, before Mr. Browne and I should start for the interior, to remove the camp to the upper part of the glen. On the 4th we struck our tents and again pitched them close to the acacias. Early on the morning of the 5th, I sent Flood with Lewis and Sullivan, having the cart full of water, to preserve a certain course until I should overtake them, being myself detained in camp with Mr. Browne, in consequence of the arrival of several natives from whom we hoped to glean some information; but in this we were disappointed. Toonda had continued with us as far as "Parnari"; but on our moving up higher into the hills, his heart failed him, and he returned to Cawndilla.

At eleven, Mr. Browne and I took leave of Mr. Poole, and pursuing a course of 140° to the west of south, rode on to overtake the cart. At about four miles from the camp we crossed a small ironstone range, from which we saw Flood and his party nearly at the foot of the hill on which I had directed him to move, and at which I intended to cross the ranges if the place was favourable. In this, however, we were disappointed, for the hills were too rugged, although of no great breadth or height. We were consequently obliged to turn to the south, and in going over the rough uneven ground, had the misfortune to burst our tank. I therefore desired Lewis to stop, and gave the horses as much water as they would drink, still leaving a considerable quantity in the tank, of which I hoped we might yet avail ourselves. Although we had found it impracticable to cross the ranges at the proposed point, Mr. Browne and I had managed to scramble up the most elevated part of them. We appeared still to be amidst broken stony hills, from which there was no visible outlet. There was a line of gum-trees, however, in a valley to the south-west of us, as if growing on the side of a creek that would in such case be tributary to the main creek on which our tents were pitched, and we hoped, by running along the base of the hills to the south and turning into the valley, to force our way onwards. At about three and a half miles our anticipations were verified by our arriving opposite to an opening leading northwards into the hills. This proved to be the valley we had noticed. A line of gum-trees marked the course of a small creek, which passing behind a little hill at the entrance of the valley, reappeared on the other side, and then trended to the N.W. Entering the valley and pursuing our way up it, at two miles we crossed another small creek, tributary to the first, and at a mile beyond halted for the night, without having found water. Although there was a little grass on the plains between the camp and the ranges, there was none in the valley in which we stopped. Low bushes of rhagodia and atriplex were alone to be seen, growing on a red, tenacious, yet somewhat sandy soil, whilst the ranges themselves were covered with low brush.

The water had almost all leaked out of the tank when we examined it, so that it was no longer of any service to us. On the morning of the 7th, therefore, I sent Lewis and Sullivan with the cart back to the camp, retaining Flood and Morgan to attend to Mr. Browne and myself.

When we started I directed them to follow up the creek, which did not appear to continue much further, and on arriving at the head of it to cross the range, where it was low, in the hope that they would strike the opposite fall of waters in descending on the other side, whilst I went with Mr. Browne to a hill from which I was anxious to take bearings, although Lewis, who had already been on the top of it, assured me that there was nothing new to be seen. However, we found the view to be extensive enough to enable us to judge better of the character of the country than from any other point on which we had yet been. It was traversed by numerous rocky ridges, that extended both to the north and south beyond the range of vision. Many peaks shewed themselves in the distance, and I was enabled to connect this point with "Coonbaralba," the hill above the camp. The ridge I had directed Flood to cross was connected with this hill, and appeared to create a division of the waters thereabouts. All however to the north or north-west was as yet confused. There was no visible termination of the ranges in any direction, nor could we see any feature to guide us in our movements.

The rock formation of this hill was a fine grained granite, and was in appearance a round and prominent feature. Although its sides were covered with low dark brush, there was a considerable quantity of oat-grass in its deep and sheltered valleys. We soon struck on Flood's track after leaving this hill, which, as Lewis had been the first to ascend, I called "Lewis's Hill"; and riding up the valley along which the men had already passed, at six miles crossed the ridge, which (as we had been led to hope) proved to be the range dividing the eastern and western waters. On our descent from this ridge we proceeded to the north-west, but changed our course to north in following the cart tracks, and at four miles overtook Flood and Morgan on the banks of a creek, the channel of which, and the broad and better grassed valley through which it runs, we ourselves had several times crossed on our way down, and from the first had hoped to find it the main creek on the west side of the ranges.

At the point where we overtook Flood it had increased greatly in size, but we searched its hopeless bed in vain for water, and as it there turned too much to the eastward, for which reason Flood had stopped until we should come up, we left it and crossed the low part of a range to our left; but as we were going too much to the south-west, I turned shortly afterwards into a valley that led me more in the direction in which I was anxious to proceed. The country had been gradually improving from the time we crossed the little dividing range, not so much in soil as in appearance, and in the quality of its herbage. There was a good deal of grass in the valleys, and up the sides of the hills, which were clear and open on the slopes but stony on their summits. After proceeding about two and a half miles, we got into a scrubby part of the hills, through which we found it difficult to push our way, the scrub being eucalyptus dumosa, an unusual tree to find in those hills. After forcing through the scrub for about half a mile, we were suddenly stopped by a succession of precipitous sandstone gullies, and were turned to the eastward of north down a valley the fall of which was to that point. This valley led us to that in which we had rejoined Flood, but lower down; in crossing it we again struck on the creek we had then left, much increased in size, and with a row of gum-trees on either side of it, but its even broad bed composed of the cleanest gravel and sand, precluded the hope of our finding water. At about a mile, however, it entered a narrow defile in the range, and the hills closed rapidly in upon it. Pursuing our way down the defile it gradually narrowed, the bed of the creek occupied its whole breadth, and the rocks rose perpendicularly on either side. We searched this place for water with the utmost care and anxiety, and I was at length fortunate enough to discover a small clear basin not a yard in circumference, under a rock on the left side of the glen. Suspecting that this was supplied by surface drainage, we enlarged the pool, and obtained from it an abundance of the most delicious water we had tasted during our wanderings. Mr. Browne will I am sure bear the Rocky Glen in his most grateful remembrance. Relieved from further anxiety with regard to our animals, he hastened with me to ascend one of the hills that towered above us to the height of 600 feet, before the sun should set, but this was no trifling task, as the ascent was exceedingly steep. The view from the summit of this hill presented the same broken country to our scrutiny which I have before described, at every point excepting to the westward, in which direction the ranges appeared to cease at about six miles, and the distant horizon from S.W. to N.W. presented an unbroken level. The dark and deep ravine through which the creek ran was visible below us, and apparently broke through the ranges at about four miles to the W.N.W., but we could not see any water in its bed. It was sufficiently cheering to us however to know that we were near the termination of the ranges to the westward, and that the country we should next traverse was of open appearance.

We started at eight to pursue our journey, and kept for some time in its bed. The rock formation near and at our camp was trap, but at about a mile below it changed to a coarse grey granite, huge blocks of which, traversed by quartz, were scattered about. The defile had opened out a little below where we had slept, but it soon again narrowed, and the hills closed in upon it nearer than before. The bed of the creek at the same time became rocky, and blocked up with immense fragments of granite. We passed two or three pools of water, one of which was of tolerable size, and near it there were the remains of a large encampment of natives. Near to it also there was a well, a sure sign that however deep the water-holes in the glen might now be, there are times when they are destitute of any. There can be no doubt, indeed, but that we owed our present supply of water both at this place and at the Coonbaralba pass, to the rains that fell in the hills during the week we remained at Williorara.

Soon after passing the native camp, our further progress was completely stopped by large blocks of granite, which, resting on each other, prevented the possibility of making a passage for the cart or even of advancing on horseback. In this predicament I sent Flood to climb one of the hills to our left, to see if there was a leading spur by which we could descend to the plains; but on his return to us he said that the country was wholly impracticable, but that he thought we should see more of it from a hill he had noticed about three miles to the north-east. We accordingly left Morgan with the horses and walked to it. We reached the summit after a fatiguing walk of an hour, but neither were we repaid for our trouble, nor was there anything in the view to lead us to hope for any change for the better. The character of the country had completely changed, and in barrenness it far exceeded that through which we had already passed. The line of hills extended from S.E. by S. to the opposite point of the compass, and formed a steep wall to shut out the level country below them.

One might have imagined that an ocean washed their base, and I would that it really had been so, but a very different hue spread between them and the distant horizon than the deep blue of the sea. The nearer plains appeared of a lighter shade than the rest of the landscape, but there were patches of trees or shrubs upon them, which in the distance were blended together in universal scrub. A hill, which I had at first sight taken to be Mount Lyell of Sir Thomas Mitchell, bore 7° to the east of north, distant 18 miles, but as our observations placed us in 31° 32′ 00″ S. only, it could not have been that hill. To the south and east our view was limited, as the distant horizon was hid from our sight by higher ground near us, but there was a confused succession of hills and valleys in those directions, the sides of both being covered with low brush and huge masses of granite, and a dark brown sombre hue pervaded the whole scene. We could not trace the windings of the creek, but thought we saw gum-trees in the plains below us, to the N.E., indicating the course of a creek over them. Some of the same trees were also visible to our left (looking westward), and the ranges appeared less precipitous and lower in the same direction. We cast our eyes therefore to that point to break through them, and returned to Morgan with at least the hope of success. In the view I had just then been contemplating, however, I saw all realized of what I had imagined of the interior, and felt assured that I had a work of extreme difficulty before me in the task of penetrating towards the centre.

As soon as we had got well into the plains, we pursued a course of half a point to the eastward of north, nearly parallel to the ranges, until we reached the glen from which the creek issues, and formed our little camp on its banks. The water

I. D.   y however was not good, so that we were obliged to send for some from a pool a little above us. In the bed of this creek we found beautiful specimens of Solani, and a few new plants.

I halted at this place in consequence of the resolution I had taken to push into the interior on the following morning. I was therefore anxious that the horses should start as fresh as possible, as we could not say where we should again find water.

The direction of the hills was nearly north and south, extending at either hand to a distance beyond the range of vision or telescope. Our observations here placed us in latitude 31° 23′ 20″ S., so that we were still nearly half a degree to the south of Mount Lyell, and a degree to the south of Mount Serle. I had little prospect of success, however, in pursuing a direct westerly course, as it would have led me into the visible scrub there; on the other hand I did not wish to move exactly parallel to the ranges, but, in endeavouring to gain a knowledge of the more remote interior, to keep such a course as would not take me too far from the hills in the event of my being obliged to fall back upon them. We started on the 11th, therefore, on a N.N.W. course, and on the bearing of the low hills we had seen to the westward, and which were now distinctly visible. For the first five miles we travelled over firm and open plains of clay and sand, similar to the soil of the plains of the Murray. At length the ground became covered with fragments of quartz rock, iron-stone, and granite. It appeared as if M'Adam had emptied every stone he ever broke to be strewed over this metalled region. The edges of the stones were not, however, rounded by attrition, or mixed together, but laid on the plains in distinct patches, as if large masses of the different rocks had been placed at certain distances from each other and then shivered into pieces. The plains were in themselves of undulating surface, and appeared to extend to some low elevations on our left, connecting them with the main range as outer features; although in the distance they only shewed as a small and isolated line of hills detached about eleven miles from the principal groups, from which we were gradually increasing our distance. This outer feature prevented our seeing the north-west horizon until we gained an elevated part of it, whence it appeared that we should soon have to descend to lower ground than that on which we had been travelling. There was a small eminence that just shewed itself above the horizon to the N.N.W., and was directly in our course, enabling us to keep up our bearings with the loftier and still visible peaks on the ranges. We found the lower ground much less stony and more even than the higher ground, and our horses got well over it. At 4 p.m., we observed a line of gum-trees before us, evidently marking the line of a creek, the upper branch of which we had already noticed as issuing from a deep recess in the range. At the distance we were from the hills, we had little hope of finding water; on approaching it, however, we alarmed some cockatoos and other birds, and observed the recent tracks of emus in the bed of the creek. Flood, who had ridden a-head, went up it in search for water. Mr. Browne and I went downwards, and from appearances had great hopes that at a particular spot we should succeed by digging, more especially as on scraping away a little of the surface gravel with our hands, there were sufficient indications to induce us to set Morgan to work with a spade, who in less than an hour dug a hole from which we were enabled to supply both our own wants and those of our animals; and as there was good grass in the creek, we tethered them out in comfort. This discovery was the more fortunate, as Flood returned unsuccessful from his search.

The gum-trees on this creek were of considerable size; and many of the shrubs we had found in the creek, at the glen, were in beautiful flower in its broad and gravelly bed, along which the Clyanthus was running with its magnificent blossoms; a situation where I certainly did not expect to find that splendid creeper growing. It was exceedingly curious to observe the instinct which brought the smaller birds to our well. Even whilst Morgan was digging, and Mr. Browne and I sitting close to him, some Diamond birds (Amandina) were bold enough to perch on his spade; we had, in the course of the day, whilst passing over the little stony range, been attracted to a low Banksia, by seeing a number of nests of these little birds in its branches, and of which there were no less than fourteen. In some of them were eggs, and in others young birds; so that it appeared they lived in communities, or congregated together to breed. But we had numberless opportunities of observing the habits of this interesting little bird, whose note cheered us for months, and was ever the forerunner of good, as indicating the existence of water.

We placed the cart under a gum-tree, in which the cockatoos we had alarmed when descending into the creek had a nest. These noisy birds (*Plyctolophus* Leadbeaterii) kept incessantly screeching to their young, which answered them in notes that resembled the croaking of frogs, more than anything else.

On the 11th we left the creek, well satisfied with our night's occupation of it, as also, I believe, to the still greater satisfaction of our noisy friends. For about two and a half or three miles there was every appearance of an improving country. It was open, and in many places well covered with grass; and although at three miles it fell off a little, still the aspect on the northern side of the creek was, to a considerable distance, preferable to that on the south side. At 11 a.m. we gained the crest of the little stony hill we had seen the day before to the N.N.W., and from it were enabled not only to take back bearings, but to carry others forward. We were fast losing sight of the hills, whose loftier summits alone were visible, yet we now saw fresh peaks to the north, which satisfied me that they continued in that direction far beyond the most distant one we had seen. From this circumstance I was led to hope that we might fall on another creek, and so gradually, but surely, work our way to the N.W.

On descending from the little hill, however, we traversed an inferior country, and at two miles saw a few scattered pine-trees. Shortly afterwards, on breaking through a low scrub, we crossed a ridge of sand, on which numerous pine-trees were growing. These ridges then occurred in rapid succession, separated by narrow flats only; the soil being of a bright red clay covered with Rhagodiae, and having bare patches on them. The draught over this kind of country becomes a serious hindrance to our movements; as it was very heavy, and the day excessively hot, the horses in the team suffered much. I therefore desired Morgan to halt, and, with Mr. Browne, rode forward in the hope of finding water, for he had shot a new and beautiful pigeon, on the bill of which some moist clay was adhering; wherefore we concluded that he had just been drinking at some shallow, but still unexhausted, puddle of water near us; we were, however, unsuccessful in our search; but crossed pine ridge after pine ridge, until at length I thought it better to turn back to the cart, and, as we had already travelled some 25 miles, to halt until the morning; more especially as there was no deficiency of grass on the sand ridges, and I did not apprehend that our horses would suffer much from the want of water.

Whatever idea I might have had of the character of the country into which we had penetrated, I certainly was not prepared for any so singular as that we encountered. The sand ridges, some partially, some thickly, covered with Pine-trees, were from thirty to fifty feet high, and about eighty yards at their base, running nearly longitudinally from north to south.

They were generally well covered with grass, which appeared to have been the produce of recent rains; and several very beautiful leguminous plants were also growing on them. I did not imagine that these ridges would continue much longer, and I therefore determined, the following morning to push on. Our position was in lat. 30° 40′ S., and in longitude 140° 51′ E. nearly.

On the morning of the 12th we commenced our day's journey on a N.W. course, as I had proposed to Mr. Browne. Flood had been about half a mile to the eastward, in the hope of finding water before we rose, but was disappointed; the horses did not, however, appear to have suffered from the want of it during the night. On starting I requested Mr. Browne to make a circuit to the N.E. for the same purpose, as we had observed many birds fly past us in that direction; and I sent Flood to the westward, but both returned unsuccessful. Nevertheless, although we could not find any water, the country improved.

The soil was still clay and sand, but we crossed some very fine flats, and only wanted water to enjoy comparative luxury. Both the flats and the ridges were well clothed with grass, and the former had box-trees and hakeas scattered over them; but these favourable indications soon ceased. The pine ridges closed upon each other once more, and the flats became covered with salsolaceous plants. The day was exceedingly hot, and still more oppressive in the brushes, so that the horses began to flag. At 2 p.m. no favourable change had taken place. Our view was limited to the succeeding sand hill; nor, by ascending the highest trees, could we see any elevated land at that hour; therefore I stopped, as the cart got on so slowly, and as the horses would now, under any circumstances, be three days without water, I determined on retracing my steps to the creek in which we had dug the well. I directed Mr. Browne, with Flood, however, to push on, till sunset, in the hope that he might see a change. At sunset I commenced my retreat, feeling satisfied that I had no hope of success in finding water so far from the hills. Turning back at so late an hour in the afternoon, it was past midnight when we reached the sand ridge from which we had started in the morning; where we again stopped until dawn, when proceeding onwards, and passing a shallow puddle of surface water, that was so thick with mud and animalculae as to be unfit to drink, we gained the creek at half-past 4 p.m. Mr. Browne and Flood joined us some little time after sunset, having ridden about 18 miles beyond the point at which we had parted, but had not noticed any change. The sandy ridge, Mr. Browne informed me, continued as far as he went; and, to all appearance, for miles beyond. The day we returned to the creek was one of most overpowering heat, the thermometer at noon being 117° in the shade. I had promised to wait for Mr. Browne at the shallow puddle, but the sun's rays fell with such intense effect on so exposed a spot that I was obliged to seek shelter at the creek. It blew furiously during the night of the 13th, in heated gusts from the north-east, and on the morning of the 14th the gale continued with unabated violence, and eventually became a hot wind. We were, therefore, unable to stir. The flies being in such myriads around us, so that we could do nothing. It is, indeed, impossible for me to describe the intolerable plague they were during the whole of that day from early dawn to sunset.

On the night of the 14th it rained a little. About 3 a.m. the wind blew round to the north-west, and at dawn we had a smart shower which cooled the air, reducing the temperature to something bearable. The sun rose amidst heavy clouds, by which his fiery beams were intercepted in their passage to the earth's surface. Before we quitted our ground I sent Flood up the creek, to trace it into the hills, an intention I was myself obliged to forego, being anxious to remain with the cart. The distance between the two creeks is about 26 miles, but, as I have already described the intervening country, it may not be necessary to notice it further. I was unable to take many back bearings, as the higher portions of the ranges were enveloped in mist. We reached the glen at half-past 5 p.m., and took up our old berth just at the gorge, preparatory to ascending the hills on the following day. Flood had already arrived there, and informed me that he had not followed the creek to where it issued from the ranges, but had approached very nearly, and could see the point from which it broke through them. That he had not found any surface water, but had tried the ground in many places, and always found water at two or three inches depth, and that where the water was the most abundant the feed was also the most plentiful. . . .

As the reader will have learnt from what I have stated at the conclusion of the last chapter, we pitched our tents at the place to which I have led him, and which I shall henceforth call the "Depot," on the 27th of January, 1845. They were not struck again until the 17th of July following.

This ruinous detention paralyzed the efforts and enervated the strength of the expedition, by constitutionally affecting both the men and animals, and depriving them of the elasticity and energy with which they commenced their labours. It was not however until after we had run down every creek in our neighbourhood, and had traversed the country in every direction, that the truth flashed across my mind, and it became evident to me, that we were locked up in the desolate and heated region, into which we had penetrated, as effectually as if we had wintered at the Pole. It was long indeed ere I could bring myself to believe that so great a misfortune had overtaken us, but so it was. Providence had, in its all-wise purposes, guided us to the only spot, in that wide-spread desert, where our wants could have been permanently supplied, but had there stayed our further progress into a region that almost appears to be forbidden ground. The immediate effect, however, of our arrival at the Depot, was to relieve my mind from anxiety as to the safety of the party. There was now no fear of our encountering difficulties, and perhaps perishing from the want of that life-sustaining element, without which our efforts would have been unavailing, for independently of the beautiful sheet of water, on the banks of which the camp was established, there was a small lagoon to the S.E. of us, and around it there was a good deal of feed, besides numerous water-holes in the rocky gully. The creek was marked by a line of gum-trees, from the mouth of the glen to its junction with the main branch, in which, excepting in isolated spots, water was no longer to be found. The Red Hill (afterwards called Mount Poole) bore N.N.W. from us, distant 3½ miles; between us and it there were undulating plains, covered with stones or salsolaceous herbage, excepting in the hollows, wherein there was a little grass. Behind us were level stony plains, with small sandy undulations, bounded by brush, over which the Black Hill, bearing S.S.E. from the Red Hill, was visible, distant 10 miles. To the eastward the country was, as I have described it, hilly. Westward at a quarter of a mile the low range, through which Depot Creek forces itself, shut out from our view the extensive plains on which it rises. This range extended longitudinally nearly north and south, but was nowhere more than a mile and a half in breadth. The geological formation of the range was slate, traversed by veins of quartz, its interstices being filled with magnesian limestone. Steep precipices and broken rugged gullies alternated on either side of this creek, and in its bed there were large slabs of beautiful slate. The precipices shewed the lateral formation with the rock split into the finest laminae, terminating in sharp points.

But neither on the ranges or on the plains behind the camp was there any feed for the cattle, neither were the banks of the creek or its neighbourhood to be put in comparison with Flood's Creek in this respect, for around it there was an abundance as well as a variety of herbage. Still the vegetation on the Depot Creek was vigorous, and different kinds of seeds were to be procured.

The morning we started to pay a visit to the blacks was more than usually oppressive even at daybreak, and about 9 it blew a hot wind from the N.E. As we rode across the stony plain lying between us and the hills, the heated and parching blasts that came upon us were more than we could bear. We were in the centre of the plain, when Mr. Browne drew my attention to a number of small black specks in the upper air. These spots increasing momentarily in size, were evidently approaching us rapidly. In an incredibly short time we were surrounded by several hundreds of the common kite, stooping down to within a few feet of us, and then turning away, after having eyed us steadily. Several approached us so closely, that they threw themselves back to avoid contact, opening their beaks and spreading out their talons. The long flight of these birds, reaching from the ground into the heavens, put me strongly in mind of one of Martin's beautiful designs, in which he produces the effect of distance by a multitude of objects gradually vanishing from the view. Whatever the reader may think, these birds had a most formidable aspect, and were too numerous for us to have overpowered, if they had really attacked us. That they came down to see what unusual object was wandering across the lonely deserts over which they soar, in the hope of prey, there can be no doubt; but seeing that we were likely to prove formidable antagonists, they wheeled from us in extensive sweeps, and were soon lost to view in the lofty region from whence they had descended. . . .

The three last days of February were cool in comparison to the few preceding ones. The wind was from the south, and blew so heavily that I anticipated rough weather at the commencement of March. But that rough month set in with renewed heat, consequent on the wind returning to its old quarter the E.S.E. There were however some heavy clouds floating about, and from the closeness of the atmosphere I hoped that rain would have fallen, but all these favourable signs vanished, the thermometer ascending to more than 100°.

When we first pitched our tents at the Depot the neighbourhood of it teemed with animal ife. The parrots and paroquets flew up and down the creeks collecting their scattered thousands, and making the air resound with their cries. Pigeons congregated together; bitterns, cockatoos, and other birds; all collected round as preparatory to migrating. In attendance on these were a variety of the Accipitrine class, hawks of different kinds, making sad havoc amongst the smaller birds. About the period of my return from the north they all took their departure, and we were soon wholly deserted. We no longer heard the discordant shriek of the parrots, or the hoarse croaking note of the bittern. They all passed away simultaneously in a single day; the line of migration being directly to the N.W., from which quarter we had small flights of ducks and pelicans.

On the 6th I sent Flood to the eastward to see if he could recover the channel of the main creek on the other side of the plain on which Mr. Poole had lost it; he returned the following day, with information that at 25 miles from the Depot he had recovered it, and found more water than he could have supposed. The day of Flood's return was exceedingly hot and close, and in the evening we had distant thunder, but no rain.

In consequence of his report, I now determined on a journey to the eastward to ascertain the character of the country between us and the Darling, and left the camp with this intention on the 12th instant. I should have started earlier than that day had not Mr. Poole's illness prevented me, but as he rallied, I proceeded on my excursion, accompanied by Mr. Browne, Flood, and another of the men. We observed several puddles near our old camp on the main creek as we rode away, so that rain must have fallen there though not at the Depot. After passing the little conical hill, of which I have already spoken, we traced the creek down until we saw plains of great extent before us, and as the creek trended to the south, skirting them on that side, we rode across them on a bearing of 322° or N.W.½N. They were 7 or 8 miles in breadth, and full 12 miles in length from east to west; their soil was rich and grassed in many places. At the extremity of the plains was a sand hill, close to which we came again on the creek, but without water, that which Flood had found being a little more to the eastward. Its channel at this place was deep, shaded, and moist, but very narrow. I was quite surprised when we came to the creek where Flood had been to find so much water; there was a serpentine sheet, of more than a quarter of a mile in length, which at first sight appeared to be as permanent as that at the Depot. The banks were high and composed of light rich alluvial soil, on which there were many new shrubs growing; the whole vegetation seemed to be more forward on this side of the hills than on that where the Depot was. Just as we halted we saw a column of smoke rise up due south, and on looking in that direction observed some grassy plains spreading out like a boundless stubble, the grass being of the kind from which the natives collect seed for subsistence at this season of the year.

Early on the morning of the 14th March we again saw smoke in the same direction as before, but somewhat to the eastward, as if the grass or brush had been fired. In hopes that we should come upon some of the natives of the plains, through which the creek appeared to run, I determined on examining them before I proceeded to the eastward. We accordingly crossed its channel when we mounted our horses after breakfast, and rode at some little distance from it on a course of 80° or nearly east, over flooded lands of somewhat sandy soil, covered with different kinds of grass, of which large heaps that had been thrashed out by the natives were piled up like hay-cocks. At about two and a half miles we ascended a sandy rise of about fifty feet in elevation, whence we obtained bearings of the little conical hill at the western termination of the plain, and of the hill we had called the Black Hill. These bearings with our latitude made the distance we had travelled 33 miles. From the sand hill we overlooked plains of great extent to the N.E.; partly grassed and partly bare, but to the eastward there was low brush and a country similar to that we had traversed before the commencement of the sandy ridges. There were low sandy undulations to be seen; but of no great height. I now turned for the smoke on a bearing of 187°, or nearly south, traversing a barren sandy level intermediate between the sand hill and the plains now upon our right; at length we entered upon the flooded ground, it was soft and yielding, and marked all over with the tracks of the natives; at 7 miles arrived at a large clump of gum-trees, and under them the channel of the creek which we had lost on the upper part of the plains was again visible. It was here very broad, but quite bare, except a belt of polygonum growing on either side, which had been set on fire, and was now in flames. We were fortunate enough soon after to find a long shallow sheet of water, in the bed of the creek, where we rested ourselves. It was singular enough that we should have pulled up close to the camp of some natives, all of whom had hidden themselves in the polygonum, except an old woman who was fast asleep, but who did not faint on seeing Mr. Browne close to her when she awoke. With this old lady we endeavoured to enter into conversation, and in order to allay her fears gave her five or six cockatoos we had shot, on which two other fair ones crept from behind the polygonum and advanced towards us. Finding that the men were out hunting, and only the women with the children were present, I determined to stop at this place until the following morning; we therefore unloaded the horses and allowed them to go and feed. A little before sunset, the two men returned to their families. They were much astonished at seeing us quietly seated before their huts, and approached us with some caution, but soon got reconciled to our presence. One of them had caught a talpero and a lizard, but the other had not killed any thing, so we gave him a dinner of mutton. The language of these people was a mixture between that of the river and hill tribes; but from what reason I am unable to say, although we understood their answers to general questions, we could not gather any lengthened information from them. I gave the elder native a blanket, and to the other a knife, with both of which they seemed highly delighted, and in return I suppose paid us the compliment of sending their wives to us as soon as it became dusk, but as we did not encourage their advances they left us after a short visit. The native who had killed the talpero, skinned it the moment he arrived in the camp, and, having first moistened them, stuffed the skin with the leaves of a plant of very astringent properties. All these natives were very poor, particularly the men, nor do I think that at this season of the year they can have much animal food of any kind to subsist on. Their principal food appeared to be seeds of various kinds, as of the box-tree, and grass seeds, which they pound into cakes and bake, together with different kinds of roots.

On the 15th we started at 7 a.m., and crossing at the head of the water, pursued a south course over extensive flooded plains, on which we again lost the channel of the creek, as, after winding round a little contiguous sand hill, it split into numberless branches; but although the plains hereabouts were well grassed, the soil was not so good as that on the plains above them. At six miles we ascended a sand hill, from which we could see to the extremity of the plain; but it had no apparent outlet excepting to the E.S.E. I therefore proceeded on that course for three miles, when we lost sight of all gum-trees, and found ourselves amongst scrub. Low bushes bounded the horizon all round, and hid the grassy plains from our view; but they were denser to the south and east than at any other point. Mount Lyell, the large hill south, bore 140° to the east of north, distant between forty and fifty miles. A short time after we left the grassy flats we crossed the dry bed of a large lagoon, which had been seen by Mr. Poole on a bearing of 77° from the Magnetic Hill. In the richer soil, a plant with round, striped fruit upon it, of very bitter taste, a species of cucumber, was growing. We next proceeded to the eastward, and surveying the country from higher ground, observed that the creek had no outlet from the plains, and that it could not but terminate on them.

As I had no object in a prolonged journey to the south, I turned back from this station, and retracing my steps to the water where we had left the natives, reached it at half-past six. All our friends were still there; we had, therefore, the pleasure of passing another afternoon with them, during which they were joined by two other natives, with their families, who had been driven in from the south, like ourselves, by the want of water. They assured us that all the water in that quarter had disappeared, "that the sun had taken it," and that we should not find a drop to the eastward, where I told them I was going. All these men, excepting one, had been circumcised. The single exception had the left fore-tooth of his upper jaw extracted, and I therefore concluded that he belonged to a different tribe. I had hoped to have seen many more natives in this locality; but it struck me, from what I observed, that they were dispersed at the different water-holes, there being no one locality capable of supporting any number.

The low and flooded track I have been describing must be dreadfully cold during the winter season, and the natives, who are wholly unprovided for inclemency of any kind, must suffer greatly from exposure; but at this time the temperature still continued very high, and the constant appearance of the deep purple tint opposite to the rising and setting sun seemed to indicate a continuance of it.

As our horses had had some long journeys for the last three days, we merely returned to our first bivouac on the creek, when we left the natives, with whom we parted on very good terms, and a promise on their part to come and see us. On the 17th started at quarter-past six for the eastward, with as much water as we could carry in the cart, as from the accounts of the natives we scarcely hoped to find any. For the first five miles we kept a course rather to the north of east, nearly E.N.E. indeed, to round some sand hills we should otherwise have been obliged to cross. There were very extensive plains to our left, on which water must lie during winter; but their soil was not good, or the vegetation thick upon them. We could just see the points of the northern flat-topped ranges beyond them. At five miles we turned due east, and crossed several small plains, separated by sandy undulations, not high enough to be termed ridges; the country, both to the south and east, appearing to be extremely low. At about fifteen miles, just as we were ascending a sand hill, Mr. Browne caught sight of a native stealing through the brush, after whom he rode; but the black observing him, ran away. On this Mr. Browne called out to him, when he stopped; but the horse happening to neigh at the moment, the poor fellow took to his heels, and secreted himself so adroitly, that we could not find him. He must, indeed, have been terribly alarmed at the uncouth sound he heard.

A short time before our adventure with the native we had seen three pelicans coming from the north. They kept very low to the ground, and wheeled along in circles in a very remarkable manner, as if they had just risen from water; but at length they soared upwards, and flew straight for the lagoon where we had left the natives. With the exception of these three birds, no other was to be seen in those dreary regions. Both Mr. Browne and I, however, rode over a snake, but our horses fortunately escaped being bitten; this animal had seized a mouse, which it let go on being disturbed, and crept into a hole; it was very pretty, being of a bright yellow colour with brown specks. Arriving at the termination of the sand hills, we looked down upon an immense shallow basin, extending to the north and south-east further than the range of vision, which must, I should imagine, be wholly impassable during the rainy season. There was scarcely any vegetation, a proof, it struck me, that it retains water on its surface till the summer is so advanced that the sun's rays are too powerful for any plants that may spring up, or that the heat bakes the soil so that nothing can force itself through. There was little, if any grass to be seen; but the mesembryanthemum reappeared upon it, with other salsolaceous plants. The former was of a new variety, with flowers on a long slender stalk, heaps of which had been gathered by the natives for the seed. Of the timber of these regions there was none; a few gum-trees near the creeks, with box-trees on the flats, and a few stunted acacia and hakea on the small hills, constituted almost the whole. Water boiled on this plain at 212°; that is to say, at our camp where we slept, about two miles advanced into it, but the plain extended about five miles further to the eastward. After crossing this on the following

morning, we traversed a country which Mr. Browne informed me
was very similar to that near Lake Torrens. It consisted of sand
banks, or *drifts*, with large bare patches at intervals: the whole
bearing testimony to the violence of the rains that must sometimes deluge it. We then traversed a succession of flats (I call
them so because they did not deserve the name of plains) separated from each other by patches of red sand and clay, that were
not more than a foot and a half above the surface of the flats.
At nine miles the country became covered with low scrub, and
we soon passed the dry bed of a lagoon, about a mile in circumference, on which there was a coating of salt and gypsum resting
on soft black mud. About a mile from this we passed a new tree,
similar to one we had seen on the Cawndilla plain. From this
point the land imperceptibly rose, until at length we found ourselves on some sandy elevations thickly covered with scrub of
acacia, almost all dead, but there was a good deal of grass around
them, and the spot might at another season, and if the trees had
been in leaf, have looked pretty. We pushed through this scrub,
the soil being a bright red sand for nine miles, when we suddenly
found ourselves at the base of a small stony hill, of about fifty
feet in height. From the summit we overlooked the region round
about. To the eastward, as a medium point, it was covered with
a dense scrub, that extended to the base of a range of hills,
distant about 33 miles, the extremities of which bore 71° and
152° respectively from us. But although the country under them
was covered with brush, the hills appeared to be clear and denuded of brushes of any kind. Our position here was about 138
miles from the Darling, and about 97 from the Depot. My object
in this excursion had been to ascertain the characteristic of the
country between us and the Darling, but I did not think it
necessary to run any risks with my horses, by pushing on for the
hills, as I could not have reached them until late the following
day, when, in the event of not finding water, their fate would
have been sealed; for we could not have returned with them to
the creek. They had already been two days without, if I except
the little we had spared them from the casks. I had deemed it
prudent to send Joseph and Lewis back to the creek for a fresh
supply, with orders to return and meet at a certain point, and
there to await our arrival, for without this supply I felt satisfied
we should have great difficulty as it was in getting our animals
back to the creek. We descended from the hill therefore to some
green-looking trees, of a foliage new to me, to rest for an hour
before we turned back again. There were neither flowers or fruit

on the trees, but from their leaf and habit, I took them to be a species of the Juglans. At sunset we mounted our horses and travelled to the edge of the acacia scrub to give our horses some of the grass, and halted in it for the night, but started early on the following morning to meet Joseph. We reached the appointed place, about 10, but not finding him there continued to journey onwards, and at five miles met him. We then stopped and gave the horses 12 gallons of water each, after which we tethered them out, but they were so restless that I determined to mount them, and pushing on reached the creek at half-past 1 a.m. The animals requiring rest I remained stationary the next day, and was myself glad to keep in the shade, not that the day was particularly hot, but because I began to feel the effects of constant exposure. Having expressed some opinion, however, that there might have been water to the north of us, in the direction whence the pelicans came, Mr. Browne volunteered to ride out, and accordingly with Flood left me about 10, but returned late in the afternoon without having found any. He ascertained that the creek I had sent Flood to trace when Mr. Stuart went to sketch in the ranges, terminated in the barren plain we had crossed, and such, the reader will observe, is the general termination of all the creeks of these singular and depressed regions.

The month of April set in without any indication of a change in the weather. It appeared as if the flood gates of Heaven were closed upon us for ever. We now began to feel the effects of disappointment, and watched the sky with extreme anxiety, insomuch that the least cloud raised all our hopes. The men were employed in various ways to keep them in health. We planted seeds in the bed of the creek, but the sun burnt them to cinders the moment they appeared above the ground. On the evening of the 3rd there was distant thunder, and heavy clouds to the westward. I thought it might have been that some shower had approached sufficiently near for me to benefit by the surface water it would have left to push towards Lake Torrens, and therefore mounted my horse and rode away to the westward on the 4th, but returned on the night of the 7th in disappointment. Time rolled on fast, and still we were unable to stir. Mr. Piesse, who took great delight in strolling out with my gun, occasionally shot a new bird.

On the 4th the wind blew strong from the south; but although the air was cooled, no rain fell, nor indeed was there any likelihood of rain with the wind in that quarter. Still as this was the first decided shift from the points to which it had kept so steadily, we augured good from it. On the 7th a very bright meteor was seen to burst in the south-east quarter of the heavens; crossing the sky with a long train of light, and in exploding seemed to form numerous stars. Whether it was fancy or not we thought the temperature cooled down from this period. On this day also we had a change of moon, but neither produced a variation of wind or weather of any immediate benefit to us. On the 14th we tried to ascertain the dew point, but failed, as in previous instances. The thermometer in our underground room stood at 78° of Farenheit, but we could not reduce the moist bulb below 49°; nor was I surprised at this, considering we had not had rain for nearly four months, and that during our stay at the Depot we had never experienced a dew. The ground was thoroughly heated to the depth of three or four feet, and the tremendous heat that prevailed had parched vegetation and drawn moisture from everything. In an air so rarified, and an atmosphere so dry, it was hardly to be expected that any experiment upon it would be attended with its usual results, or that the particles of moisture so far separated, could be condensed by ordinary methods. The mean of the thermometer for the months of December, January, and February had been 101°, 104°, and 101° respectively in the shade. Under its effects every screw in our boxes had been drawn, and the horn handles of our instruments, as well as our combs, were split into fine laminae. The lead dropped out of our pencils, our signal rockets were entirely spoiled; our hair, as well as the wool on the sheep, ceased to grow, and our nails had become as brittle as glass. The flour lost more than eight per cent. of its original weight, and the other provisions in a still greater proportion. The bran in which our bacon had been packed was perfectly saturated, and weighed almost as heavy as the meat; we were obliged to bury our wax candles; a bottle of citric acid in Mr. Browne's box became fluid, and, escaping, burnt a quantity of his linen; and we found it difficult to write or draw, so rapidly did the fluid dry in our pens and brushes. It was happy for us, therefore, that a cooler season set in, otherwise I do not think that many of us could much longer have survived. But, although it might be said that the intense heat of the summer had passed, there still were intervals of most oppressive weather.

About the beginning of March I had had occasion to speak to Mr. Browne as to certain indications of disease that were upon me. I had violent headaches, unusual pains in my joints, and a coppery taste in my mouth. These symptoms I attributed to having slept so frequently on the hard ground and in the beds of creeks, and it was only when my mouth became sore, and my gums spongy, that I felt it necessary to trouble Mr. Browne, who at once told me that I was labouring under an attack of scurvy, and I regretted to learn from him that both he and Mr. Poole were similarly affected, but they hoped I had hitherto escaped. Mr. Browne was the more surprised at my case, as I was very moderate in my diet, and had taken but little food likely to cause such a malady. Of we three Mr. Poole suffered most, and gradually declined in health. For myself I immediately took double precautions, and although I could not hope soon to shake off such a disease, especially under such unfavourable circumstances as those in which we were placed, I was yet thankful that I did not become worse. For Mr. Browne, as he did not complain, I had every hope that he too had succeeded in arresting the progress of this fearful distemper. It will naturally occur to the reader as singular, that the officers only should have been thus attacked; but the fact is, that they had been constantly absent from the camp, and had therefore been obliged to use bacon, whereas the men were living on fresh mutton; besides, the same men were seldom taken on a second journey, but were allowed time to recover from the exposure to which they had been subjected, but for the officers there was no respite.

On the 18th the wind, which had again settled in the S.E., changed to the N.E., and the sky became generally overcast. Heavy clouds hung over the Mount Serle chain, and I thought that rain would have fallen, but all these favourable indications vanished before sunset. At dawn of the morning of the 19th, dense masses of clouds were seen, and thunder heard to the west; and the wind shifting to that quarter, we hoped that some of the clouds would have been blown over to us, but they kept their place for two days, and then gradually disappeared. These distant indications, however, were sufficient to rouse us to exertion, in the hope of escaping from the fearful captivity in which we had so long been held. I left the camp on the 21st with Mr. Browne and Flood, thinking that rain might have extended to the eastward from Mount Serle, sufficiently near to enable us to push into the N.W. interior, and as it appeared to me that a W. by N. course would take me abreast of Mount Hopeless, I ran upon it. At 16 miles I ascended a low range, but could not observe anything from it to the westward but scrub. Descending from this range we struck the head of a creek, and at six miles came on the last dregs of a pool of water, so thick that it was useless to us. We next crossed barren stony undulations and open

I. D.   z

plains, some of them apparently subject to floods; and halted at half-past six, after a journey of between thirty and forty miles without water, and with very little grass for our horses to eat. Although the course we kept had taken us at times to a considerable distance from the creek, we again came on it before sunset, and consequently halted upon its banks; but in tracing it down on the following morning we lost its channel on an extensive plain, and therefore continued our journey to the westward. At seven miles we entered a dense scrub, and at fifteen ascended a sand hill, from which we expected to have had a more than usually extensive view, but it was limited to the next sand hill, nor was there the slightest prospect of a change of country being at hand. At four miles from this position we came upon a second creek seemingly from the N.E., whose appearance raised our hopes of obtaining water; but as its channel became sandy, and turned southwards, I left it, and once more running on our old course, pulled up at sunset under a bank of sand, without anything either for ourselves or our horses to drink. During the latter part of the evening we had observed a good deal of grass on the sand hills, nor was there any deficiency of it round our bivouac; but, notwithstanding that there was more than enough for the few horses we had, a herd of cattle would have discussed the whole in a night. It was evident from the state of the ground that no rain had fallen hereabouts, and I consequently began to doubt whether it had extended beyond the mountains. Comparing the appearance of the country we were in, with that through which Mr. Browne had passed for 50 miles before he came upon Lake Torrens, and concluding that some such similar change would have taken place here if we had approached within any reasonable distance of that basin, I could not but apprehend that we were still a long way from it.

The horses having refused the water we had found in the creek, I could hardly expect they would drink it on their return, so that I calculated our distance from water at about 68 miles; and I foresaw that unless we should succeed in finding some early in the day following, it would be necessary for us to make for the Depot again. Close to where we stopped there was a large burrow of Talperos, an animal, as I have observed, similar to the rabbit in its habits, and one of which the natives are very fond, as food. The sandy ridges appeared to be full of them, and other animals, that must live for many months at a time without water. Whilst we were sitting in the dusk near our fire, two beautiful parrots attracted by it, I suppose, pitched close to us; but immediately took wing again, and flew away to the N.W. They, no doubt, thought that we were near water, but like ourselves were doomed to disappointment. During the evening also some plovers flew over us, and we heard some native dogs howling to the south-west. At daylight, therefore, we rode in that direction, with the hope of finding the element we now so much required. At three miles a large grassy flat opened out to view upon our right, similar to that at the termination of the Depot creek. It might have contained 1000 acres, but there was not at the first glance a tree to be seen upon it. This flat was bounded to the S.W. by a sand bank, lying at right angles to the sand ridges we had been crossing. The latter, therefore, ran down upon this bank in parallel lines, some falling short of, and others striking it; so that, as the drainage was towards the embankment, the collected waters lodged against it. After crossing a portion of the plain we saw some box-trees in a hollow, towards which we rode, and then came upon a deep dry pond, in whose bottom the natives had dug several wells, and had evidently lingered near it as long as a drop of water remained. It was now clear that our further search for water would be useless. I therefore turned on a course of 12° to the north of east for the muddy water we had passed two days before, and halted there about an hour after sunset, having journeyed 42 miles. We fell into our tracks going out about four miles before we halted, and were surprised to observe that a solitary native had been running them down. On riding a little further, however, we noticed several tracks of different sizes, as if a family of natives had been crossing the country to the north-west. It is more than probable that their water having failed in the hills, they were on their way to some other place where they had a well.

Although we had ourselves been without water for two days, the mud in the creek was so thick that I could not swallow it, and was really astonished how Mr. Browne managed to drink a pint of it made into tea. It absolutely fell over the cup of the panakin like thick cream, and stuck to the horses' noses like pipe-clay. They drank sparingly however, and took but little grass during the night. As we pursued our journey homewards on the following day, we passed several flights of dotterel making to the south, this being the first migration we had observed in that direction. These birds were in great numbers on the plains of Adelaide the year preceding, and had afforded good sport to my friend Torrens; we also observed a flight of pelicans, wheeling about close to the ground, as they had before done to the eastward, as well as a flight of the black-shouldered hawks hovering in the air. Our day's ride had been very long and fatiguing, as the horses were tired, but we got relieved by our arrival at the camp a little before sunset on the 25th: and thus terminated another journey in disappointment. We regretted to find that Mr. Poole was seriously indisposed. His muscles were now attacked and he was suffering great pain, but, as the disease appeared inclined to make to the surface, Mr. Browne had some hopes of a favourable change. Both Mr. Browne and myself found that the sameness of our diet began to disagree with us, and were equally anxious for the reappearance of vegetation, in the hope that we should be able to collect sow-thistles or the tender shoots of the rhagodia as a change. We had, whilst it lasted, taken mint tea, in addition to the scanty supply of tea to which we were obliged to limit ourselves, but I do not think it was wholesome.

The moon entered her third quarter on the 27th, but brought no change; on the contrary she chased away the clouds as she rose, and moved through the heavens in unshrouded and dazzling brightness. Sometimes a dark mass of clouds would rise simultaneously with her, in the west, but as the queen of night advanced in her upward course they gradually diminished the velocity with which they at first came up; stopped, and fell back again, below the horizon. Not once, but fifty times we watched these apparently contending forces, but whether I am right in attributing the cause I will not say.

At this time (the end of April) the weather was very fine, although the thermometer ranged high. The wind being steady at south accounted for the unusual height of the barometrical column, which rose to 30.600. On the night of the 20th we had a very heavy dew, the first since our departure from the Darling. On the morning of the 28th it thundered, and a dense cloud passed over to the north, the wind was unsteady, and I hoped that the storm would have worked round, but it did not. At ten the wind sprung up from the south, the sky cleared and all our hopes were blighted.

Notwithstanding that we treated the natives who came to the creek with every kindness, none ever visited us, and I was the more surprised at this, because I could not but think that we were putting them to great inconvenience by our occupation of this spot. Towards the end of the month, it was so cold that we were glad to have fires close to our tents. Mr. Poole had gradually become worse and worse, and was now wholly confined to his bed, unable to stir, a melancholy affliction both to himself and us, rendering our detention in that gloomy region still more painful. My men generally were in good health, but almost all had bleeding at the nose; I was only too thankful that my own health did not give way, though I still felt the scurvy in a mitigated form, but Mr. Browne had more serious symptoms about him.

The 10th of May completed the ninth month of our absence from Adelaide, and still we were locked up without the hope of escape, whilst every day added fresh causes of anxiety to those I had already to bear up against. Mr. Poole became worse, all his skin along the muscles turned black, and large pieces of spongy flesh hung from the roof of his mouth, which was in such a state that he could hardly eat. Instead of looking with eagerness to the moment of our liberation, I now dreaded the consequent necessity of moving him about in so dreadful a condition. Mr. Browne attended him with a constancy and kindness that could not but raise him in my estimation, doing every thing which friendship or sympathy could suggest.

On the 11th about 3 p.m. I was roused by the dogs simultaneously springing up and rushing across the creek, but supposing they had seen a native dog, I did not rise; however, I soon knew by their continued barking that they had something at bay, and Mr. Piesse not long after came to inform me a solitary native was on the top of some rising ground in front of the camp. I sent him therefore with some of the men to call off the dogs, and to bring him down to the tents. The poor fellow had fought manfully with the dogs, and escaped injury, but had broken his waddy over one of them. He was an emaciated and elderly man, rather low in stature, and half dead with hunger and thirst; he drank copiously of the water that was offered to him, and then ate as much as would have served me for four and twenty dinners. The men made him up a screen of boughs close to the cart near the servants, and I gave him a blanket in which he rolled himself up and soon fell fast asleep. Whence this solitary stranger could have come from we could not divine. No other natives approached to look after him, nor did he shew anxiety for any absent companion. His composure and apparent self-possession were very remarkable, for he neither exhibited astonishment or curiosity at the novelties by which he was surrounded. His whole demeanour was that of a calm and courageous man, who finding himself placed in unusual jeopardy, had determined not to be betrayed into the slighest display of fear or timidity.

From the period of our return from the eastward, I had remained quiet in the camp, watching every change in the sky; I was indeed reluctant to absent myself for any indefinite period, in consequence of Mr. Poole's precarious state of health. He had now used all the medicines we had brought out, and none therefore remained either for him or any one else who might subsequently be taken ill. As however he was better, on the 12th, I determined to make a second excursion to the eastward, to see if there were any more natives in the neighbourhood of the grassy plains than when I was last there. Wishing to get some samples of wood I took the light cart and Tampawang also, in the hope that he would be of use.

Although the water in the creek had sunk fearfully there was still a month's supply remaining, but if it had been used by our stock it would then have been dry. Close to the spot where we had before stopped, there were two huts that had been recently erected. Before these two fires were burning, and some troughs of grass seed were close to them, but no native could we see, neither did any answer to our call. Mr. Browne, however, observing some recent tracks, ran them down, and discovered a native and his lubra who had concealed themselves in the hollow of a tree, from which they crept as soon as they saw they were discovered. The man we had seen before, and the other proved to be the frail one who exhibited such indignation at our rejecting her addresses on a former occasion; being a talkative damsel, we were glad to renew our acquaintance with her. We learnt from them that the second hut belonged to an absent native who was out hunting, the father of a pretty little girl who now obeyed their signal and came forth. They said the water on the plain had dried up, and that the only water-holes remaining were to the west, viz., at our camp, and to the south, where they said there were two water-holes. As they had informed us, the absent native made his appearance at sunset, but his bag was very light, so we once more gave them all our mutton; he proved to be the man Mr. Browne chased on the sand hills, the strongest native we had seen; he wanted the front tooth, but was not circumcised.

In the evening we had a thunder-storm, but could have counted the drops of rain that fell, notwithstanding the thunder was loud and the lightning vivid. We returned to the Depot on 13th, and on crossing the plain Mr. Browne had well nigh captured a jerboa, which sprang from under my horse's legs, but managed to elude him, and popped into a little hole before he could approach sufficiently near to strike at it. On reaching the tents we had the mortification to find Mr. Poole still worse, but

I attributed his relapse in some measure to a depression of spirits. The old man who had come to the camp the day before we left it was still there, and had apparently taken up his quarters between the cart and my tent. During our absence the men had shewn him all the wonders of the camp, and he in his turn had strongly excited their anticipations by what he had told them.

He appeared to be quite aware of the use of the boat, intimating that it was turned upside down, and pointed to the N.W. as the quarter in which we should use her. He mistook the sheep net for a fishing net, and gave them to understand that there were fish. in those waters so large that they would not get through the meshes. Being anxious to hear what he had to say I sent for him to my tent, and with Mr. Browne cross-questioned him.

It appeared quite clear to us that he was aware of the existence of large water somewhere or other to the northward and westward. He pointed from W.N.W. round to the eastward of north, and explained that large waves higher than his head broke on the shore. On my shewing him the fish figured in Sir Thomas Mitchell's work he knew only the cod. Of the fish figured in Cuvier's works he gave specific names to those he recognised, as the hippocampus, the turtle, and several sea fish, as the chetodon, but all the others he included under one generic name, that of "guia," fish.

He put his hands very cautiously on the snakes, and withdrew them suddenly as if he expected they would bite him, and evinced great astonishment when he felt nothing but the soft paper. On being asked, he expressed his readiness to accompany us when there should be water, but said we should not have rain yet. I must confess this old native raised my hopes, and made me again anxious for the moment when we should resume our labours, but when that time was to come God only knew.

It had been to no purpose that we had traversed the country in search for water. None any longer remained on the parched surface of the stony desert, if I except what remained at the Depot, and the little in the creek to the eastward. There were indeed the ravages of floods and the vestiges of inundations to be seen in the neighbourhood of every creek we had traced, and upon every plain we had crossed, but the element that had left such marks of its fury was nowhere to be found.

From this period I gave up all hope of success in any future effort I might make to escape from our dreary prison. Day after day, and week after week passed over our heads, without any apparent likelihood of any change in the weather. The consequences of our detention weighed heavily on my mind, and depressed my spirits, for in looking over Mr. Piesse's monthly return of provisions on hand, I found that unless some step was taken to enable me to keep the field, I should on the fall of rain be obliged to retreat. I had by severe exertion gained a most commanding position, the wide field of the interior lay like an open sea before me, and yet every sanguine hope I had ever indulged appeared as if about to be extinguished. The only plan for me to adopt was to send a portion of the men back to Adelaide. I found by calculation that if I divided the party, retaining nine in all, and sending the remainder home, I should secure the means of pushing my researches to the end of December, before which time I hoped (however much it had pleased Providence to stay my progress hitherto,) to have performed my task, or penetrated the heartless desert before me to such a distance as would leave no doubt as to the question I had been directed to solve.

The old man left us on the 17th with the promise of returning, and from the careful manner in which he concealed the different things that had been given to him I thought he would have done so, but we never saw him more, and I cannot but think that he perished from the want of water in endeavouring to return to his kindred.

I have repeatedly remarked that we had been deserted by all the feathered tribes. Not only was this the case, but we had witnessed a second migration of the later broods; after these were gone, there still remained with us about fifty of the common kites and as many crows: these birds continued with us for the offals of the sheep, and had become exceedingly tame; the kites in particular came flying from the trees when a whistle was sounded, to the great amusement of the men, who threw up pieces of meat for them to catch before they fell to the ground. When the old man first came to us, we fed him on mutton, but one of the men happening to shoot a crow, he shewed such a decided preference for it, that he afterwards lived almost exclusively upon them. He was, as I have stated, when he first came to us a thin and emaciated being, but at the expiration of a fortnight when he rose to depart, he threw off his blanket and exhibited a condition that astonished us all. He was absolutely fat, and yet his face did not at all indicate such a change. If he had been fed in the dark like capons, he could not have got into better condition. Mr. Browne was anxious to accompany him, but I thought that if his suspicions were aroused he would not return, and I therefore let him depart as he came. With him all our hopes vanished, for even the presence of that savage was soothing to us, and so long as he remained, we indulged in anticipations as to the future. From the time of his departure a gloomy silence pervaded the camp; we were, indeed, placed under the most trying circumstances; everything combined to depress our spirits and exhaust our patience. We had gradually been deserted by every beast of the field, and every fowl of the air. We had witnessed migration after migration of the feathered tribes, to that point to which we were so anxious to push our way. Flights of cockatoos, of parrots, of pigeons, and of bitterns, birds also whose notes had cheered us in the wilderness, all had taken the same high road to a better and more hospitable region. The vegetable kingdom was at a stand, and there was nothing either to engage the attention or attract the eye. Our animals had laid the ground bare for miles around the camp, and never came towards it but to drink. The axe had made a broad gap in the line of gum-trees which ornamented the creek, and had destroyed its appearance. We had to witness the gradual and fearful diminution of the water, on the possession of which our lives depended; day after day we saw it sink lower and lower, dissipated alike by the sun and winds. From its original depth of nine feet, it now scarcely measured two, and instead of extending from bank to bank it occupied only a narrow line in the centre of the channel. Had the drought continued for a month longer than it pleased the Almighty to terminate it, that creek would have been as dry as the desert on either side. Almost heart-broken, Mr. Browne and I seldom left our tents, save to visit our sick companion. Mr. Browne had for some time been suffering great pain in his limbs, but with a generous desire to save me further anxiety carefully concealed it from me; but it was his wont to go to some acacia trees in the bed of the creek to swing on their branches, as he told me to exercise his muscles, in the hope of relaxing their rigidity.

One day, when I was sitting with Mr. Poole, he suggested the erection of two stations, one on the Red Hill and the other on the Black Hill, as points for bearings when we should leave the Depot. The idea had suggested itself to me, but I had observed that we soon lost sight of the hills in going to the north-west; and that, therefore, for such a purpose, the works would be of little use, but to give the men occupation; and to keep them in health I employed them in erecting a pyramid of stones on the summit of the Red Hill. It is twenty-one feet at the base, and eighteen feet high, and bears 329° from the camp, or 31° to the west of north. I little thought when I was engaged in that work, that I was erecting Mr. Poole's monument, but so it was, that rude structure looks over his lonely grave, and will stand for ages as a record of all we suffered in the dreary region to which we were so long confined.

The months of May and June, and the first and second weeks of July passed over our heads, yet there was no indication of a change of weather. It had been bitterly cold during parts of this period, the thermometer having descended to 24°; thus making the difference between the extremes of summer heat and winter's cold no less than 133°.

About the middle of June I had the drays put into serviceable condition, the wheels wedged up, and every thing prepared for moving away.

Anxious to take every measure to prevent unnecessary delay, when the day of liberation should arrive, I had sent Mr. Stuart and Mr. Piesse, with a party of chainers, to measure along the line on which I intended to move when the Depot was broken up. I had determined, as I have elsewhere informed the reader, to penetrate to the westward, in the hope of finding Lake Torrens connected with some more extensive and more central body of water; and I thought it would be satisfactory to ascertain, as nearly as possible, the distance of that basin from the Darling, and in so doing to unite the eastern and western surveys. I had assumed Sir Thomas Mitchell's position at Williorara as correct, and had taken the most careful bearings from that point to the Depot, and the position in which they fixed it differed but little from the result of the many lunars I took during my stay there. As I purpose giving the elements of all my calculations, those more qualified than myself to judge on these matters will correct me if I have been in error; but, as the mean of my lunars was so close to the majority of the single lunars, I cannot think they are far from the truth. Be that as it may, I assumed my position at the Depot to be in lat. 29° 40' 14" S. and in long. 141° 29' 41" E., the variation being 5° 14' East. Allowing for the variation, I directed Mr. Stuart to run the chain line on a bearing of 55° to the west of north, which I intended to cut a little to the west of the park-like and grassy plain at the termination of the creek I had traced in that direction. By supplying the party with water from the camp, I enabled them to prolong the line to 30 miles.

On the 15th of June I commenced my preparations for moving; not that I had any reason so to do, but because I could not bring myself to believe that the drought would continue much longer. The felloes and spokes of the wheels of the drays had shrunk to nothing, and it was with great difficulty that we wedged them up; but the boat, which had been so long exposed to an ardent sun, had, to appearance at least, been but little injured.

As it became necessary to point out the drays that were to go with the home returning party, I was obliged to break my intentions to Mr. Poole, who I also proposed sending in charge of them. He was much affected, but, seeing the necessity of the measure, said that he was ready to obey my orders in all things. I directed Mr. Piesse to weigh out and place apart the supplies that would be required for Mr. Poole and his men, and to pack the provisions we should retain in the most compact order. On examining our bacon we found that it had lost more than half its weight, and had now completely saturated the bran in which it had been packed. Our flour had lost more than 8 per cent., and the tea in a much greater proportion.

The most valuable part of our stock were the sheep, they had kept in excellent condition, and seldom weighed less than 55 lbs. or 65 lbs.; but their flesh was perfectly tasteless. Still they were a most valuable stock, and we had enough remaining to give the men a full allowance; for the parties employed on detached excursions could only take a day or two's supply with them, and in consequence a quantity of back rations, if I may so term them, were constantly accumulating.

Mr. Poole's reduced state of health rendered it necessary that a dray should be prepared for his transport, and I requested Mr. Browne to superintend every possible arrangement for his comfort. A dray was accordingly lined with sheep skins, and had a flannel tilt, as the nights were exceedingly cold, and he could not be moved to a fire. I had also a swing cot made, with pullies to raise him up when he should feel disposed to change his position.

Whilst these necessary preparations were being forwarded, I was engaged writing my public despatches.

In my communication to the Governor of South Australia, I expressed a desire that a supply of provisions might be forwarded to Williorara by the end of December, about which period I hoped I should be on my return from the interior. I regretted exceedingly putting her Majesty's Government to this additional cost, but I trust a sufficient excuse will have been found for me in the foregoing pages. I would rather that my bones had been left to bleach in that desert than have yielded an inch of the ground I had gained at so much expense and trouble.

The 27th of June completed the fifth month of our detention at the Depot, and the prospect of our removal appeared to be as distant as ever; there were, it is true, more clouds, but they passed over us without breaking. The month of July, however, opened with every indication of a change, the sky was generally overcast, and although we had been so often disappointed, I had a presentiment that the then appearances would not vanish without rain.

About this time Mr. Poole, whose health on the whole was improving, had a severe attack of inflammation, which Mr. Browne subdued with great difficulty. After this attack he became exceedingly restless, and expressed a desire to be moved from the tent in which he had so long been confined, to the underground room, but as that rude apartment was exceedingly cold at night, I thought it advisable to have a chimney built to it before he was taken there. It was not until the 12th that it was ready for him. As the men were carrying him across the camp towards the room he was destined to occupy for so short a time, I pointed out the pyramid to him, and it is somewhat singular, that the first drops of rain, on the continuance of which our deliverance depended, fell as the men were bearing him along.

Referring back to the early part of the month, I may observe that the indications of a breaking up of the drought became every day more apparent.

It was now clear, indeed, that the sky was getting surcharged with moisture, and it is impossible for me to describe the intense anxiety that prevailed in the camp. On the morning of the 3rd the firmament was again cloudy, but the wind shifted at noon to west, and the sun set in a sky so clear that we could hardly believe it had been so lately overcast. On the following morning he rose bright and clear as he had set, and we had a day of surpassing fineness, like a spring day in England.

The night of the 6th was the coldest night we experienced at the Depot, when the thermometer descended to 24°. On the 7th a south wind made the barometer rise to 30° 180′, and with it despair once more stared us in the face, for with the wind in that quarter there was no hope of rain. On the 8th it still blew heavily from the south, and the barometer rose to 30° 200′; but the evening was calm and frosty, and the sky without a cloud. I may be wearying my reader by entering thus into the particulars of every change that took place in the weather at this, to us, intensely anxious period, but he must excuse me; my narrative may appear dull, and should not have been intruded on the notice of the public, had I not been influenced by a sense of duty to all concerned.

No one but those who were with me at that trying time and in that fearful solitude can form an idea of our feelings. To continue then, on the morning of the 9th it again blew fresh from the south, the sky was cloudless even in the direction of Mount Serle, and all appearance of rain had passed away.

On the 10th, to give a change to the current of my thoughts, and for exercise, I walked down the Depot creek with Mr. Browne, and turning northwards up the main branch when we reached the junction of the two creeks, we continued our ramble for two or three miles. I know not why it was, that, on this occasion more than any other, we should have contemplated the scene around us, unless it was that the peculiar tranquility of the moment made a greater impression on our minds. Perhaps the deathlike silence of the scene at that moment led us to reflect, whilst gazing on the ravages made by the floods, how fearfully that silence must sometimes be broken by the roar of waters and of winds. Here, as in other places, we observed the trunks of trees swept down from the hills, lodged high in the branches of the trees in the neighbourhood of the creek, and large accumulations of rubbish lying at their butts, whilst the line of inundation extended so far into the plains that the country must on such occasions have the appearance of an inland sea. The winds on the other hand had stripped the bark from the trees to windward (a little to the south of west), as if it had been shaved off with an instrument, but during our stay at the Depot we had not experienced any unusual visitation, as a flood really would have been; for any torrent, such as that which it was evident sometimes swells the creek, would have swept us from our ground since the marks of inundation reached more than a mile beyond our encampment, and the trunk of a large gum-tree was jambed between the branches of one overhanging the creek near us at an altitude exceeding the height of our tents.

On the 11th the wind shifted to the east, the whole sky becoming suddenly overcast, and on the morning of the 12th it was still at east, but at noon veered round to the north, when a gentle rain set in, so gentle that it more resembled a mist, but this continued all the evening and during the night. It ceased

however at 10 a.m. of the 13th, when the wind shifted a little
to the westward of north. At noon rain again commenced, and
fell steadily throughout the night, but although the ground
began to feel the effects of it, sufficient had not fallen to enable
us to move. Yet, how thankful was I for this change, and how
earnestly did I pray that the Almighty would still farther extend
his mercy to us, when I laid my head on my pillow. All night it
poured down without any intermission, and as morning dawned
the ripple of waters in a little gully close to our tents was a
sweeter and more soothing sound than the softest melody I ever
heard. On going down to the creek in the morning I found that
it had risen five inches, and the ground was now so completely
saturated that I no longer doubted the moment of our liberation
had arrived.

I had made every necessary preparation for Mr. Poole's departure on the 13th, and as the rain ceased on the morning of the
14th the home returning party mustered to leave us. Mr. Poole
felt much when I went to tell him that the dray in which he was
to be conveyed was ready for his reception. I did all that I could
to render his mind easy on every point, and allowed him to
select the most quiet and steady bullocks for the dray he was to
occupy; together with the most careful driver in the party. I
also consented in his taking Joseph, who was the best man I
had, to attend him personally, and Mr. Browne put up for his
use all the little comforts we could spare. I cheered him with
the hope of returning to meet us after we should have terminated
our labours, and assured him that I considered his services on
the duty I was about to send him as valuable and important as
if he continued with me. He was lifted on his stretcher into the
dray, and appeared gratified at the manner in which it had been
arranged. I was glad to see that his feelings did not give way at
this painful moment; on my ascending the dray, however, to bid
him adieu, he wept bitterly, but expressed his hope that we
should succeed in our enterprise.

As I knew his mind would be agitated, and that his greatest
trial would be on the first day, I requested Mr. Browne to accompany him, and to return to me on the following day. On Mr.
Poole's departure I prepared for our own removal, and sent
Flood after the horses, but having an abundance of water everywhere, they had wandered, and he returned with them too late
for me to move. He said, that in crossing the rocky range he
heard a roaring noise, and that on going to the glen he saw the
waters pouring down, foaming and eddying amongst the rocks,

adding that he was sure the floods would be down upon us ere long. An evident proof that however light the rain appeared to be, an immense quantity must have fallen, and I could not but hope and believe that it had been general.

Before we left the Depot Flood's prediction was confirmed, and the channel which, if the drought had continued a few days longer, would have been perfectly waterless, was thus suddenly filled up to the brim; no stronger instance of the force of waters in these regions can be adduced than this, no better illustration of the character of the creeks can be given. The head of the Depot creek was not more than eight miles from us, its course to its junction with the main creek was not ten, yet it was a watercourse that without being aware of its commencement or termination might have been laid down by the traveller as a river. Such however is the uncertain nature of the rivers of those parts of the continent of Australia over which I have wandered. I would not trust the largest farther than the range of vision; they are deceptive all of them, the offsprings of heavy rains, and dependent entirely on local circumstances for their appearance and existence.

Having taken all our circumstances into consideration, our heart-breaking detention, the uncertainty that involved our future proceedings, and the ceaseless anxiety of mind to which we should be subjected, recollecting also that Mr. Browne had joined me for a limited period only, and that a protracted journey might injure his future prospects, I felt that it was incumbent on me to give him the option of returning with Mr. Poole if he felt disposed to do so, but he would not desert me, and declined all my suggestions.

On the morning of the 16th I struck the tents, which had stood for six months less eleven days, and turned my back on the Depot in grateful thankfulness for our release from a spot where my feelings and patience had been so severely tried. When we commenced our journey, we found that our progress would be slow, for the ground was dreadfully heavy, and the bullocks, so long unaccustomed to draught, shrunk from their task. One of the drays stuck in the little gully behind our camp, and we were yet endeavouring to get it out, when Mr. Browne returned from his attendance on Mr. Poole, and I was glad to find that he had left him in tolerable spirits, and with every hope of his gradual improvement.

As we crossed the creek, between the Depot and the glen, we found that the waters, as Flood predicted, had descended so far, and waded through them to the other side. We then rode to the glen, to see how it looked under such a change, and remained some time watching the current as it swept along.

On our return to the party I found that it would be impossible to make a lengthened journey; for, having parted with two drays, we had necessarily been obliged to increase the loads on the others, so that they sank deep into the ground. I therefore halted, after having gone about four miles only.

About seven o'clock p.m. we were surprised by the sudden return of Joseph, from the home returning party; but, still more so at the melancholy nature of the information he had to communicate. Mr. Poole, he said, had breathed his last at three o'clock. This sad event necessarily put a stop to my movements, and obliged me to consider what arrangements I should now have to make.

It appeared, from Joseph's account, that Mr. Poole had not shewn any previous indications of approaching dissolution. About a quarter before three he had risen to take some medicine, but suddenly observed to Joseph that he thought he was dying, and falling on his back, expired without a struggle.

Early on the morning of this day, and before we ourselves started, I had sent Mr. Stuart and Mr. Piesse in advance with the chainers to carry on the chaining. On the morning of the 17th, before I mounted my horse to accompany Mr. Browne to examine the remains of our unfortunate companion, which I determined to inter at the Depot, I sent a man to recall them.

The suddenness of Mr. Poole's death surprised both Mr. Browne and myself; but the singular fairness of his countenance left no doubt on his mind but that internal hæmorrhage had been the immediate cause of that event.

On the 17th the whole party, which had so lately separated, once more assembled at the Depot. We buried Mr. Poole under a Grevillia that stood close to our underground room; his initials, and the year, are cut in it above the grave, "J. P. 1845," and he now sleeps in the desert.

The sad event I have recorded, obliged me most reluctantly to put Mr. Piesse in charge of the home returning party, for I had had every reason to be satisfied with him, and I witnessed his departure with regret. A more trustworthy or a more anxious officer could not have been attached to such a service as that in which he was employed.

The funeral of Mr. Poole was a fitting close to our residence at the Depot. At the conclusion of that ceremony the party again

(*By permission of John Murray.*)

STURT'S EXPEDITION INTO CENTRAL AUSTRALIA, 1844–5–6.
From " The Life of Charles Sturt."

separated, and I returned to my tent, to prepare for moving on the morrow.

At 9 a.m. accordingly of the 18th we pushed on to the N.W. The ground had become much harder, but the travelling was still heavy. At three miles we passed a small creek, about seven miles from the Depot, at which I intended to have halted on leaving that place. We passed over stony plains, or low, sandy, and swampy ground, since the valleys near the hills opened out as we receded from them. On the 19th I kept the chained line, but in consequence of the heavy state of the ground we did not get more than 8½ miles. The character of the country was that of open sandy plains, the sand being based upon a stiff, tenacious clay, impervious to water. With the exception of a few solsolae and a triplex, the plains were exceedingly bare, and had innumerable patches of water over them, not more than two or three inches deep. At intervals pure sand hills occurred, on which there were a few stunted casuarina and mimosae, but a good deal of grass and thousands of young plants already springing up. As the ground was still very soft, I should not have moved on the 20th, but was anxious to push on. Early in the day, and at less than 18 miles from the hills, we encountered the sandy ridges, and found the pull over them much worse than over the flats. The wheels of the drays sank deep into the ground, and in straining to get them clear we broke seven yokes. Two flights of swans, and a small flight of ducks, passed over our heads at dusk, coming from the W.N.W. The brushes were full of the Calodera, but being very wild we could not procure a specimen.

The chainers had no difficulty in keeping pace with us, and on the 26th we found ourselves in lat. 29° 6′, having then chained 61 miles on a bearing of 55° to the west of north, as originally determined upon. Finding that I had thus passed to the southwest of the grassy plain, I halted, and rode with Flood to the eastward; when at seven miles we descended into it, and finding that there was an abundance of water in the creek (the channel we had before noticed), I returned to Mr. Browne; but as it was late in the afternoon when we regained the tents, we did not move that evening, and the succeeding day being Sunday we also remained stationary. We had halted close to one of those clear patches on which the rain water lodges, but it had dried up, and there was only a little for our use in a small gutter not far distant. Whilst we were here encamped a little jerboa was chased by the dogs into a hole close to the drays; which, with four others, we succeeded in capturing, by digging for them.

This beautiful little animal burrows in the ground like a mouse, but their habitations have several passages, leading straight, like the radii of a circle, to a common centre, to which a shaft is sunk from above, so that there is a complete circulation of air along the whole. We fed our little captives on oats, on which they thrived, and became exceedingly tame. They generally huddled together in a corner of their box, but, when darting from one side to the other, they hopped on their hind legs, which, like the kangaroo, were much longer than the fore, and held the tail perfectly straight and horizontal. At this date they were a novelty to us, but we subsequently saw great numbers of them, and ascertained that the natives frequented the sandy ridges in order to procure them for food. Those we succeeded in capturing were, I am sorry to say, lost from neglect.

On Monday I conducted the whole party to the new depot, which for the present I shall call the Park, but as I was very unwilling that any more time should be lost in pushing to the west, I instructed Mr. Stuart to change the direction of the chained line to 75° to the west of south, direct upon Mount Hopeless, and to continue it until I should overtake him. In this operation Mr. Browne kindly volunteered to assist Mr. Stuart, as the loss of Mr. Piesse had so reduced my strength.

By the 30th I had arranged the camp in its new position, and felt myself at liberty to follow after the chainers. Before I left, however, I directed a stockyard to be made, in which to herd the cattle at night, and instructed Davenport to prepare some ground for the garden, with a view to planting it out with vegetables—pumpkins and melons. I left the camp with Flood, at 10 a.m. on the above day, judging that Mr. Browne was then about 42 miles a-head of me, and stopped for the night in a little sheltered valley between two sand hills, after a ride of 28 miles. The country continued unchanged. Valleys or flats, more or less covered with water, alternated with sandy ridges, on some of which there was no scarcity of grass.

We had not ridden far on the following morning when a partial change was perceptible in the aspect of the country. The flats became broader and the sand hills lower, but this change was temporary. We gradually rose somewhat from the general level and crossed several sand hills, higher than any we had seen. These sand hills had very precipitous sides and broken summits, and being of a bright red colour, they looked in the distance like long lines of dead brick walls, being perfectly bare, or sparingly covered with spinifex at the base. They succeeded each other so rapidly, that it was like crossing the tops of houses in some street; but they were much steeper to the eastward than to the westward, and successive gales appeared to have lowered them, and in some measure to have filled up the intervening flats with the sand from their summits.

On the 1st of August we did not find the country so heavy or so wet as it had been. It was indeed so open and denuded of every thing like a tree or bush, that we had some difficulty in finding wood to boil our tea. In the afternoon when we halted the men had chained 46 miles on the new bearing, but as yet we could not see any range or hill to the westward.

About two hours before we halted Mr. Browne and I surprised some natives on the top of a sand hill; two of them saw us approaching and ran away, the third could not make his escape before we were upon him, but he was dreadfully alarmed. In order to allay his fears Mr. Browne dismounted and walked up to him, whilst I kept back. On this the poor fellow began to dance, and to call out most vehemently, but finding that all he could do was to no purpose he sat down and began to cry. We managed however to pacify him, so much that he mustered courage to follow us, with his two companions, to our halting place. These wanderers of the desert had their bags full of jerboas which they had captured on the hills. They could not indeed have had less than from 150 to 200 of these beautiful little animals, so numerous are they on the sand hills, but it would appear that the natives can only go in pursuit of them after a fall of rain, such as that we had experienced. There being then water, the country, at other times impenetrable, is then temporarily thrown open to them, and they traverse it in quest of the jerboa and other quadrupeds. Our friends cooked all they had in hot sand, and devoured them entire, fur, skin, entrails and all, only breaking away the under jaw and nipping off the tail with their teeth.

They absolutely managed before sunset to finish their whole stock, and then took their departure, having, I suppose, gratified both their appetite and their curiosity. They were all three circumcised and spoke a different language from that of the hill natives, and came, they told us, from the west.

As we advanced the country became extremely barren, and surface water was very scarce, and the open ground, entirely denuded of timber, wore the most desolate appearance. If we had hitherto been in a region destitute of inhabitants it seemed as if we were now getting into a more populous district. About noon of the 2nd, as Mr. Browne and I were riding in front of the chainers, we heard a shout to our right, and on looking in that direction saw a party of natives assembled on a sand hill, to the number of fourteen. As we advanced towards them they retreated, but at length made a stand as if to await our approach. They were armed with spears, and on Mr. Browne dismounting to walk towards them, formed themselves into a circle, in the centre of which were two old men, round whom they danced. Thinking that Mr. Browne might run some risk if he went near, I called him back, and as I really had not time for ceremonies, we rejoined the chainers, being satisfied also that if the natives felt disposed to communicate with us, they would do so of their own accord; nor was I mistaken in this, for judging, I suppose, from our leaving them that we did not meditate any hostility, seven of their number followed us, and as Mr. Browne was at that time in advance, I gave my horse to one of the men and again went towards them, but it was with great difficulty that I got them to a parley, after which they sat down and allowed me to approach, though from the surprise they exhibited I imagine they had never seen a white man before. They spoke a language different from any I had heard, had lost two of the front teeth of the upper jaw, and had large scars on the breast. I could not gather any information from them, or satisfactorily ascertain from what quarter they came; staying with them for a short time therefore, and giving them a couple of knives, I left them, and after following abreast of us for a mile or two, they also turned to the north and disappeared.

The night of the 2nd August was exceedingly cold, with the wind from the N.E. (an unusual quarter from which to have a low temperature) and there was a thick hoar frost on the morning of the 3rd. Why the winds should have been so cold blowing from that quarter, whence our hottest winds also came, it is difficult to say; but at this season of the year, and in this line, they were invariably so.

Near the flat on which we stopped on the evening of the 2nd there was a hill considerably elevated above the others; which, after unsaddling and letting out the horses, Mr. Browne and I were induced to ascend. From it we saw a line of high and broken ranges to the S.S.W., but they were very distant. At three and a half miles from this point we crossed a salt water creek, having pools in it of great depth, but so clear that we could see to the bottom; and wherever our feet sank in the mud, salt water immediately oozed up. There were some box-trees growing near this creek, which came from t1e north, and fell towards the ranges. At half a mile further we crossed a small fresh water creek, and intermediate between the two was a lagoon of about a mile in length, but not more than three inches in depth. This lagoon, if it might so be called, from its size only, had been filled by the recent rains; but was so thick and muddy, from being continually ruffled by the winds, that it was unfit for use. The banks of the fresh water creek were crowded with water-hens, similar to those which visited Adelaide in such countless numbers the year before I proceeded into the interior (1843). They were running about like so many fowls; but, on being alarmed, took flight and went south.

The fresh water creek (across which it was an easy jump) joined the salt water creek a little below where we struck it, and was the first creek of the kind we had seen since we left the Depot, in a distance of more than 100 miles, and up to this point we had entirely subsisted on the surface water left by the rains. The country we now passed through was of a salsolaceous character, like a low barren sea coast. The sand hills were lower and broader than they had been, and their sides were cut by deep fissures made by heavy torrents. From a hill, about a mile from our halting place on this day, we again saw the ranges, which had been sighted the day before. South of us, and distant about a mile, there was a large dry lagoon, white with salt, and another of a similar kind to the west of it.

These changes in the character of the country convinced me that we should soon arrive at some more important one. On the 4th we advanced as usual on a bearing of 75° to the west of south, having then chained 65 miles upon it. At about three miles we observed a sand hill in front of us, beyond which no land was to be seen, as if the country dipped, and there was a great hollow. On arriving at this sand hill our further progress westward was checked by the intervention of an immense shallow and sandy basin, upon which we looked down from the place where we stood. The hills we had seen the day before were still visible through a good telescope, but we could only distinguish their outlines; in addition to them, however, there was a nearer flat-topped range, more to the northward and westward of the main range, which latter still bore S.S.W., and appeared to belong to a high and broken chain of mountains. The sandy basin was from ten to twelve miles broad, but destitute of water opposite to us, although there were, both to the southward and northward, sheets of water as blue as indigo and as salt as brine. These detached sheets were fringed round with samphire bushes with which the basin was also speckled over. There was a gradual descent of about a mile and a half, to the margin of the basin, the intervening ground being covered with low scrub. My first object was, to ascertain if we could cross this feature, which extended southwards beyond the range of vision, but turned to the westward in a northerly direction, in the shape in which Mr. Eyre has laid Lake Torrens down. For this purpose Mr. Browne and I descended into it. The bed was composed of sand and clay, the latter lying in large masses, and deeply grooved by torrents of rain. There was not any great quantity of salt to be seen, but it was collected at the bottom of gutters, and, no doubt, was more or less mixed with the soil. At about four miles we were obliged to dismount; and, tying our horses so as to secure them, walked on for another mile, when we found the ground too soft for our weight and were obliged to return; and, as it was now late, we commenced a search for water, and having found a small supply in a little hollow, at a short distance from the flag, we went to it and encamped. The length of the chain line to the flag staff was 70¾ miles, which with the 61 we had measured from the Depot, made 131¼ miles in all; the direct distance, therefore, from the Depot to the flag staff, was about 115 miles, on a bearing of 9½° to the North of West or W. ¾ N.

My object in the journey I had thus undertaken, was not so much to measure the distance between the two places, as to ascertain if the country to the north-west of Lake Torrens, on the borders of which I presumed I had arrived, was practicable or not, and whether it was connected with any more central body of water. It behoved me to ascertain these two points with as little delay as possible, for the surface water was fast drying up, and we were in danger of having our retreat cut off. Whether the country was practicable or not, in the direction I was anxious to take, it was clear that I could not have penetrated as far as I then was, with the heavy drays, with any prudence.

To be more satisfied, however, as to the nature of the country to the westward, I rode towards the N.E. angle of the Sandy Basin, on the morning of the 4th, sending Mr. Stuart southwards, to examine it in that direction; but, neither of these journeys proving satisfactory, I determined on fixing the position of the hills in reference to our chained line, and then return to the Depot, to prepare for a more extensive exploration of the N.W. interior. I found the country perfectly impracticable to the N.W., and that it was impossible to ascertain the real character of this Sandy Basin. On the other side of it the country appeared to be wooded; beyond the wood there was a sudden fall; and, as far as I could judge, this singular feature must have been connected with Spencer's Gulf, before the passage that evidently existed once between them was filled up. . . .

To that man who is really earnest in the performance of his duty to the last, and who has set his heart on the accomplishment of a great object, the attainment of which would place his name high up in the roll of Fame; to him who had well nigh reached the topmost step of the ladder, and whose hand had all but grasped the pinnacle, the necessity must be great, and the struggle of feeling severe, that forces him to bear back, and abandon his task.

Let any man lay the map of Australia before him, and regard the blank upon its surface, and then let me ask him if it would not be an honourable achievement to be the first to place foot in its centre.

Men of undoubted perseverance and energy in vain had tried to work their way to that distant and shrouded spot. A veil hung over Central Australia that could neither be pierced or raised. Girt round about by deserts, it almost appeared as if Nature had intentionally closed it upon civilized man, that she might have one domain on the earth's wide field over which the savage might roam in freedom.

I had traced down almost every inland river of the continent, and had followed their courses for hundreds of miles, but, they had not led me to its central regions. I had run the Castlereagh, the Macquarie, the Lachlan, the Murrumbidgee, the Hume, the Darling, and the Murray down to their respective terminations, but beyond them I had not passed—yet—I looked upon Central Australia as a legitimate field, to explore which no man had a greater claim than myself, and the first wish of my heart was to close my services in the cause of Geography by dispelling the mists that hung over it.

True it is that my friend Eyre had penetrated high up to the north of Mount Arden, and there can be no doubt but that his ardent and chivalrous spirit would have carried him far beyond the point he attained, if he had not met unconquerable difficulties. I thought that a cooler and more leisurely progress would enable me to feel my way into a country, whose inhospitable character developed itself more the more it was penetrated. I had adopted certain opinions, the correctness of which I was anxious to test, and I thought the investigations I desired to make, were not only worthy the pursuit of private ambition, but deserving the attention of Her Majesty's Government. With these feelings I could not but be grateful to Lord Stanley, for having entertained my proposition, and given me an opportunity to distinguish myself. It is not because his Lordship is no longer at the head of the Colonial Office, that I should refrain from making my acknowledgements to him, and expressing the sense I entertain of the obligation under which he has laid me. It so happened that the course pointed out to me by Lord Stanley, and that in which I desired to go, were the same, and I had hoped that in following up my instructions, I should ultimately have gained the spot I so ardently desired to reach, and to have left the flag of my native country flying over it.

The feelings then with which I returned to the creek after the failure of our last attempt to penetrate to the north may well be imagined. I returned to it, as I have said, with perhaps a sullen determination to stand out the drought; but, on calm reflection, I found that I could not do so. I could not indeed hide from myself that in the course of a few days my retreat to the Depot would unavoidably be cut off if rain should not fall. Looking to the chance of our being delayed until our provisions should be consumed, and to the fact that we could not expect to get back to the Depot in less than three weeks, and that I could not hope for any amendment either in Mr. Browne or my men, so long as they were confined to the scanty diet we then had, I determined on my return to the Park, thence to take out fresh hands, and to make another attempt to penetrate across the Desert in some other direction; but, as this measure, like our detention at the Depot, would involve a great loss of time, I proposed to myself again to divide the party, and to send Mr. Browne home with all the men, except Mr. Stuart and two others. I saw no objection to such a course, and certainly did not anticipate any opposition to it on the part of my companion. I resolved then, with a due regard to his state, to retrace my steps with all possible expedition; and, accordingly, directed that everything should be prepared for our retreat on the morning of the 14th, for the sky had cleared, and all prospect of rain had again vanished. Although we were here so close to the Tropic, the climate was not oppressive. The general temperature after noon was 84°, the morning 46°. The prevailing wind was from S.S.E. to E.S.E. and it was invariably cold; at least we felt it so, and I regretted to observe, that in Mr. Browne's case it caused a renewed attack of violent pains in the muscles and joints, from which he had before been somewhat free. It is also remarkable, that up to this distant point, no material change had taken place in the character of the vegetation; with the exception of the few trees and plants I have mentioned the herbage of these sterile regions and of the Darling were essentially the same, only with this difference, that here they were all more or less stunted, whereas, in the month of October, when we passed up the Darling, they were only just flowering, now in the month of September they had ripened their seed.

Before we commenced our journey back to the Depot, I named this " Eyre's Creek." No doubt it is an important feature in the country where it exists. Like the other creeks, however, it rises in plains, and either terminates in such or falls into the Stony Desert. There can be no doubt, however, that to any one desiring to cross the continent to the north, Eyre's Creek would afford great facilities; and if the traveller happened fortunately to arrive on it at a favourable moment he would have every chance of success.

For twelve miles below the salt lagoon there is not a blade of grass either in the bed of the creek or on the neighbouring flats, the soil of both being a stiff cold clay. We passed this ungenial line, therefore, and encamped near a fine pool of water, where both our own wants and those of our horses, as far as feed and water went, were abundantly supplied.

In going along one of the flats, before we discovered the creek, Mr. Browne and I had chased a Dipus into a hollow log, and there secured it. This pretty animal we put into a box; but as it appeared to eat but little grass, we gave it some small birds, which it always devoured at night. Our dogs had killed one on the banks of the Darling, but had so mutilated it that we could not preserve it. We hoped, however, to keep this animal alive, and up to the present time there was every chance of our doing so. It was an exceedingly pretty animal, of a light grey colour, having a long tail, feathered at the end, insectivorous, and not marsupial. On the 16th we turned from the creek to the south, and passed down the long flat up which we had previously come. On the following day we passed several of the hollows scraped by the natives, and in one of them found a little water, that must have accumulated in it from the drizzly showers that fell on the night of the 8th, and which might have been heavier here than with us. On the 19th we arrived at the creek where Flood's horse was lost, but could not make out any track to betray that he had been to water, and as there was not enough remaining in the pond for our use, we crossed the plain, over which we had had so much difficulty in travelling, and halted for a short time at the native well, out of which numbers of birds flew as we approached. From the Box-tree Forest we pushed on down the polygonum flat, where we had seen the native woman who had secreted herself in the bush. A whole family was now in the same place, but an old man only approached us. We were, indeed, passing, when he called to us, expressly for the purpose of telling us that the horse (Flood's) had gone away to the eastward. This native came out of his way, and evidently under considerable alarm, to tell us this, and to point out the direction in which he had gone. Our stock of presents being pretty nearly exhausted, Mr. Browne, with his characteristic good nature, gave him a striped handkerchief, with which he was much pleased. As it was evident that the poor horse had kept along the edge of the Desert, and as he was a wandering brute, not caring for companions, it was uncertain to what distance he had rambled, I did not, therefore, lose time by attempting to recover him. We were all of us sure that he would not face the Stony Desert, but he may still be alive and wandering over that sterile country. We stopped for the night on the long channel near the sandy rise where we had before rested, about ten miles short of our camp, and the trees on the muddy plain; and having effected our passage across that plain and the Stony Desert, over which it was with extreme difficulty that we kept our track, found ourselves, on the 22nd, in the little grassy valley, from which we had entered upon it; little water was remaining, however, at the place where we had then stopped, so that I sent over to the sequestered spot Lewis had discovered, but the water there had entirely disappeared. Flood managed to shoot a couple of ducks (Teal), of which there were four or five that flew away to the south-east. These two birds were, I may truly say, a God-send, and I beg to assure the reader they were uncommonly good.

From this valley we had to cross the heavy sand ridges which had so fatigued our horses before, and I hardly expected we should find water nearer than the Fish Pond. We therefore started early to get over the distance as soon as possible, and, as on the outward journey, had a most severe task of it. The ridges were certainly most formidable, although they were not of such size as those from which we had retreated. At six miles we crossed the salt lagoon, and late in the afternoon descended to the box-tree forest before mentioned, having the grassy plains now upon the left-hand side. The sandy ridges overlooked these plains, so that in riding along we noticed some natives, seven in number, collecting grass seeds upon them, on which alone, it appears to me, they subsist at this season of the year. However, as soon as they saw us, they all ran away in more than usual alarm, perhaps from the recollection of our misunderstanding with Mr. Popinjay. Their presence, however, assured us that there must be water somewhere about, and as on entering the plain, more to the west than before, we struck on a track, I directed Mr. Browne to run it down, who, at about half-a-mile, came to a large well similar to that in the creek on the other side of the Stony Desert, but not of the same dimensions. We had lost sight of him for some little time, when suddenly his horse made his appearance without a rider, and caused me great anxiety for the moment, for my mind immediately reverted to our sulky friend, and my fears were at once raised that my young companion had been speared; riding on, therefore, I came at length to the well, down which, to my inexpressible relief, I saw Mr. Browne, who was examining it, and who came out on my calling to him. There was not sufficient water to render it worth our while to stop; but the well being nine feet deep, shewed the succession of strata as follows: four feet of good alluvial soil; three feet of white clay; and two feet of sea sand.

I should perhaps have been more particular in the description of our interview with the old man and his family on the northern side of the earthy plain. As I have stated, he called out to us, and in order to discover what he wanted, I held Mr. Browne's horse, while he dismounted and went to him. The old native would not, however, sit down, but pointed to the S.E. as the direction in which, as far as we could understand, the horse, "cadli" (dog), as he called him, the only large four-legged brute of which he knew any thing, had gone. The poor fellow cried, and the tears rolled down his cheeks when he first met Mr. Browne, and the women chanted a most melancholy air during the time we remained, to keep the evil spirits off, I suppose; but they had nothing to fear from us, if they could only have known it. This confusion of tongues is a sad difficulty in travelling the wilds of Australia. Both the old man and the women wanted the two front teeth of the upper jaw, and as the former had worn his down almost to a level with his gums like an old horse, he looked sadly disfigured.

We halted about three miles short of the place at which we had before stopped, but as Joseph followed some pigeons to a clump of trees across the plain at about a mile distance, and there found a small pond of water, we moved over to it, and remained stationary on the following day to rest our wearied animals.

The 24th again saw us at the Fish Pond, where Mr. Browne

again exhibited his skill in the gentle craft, and caught a good dish of the finny tribe. The mystery as to how these fish could have got into so isolated a spot was not yet cleared up, and I was really puzzled on the subject.

On the 27th, as we were crossing the country between the creeks, some natives came in from the north and called out to us, in consequence of which Mr. Browne and I rode up to them. They were in a sad state of suffering from the want of water; their lips cracked, and their tongues swelled. They had evidently lingered at some place or other until all the water intermediate between them and the creeks had dried up. The little water we had was not sufficient to allay their thirst, so they left us, and at a sharp trot disappeared over the sand hill.

On the 29th our journey over the sandy ridges was very distressing. They appeared to me to be much more numerous, and the valleys between them much more sandy than when we first passed over them, and were thickly covered with spinifex, although grass was also tolerably abundant in the flats. At this stage of our journey, I was the only one of the party who was not ill; Mr. Browne and all the men were suffering, added to which, the men were fairly knocked up. Their labours were now, however, drawing to a close, and I was only too thankful, that I retained my strength. . . .

By half past eleven of the 9th November we had again got quietly settled, and I then found leisure to make such arrangements as might suggest themselves for our further retreat. To insure the safety of the animals as much as possible, I determined to leave all my spare provisions and weightier stores behind, and during the afternoon we were engaged making the loads as compact and as light as we could.

It was not, however, the fear of the water in Strzelecki's Creek having dried up, that was at this moment the only cause of anxiety to me, for I thought it more than probable that Mr. Browne had been obliged to retreat from Fort Grey, in which case I should still have a journey before me to the old Depot of 170 miles or more, under privations, to the horses at least, of no ordinary character; and I had great doubts as to the practicability of our final retreat upon the Darling. The drought had now continued so long, and the heat been so severe, that I apprehended we might be obliged to remain another summer in these fearful solitudes. The weather was terrifically hot, and appeared to have set in unusually early.

Under such circumstances, and with so many causes to render

my mind anxious, the reader will believe I did not sleep much. The men were as restless as myself, so that we commenced our journey before the sun had risen on the morning of the 10th of November, to give the horses time to take their journey leisurely. Slowly we retraced our steps, nor did I stop for a moment until we had got to within five miles of our destination, at which distance we saw a single native running after us, and taking it into my head that he might be a messenger from Mr. Browne, I pulled up to wait for him, but curiosity alone had induced him to come forward. When he got within a hundred yards, he stopped and approached no nearer. This little delay made it after sunset before we reached the upper pool (not the one Mr. Browne and I had discovered), and were relieved from present anxiety by finding a thick puddle still remaining in it, so that I halted for the night. Slommy, Bawley, and the colt had hard work to keep up with the other horses, and it really grieved me to see them so reduced. My own horse was even now beginning to give way, but I had carried a great load upon him.

As we approached the water, three ducks flew up and went off down the creek southwards, so I was cheered all night by the hope that water still remained at the lower pool, and that we should be in time to benefit by it. On the 11th, therefore, early we pushed on, as I intended to stop and breakfast at that place before I started for the Depot. We had scarcely got there, however, when the wind, which had been blowing all the morning hot from the N.E., increased to a heavy gale, and I shall never forget its withering effect. I sought shelter behind a large gum-tree, but the blasts of heat were so terrific, that I wondered the very grass did not take fire. This really was nothing ideal: every thing, both animate and inanimate, gave way before it; the horses stood with their backs to the wind, and their noses to the ground, without the muscular strength to raise their heads; the birds were mute, and the leaves of the trees, under which we were sitting, fell like a snow shower around us. At noon I took a thermometer, graduated to 127°, out of my box, and observed that the mercury was up to 125°. Thinking that it had been unduly influenced, I put it in the fork of a tree close to me, sheltered alike from the wind and the sun. In this position I went to examine it about an hour afterwards, when I found that the mercury had risen to the top of the instrument, and that its further expansion had burst the bulb, a circumstance that I believe no traveller has ever before had to record. I cannot find language to convey to the reader's mind an idea of the intense and oppressive nature of the heat that prevailed. We had reached our destination however before the worst of the hot wind set in; but all the water that now remained in the once broad and capacious pool to which I have had such frequent occasion to call the attention of the reader, was a shining patch of mud nearly in the centre. We were obliged to dig a trench for the water to filter into during the night, and by this means obtained a scanty supply for our horses and ourselves.

About sunset the wind shifted to the west, a cloud passed over us, and we had heavy thunder; but a few drops of rain only fell. They partially cooled the temperature, and the night was less oppressive than the day had been. We had now a journey of 86 miles before us: to its results I looked with great anxiety and doubt. I took every precaution to fortify the horses, and again reduced the loads, keeping barely a supply of flour for a day or two. Before dawn we were up, and drained the last drop of water, if so it could be called, out of the little trench we had made, and reserving a gallon for the first horse that should fall, divided the residue among them. Just as the morning was breaking, we left the creek, and travelled for 36 miles. I then halted until the moon should rise, and was glad to see that the horses stood it well. At seven we resumed the journey, and got on tolerably well until midnight, when poor Bawley, my favourite horse, fell; but we got him up again, and abandoning his saddle, proceeded onwards. At a mile, however, he again fell, when I stopped, and the water revived him. I now hoped he would struggle on, but in about an hour he again fell. I was exceedingly fond of this poor animal, and intended to have purchased him at the sale of the remnants of the expedition, as a present to my wife. We sat down and lit a fire by him, but he seemed fairly worn out. I then determined to ride on to the Depot, and if Mr. Browne should still be there, to send a dray with water to the relief of the men. I told them, therefore, to come slowly on, and with Mr. Stuart pushed for the camp. We reached the plain just as the sun was descending, without having dismounted from our horses for more than fifteen hours, and as we rode down the embankment into it, looked around for the cattle, but none were to be seen. We looked towards the little sandy mound on which the tents had stood, but no white object there met our eye; we rode slowly up to the stockade, and found it silent and deserted. I was quite sure that Mr. Browne had had urgent reasons for retiring. I had indeed anticipated the measure: I hardly hoped to find him at the Fort, and had given him instructions on the subject of his removal, yet a sickening feeling came over me when I saw that he was really gone; not on my own account, for, with the bitter feelings of disappointment with which I was returning home, I could calmly have laid my head on that desert, never to raise it again. The feeling was natural, and had no mixture whatever of reproach towards my excellent companion.

We dismounted and led our horses down to water before I went to the tree under which I had directed Mr. Browne to deposit a letter for me. A good deal of water still remained in the channel, but nevertheless a large pit had been dug in it as I had desired. I did not drink, nor did Mr. Stuart, the surface of the water was quite green, and the water itself was of a red colour, but I believe we were both thinking of any thing but ourselves at that moment. As soon as we had unsaddled the horses, we went to the tree and dug up the bottle into which, as agreed upon, Mr. Browne had put a letter; informing me that he had been most reluctantly obliged to retreat; the water at the Depot having turned putrid, and seriously disagreed with the men; he said that he should fall back on the old Depot along the same line on which we had advanced, and expressed his fears that the water in Strzelecki's Creek would have dried, on the permanence of which he knew our safety depended. Under present circumstances the fate of poor Bawley, if not of more of our horses, was sealed. Mr. Stuart and I sat down by the stockade, and as night closed in lit a fire to guide Morgan and Mack on their approach to the plain. They came up about 2 p.m. having left Bawley on a little stony plain, and the Colt on the sand ridges nearer to us, and in the confusion and darkness had left all the provisions behind; it therefore became necessary to send for some, as we had not had anything for many hours. The horses Morgan and Mack had ridden were too knocked up for further work, but I sent the latter on my own horse with a leather bottle that had been left behind by the party, full of water for poor Bawley, if he should still find him alive. Mack returned late in the afternoon, having passed the Colt on his way to the Depot, towards which he dragged himself with difficulty, but Bawley was beyond recovery; he gave the poor animal the water, however, for he was a humane man, and then left him to die.

We had remained during the day under a scorching heat, but could hardly venture to drink the water of the creek without first purifying it by boiling, and as we had no vessel until Mack should come up we had to wait patiently for his arrival at 7 p.m. About 9 we had a damper baked, and broke our fast for the first time for more than two days.

While sitting under a tree in the forenoon Mr. Stuart had observed a crow pitch in the little garden we had made, but which never benefited us, since the sun burnt up every plant the moment it appeared above the ground. This bird scratched for a short time in one of the soft beds, and then flew away with something in his bill. On going to the spot Mr. Stuart scraped up a piece of bacon and some suet, which the dogs of course had buried. These choice morsels were washed and cooked, and Mr. Stuart brought me a small piece of bacon, certainly not larger than a dollar, which he assured me had been cut out of the centre and was perfectly clean. I had not tasted the bacon since February, nor did I now feel any desire to do so, but I ate it because I thought I really wanted it in the weak state in which I was.

Perhaps a physician would laugh at me for ascribing the pains I felt the next morning to so trifling a cause, but I was attacked with pains at the bottom of my heels and in my back. Although lying down I felt as if I was standing balanced on stones; these pains increased during the day, insomuch that I anticipated some more violent attack, and determined on getting to the old Depot as soon as possible; but as the horses had not had sufficient rest, I put off my journey to 5 p.m. on the following day, when I left Fort Grey with Mr. Stuart, directing Mack and Morgan to follow at the same hour on the following day, and promising that I would send a dray with water to meet them. I rode all that night until 3 p.m. of the 17th, when we reached the tents, which Mr. Browne had pitched about two miles below the spot we had formerly occupied. If I except two or three occasions on which I was obliged to dismount to rest my back for a few minutes we rode without stopping, and might truly be said to have been twenty hours on horseback.

Sincere I believe was the joy of Mr. Browne, and indeed of all hands, at seeing us return, for they had taken it for granted that our retreat would have been cut off. I too was gratified to find that Mr. Browne was better, and to learn that everything had gone on well. Davenport had recently been taken ill, but the other men had recovered on their removal from the cause of their malady.

When I dismounted I had nearly fallen forward. Thinking that one of the kangaroo dogs in his greeting had pushed me between the legs, I turned round to give him a slap, but no dog was there, and I soon found out that what I had felt was nothing more than strong muscular action brought on by hard riding.

Mr. Browne informed me that the natives had frequently

EDWARD JOHN EYRE.
From an engraving by J. Brown after a photograph by H. Hering.

visited the camp during my absence. He had given them to
understand that we were going over the hills again, on which they
told him that if he did not make haste all the water would be
gone. It now behoved us therefore to effect our retreat upon the
Darling with all expedition. Our situation was very critical, for
the effects of the drought were more visible now than before the
July rain,—no more indeed had since fallen, and the water in the
Depot creek was so much reduced that we had good reason to
fear that none remained anywhere else. On the 18th I sent Flood
to a small creek, between us and the Pine forest, but he returned
on the following day with information that it had long been dry.
Thus then were my fears verified, and our retreat to the Darling
apparently cut off. About this time too the very elements, against
which we had so long been contending, seemed to unite their
energies to render our stay in that dreadful region still more
intolerable. The heat was greater than that of the previous
summer; the thermometer ranging between 110° and 123° every
day; the wind blowing heavily from N.E. to E.S.E. filled the air
with impalpable red dust, giving the sun the most foreboding and
lurid appearance as we looked upon him. The ground was so
heated that our matches falling on it, ignited; and, having occasion to make a night signal, I found the whole of our rockets had
been rendered useless, as on being lit they exploded at once
without rising from the ground.

XV. EYRE'S JOURNEY FROM FOWLER'S BAY TO ALBANY IN 1841

[THE purpose of the expeditions commanded by Edward John Eyre was to explore the territory north and west of Adelaide in the hope of discovering good grazing grounds and stock routes. He made two journeys with this object in view in 1839. In 1840 he set out from Adelaide to explore the Lake Torrens country. Coming to the conclusion that it was useless to attempt to proceed beyond Mount Hopeless, he sent to Adelaide for a fresh supply of provisions, and moved his party down to Fowler's Bay. The following narrative relates his adventures after he sent back the main body of his expedition, and determined to take pack-horses and try to reach Albany (King George's Sound) by a direct route round the shores of the Great Australian Bight.]

Upon maturely considering our circumstances and position, I decided to attempt to force a passage round the Great Bight, with pack-horses only, sending, upon the return of the cutter, all our heavy stores and drays in her to Cape Arid, if I found, upon her arrival, the instructions I might receive would justify me in taking her so far beyond the boundaries of South Australia. This was the only plan that appeared to me at all feasible, and I determined to adopt it as soon as our horses were sufficiently recruited to commence their labours again. . . .

The native boys I intended to accompany me in my journey, as they would be better able to put up with the fatigues and privations we should have to go through, than Europeans; whilst their quickness of sight, habit of observation, and skill in tracking, might occasionally be of essential service to me. The native who had lately joined me from Adelaide, and whose country was around King George's Sound, would, I hoped, be able to interpret to any tribes we might meet with, as it appeared to me that some of the words we had heard in use among the natives of this part of the coast were very similar to some I had heard among the natives of King George's Sound. Three natives, however, were more than I required, and I would gladly have

338

sent the youngest of them back to Adelaide, but he had been with me several years, and I did not like to send him away whilst he was willing to remain; besides, he was so young and so light in weight, that if we were able to get on at all, his presence could cause but little extra difficulty. I therefore decided upon taking him also.

There remained now only the overseer; a man who had been in my service for many years, and whose energy, activity, and many useful qualities, had made him an invaluable servant to me at all times; whilst his courage, prudence, good conduct, and fidelity, made me very desirous to have him with me in this last effort to cross to the westward. Having sent for him, I explained to him most fully the circumstances in which I was placed, the utter impossibility of taking on the whole party through so inhospitable a region as that before us, my own firm determination never to return unsuccessful, but either to accomplish the object I had in view, or perish in the attempt. I pointed out to him that there were still eight hundred and fifty miles of an unknown country yet to be traversed and explored; that, in all probability, this would consist principally, if not wholly, of an all but impracticable desert. I reminded him of the fatigues, difficulties, and losses we had already experienced in attempting to reconnoitre the country only as far as the head of the Great Bight; and stated to him my own conviction, that from the knowledge and experience we had already acquired of the nature of the country, the journey before us must of necessity be a long and harassing one—one of unceasing toil, privation, and anxiety, whilst, from the smallness of our party, the probable want of water, and other causes, it would be one, also, of more than ordinary risk and danger. I then left him to determine whether he would return to Adelaide, in the cutter, or remain and accompany me. His reply was, that although he had become tired of remaining so long away in the wilds, and should be glad when the expedition had terminated, yet he would willingly remain with me to the last, and would accompany me to the westward at every hazard. . . .

February 24.—This being the day I had appointed to enter upon the arduous task before me, I had the party up at a very early hour. Our loads were all arranged for each of the horses; our blankets and coats were all packed up, and we were in the act of burying in a hole under ground the few stores we could not take with us, when to our surprise a shot was heard in the direction of Fowler's Bay, and shortly after a second; we then

observed two people in the distance following up the dray
tracks leading to the depot. Imagining that some whaler had
anchored in the bay, and being anxious to prevent our underground store from being noticed, we hastily spread the tarpaulins over the hole, so that what we were about could not be
observed, and then fired shots in reply. . . .

February 25.—Having finished my letters, and buried all the
spare stores, I sent the native boys away early with the sheep,
that they might travel more slowly than we should do with the
horses. About two we loaded the pack animals, and wishing
Mr. Scott a final adieu, set off upon our route. The party consisted of myself, the overseer, three native boys, nine horses,
one Timor pony, one foal, born at Streaky Bay, and six sheep;
our flour, which was buried at the sand-hills to the north-west,
was calculated for nine weeks, at an allowance of six pounds of
flour each weekly, with a proportionate quantity of tea and
sugar. The long rest our horses had enjoyed, and the large
supply of oats and bran we had received for them, had brought
them round wonderfully, they were now in good condition, and
strong, and could not have commenced the journey under more
favourable circumstances, had it been the winter instead of the
summer season.

Two of the native boys having gone on early in the morning
with the sheep, there remained only myself, the overseer, and
one native, to manage ten horses, and we were consequently
obliged to drive some of the pack-horses loose; at first they went
well and quietly, but something having unluckily startled one
of them, he frightened the others, and four out of the number
set off at full gallop, and never stopped for five miles, by which
time they had got rid of all their loads except the saddles.
Sending the black boy back to the depot with the four horses
that had not got away, I and the overseer went on horseback
after the others, picking up the baggage they had been carrying,
scattered about in every direction; luckily no great damage was
done, and at sunset we were all assembled again at the depot,
and the animals reloaded. Leaving a short note for Mr. Scott,
who had gone on board the cutter, we again recommenced our
journey, and, travelling for five miles, halted at the well in the
plains. I intended to have made a long stage, but the night set
in so dark that I did not like to venture amongst the scrub
with the pack-horses now they were so fresh, and where, if they
did get frightened and gallop off, they would cause us much
greater trouble and delay than they had done in the daytime.

February 26.—Moving on very early, we arrived at the grassy plain under the sand-hills, a little after three in the afternoon, just in time to save the gun and clothes of the black boys, which they had imprudently left there whilst they took the sheep to water, a mile and a half away. At the very instant of our arrival, a native was prowling about the camp, and would, doubtless, soon have carried off every thing. Upon examining the place at which we had buried our flour on the 31st December, and upon which we were now dependent for our supply, I found that we had only just arrived in time to save it from the depredations of the natives; it seems, that having found where the cask containing it was buried, and being unable, from its weight, to get it out of the ground, they had broken a square hole in one of the staves (by what means I could not discover), and though, as yet, every thing was safe and uninjured inside, I have no doubt, that, had we been one day later in coming, they would have enlarged the opening in the cask, and scattered or destroyed the contents, and we should have then had the unpleasant and laborious task of returning to that we had buried at Fowler's Bay for a fresh supply. A bucket, which we had also left buried, was broken to pieces, a two-gallon keg carried off, and a twenty-five-gallon cask full of water had been dug up, and the water drank or emptied, so that we were very fortunate in arriving when we did to prevent further loss.

The black boys, who had gone a-head with the sheep, returned soon after our arrival, tired and hungry, having only had one meal since they left us on the 25th. They had been over the sand-hills to fetch water, and were now coming to try and find the flour which they knew we had left buried at these plains. After dark, accompanied by the overseer, I took the horses down to the water, but the sand had slipped in, and we could not get them watered to-night.

February 27.—Sending the overseer and two boys down with the horses to the well this morning, I and the other boy set to work, and dug out the cask with the flour, which we then weighed out, and subdivided into packages of fifty pounds each, for the convenience of carrying. The native I had seen about the camp, on our approach, yesterday, had returned, and slept near us at night; but upon inquiring from him this morning, where our two-gallon keg was, he took the very earliest opportunity of decamping, being probably afraid that we should charge him with the robbery, or punish him for it. The natives, generally, are a strange and singular race of people, and their customs and habits are often quite inexplicable to us. Sometimes, in barely passing through a country, we have them gathering from all quarters, and surrounding us, anxious and curious to observe our persons, or actions; at other times, we may remain in camp for weeks together without seeing a single native, though many may be in the neighbourhood; when they do come, too, they usually depart as suddenly as their visit had been unexpected. Among all who had come under my observation, hitherto, along this coast, I found that every male had undergone the singular ceremony I have described as prevailing in the Port Lincoln peninsula; each, too, had the cartilage of the nose perforated, but none had lost the front teeth, nor did I see any (with one exception) having scars raised on the back, breast, or arms, as is frequently the case with many tribes in Australia.

February 28.—As we had a long distance to travel to the next water, and the sheep could not keep pace with the horses, I left the overseer and two natives to bring the latter after us, whilst I and the younger boy set off with the sheep to the undulating plains, arriving there between ten and eleven at night. After hobbling the horses, and making a brush-yard for the sheep, we laid down, tired with the labours of the day.

March 2.—A hot day, with the wind north-east. Between eleven and twelve we arrived at the first water, at the head of the Bight, and had a long and arduous task to get the sheep and horses watered, no natives being here to help us now, and the sand rushing in as fast as we could throw it out. By great exertion we effected our object, and then getting some tea, and leaving a note to tell the overseer not to halt at this difficult watering-place, if he could possibly avoid it, we pushed on again, and took up our position at Yeerkumban kauwe, in time to dig holes, and water the sheep, before dark.

March 3.—Having got up and watered the horses and sheep, I sent the boy out to tend them at grass, whilst I commenced digging two large holes to water the pack-horses, that there might be no delay when the overseer came up with them. I had nothing but a shell to dig with, and, as a very large excavation was required to enable a bucket to be dipped, my occupation was neither a light nor a short one. Having completed my work, I killed a sheep, well knowing the party would be fatigued and hungry when they came up. About three they made their appearance, and thus, upon the whole, we had very successfully got over this our first push, and were soon very comfortably established at Yeerkumban kauwe. The holes I had dug enabled us easily and speedily to water the horses, and the sheep I had killed afforded a refreshing meal to the overseer and boys, after their harassing journey. In the afternoon the sand blew about in a most annoying manner, covering us from head to foot, and filling everything we put down, if but for an instant. This sand had been our constant torment for many weeks past; condemned to live among the sandhills for the sake of procuring water, we were never free from irritation and inconvenience. It floated on the surface of the water, penetrated into our clothes, hair, eyes, and ears, our provisions were covered over with it, and our blankets half buried when we lay down at nights,—it was a perpetual and never-ceasing torment, and as if to increase our miseries we were again afflicted with swarms of large horse-flies, which bit us dreadfully. On the 4th, we remained in camp to rest the horses, and I walked round to reconnoitre. Upon the beach I found the fragments of a wreck, consisting of part of a mast, a tiller wheel, and some copper sheathings, the last sad records of the fate of some unfortunate vessel on this wild and breaker-beaten shore. There was nothing to indicate its size, or name, or the period when the wreck occurred.

Knowing from the accounts of the natives that upon leaving Yeerkumban kauwe, I should have a task before me of no ordinary difficulty to get either the sheep or the horses to the next water, I determined to proceed myself in advance, with the sheep, that by travelling slowly, at the same time that we kept steadily advancing, every chance might be given to them of accomplishing the journey in safety. I was anxious too to precede my party, in order that by finding out where the water was, I might be on the look out for them, to guide them to it, and that thus, when in their greatest difficulty, no time should be lost in searching for water. Having given the overseer orders to keep the tracks of my horses, when he had travelled about seventy miles along the coast, I set off on the 7th March, with the youngest of the natives to assist me in driving the sheep, leaving the two elder ones with the overseer, to aid in managing the pack-horses. As before we took two horses with us, one to carry our provisions and water, and the other to ride upon in turn, the boy however, being young, and incapable of much fatigue, the greater portion of the walking naturally fell to my share. The day was cool and favourable, and we accomplished a stage of twenty-four miles; the afternoon became dark and lowering, and I fully expected rain, but towards sunset two or three drops fell, and the clouds cleared away. Our horses fed tolerably upon the little withered grass that we found, but the sheep were too tired to eat, and lay down; we put them therefore into a yard we had made for them for the night.

March 8.—Having turned the sheep out of the yard three hours before daylight, I was in hopes they would have fed a little before we moved on, but they would not touch such food as we had for them, and at six I was obliged to proceed onwards; the morning was dark and looked like rain, but as was the case yesterday, a drop or two only fell. We made a stage to-day of twenty-six miles, through a level country, generally open, but near the sea covered with a very low dwarf tea-tree, small prickly bushes, and salsolae, and having the surface almost every where sprinkled over with fresh-water shells; further from the coast the plains extending to the north were very extensive, level, and divided by belts of scrub or shrubs. There was no perceptible inclination of the country in any direction, the level land ran to the very borders of the sea, where it abruptly ter-minated, forming the steep and precipitous cliffs, observed by Captain Flinders, and which it was quite impossible to descend anywhere. The general elevation of this table land was from three to four hundred feet.

The day turned out fine and clear, and the effect produced by refraction in these vast plains was singular and deceptive: more than once we turned considerably out of our way to examine some large timber, as we thought it to be, to the north of us, but which, upon our approach, proved to be low scrubby bushes. At another time we imagined we saw two natives in the distance, and went towards them as carefully and cautiously as we could; instead, however, of our having seen the heads of natives, as we supposed, above the bushes, it turned out to be only crows. Yet the native boy, whose quickness and accuracy of vision had often before surprised me, was equally deceived with myself. Upon halting in the evening our sheep again were very tired, and refused to eat. The horses too were now beginning to feel the want of water, and fed but little. I therefore sat up and watched them until half-past eight, after which I tied them up to some bushes. At one o'clock I again got up and let them loose, hoping they might feed a little better in the cool of the night. The scud was rapidly passing the moon, and I watched for hours the clouds gathering to the south and passing to the north, but no rain fell.

March 9.—The day was cloudy and gathering for rain, but none fell. After travelling twenty-five miles we halted for an hour or two to rest the sheep and horses, feeding was out of the question, for they were too much in want of water to attempt to eat the dry and withered grass around us. We now lay down to rest ourselves, and the boy soon fell asleep; I was however feverish and restless and could not close my eyes. In an hour and a half I arose, got up the horses and saddled them, and then, awaking my companion, we again pushed on by moonlight. At ten miles we crossed a well-beaten native pathway, plainly discernible even then, and this we followed down towards the cliffs, fully hoping it would lead to water. Our hopes however had been excited but to render our disappointment the greater, for upon tracing it onwards we found it terminate abruptly at a large circular hole of limestone rock, which would retain a considerable quantity of water after rains, but was now without a single drop. Gloomily turning away we again pushed on for eight miles further, and at three in the morning of the 10th were compelled to halt from downright exhaustion and fatigue. The horses and sheep were knocked up. The poor boy was so tired and sleepy that he could scarcely sit upon his horse, and I found myself actually dosing as I walked: mechanically my legs kept moving forwards, but my eyes were every now and then closed in forgetfulness of all around me, until I was suddenly thrown down by getting entangled amongst the scrub, or aroused by a severe blow across the face from the recoil of a bough after the passage of the boy's horse. I now judged we had come about ninety-three miles from Yeerkumban-kauwe, and hoped that we could not be very far from water. Having tied up the horses for an hour or two, and without making a fire, or even unrolling our cloaks to cover us, we stretched ourselves on the ground, and were in a few moments fast asleep.

March 10.—At five we were again on our route, every moment expecting to see a break in the line of cliffs along which we had now travelled so far. Alas! they still continued stretching as far as the eye could see to the westward, and as fast as we arrived at one point which had bounded our vision (and beyond which we hoped a change might occur), it was but to be met with the view of another beyond. Distressing and fatal as the continuance of these cliffs might prove to us, there was a grandeur and sublimity in their appearance that was most imposing, and which struck me with admiration. Stretching out before us in lofty unbroken outline, they presented the singular and romantic appearance of massy battlements of masonry, supported by huge buttresses, and glittering in the morning sun which had now risen upon them, and made the scene beautiful even amidst the dangers and anxieties of our situation. It was indeed a rich and gorgeous view for a painter, and I never felt so much regret at my inability to sketch as I did at this moment. Our sheep still travelled, but they were getting so tired, and their pace was so slow, that I thought it would be better to leave them behind, and by moving more rapidly with the horses endeavour at least to save their lives. Foreseeing that such a contingency as this might occur, I had given the overseer strict orders to keep the tracks of my horses, that if I should be compelled to abandon the sheep he might find them and bring them on with his party.

Having decided upon this plan we set to work and made a strong high yard of such shrubs as we could find, and in this we shut up the sheep. I then wrote a note for the overseer, directing him to bury the loads of the horses, and hastening on with the animals alone endeavour to save their lives. To attract attention I raised a long stick above the sheep-yard, and tied to it a red handkerchief, which could be seen a long way off. At one we again proceeded, and were able to advance more rapidly than we could whilst the sheep were with us. In a few miles we came to a well-beaten native road, and again our hopes were raised of speedily terminating the anxiety and suspense we were in. Following the road for ten miles it conducted us to where the cliffs receded a little from the sea, leaving a small barren valley between them and the ocean, of low, sandy ground; the road ceased here at a deep rocky gorge of the cliffs, where there was a breach leading down to the valley. There were several deep holes among the rocks where water would be procurable after rains, but they were now all dry. The state of mind in which we passed on may be better imagined than described. We had now been four days without a drop of water for our horses, and we had no longer any for ourselves, whilst there appeared as little probability of our shortly procuring it as there had been two days ago. A break, it is true, had occurred in the line of the cliffs, but this appeared of a very temporary character, for we could see beyond them the valley again abutting upon the ocean.

At dark we were fifteen miles from where we left the sheep, and were again upon a native pathway, which we twice tried to follow down the steep and rugged slopes of the table land into the valley below. We were only, however, fagging our poor horses and bewildering ourselves to no purpose, for we invariably lost all track at the bottom, and I at last became convinced that it was useless to try and trace the natives' roadway further, since it always appeared to stop at rocky holes where there was no water now. Keeping, therefore, the high ground, we travelled near the top of the cliffs, bounding the sandy valley, but here again a new obstacle impeded our progress. The country, which had heretofore been tolerably open, was now become very scrubby, and we found it almost impossible either to keep a straight course, or to make any progress through it in the dark. Still we kept perseveringly onwards, leading our horses and forcing our way through in the best way we could. It was, however, all in vain; we made so little headway, and were so completely exhausting the little strength we had left, that I felt compelled to desist. The poor boy was quite worn out, and could scarcely move. I was myself but little better, and we were both suffering from a parching thirst; under such obstacles labour and perseverance were but thrown away, and I determined to await the daylight. After tying up the horses the boy lay down, and was soon asleep, happy in his ignorance of the dangers which threatened him. I lay down, too, but not to sleep; my own distresses were lost in the apprehensions which I entertained for those who were behind. We were now about one hundred and twenty-eight miles from the last water; we had been four whole days and nights without a drop for our horses, and almost without food also, (for parched as they were they could not feed upon the dry and withered grass we found). The state the poor animals were in was truly pitiable; what then was likely to be the condition of those that were coming after us, and carrying heavy packs. It was questionable, even, if they would reach the distance we had already attained in safety; and it was clear, that unless I discovered water early in the morning, the whole of our horses must perish, whilst it would be very doubtful if we could succeed even in saving our own lives.

March 11.—Early this morning we moved on, leading slowly our jaded animals through the scrub. The night had been one of painful suspense and gloomy forebodings; and the day set in dark and cloudy, as if to tantalise us with the hope of rain which was not destined to fall. In a few miles we reached the edge of the cliffs, from which we had a good view of the sandy valley we had been travelling round, but which the thick scrub had prevented our scrutinising sooner.

For a few minutes I carefully scanned the line of coast before me. In the distance beyond a projecting point of the cliffs, I fancied I discerned a low sandy shore, and my mind was made up at once, to advance in the line we were pursuing. After a little while, we again came to a well beaten native pathway, and following this along the summit of the cliffs, were brought by it, in seven miles, to the point where they receded from the sea-shore; as they inclined inland, leaving a low sandy country between them and some high bare sand-hills near the sea. The road now led us down a very rocky steep part of the cliffs, near the angle where they broke away from the beach, but upon reaching the bottom we lost it altogether on the sandy shore; following along by the water's edge, we felt cooled and refreshed by the sea air, and in one mile and a half from where we had descended the cliffs, we reached the white sand-drifts. Upon turning into these to search for water, we were fortunate enough to strike the very place where the natives had dug little wells; and thus on the fifth day of our sufferings, we were again blessed with abundance of water,—nor could I help considering it as a special instance of the goodness of Providence, that we had passed the sandy valley in the dark, and had thereby been deterred from descending to examine the sand-hills it contained; had we done so, the extra fatigue to our horses and the great length of time it would have taken up, would probably have prevented the horses from ever reaching the water we were now at. It took us about two hours to water the animals, and get a little tea for ourselves, after which the boy laid down to sleep, and I walked round to search for grass. A little grew between the sand-drifts and the cliffs, and though dry and withered, I was most thankful to find it.

March 12.—The first streak of daylight found us on our way to meet the party, carrying with us three gallons of water upon one of the horses, the other was ridden by the boy.

At night, the whole party were, by God's blessing, once more together, and in safety, after having passed over one hundred and thirty-five miles of desert country, without a drop of water in its whole extent, and at a season of the year the most unfavour-able for such an undertaking. In accomplishing this distance, the sheep had been six and the horses five days without water, and both had been almost wholly without food for the greater part of the time. The little grass we found was so dry and withered that the parched and thirsty animals could not eat it after the second day. The day following our arrival at the water was one of intense heat, and had we experienced such on our journey, neither men nor horses could ever have accomplished it; most grateful did we feel, therefore, to that merciful Being who had shrouded us from a semi-tropical sun, at a time when our exposure to it would have ensured our destruction.

From the 12th to the 18th we remained at the sand-drifts, during which time we were engaged in attending to the horses, in sending back to recover the stores that had been left by the overseer, and in examining the country around.

Being now at a part of the cliffs where they receded from the sea, and where they had at last become accessible, I devoted some time to an examination of their geological character. The part that I selected was high, steep, and bluff towards the sea, which washed its base; presenting the appearance described by Captain Flinders, as noted before. By crawling and scrambling among the crags, I managed, at some risk, to get at these singular cliffs. The brown or upper portion consisted of an exceedingly hard, coarse grey limestone, among which some few shells were embedded, but which, from the hard nature of the rock, I could not break out; the lower or white part consisted of a gritty chalk, full of broken shells and marine productions, and having a somewhat saline taste: parts of it exactly resembled the formation that I had found up to the north, among the fragments of table-land; the chalk was soft and friable at the surface, and easily cut out with a tomahawk, it was traversed horizontally by strata of flint, ranging in depth from six to eighteen inches, and having varying thicknesses of chalk between the several strata. The chalk had worn away from beneath the harder rock above, leaving the latter most frightfully overhanging and threatening instant annihilation to the intruder. Huge mis-shapen masses were lying with their rugged pinnacles above the water, in every direction at the foot of the cliffs, plainly indicated the frequency of a falling crag, and I felt quite a relief when my examination was completed, and I got away from so dangerous a post.

On the 18th we moved on, making a short stage of fourteen miles, through a heavy, sandy, and scrubby country. At first I tried the beach, but finding the sand very loose and unsuitable for travelling, I was again compelled to enter the scrub behind the sea-shore ridge, travelling through a succession of low scrubby undulations, with here and there the beds of dried-up lakes. The day was cloudy, and likely for rain, but after a few drops had fallen, the clouds passed away. In the afternoon the overseer dug behind the sand-ridge, and at six feet came to water, but perfectly salt.

March 19.—To-day we travelled onwards for twenty-six miles, through a country exactly similar to that we had passed through yesterday. At three in the afternoon we halted at an opening where there was abundance of grass, though dry and withered. The indications of natives having recently passed still continued, and confirmed me in my impression, that they were on a journey to the westward, and from one distant water to another, and principally for the purpose of gathering the fruit. We were now forty miles from the last water, and I became assured that we had very far to go to the next; I had for some time given over any hope of finding the second water spoken of by the natives at the head of the Bight, and considered that we must have passed it if it existed, long ago, perhaps even in that very valley, or among those very sand-hills where we had searched so unsuccessfully on the 12th. There was now the prospect of a long journey before us without water, as we had brought only a little with us for ourselves, and which was nearly exhausted, whilst our horses had been quite without, and were already suffering from thirst. Consulting with the overseer, I resolved to leave our baggage where we were, whilst the horses were sent back to the water (forty miles) to rest and recruit for three or four days; by this means I expected they would gather strength, and as they would have but little weight to carry until they reached our present position, when they returned we should be better able to force a passage through the waste before us, at the same time that we should be able to procure a fresh and larger stock of water for ourselves. At midnight I sent the whole party back to the last water, but remained myself to take care of the baggage and sheep. I retained an allowance of a pint of water per day for six days, this being the contemplated period of the overseer's absence. My situation was not at all enviable, but circumstances rendered it unavoidable.

From the departure of my party, until their return, I spent a miserable time, being unable to leave the camp at all. This gave me a little time to examine my maps, and to reflect upon my position and prospects, which involved the welfare of others, as well as my own. We had still 600 miles of country to traverse, measured in straight lines across the chart, but taking into account the inequalities of the ground, and the circuit we were frequently obliged to make, we could not hope to accomplish this in less than 800 miles of distance. With every thing in our favour we could not expect to accomplish this in less than eight weeks; but with all the impediment and embarrassments we were likely to meet with, it would probably take us twelve. Our sheep were reduced to three in number, and our sole stock of flour now amounted to 142 pounds, to be shared out amongst five persons, added to which the aspect of the country before us was disheartening in the extreme; the places at which there was any likelihood of finding water were probably few and far apart, and the strength of our horses was already greatly reduced by the hardships they had undergone. Ever since we had left Fowler's Bay, the whole party, excepting the youngest boys, had been obliged chiefly to walk, and yet every care and precaution we could adopt were unable to counteract the evil effects of a barren country, and an unfavourable season of the year. The task before us was indeed a fearful one, but I firmly hoped by patience and perseverance, safely and successfully to accomplish it at last.

During nearly the whole time that my party were away the weather was cool and cloudy. Occasionally there was a great deal of thunder and lightning, accompanied by a few drops of rain, but it always cleared away without heavy showers. The storms came up from seawards, and generally passed inland to the north-east; which struck me as being somewhat singular, especially when taken in conjunction with the fact that on one or two occasions, when the wind was from the north-east, it was comparatively cool, and so unlike any of those scorching blasts we had experienced from the same quarter when on the western side of the Great Bight. There was another thing connected with my present position which equally surprised me, and was quite as inexplicable: whilst engaged one morning rambling about the encampment as far as I could venture away, I met with several flights of a very large description of parrot, quite unknown to me, coming apparently from the north-east, and settling among the shrubs and bushes around. They had evidently come to eat the fruit growing behind the sand-hills, but being scared by my following them about, to try and shoot one, they took wing and went off again in the direction they had come from.

March 26.—Upon moving on this morning we passed through the same wretched kind of country for eighteen miles, to an opening in the scrub where was a little grass, and at which we halted to rest. Leaving the natives to enjoy a sleep, the overseer and I opened and re-sorted all our baggage, throwing away every thing that we could at all dispense with; our great coats, jackets, and other articles of dress were thrown away; a single spare shirt and pair of boots and socks being all that were kept for each, besides our blankets and the things we stood in, and which consisted only of trowsers, shirt, and shoes. Most of our pack-saddles, all our horse-shoes, most of our kegs for holding water, all our buckets

but one, our medicines, some of our fire-arms, a quantity of ammunition, and a variety of other things, were here abandoned.
Among the many things that we were compelled to leave behind
there was none that I regretted parting with more than a copy of
Captain Sturt's Expeditions, which had been sent to me by the
author to Fowler's Bay to amuse and cheer me on the solitary
task I had engaged in; it was the last kind offering of friendship
from a highly esteemed friend, and nothing but necessity would
have induced me to part with it. Could the donor, however, have
seen the miserable plight we were reduced to, he would have
pitied and forgiven an act that circumstances alone compelled
me to.

After all our arrangements were made, and every thing rejected that we could do without, I found that the loads of the
horses were reduced in the aggregate about two hundred pounds;
but this being divided among ten, relieved each only a little. Myself, the overseer, and the King George's Sound native invariably
walked the whole way, but the two younger natives were still permitted to ride alternately upon one of the strongest horses. As our
allowance of flour was very small, and the fatigue and exertion we
were all obliged to undergo very great, I ordered a sheep to be
killed before we moved on again. We had been upon short allowance for some time, and were getting weak and hardly able to go
through the toils that devolved upon us. Now, I knew that our
safety depended upon that of our horses, and that their lives again
were contingent upon the amount of fatigue we were ourselves
able to endure, and the degree of exertion we were capable of
making to relieve them in extremity. I did not therefore hesitate
to make use of one of our three remaining sheep to strengthen us.
for coming trials, instead of retaining them until perhaps they
might be of little use to us. The whole party had a hearty meal,
and then, watching the horses until midnight, we moved on when
the moon rose.

March 27.—During the night we travelled slowly over dense
scrubby and sandy ridges, occasionally crossing large sheets of
oolitic limestone, in which were deep holes that would most likely
retain water after rains, but which were now quite dry. As the daylight dawned the dreadful nature of the scrub drove us to the sea
beach; fortunately it was low water, and we obtained a firm hard
sand to travel over, though occasionally obstructed by enormous
masses of sea-weed, thrown into heaps of very many feet in
thickness and several hundreds of yards in length, looking exactly like hay cut and pressed ready for packing.

To-day we overtook the natives, whose tracks we had seen so frequently on our route. There was a large party of them, all busily engaged in eating the red berries which grew behind the coast ridge in such vast quantities; they did not appear so much afraid of us as of our horses, at which they were dreadfully alarmed, so that all our efforts to communicate with them were fruitless; they would not come near us, nor would they give us the opportunity of getting near them, but ran away whenever I advanced towards them, though alone and unarmed.

Whilst in camp, during the heat of the day, the native boys shewed me the way in which natives procure water for themselves, when wandering among the scrubs, and by means of which they are enabled to remain out almost any length of time, in a country quite destitute of surface water. I had often heard of the natives procuring water from the roots of trees, and had frequently seen indications of their having so obtained it, but I had never before seen the process actually gone through. Selecting a large healthy looking tree out of the gum-scrub, and growing in a hollow, or flat between two ridges, the native digs round at a few feet from the trunk, to find the lateral roots; to one unaccustomed to the work, it is a difficult and laborious thing frequently to find these roots, but to the practised eye of the native, some slight inequality of the surface, or some other mark, points out to him their exact position at once, and he rarely digs in the wrong place. Upon breaking the end next to the tree, the root is lifted, and run out for twenty or thirty feet; the bark is then peeled off, and the root broken into pieces, six or eight inches long, and these again, if thick, are split into thinner pieces; they are then sucked, or shaken over a piece of bark, or stuck up together in the bark upon their ends, and water is slowly discharged from them; if shaken, it comes out like a shower of very fine rain. The roots vary in diameter from one inch to three; the best are those from one to two and a half inches, and of great length. The quantity of water contained in a good root would probably fill two-thirds of a pint. I saw my own boys get one-third of a pint out in this way in about a quarter of an hour, and they were by no means adepts at the practice, having never been compelled to resort to it from necessity.

March 28.—At daylight we moved on, every one walking, even the youngest boy could not ride now, as the horses were so weak and jaded. Soon after leaving the camp, one of them laid down, although the weight upon his back was very light; we were consequently obliged to distribute the few things he carried among

I. D.   *c c*

the others, and let him follow loose. We had scarcely advanced six miles from our last night's camp when the little Timor pony I had purchased at Port Lincoln broke down completely; for some time it had been weak, and we were obliged to drive it loose, but it was now unable to proceed further, and we were compelled to abandon it to a miserable and certain death, that by pushing on, we might use every exertion in our power to relieve the others, though scarcely daring to hope that we could save even one of them. It was, indeed, a fearful and heart-rending scene to behold the noble animals which had served us so long and so faithfully, suffering the extremity of thirst and hunger, without having it in our power to relieve them.

The country we had already passed through, precluded all hope of our recrossing it without the horses to carry water for us, and without provisions to enable us to endure the dreadful fatigue of forced marches across the desert. The country before us was, it is true, quite unknown, but it could hardly be worse than that we had traversed, and the chance was that it might be better. We were now pushing on for some sand-hills, marked down in Captain Flinders' chart at about 126½° of east longitude; I did not expect to procure water until we reached these, but I felt sure we should obtain it on our arrival there. After this point was passed, there appeared to be one more long push without any likelihood of procuring water, as the cliffs again became the boundary of the ocean; but beyond Cape Arid, the change in the character and appearance of the country, as described by Flinders, indicated the existence of a better and more practicable line of country than we had yet fallen in with.

My overseer, however, was now unfortunately beginning to take up an opposite opinion, and though he still went through the duty devolving upon him with assiduity and cheerfulness, it was evident that his mind was ill at ease, and that he had many gloomy anticipations of the future. He fancied there were no sand-hills ahead, that we should never reach any water in that direction, and that there was little hope of saving any of the horses. In this latter idea I rather encouraged him than otherwise, deeming it advisable to contemplate the darker side of the picture, and by accustoming ourselves to look forward to being left entirely dependent upon our own strength and efforts, in some measure to prepare ourselves for such an event, should it unfortunately befal us.

March 29.—After calling up the party, I ascended the highest sand-hill near me, from which the prospect was cheerless and gloomy, and the point and sandy cones we imagined we had seen last night had vanished. Indeed, upon examining the chart, and considering that as yet we had advanced only one hundred and twenty-six miles from the last water, I felt convinced that we had still very far to go before we could expect to reach the sand-drifts. The supply of water we had brought for ourselves was nearly exhausted, and we could afford none for breakfast to-day; the night, however, had been cool, and we did not feel the want of it so much. Upon moving, I sent one of the natives back to the horse I had tied up, about four miles from our camp, to try to bring him on to where we should halt in the middle of the day.

March 30.—Getting up as soon as the day dawned, I found that some of the horses had crossed the sand ridge to the beach, and rambled some distance backwards. I found, too, that in the dark we had missed a patch of tolerable grass among the scrub, not far from our camp. I regretted this the more, as during the night a very heavy dew had fallen, and the horses might perhaps have fed a little.

Leaving the overseer to search for those that had strayed, I took a sponge, and went to try to collect some of the dew which was hanging in spangles upon the grass and shrubs; brushing these with the sponge, I squeezed it, when saturated, into a quart pot, which, in an hour's time, I filled with water. The native boys were occupied in the same way; and by using a handful of fine grass, instead of a sponge, they collected about a quart among them. Having taken the water to the camp, and made it into tea, we divided it amongst the party, and never was a meal more truly relished, although we all ate the last morsel of bread we had with us, and none knew when we might again enjoy either a drink of water or a mouthful of bread. We had now demonstrated the practicability of collecting water from the dew. I had often heard from the natives that they were in the habit of practising this plan, but had never before actually witnessed its adoption. It was, however, very cold work, and completely wet me through from head to foot, a greater quantity of water by far having been shaken over me, from the bushes, than I was able to collect with my sponge. The natives make use of a large oblong vessel of bark, which they hold under the branches, whilst they brush them with a little grass, as I did with the sponge; the water thus falls into the trough held for it, and which, in consequence of the surface being so much larger than the orifice of a quart pot, is proportionately sooner filled. After the sun once rises, the

spangles fall from the boughs, ar d no more water can be collected;
it is therefore necessary to be at work very early, if success is an
object of importance.

I took the overseer up one of the ridges to reconnoitre the
country for the purpose of ascertaining whether there was no
place near us where water might be procured by digging. After
a careful examination a hollow was selected between the two front
ridges of white sand, where the overseer thought it likely we
might be successful. The boys were called up to assist in digging,
and the work was anxiously commenced; our suspense increasing
every moment as the well was deepened. At about five feet the
sand was observed to be quite moist, and upon its being tasted
was pronounced quite free from any saline qualities. This was
joyous news, but too good to be implicitly believed, and though
we all tasted it over and over again, we could scarcely believe
that such really was the case. By sinking another foot the question was put beyond all doubt, and to our great relief fresh water
was obtained at a depth of six feet from the surface, on the
seventh day of our distress, and after we had travelled one
hundred and sixty miles since we had left the last water. Words
would be inadequate to express the joy and thankfulness of my
little party at once more finding ourselves in safety, and with
abundance of water near us. A few hours before hope itself
seemed almost extinguished, and those only who have been
subject to a similar extremity of distress can have any just idea
of the relief we experienced. The mind seemed to have been
weighed down by intense anxiety and over-wrought feelings.
At first the gloomy restlessness of disappointment or the feverish
impatience of hope had operated upon our minds alternately,
but these had long since given way to that calm settled determination of purpose, and cool steady vigour of action which
desperate circumstances can alone inspire. Day by day our
prospects of success had gradually diminished; our horses had
become reduced to so dreadful a state that many had died, and
all were likely to do so soon; we ourselves were weak and
exhausted by fatigue, and it appeared impossible that either could
have gone many miles further. In this last extremity we had been
relieved. That gracious God, without whose assistance all hope
of safety had been in vain, had heard our earnest prayers for his
aid, and I trust that in our deliverance we recognised and
acknowledged with sincerity and thankfulness his guiding and
protecting hand. It is in circumstances only such as we had lately
been placed in that the utter hopelessness ot all human efforts is

truly felt, and it is when relieved from such a situation that the hand of a directing and beneficent Being appears most plainly discernible, fulfilling those gracious promises which he has made, to hear them that call upon him in the day of trouble.

As soon as each had satisfied his thirst, the pots were filled and boiled for tea, and some bread was baked, whilst the overseer and natives were still increasing the size of the well to enable us to water the horses. We then got a hasty meal that we might the better go through the fatigue of attending to the suffering animals. Our utmost caution now became necessary in their management; they had been seven days without a drop of water, and almost without food also, and had suffered so much that with abundance of water near us, and whilst they were suffering agonies from the want of it, we dared not give it to them freely. Having tied them up to some low bushes, we gave each in turn about four gallons, and then driving them away for half a mile to where there was a little withered grass, we watched them until the evening, and again gave each about four gallons more of water.

March 31.—The morning broke wild and lowering, and the sand blew fearfully about from the drifts among which the water was. Our well had tumbled in during the night, and we had to undergo considerable labour before we could water the horses. After clearing it out, we gave each of them seven gallons, and again sent them away to the grass, letting the native boys watch them during the day, whilst we rested for a few hours, shifted our camp to a more sheltered place, weighed out a week's allowance of flour at half a pound each per day, and made sundry other necessary arrangements.

April 1.—The last night had been bitterly cold and frosty, and as we were badly clad, and without the means of making a large or permanent fire, we all felt acutely the severity of the weather.

April 2.—Another severe cold frosty night made us fully sensible that the winter was rapidly closing in upon us, notwithstanding the ill-provided and unprotected state we were in to encounter its inclemencies. Our well had again tumbled in, and gave us a good deal of trouble, besides, each successive clearing out deepened it considerably, and this took us to a level where the brackish water mixed with the fresh; from this cause the water was now too brackish to be palatable, and we sunk another well apart from that used for the horses, at which to procure any water we required for our own use.

On the 3rd, I sent the overseer out in one direction and I went myself out in another, to examine the country and try to procure wallabies for food. We both returned late, greatly fatigued with walking through dense scrubs and over steep heavy sand ridges, but without having fired a shot.

Our mutton (excepting the last sheep) being all used on the 4th, we were reduced to our daily allowance of half a pound of flour each, without any meat.

On the 5th, the overseer and one of the native boys got ready to go back for some of the stores and other things we had abandoned, forty-seven miles away. As they were likely to have severe exercise, and to be away for four days, I gave them five pounds extra of flour above their daily allowance, together with the wallabie which I had shot, and which had not yet been used; they drove before them three horses to carry their supply of water, and bring back the things sent for.

As soon as they were gone, with the assistance of the two native boys who were left, I removed the camp to the white sand-drifts five miles further west. Being anxious to keep as near to the grass as I could, I commenced digging at some distance away from where the natives procured their water, but at a place where there were a great many rushes. After sinking to about seven feet, I found the soil as dry as ever, and removing to the native wells, with some little trouble opened a hole large enough to water all the horses. The single sheep gave us a great deal of trouble and kept us running about from one sand-hill to another, until we were tired out, before we could capture it; at last we succeeded, and I tied him up for the night, resolved never to let him loose again.

April 6.—The severe frost and intense cold of last night entirely deprived me of sleep, and I was glad when the daylight broke, though still weary and unrefreshed. After clearing out the well, and watering the horses, I sent one of the boys out to watch them, and gave the other the gun to try and shoot a wallabie, but after expending the only two charges of slugs I had left, he returned unsuccessful. At night we all made up our supper with the bark of the young roots of the gum-scrub. It appears to be extensively used for food by the natives in this district, judging from the remnants left at their encamping places. The bark is peeled off the young roots of the eucalyptus dumosa, put into hot ashes until nearly crisp, and then the dust being shaken off, it is pounded between two stones and ready for use. Upon being chewed, a farinaceous powder is imbibed from between the fibres of the bark, by no means unpleasant in flavour, but rather sweet, and resembling the taste of malt; how far a person could live upon this diet alone, I have no means of judging, but it certainly appeases the appetite, and is, I should suppose, nutritious.

April 7.—Another sleepless night from the intense cold. Upon getting up I put a mark upon the beach to guide the overseer to our camp on his return, then weighed out flour and baked bread for the party, as I found it lasted much better when used stale than fresh.

The weather on the 8th and 9th suddenly became mild and soft, with the appearance of rain, but none fell. I was becoming anxious about the return of my overseer and native boy, who had been absent nine tides, when they ought to have returned in eight, and I could not help fearing some mischance had befallen them, and frequently went backwards and forwards to the beach, to look for them. The tenth tide found me anxiously at my post on the look out, and after watching for a long time I thought I discerned some dark objects in the distance, slowly advancing; gradually I made out a single horse, driven by two people, and at once descended to meet them. Their dismal tale was soon told. After leaving us on the 5th, they reached their destination on the 7th; but in returning one of the horses became blind, and was too weak to advance further, when they had barely advanced thirteen miles; they were consequently obliged to abandon him, and leave behind the things he had been carrying. With the other two horses they got to within five miles of the place we first procured water at on the 30th March. Here a second horse had become unable to proceed, and the things he had carried were also obliged to be left behind. They then got both horses to the first well at the sand-hills and watered them, and after resting a couple of hours came on to join me. Short as this distance was, the jaded horse could not travel it, and was left behind a mile and a half back. Having shewn the overseer and boy the camp, I sent the other two natives to fetch up the tired horse, whilst I attended to the other, and put the solitary sheep in for the night. By a little after dark all was arranged, and the horse that had been left behind once more with the others.

From the overseer I learnt, that during the fifty miles he had retraced our route to obtain the provisions we had left, he had five times dug for water: four times he had found salt water, and once he had been stopped by rock. The last effort of this kind he had made not far from where we found water on the 30th of March, and I could not but be struck with the singular and providential circumstance of our first halting and attempting to dig for water on that day in all our distress, at the very first place, and at the only place, within the 160 miles we had traversed, where water could have been procured. It will be remembered, that in our advance we had travelled a great part of the latter portion of this distance by night, and that thus there was a probability of our having passed unknowingly some place where water might have been procured. The overseer had now travelled over the same ground in daylight, with renovated strength, and in a condition comparatively strong, and fresh for exertion. He had dug wherever he thought there was a chance of procuring water, but without success in any one single instance.

We were now about half-way between Fowler's Bay and King George's Sound, located among barren sand-drifts, and without a drop of water beyond us on either side, within a less distance than 150 miles. Our provisions were rapidly decreasing, whilst we were lying idle and inactive in camp; and yet it would be absolutely necessary for us thus to remain for some time longer, or at once abandon the horses, and endeavour to make our way without them. To the latter, however, there were many objections, one of which was, that I well knew from the experience we had already had, that if we abandoned the horses, and had those fearful long distances to travel without water, we never could accomplish them on foot, if compelled at the same time to live upon a very low diet, to carry our arms, ammunition, and provisions, and in addition to these, a stock of water sufficient to last six or seven days. The only thing that had enabled us to get through so far on our journey in safety, had been the having the horses with us, for though weak and jaded, they had yet carried the few things which were indispensable to us, and which we never could have carried ourselves under the circumstances.

There was another inducement to continue with the horses, which had considerable weight with me, and however revolting the idea might be at first, it was a resource which I foresaw the desperate circumstances we were in must soon compel us to adopt. It was certainly horrible to contemplate the destruction of the noble animals that had accompanied us so far, but ere long I well knew that such would be the only chance of saving our own lives, and I hoped that by accustoming the mind to dwell upon the subject beforehand, when the evil hour did arrive, the horror and disgust would be in some degree lessened. Upon consulting the overseer, I was glad to find that he agreed with me fully in the expediency of not abandoning the horses until it became unavoidable, and that he had himself already contemplated the probability of our being very shortly reduced to the alternative of using them for food.

April 10.—Four days' provisions having been given to each of the party, I took the King George's Sound native with me to retrace, on foot, our route to the eastward. For the first ten miles I was accompanied by one of the other native boys, leading a horse to carry a little water for us, and take back the stores the overseer had buried at that point, when the second horse knocked up with him on the morning of the 9th. Having found the things, and put them on the horse, I sent the boy with them back to the camp, together with a large sting-ray fish which he had speared in the surf near the shore. It was a large, coarse, ugly-looking thing, but circumstances had broken through many scruples and prejudices, and we were by no means particular as to what the fish might be, if it were eatable.

April 11.—Moving away long before daylight, we pushed steadily on, and about dusk arrived, after a stage of twenty-three miles, at the place where our stores were.

April 12.—To-day the weather was cloudy and sultry, and we found it very oppressive carrying the weight we had with us, especially as we had no water. By steady perseverance, we gained the place where our little keg had been buried; and having refreshed ourselves with a little tea, again pushed on for a few miles to a place where I had appointed the overseer to send a native to meet us with water. He was already there, and we all encamped together for the night, soon forgetting, in refreshing sleep, the fatigues and labours of the day.

The 13th was a dark cloudy day, with light rains in the morning. About noon we arrived at the camp, after having walked seventy-six miles in the last three days and a half, during great part of which we had carried heavy weights. We had, however, successfully accomplished the object for which we had gone, and had now anxieties only for our future progress, the provisions and other stores being all safely recovered.

April 14.—Early this morning, I sent the overseer, and one of the native boys, with three days' provision to the commencement of the cliffs to the westward, visible from the sand-hills near our camp, in order that they might ascertain the exact distance they were from us, and whether any grass or water could be procured nearer to their base than where we were.

The 15th was another cold day, with the wind at south-west, and we could neither set the lines nor spear sting-ray, whilst the supply we had before obtained was now nearly exhausted. One of the horses was taken ill, and unable to rise, from the effects of the cold; his limbs were cramped and stiff, and apparently unable to sustain the weight of his body. After plucking dry grass, and making a bed for him, placing a breakwind of boughs round, and making a fire near him, we left him for the night.

Late in the evening, the overseer and boy returned from the westward, and reported, that the cliffs were sixteen miles away; that they had dug for water; but that none could be found, and that there was hardly a blade of grass any where, whilst the whole region around was becoming densely scrubby; through much of which we should have to pass before we reached the cliffs. Altogether, the overseer seemed quite discouraged by the appearance of the country, and to dread the idea of moving on in that direction, often saying, that he wished he was back, and that he thought he could retrace his steps to Fowler's Bay, where a supply of provisions had been buried. I was vexed at these remarks, because I felt that I could not coincide in them, and because I knew that when the moment for decision came, my past experience, and the strong reasons which had produced in my own mind quite a different conviction, would compel me to act in opposition to the wishes of the only European with me, and he a person, too, whom I sincerely respected for the fidelity and devotion with which he had followed me through all my wanderings. I was afraid, too, that the native boys, hearing his remarks, and perceiving that he had no confidence in our future movements, would catch up the same idea, and that, in addition to the other difficulties and anxieties I had to cope with, would be the still more frightful one of disaffection and discontent. Another subject of uneasiness arose from the nature of our diet; —for some few days we had all been using a good deal of the stingray fish, and though at first we had found it palatable, either from confining ourselves too exclusively to it, or from eating too much, it had latterly disagreed with us. The overseer declared it made him ill and weak, and that he could do nothing whilst living upon it. The boys said the same; and yet we had nothing else to supply its place, and the small quantity of flour left would not admit of our using more than was barely necessary to sustain life. At this time we had hardly any fish left, and the whole party were ravenously hungry. In this dilemma, I determined to have the sick horse killed for food. It was impossible he could ever recover, and by depriving him of life a few hours sooner than the natural course of events would have done, we should be enabled to get a supply of food to last us over a few days more, by which time I hoped we might again be able to venture on, and attempt another push to the westward.

Early on the morning of the 16th, I sent the overseer to kill the unfortunate horse, which was still alive, but unable to rise from the ground, having never moved from the place where he had first been found lying yesterday morning. The miserable animal was in the most wretched state possible, thin and emaciated by dreadful and long-continued sufferings, and labouring under some complaint, that in a very few hours at the farthest must have terminated its life.

After a great portion of the meat had been cut off from the carcase, in thin slices, they were dipped in salt water and hung up upon strings to dry in the sun. I could not bring myself to eat any to-day, so horrible and revolting did it appear to me, but the overseer made a hearty dinner, and the native boys gorged themselves to excess, remaining the whole afternoon by the carcase, where they made a fire, cutting off and roasting such portions as had been left. They looked like ravenous wolves about their prey, and when they returned to the camp at night, they were loaded with as much cooked meat as they could carry, and which they were continually eating during the night; I made a meal upon some of the sting-ray that was still left, but it made me dreadfully sick, and I was obliged to lie down, seriously ill.

April 17.—Being rather better to-day, I was obliged to overcome my repugnance to the disagreeable food we were compelled to resort to, and the ice once broken, I found that although it was far from being palatable, I could gradually reconcile myself to it. The boys after breakfast again went down to the carcase, and spent the whole day roasting and eating, and at night they again returned to the camp loaded. Both yesterday and to-day light showers fell sufficient to moisten the grass.

April 18.—The day being much warmer, many large flies were about, and I was obliged to have a fire kept constantly around the meat, to keep them away by the smoke.

April 22.—Upon weighing the meat this morning, which as usual was left out upon the strings at night, I discovered that four pounds had been stolen by some of the boys whilst we were sleeping. I had suspected that our stock was diminishing rapidly for a day or two past, and had weighed it overnight that I might ascertain this point, and if it were so, take some means to prevent it for the future. With so little food to depend upon, and where it was so completely in the power of any one of the party to gratify his own appetite at the expense of the others, during their absence, or when they slept, it became highly necessary to enforce strict honesty towards each other; I was much grieved to find that the meat had been taken by the natives, more particularly as their daily allowance had been so great. We had, moreover, only two days' supply of meat left for the party, and being about to commence the long journey before us, it was important to economise our provisions to support us under the fatigue and labours we should then have to undergo.

Having deducted the four pounds stolen during the night, from the daily rations of the three boys, I gave them the remainder (eight pounds), telling them the reason why their quantity was less to-day than usual, and asking them to point out the thief, who alone should be punished and the others would receive their usual rations. The youngest of the three boys, and the King George's Sound native, resolutely denied being concerned in the robbery; but the other native doggedly refused to answer any questions about it, only telling me that he and the native from King George's Sound would leave me and make their way by themselves. I pointed out to them the folly, in fact the impossibility almost, of their succeeding in any attempt of the kind; advised them to remain quietly where they were, and behave well for the future, but concluded by telling them that if they were bent upon going they might do so, as I would not attempt to stop them.

For some time past the two eldest of the boys, both of whom were now nearly grown up to manhood, had been far from obedient in their general conduct. Ever since we had been reduced to a low scale of diet they had been sulky and discontented, never assisting in the routine of the day, or doing what they were requested to do with that cheerfulness and alacrity that they had previously exhibited. Unaccustomed to impose the least restraint upon their appetites or passions, they considered it a hardship to be obliged to walk as long as any horses were left alive, though they saw those horses falling behind and perishing from fatigue; they considered it a hardship, too, to be curtailed in their allowance of food, as long as a mouthful was left unconsumed; and in addition to this, they had imbibed the overseer's idea that we never should succeed in our attempt to get to the westward, and got daily more dissatisfied at remaining idle in camp whilst the horses were recruiting.

The excess of animal food they had had at their command for some few days after the horse was killed, made them forget their former scarcity, and in their folly they imagined that they could supply their own wants, and get on better and more rapidly than we did, and they determined to attempt it. Vexed as I had been at finding out they had not scrupled to plunder the small stock of provisions we had left, I was loth to let them leave me foolishly without making an effort to prevent it. One of them had been with me a great length of time, and the other I had brought from his country and his friends, and to both I felt bound by ties of humanity to prevent if possible their taking the rash step they meditated; my remonstrances and expostulations were however in vain, and after getting their breakfasts, they took up some spears they had been carefully preparing for the last two days, and walked sulkily from the camp in a westerly direction. The youngest boy had, it seemed, also been enticed to join them, for he was getting up with the intention of following, when I called him back and detained him in the camp, as he was too young to know what he was doing, and had only been led astray by the others. I had intended to have moved on myself to-day, but the departure of the natives made me change my intention, for I deemed it desirable that they should have at least three or four days' start of us. Finding that the single sheep we had left would now be the cause of a good deal of trouble, I had it killed this afternoon, that we might have the full advantage of it whilst we had plenty of water, and might be enabled to hoard our bread a little. We had still a little of the horse-flesh left, and made a point of using it all up before the mutton was allowed to be touched.

The morning of the 23rd broke cool and cloudy, with showers gathering from seawards; the wind was south-west, and the sky wild and lowering in that direction. During the forenoon light rain fell, but scarcely more than sufficient to moisten the grass; it would, however, probably afford our deserters a drink upon the cliffs. Towards evening the sky cleared, and the weather became frosty.

April 25.—During the night dense clouds, accompanied by gusts of wind and forked lightning, passed rapidly to the south-west, and this morning the wind changed to that quarter. Heavy storms gathered to seawards with much thunder and lightning, but no rain fell near us; the sea appearing to attract all the showers. The overseer shot a very large eagle to-day and made a stew of it, which was excellent. I sent the boy out to try and shoot a wallabie, but he returned without one.

In the evening, a little before dark, and just as we had finished

our tea, to my great astonishment our two runaway natives made
their appearance, the King George's Sound native being first.
He came frankly up, and said that they were both sorry for what
they had done, and were anxious to be received again, as they
found they could get nothing to eat for themselves. The other
boy sat silently and sullenly at the fire, apparently more chagrined
at being compelled by necessity to come back to us than sorry
for having gone away. Having given them a lecture, for they
both now admitted having stolen meat, not only on the night
they were detected but previously, I gave each some tea and
some bread and meat, and told them if they behaved well they
would be treated in every respect as before, and share with us our
little stock of provisions as long as it lasted.

I now learnt that they had fared in the bush but little better
than I should have done myself. They had been absent four days,
and had come home nearly starved.

Being determined to break up camp on the 27th, I sent the
King George's Sound native on a-head, as soon as he had breakfasted, that, by preceding the party, he might have time to spear
a sting-ray against we overtook him. The day was dull, cloudy,
and warm, and still looking likely for rain, with the wind at north-
east. At eleven we were ready, and moved away from a place
where we had experienced so much relief in our extremity, and
at which our necessities had compelled us to remain so long.
For twenty-eight days we had been encamped at the sand-drifts,
or at the first water we had found, five miles from them.   Daily,
almost hourly, had the sky threatened rain, and yet none fell.
We had now entered upon the last fearful push, which was to
decide our fate. This one stretch of bad country crossed, I felt
a conviction we should be safe. That we had at least 150 miles
to go to the next water I was fully assured of; I was equally
satisfied that our horses were by no means in a condition to
encounter the hardships and privations they must meet with in
such a journey; for though they had had a long rest, and in some
degree recovered from their former tired-out condition, they had
not picked up in flesh or regained their spirits; the sapless,
withered state of the grass and the severe cold of the nights
had prevented them from deriving the advantage that they ought
to have done from so long a respite from labour. Still I hoped we
might be successful. We had lingered day by day, until it would
have been folly to have waited longer; the rubicon was, however, now passed, and we had nothing to rely upon but our own
exertions and perseverance, humbly trusting that the great and

merciful God who had hitherto guarded and guided us in safety would not desert us now.

April 28.—After travelling along the beach for two miles we ascended behind the cliffs, which now came in bluff to the sea, and then keeping along their summits, nearly parallel with the coast, and passing through much scrub, low brushwood, and dwarf tea-tree growing upon the rocky surface, we made a stage of twenty miles; both ourselves and the horses greatly tired with walking through the matted scrub of tea-tree every where covering the ground.

On the morning of the 29th we moved away very early, passing over a rocky level country, covered with low brush, and very fatiguing to both ourselves and our horses. The morning was gloomy and close, and the day turned out intensely hot. After travelling only fifteen miles we were compelled to halt until the greatest heat was passed. Our stock of water and provisions only admitted of our making two meals in the day, breakfast and supper; but as I intended this evening to travel great part of the night, we each made our meal now instead of later in the day, that we might not be delayed when the cool of the evening set in. We had been travelling along the summit of the cliffs parallel with the coast line, and had found the country level and uniform in its character; the cliffs still being from two to three hundred feet in elevation, and of the same formation as I noticed before. There were patches of grass scattered among the scrub at intervals, but all were old and withered.

At four in the afternoon we again proceeded on our journey, but had not gone far before the sky unexpectedly became overcast with clouds, and the whole heavens assumed a menacing and threatening appearance. To the east and to the west, thunderclouds gathered heavily around, every indication of sudden and violent rain was present to cheer us as we advanced, and all were rejoicing in the prospects of a speedy termination of our difficulties. The wind had in the morning been north-east, gradually veering round to north and north-west, at which point it was stationary when the clouds began to gather. Towards sunset a heavy storm passed over our heads, with the rapidity almost of lightning; the wind suddenly shifted from north-west to south-west, blowing a perfect hurricane, and rendering it almost impossible for us to advance against it. A few moments before we had confidently expected a heavy fall of rain; the dark and lowering sky had gradually gathered and concentrated above and around us, until the very heavens seemed overweighted and ready every instant to burst. A briefer interval of time, accompanied by the sudden and violent change of wind, had dashed our hopes to the ground, and the prospect of rain was now over, although a few heavy clouds still hung around us.

To-night the overseer asked me which of the watches I would keep, and as I was not sleepy, though tired, I chose the first. At a quarter before six, I went to take charge of the horses, having previously seen the overseer and the natives lay down to sleep, at their respective break-winds, ten or twelve yards apart from one another. The arms and provisions, as was our custom, were piled up under an oilskin, between my break-wind and that of the overseer, with the exception of one gun, which I always kept at my own sleeping place. I have been thus minute in detailing the position and arrangement of our encampment this evening, because of the fearful consequences that followed, and to shew the very slight circumstances upon which the destinies of life sometimes hinge. Trifling as the arrangement of the watches might seem, and unimportant as I thought it at the time, whether I undertook the first or the second, yet was my choice, in this respect, the means under God's providence of my life being saved, and the cause of the loss of that of my overseer.

The night was cold, and the wind blowing hard from the south-west, whilst scud and nimbus were passing very rapidly by the moon. The horses fed tolerably well, but rambled a good deal, threading in and out among the many belts of scrub which intersected the grassy openings, until at last I hardly knew exactly where our camp was, the fires having apparently expired some time ago. It was now half-past ten, and I headed the horses back, in the direction in which I thought the camp lay, that I might be ready to call the overseer to relieve me at eleven. Whilst thus engaged, and looking steadfastly around among the scrub, to see if I could anywhere detect the embers of our fires, I was startled by a sudden flash, followed by the report of a gun, not a quarter of a mile away from me. Imagining that the overseer had mistaken the hour of the night, and not being able to find me or the horses, had taken that method to attract my attention, I immediately called out, but as no answer was returned, I got alarmed, and leaving the horses, hurried up towards the camp as rapidly as I could. About a hundred yards from it, I met the King George's Sound native (Wylie), running towards me, and in great alarm, crying out, " Oh Massa, oh Massa, come here,"—but could gain no information from him, as to what had occurred. Upon reaching the encampment, which I did in about five minutes, after the shot was fired, I was horror-struck to find my poor over-seer lying on the ground, weltering in his blood, and in the last agonies of death.

Glancing hastily around the camp I found it deserted by the two younger native boys, whilst the scattered fragments of our baggage, which I left carefully piled under the oilskin, lay thrown about in wild disorder, and at once revealed the cause of the harrowing scene before me.

Upon raising the body of my faithful but ill-fated follower, I found that he was beyond all human aid; he had been shot through the left breast with a ball, the last convulsions of death were upon him, and he expired almost immediately after our arrival. The frightful, the appalling truth now burst upon me, that I was alone in the desert. He who had faithfully served me for many years, who had followed my fortunes in adversity and in prosperity, who had accompanied me in all my wanderings, and whose attachment to me had been his sole inducement to remain with me in this last, and to him alas, fatal journey, was now no more. For an instant I was almost tempted to wish that it had been my own fate instead of his. The horrors of my situation glared upon me in such startling reality, as for an instant almost to paralyse the mind. At the dead hour of night, in the wildest and most inhospitable wastes of Australia, with the fierce wind raging in unison with the scene of violence before me, I was left, with a single native, whose fidelity I could not rely upon, and who for aught I knew might be in league with the other two, who per-haps were even now lurking about with the view of taking away my life as they had done that of the overseer. Three days had passed away since we left the last water, and it was very doubtful when we might find any more. Six hundred miles of country had to be traversed before I could hope to obtain the slightest aid or assistance of any kind, whilst I knew not that a single drop of water or an ounce of flour had been left by these murderers, from a stock that had previously been so small.

With such thoughts rapidly passing through my mind, I turned to search for my double-barelled gun, which I had left covered with an oilskin at the head of my own break wind. It was gone, as was also the double-barrelled gun that had belonged to the overseer. These were the only weapons at the time that were in serviceable condition, for though there were a brace of pistols they had been packed away, as there were no cartridges for them, and my rifle was useless, from having a ball sticking fast in the breech, and which we had in vain endeavoured to extract. A few

I. D. *d d*

days previous to our leaving the last water, the overseer had
attempted to wash out the rifle not knowing it was loaded, and
the consequence was, that the powder became wetted and partly
washed away, so that we could neither fire it off nor get out the
ball; I was, therefore, temporarily defenceless, and quite at the
mercy of the natives, had they at this time come upon me. Having hastily ripped open the bag in which the pistols had been
sewn up, I got them out, together with my powder flask, and a
bag containing a little shot and some large balls. The rifle I found
where it had been left, but the ramrod had been taken out by the
boys to load my double-barrelled gun with, its own ramrod being
too short for that purpose; I found it, however, together with
several loose cartridges, lying about near the place where the boys
had slept, so that it was evident they had deliberately loaded the
fire-arms before they tried to move away with the things they had
stolen; one barrel only of my gun had been previously loaded, and
I believe neither barrels in that of the overseer.

After obtaining possession of all the remaining arms, useless as
they were at the moment, with some ammunition, I made no
further examination then, but hurried away from the fearful
scene, accompanied by the King George's Sound native, to search
for the horses, knowing that if they got away now, no chance
whatever would remain of saving our lives. Already the wretched
animals had wandered to a considerable distance; and although
the night was moonlight, yet the belts of scrub, intersecting the
plains, were so numerous and dense, that for a long time we could
not find them; having succeeded in doing so at last, Wylie and I
remained with them, watching them during the remainder of the
night; but they were very restless, and gave us a great deal of
trouble. With an aching heart, and in most painful reflections,
I passed this dreadful night. Every moment appeared to be protracted to an hour, and it seemed as if the daylight would never
appear. About midnight the wind ceased, and the weather became
bitterly cold and frosty. I had nothing on but a shirt and a pair
of trowsers, and suffered most acutely from the cold; to mental
anguish was now added intense bodily pain. Suffering and distress
had well-nigh overwhelmed me, and life seemed hardly worth the
effort necessary to prolong it. Ages can never efface the horrors
of this single night, nor would the wealth of the world ever tempt
me to go through similar ones again.

April 30.—At last, by God's blessing, daylight dawned once
more, but sad and heart-rending was the scene it presented to my
view, upon driving the horses to what had been our last night's

camp. The corpse of my poor companion lay extended on the ground, with the eyes open, but cold and glazed in death. The stern resolution, and fearless open look, which had characterised him when living, stamped the expression of his countenance even now. He had fallen upon his breast four or five yards from where he had been sleeping, and was dressed only in his shirt. In all probability, the noise made by the natives, in plundering the camp, had awoke him; and upon his jumping up, with a view of stopping them, they had fired upon and killed him.

Around the camp lay scattered the harness of the horses, and the remains of the stores that had been the temptation to this fatal deed.

As soon as the horses were caught, and secured, I left Wylie to make a fire, whilst I proceeded to examine into the state of our baggage, that I might decide upon our future proceedings. Among the principal things carried off by the natives were, the whole of our baked bread, amounting to twenty pounds weight, some mutton, tea and sugar, the overseer's tobacco and pipes, a one gallon keg full of water, some clothes, two double-barrelled guns, some ammunition, and a few other small articles.

There were still left forty pounds of flour, a little tea and sugar, and four gallons of water, besides the arms and ammunition I had secured last night.

From the state of our horses, and the dreadful circumstances we were placed in, I was now obliged to abandon every thing but the bare necessaries of life. The few books and instruments I had still left, with many of the specimens I had collected, a saddle, and some other things, were thrown aside to lighten somewhat more the trifling loads our animals had to carry. A little bread was then baked, and I endeavoured once more to put the rifle in serviceable condition, as it was the only weapon we should have to depend upon in any dangers that might beset us. Unable in any way to take out the breech, or to extract the ball, I determined to melt it out, and for that purpose took the barrel off the stock, and put the breech in the fire, holding the muzzle in my hand. Whilst thus engaged, the rifle went off, the ball whizzing close past my head; the fire, it seems, had dried the powder, which had been wetted, not washed out; and when the barrel was sufficiently heated, the piece had gone off, to the imminent danger of my life, from the incautious way in which I held it. The gun, however, was again serviceable; and after carefully loading it, I felt a degree of confidence and security I had before been a stranger to.

At eight o'clock we were ready to proceed; there remained but to perform the last sad offices of humanity towards him whose career had been cut short in so untimely a manner. This duty was rendered even more than ordinarily painful, by the nature of the country where we happened to have been encamped. One vast unbroken surface of sheet rock extended for miles in every direction and rendered it impossible to make a grave. We were some miles away from the sea-shore, and even had we been nearer, could not have got down the cliffs to bury the corpse in the sand, I could only, therefore, wrap a blanket around the body of the overseer, and leaving it enshrouded where he fell, escape from the melancholy scene, accompanied by Wylie, under the influence of feelings which neither time nor circumstances will ever obliterate. Though years have now passed away since the enactment of this tragedy, the dreadful horrors of that time and scene are recalled before me with frightful vividness, and make me shudder even now, when I think of them. A lifetime was crowded into those few short hours, and death alone may blot out the impressions they produced.

For some time we travelled slowly and silently onwards. Wylie preceding, leading one of the horses, myself following behind and driving the others after him, through a country consisting still of the same alternations of scrub and open intervals as before. The day became very warm, and at eleven, after travelling ten miles to the west, I determined to halt until the cool of the evening. After baking some bread and getting our dinners, I questioned Wylie as to what he knew of the sad occurrence of yesterday. He positively denied all knowledge of it—said he had been asleep, and was awoke by the report of the gun, and that upon seeing the overseer lying on the ground he ran off to meet me. He admitted, however, that, after the unsuccessful attempt to leave us, and proceed alone to King George's Sound, the elder of the other two natives had proposed to him again to quit the party, and try to go back to Fowler's Bay, to the provisions buried there. But he had heard or knew nothing, he said, of either robbery or murder being first contemplated.

My own impression was, that Wylie had agreed with the other two to rob the camp and leave us:—that he had been cognisant of all their proceedings and preparations, but that when, upon the eve of their departure, the overseer had unexpectedly awoke and been murdered, he was shocked and frightened at the deed, and instead of accompanying them, had run down to meet me. My opinion upon this point received additional confirmation from the subsequent events of this day; but I never could get Wylie to admit even the slightest knowledge of the fatal occurrence, or that he had even intended to have united with them in plundering the camp and deserting. He had now become truly alarmed; and independently of the fear of the consequences which would attach to the crime, should we ever reach a civilised community again, he had become very apprehensive that the other natives, who belonged to quite a different part of Australia to himself, and who spoke a totally different language, would murder him as unhesitatingly as they had done the white man.

We remained in camp until four o'clock, and were again preparing to advance, when my attention was called by Wylie to two white objects among the scrub, at no great distance from us, and I at once recognised the native boys, covered with their blankets only, and advancing towards us. From Wylie's account of their proposal to go back towards Fowler's Bay, I fully hoped that they had taken that direction, and left us to pursue our way to the Sound unmolested. I was therefore surprised, and somewhat alarmed, at finding them so near us. With my rifle and pistols I felt myself sufficiently a match for them in an open country, or by daylight. Yet I knew that as long as they followed like blood-hounds on our tracks our lives would be in their power at any moment that they chose to take them, whilst we were passing through a scrubby country, or by night. Whatever their intention might be, I knew, that if we travelled in the same direction with them, our lives could only be safe by their destruction. Although they had taken fully one-third of the whole stock of our provisions their appetites were so ravenous, and their habits so improvident, that this would soon be consumed, and then they must either starve or plunder us; for they had already tried to subsist themselves in the bush, and had failed.

As these impressions rapidly passed through my mind, there appeared to me but one resource left, to save my own life and that of the native with me: that was, to shoot the elder of the two. Painful as this would be, I saw no other alternative, if they still persisted in following us. After packing up our few things, and putting them upon the horses, I gave the bridles to Wylie to hold, whilst I advanced alone with my rifle towards the two natives. They were now tolerably near, each carrying a double-barrelled gun, which was pointed towards me, elevated across the left arm and held by the right hand. As I attempted to approach nearer they gradually retreated.

Finding that I was not likely to gain ground upon them in this way, I threw down my weapons, and advanced unarmed, hoping that if they let me near them I might suddenly close with the eldest and wrest his gun from him. After advancing about sixty or seventy yards towards them, I found that they again began to retreat, evidently determined not to let me approach any nearer, either armed or unarmed. Upon this I halted, and endeavoured to enter into parley with them, with a view to persuading them to return towards Fowler's Bay, and thus obviate the painful necessity I should have been under of endeavouring, for my own security, to take away the life of the eldest whenever I met with him, should they still persist in going the same road as myself. The distance we were apart was almost too great for parley, and I know not whether they heard me or not; though they halted, and appeared to listen, they did not reply to what I said, and plainly wished to avoid all closer contact. They now began to call incessantly to Wylie, and in answer to my repeated efforts to get them to speak to me, only would say; "Oh Massa, we don't want you, we want Wylie." Thus fully confirming me in the opinion I had formed, that Wylie had agreed to go with them before the deed of violence was committed. It was now apparent to me that their only present object in following us had been to look for Wylie, and get him to join them. In this they were unsuccessful; for he still remained quietly where I left him holding the horses, and evidently afraid to go near them. There was no use wasting further time, as I could not get them to listen to me. The sun, too, was fast sinking in the horizon, we had been four days without finding water, and the probability was we had very far still to go before we could hope to procure any; every moment, therefore, was precious.

Having returned to Wylie, I made him lead one of the horses in advance, and I followed behind, driving the rest after him, according to the system of march I had adopted in the morning. As soon as the two natives saw us moving on, and found Wylie did not join them, they set up a wild and plaintive cry, still following along the brush parallel to our line of route, and never ceasing in their importunities to Wylie, until the denseness of the scrub, and the closing in of night, concealed us from each other.

I was now resolved to make the most of the opportunity afforded me, and by travelling steadily onwards, to gain so much distance in advance of the two natives as to preclude the possibility of their again overtaking us until we had reached the water, if indeed we were ever destined to reach water again. I knew that they would never travel more than a few miles before lying down, especially if carrying all the bread they had taken, the keg of water, guns, and other articles. We had, however, seen none of these things with them, except the fire-arms.

Our road was over scrubby and stony undulations, with patches of dry grass here and there; in other parts, we passed over a very sandy soil of a red colour, and overrun by immense tufts of prickly grass (spinifex), many of which were three and four yards in diameter. After pushing on for eighteen miles, I felt satisfied we had left the natives far behind, and finding a patch of grass for the horses, halted for the remainder of the night. It was quite impossible, after all we had gone through, to think of watching the horses, and my only means of preventing them from straying, was to close the chains of their hobbles so tight, that they could not go far; having thus secured them, we lay down, and for a few hours enjoyed uninterrupted and refreshing sleep.

Moving on again on the 1st of May, as the sun was above the horizon, we passed through a continuation of the same kind of country, for sixteen miles, and then halted for a few hours during the heat of the day. We had passed many recent traces of natives, both yesterday and to-day, who appeared to be travelling to the westward. After dividing a pot of tea between us, we again pushed on for twelve miles, completing a stage of twenty-eight miles, and halting, with a little dry grass for the horses.

One circumstance in our route to-day cheered me greatly, and led me shortly to expect some important and decisive change in the character and formation of the country. It was the appearance for the first time of the Banksia, a scrub which I had never before found to the westward of Spencer's Gulf, but which I knew to abound in the vicinity of King George's Sound, and that description of country generally. Those only who have looked out with the eagerness and anxiety of a person in my situation, to note any change in the vegetation or physical appearance of a country, can appreciate the degree of satisfaction with which I recognised and welcomed the first appearance of the Banksia. Isolated as it was amidst the scrub, and insignificant as the stunted specimens were that I first met with, they led to an inference that I could not be mistaken in, and added, in a tenfold degree, to the interest and expectation with which every mile of our route had now become invested.

May 2.—We again moved away at dawn, through a country which gradually become more scrubby, hilly, and sandy. The horses crawled on for twenty-one miles, when I halted for an hour to rest, and to have a little tea from our now scanty stock of water. The change which I had noticed yesterday in the vegetation of the country was greater and more cheering every mile we went, although as yet the country itself was as desolate and inhospitable as ever.

May 3.—The seventh day's dawn found us early commencing our journey. The poor horses still crawled on, though slowly. I was surprised that they were still alive, after the continued sufferings and privations they had been subject to. As for ourselves, we were both getting very weak and worn out, as well as lame, and it was with the greatest difficulty I could get Wylie to move, if he once sat down. I had myself the same kind of apathetic feeling, and would gladly have laid down and slept for ever. Nothing but a strong sense of duty prevented me from giving way to this pleasing but fatal indulgence.

At ten miles from where we had slept, a native road led us down a very steep part of the cliffs, and we descended to the beach. The wretched horses could scarcely move, it was with the greatest difficulty we got them down the hill, and now, although within sight of our goal, I feared two of them would never reach it. By perseverance we still got them slowly along, for two miles from the base of the cliffs, and then turning in among the sand-drifts, to our great joy and relief, found a place where the natives had dug for water; thus at twelve o'clock on the seventh day since leaving the last depot, we were again encamped at water, after having crossed 150 miles of a rocky, barren, and scrubby table land.

May 4.—After an early breakfast we gave the horses as much water as they chose to drink, and removing their hobbles gave them full liberty to range where they liked. I then left Wylie to continue his slumbers, and taking my rifle, walked about three miles among the sand-drifts to search for grass, but could find none, except the coarse vegetation that grew amongst the sand-drifts. I found two other places where the natives got water by digging, and have no doubt that it may be procured almost anywhere in these drifts, which extend for some miles, along the coast.

May 5.—Up before daybreak, and moved down to the water to breakfast, then examined carefully round the wells, and between the sand-drifts and the sea, to see if any foot-prints had been made during the night, but none had. There were many pigeons about, and as I had still some ammunition left, I felt the loss of my gun severely. During the morning a very large eagle came and settled near us, and I sent Wylie with the rifle to try to shoot it; he crept within a very few yards of it, and being a good shot, I felt sure of a hearty meal, but unfortunately the rifle missed fire, having got damp during the heavy fall of dew a few evenings before. We lost our dinner, but I received a useful lesson on the necessity of taking better care of the only gun I had left, and being always certain that it was in a fit and serviceable state; I immediately set to work, cleaned and oiled it, and in the afternoon made some oil-skin covers for the lock and muzzle to keep the damp from it at nights.

May 6.—After breakfast we carefully examined the sand-drifts and the sea-shore, to see if the two boys had passed, but there were no traces of them to be found, and I now felt that we were secure from all further interruption from them.

The youngest of the two had been with me for four years, the eldest for two years and a half, and both had accompanied me in all my travels during these respective periods. Now that the first and strong impressions naturally resulting from a shock so sudden and violent as that produced by the occurrences of the 29th April had yielded, in some measure, to calmer reflections, I was able maturely to weigh the whole of what had taken place, and to indulge in some considerations in extenuation of their offence. The two boys knew themselves to be as far from King George's Sound as they had already travelled from Fowler's Bay. They were hungry, thirsty, and tired, and without the prospect of satisfying fully their appetites, or obtaining rest for a long period of time, they probably thought, that bad and inhospitable as had been the country we had already traversed, we were daily advancing into one still more so, and that we never could succeed in forcing a passage through it; and they might have been strengthened in this belief by the unlucky and incautiously-expressed opinions of the overseer. It was natural enough, under such circumstances, that they should wish to leave the party. Having come to that determination, and knowing from previous experience that they could not subsist upon what they could procure for themselves in the bush, they had resolved to take with them a portion of the provisions we had remaining, and which they might look upon, perhaps, as their share by right. Nor would Europeans, perhaps, have acted better. In desperate circumstances men are ever apt to become discontented and impatient of restraint, each throwing off the discipline and control he had been subject to before, and each conceiving himself to have a right to act independently when the question becomes one of life and death.

Having decided upon leaving the party, and stealing a portion of the provisions, their object would be to accomplish this as effectually and as safely as they could; and in doing this, they might, without having had the slightest intention originally of injuring either myself or the overseer, have taken such precautions, and made such previous arrangements as led to the fatal tragedy which occurred. I have no doubt that they first extinguished the fires, and then, possessing themselves of the fire-arms, proceeded to plunder the baggage and select such things as they required. In doing this they must have come across the ammunition, and loaded the guns preparatory to their departure, but this might have been without any premeditated intention of making use of them in the way they did. At this unhappy juncture it would seem that the overseer must have awoke, and advanced towards them to see what was the matter, or to put a stop to their proceedings, when they fired on him, to save themselves from being caught in their act of plunder. That either of the two should have contemplated the committal of a wilful, barbarous, cold-blooded murder, I cannot bring myself to believe—no object was to be attained by it; and the fact of the overseer having been pierced through the breast, and many yards in advance of where he had been sleeping, in a direction towards the sleeping-place of the natives, clearly indicated that it was not until he had arisen from his sleep, and had been closely pressing upon them, that they had fired the fatal shot. Such appeared to me to be the most plausible and rational explanation of this melancholy affair—I would willingly believe it to be the true one.

May 8.—About two hours before daylight, rain began to fall, and continued steadily though lightly for three hours, so that enough had fallen to deposit water in the ledges or holes of the rocks. The day was wild and stormy, and we did not start until late. Even then we could only get the tired horse along for three miles, and were again compelled to halt.

May 9.—The day was cold and cloudy, and we remained in camp to rest the horses, and diminished the weight of meat, which was greater than our horses could well carry in their present state.

Our progress was slow, and at eight miles I halted. Here we found a little dry grass not far from the sea, and as the horses did not require water, they fared tolerably well. This was the first grass we had met with since we descended the cliffs on the 3rd instant, the horses having entirely subsisted since then on the wiry vegetation which binds the sand-drifts together.

May 11.—Upon moving away this morning, I kept behind the sea-shore along the borders of the salt swamp, steering for some sand-hills which were seen a-head of us. In our approach to them we passed through a fine plain full of grass, and of a much better description than we had met with since leaving Fowler's Bay. Not only was it long and in the greatest abundance, but there were also mixed with the old grass many stalks of new and green, the whole forming a rich and luxurious feast for our horses, such as they had not enjoyed for many a long day. Nearer to the sand-hills we obtained excellent water by digging, at a depth of five feet, and only half a mile away from the grass. This place was too favourable not to be made the most of, and I determined to halt for a day or two to give our horses the benefit of it, and to enable us to diminish the weight of meat they had to carry. Whilst here I gave Wylie free permission to eat as much as he could—a privilege which he was not long in turning to account. Between last night's supper and this morning's breakfast he had got through six-and-a-half pounds of solid cooked flesh, weighed out and free from bone, and he then complained, that as he had so little water (the well had fallen in and he did not like the trouble of cleaning it out again), he could hardly eat at all. On an average he would consume nine pounds of meat per day.

June 2.—As we had made a shorter stage yesterday than I intended to have done, and the quantity of flour we had now remaining was very small, I did not dare to make use of any this morning, and we commenced our journey without breakfast. Being now near Thistle Cove, where I intended to halt for some time, and kill the little foal for food, whilst the other horses were recruiting, and as I hoped to get there early this afternoon, I was anxious to husband our little stock of flour in the hope, that at the little fresh-water lake described by Flinders as existing there, we should find abundance of the flag-reed for our support. Keeping a little behind the shore for the first hour, we crossed over the sandy ridge bounding it, and upon looking towards the sea, I thought I discovered a boat sailing in the bay. Upon pointing this object out to Wylie, he was of the same opinion with myself, and we at once descended towards the shore, but on our arrival were greatly disappointed at not being able again to see the object of our search. In the course of half an hour, however, whilst resting ourselves and watching the surface of the ocean, it again became visible, and soon after a second appeared. It was now evident that both these were boats, and that we had noticed them only when standing off shore, and the light shone upon their sails, and had lost them when upon the opposite tack. It was equally apparent that they were standing out from the main land for the islands. I imagined them to be sealers, who having entered the bay to procure water or firewood, were again steering towards the islands to fish. Having hastily made a fire upon one of the sand-hills, we fired shots, shouted, waved handkerchiefs, and made every signal we could to attract attention, but in vain. They were too far away to see, or too busy to look towards us. The hopes we had entertained were as suddenly disappointed as they had been excited, and we stood silently and sullenly gazing after the boats as they gradually receded from our view.

Whilst thus occupied and brooding over our disappointment, we were surprised to see both boats suddenly lower their sails, and apparently commence fishing. Watching them steadily we now perceived that they were whale-boats, and once more our hearts beat with hope, for I felt sure that they must belong to some vessel whaling in the neighbourhood. We now anxiously scanned the horizon in every direction, and at last were delighted beyond measure to perceive to the westward the masts of a large ship, peeping above a rocky island which had heretofore concealed her from our view. She was apparently about six miles from us, and as far as we could judge from so great a distance, seemed to be at anchor near the shore.

Poor Wylie's joy now knew no bounds, and he leapt and skipped about with delight as he congratulated me once more upon the prospect of getting plenty to eat. I was not less pleased than he was, and almost as absurd, for although the vessel was quietly at anchor so near us, with no sails loose and her boats away, I could not help fearing that she might disappear before we could get to her, or attract the notice of those on board. To prevent such a calamity, I mounted one of the strongest horses and pushed on by myself as rapidly as the heavy nature of the sands would allow, leaving Wylie at his own especial request to bring on the other horses. In a short time I arrived upon the summit of a rocky cliff, opposite to a fine large barque lying at anchor in a well-sheltered bay, (which I subsequently named Rossiter Bay, after the captain of the whaler,) immediately east of Lucky Bay, and at less than a quarter of a mile distant from the shore. The people on board appeared to be busily engaged in clearing their cables, which were foul, and did not observe me at all. I tied up my horse, therefore, to a bush, and waited for Wylie, who was not long in coming after me, having driven the poor horses at a pace they had not been accustomed to for many a long day. I now made a smoke on the rock where I was, and hailed the vessel, upon which a boat instantly put off, and in a few moments

I had the inexpressible pleasure of being again among civilised beings, and of shaking hands with a fellow-countryman in the person of Captain Rossiter, commanding the French Whaler "Mississippi."

Our story was soon told, and we were received with the greatest kindness and hospitality by the captain.

June 2.—After watering the horses at a deposit left by the rains, in the sheets of granite near us, and turning them loose, we piled up our little baggage, and in less than an hour we were comfortably domiciled on board the hospitable Mississippi—a change in our circumstances so great, so sudden, and so unexpected, that it seemed more like a dream than a reality; from the solitary loneliness of the wilderness, and its attendant privations, we were at once removed to all the comforts of a civilised community.

After we had done ample justice to the good cheer set before us by our worthy host, he kindly invited us to remain on board as long as we pleased, to recruit our horses, and told us, that when we felt refreshed sufficiently to renew the journey, he would supply us with such stores and other articles as we might require. I learnt that the Mississippi had but recently arrived from France, and that she had only been three weeks upon the ground she had taken up for the season's whaling. As yet no whales had been seen, and the season was said not to commence before the end of June or beginning of July. The boats I saw in the morning belonged to her, and had been out chasing what they thought to be a whale, but which proved to be only a fin-back, a species which was not thought to repay the trouble of trying out.

Early in the evening the whalers retired to rest, and I had a comfortable berth provided for me in the cabin, but could not sleep; my thoughts were too much occupied in reflecting upon the great change which the last few hours had wrought in the position of myself and my attendant. Sincerely grateful to the Almighty for having guided us through so many difficulties, and for the inexpressible relief afforded us when so much needed, but so little expected, I felt doubly thankful for the mercy we experienced, when, as I lay awake, I heard the wind roar, and the rain drive with unusual wildness, and reflected that by God's blessing we were now in safety, and under shelter from the violence of the storm, and the inclemency of the wet season, which appeared to be setting in, but which, under the circumstances we were in but a few short hours ago, we should have been so little able to cope with, or to endure.

June 5.—From this time until the fourteenth of June I remained on board the Mississippi, enjoying the hospitality of Captain Rossiter. Wylie went out once or twice to try to shoot a kangaroo for the ship, but he never succeeded; he had so much to eat on board that he had no stimulus to exertion, and did not take the trouble necessary to insure success. During almost the whole of the time that I remained on board the Mississippi, the weather was exceedingly boisterous, cold, and wet, and I could not but feel truly thankful that I had not been exposed to it on shore; even on board the ship, with shelter and extra clothing, I felt very sensibly the great change which had taken place in the temperature.

June 15.—Early this morning the boat came on shore for me, and I went on board to take a farewell breakfast, in the Mississippi, and to wish good-bye to her kind-hearted people. At eight I landed with the Captain, got up my horses and loaded them, a matter of some little time and trouble, now my stock of provisions and other things was so greatly augmented; in addition too to all I had accumulated before, the Captain insisted now upon my taking six bottles of wine and a tin of sardines.

Having received a few letters to be posted at Albany for France, I asked the Captain if there was anything else I could do for him, but he said there was not. The only subject upon which he was at all anxious, was to ascertain whether a war had broken out between France and England or not. In the event of this being the case, he wished me not to mention having seen a French vessel upon the coast, and I promised to comply with his request.

After wishing my kind host good-bye, and directing Wylie to lead one of the horses in advance, I brought up the rear, driving the others before me. Once again we had a long and arduous journey before us, and were wending our lonely way through the unknown and untrodden wilds. We were, however, in very different circumstances now, to what we had been in previous to our meeting with the French ship. The respite we had had from our labours, and the generous living we had enjoyed, had rendered us comparatively fresh and strong. We had now with us an abundance, not only of the necessaries, but of the luxuries of life; were better clothed and provided against the inclemency of the weather than we had been; and entered upon the continuation of our undertaking with a spirit, an energy, and a confidence that we had long been strangers to.

July 7.—Getting up the horses early, we proceeded up the

King's river, with a view of attempting to cross, but upon sounding the depths in one or two places, I found the tide, which was rising, was too high; I had only the alternative, therefore, of waiting for several hours until the water ebbed, or else of leaving the horses, and proceeding on without them. Under all the circumstances, I decided upon the latter; the rain was still falling very heavily, and the river before us was so wide and so dangerous for horses, from its very boggy character, that I did not think it prudent to attempt to force a passage, or worth while to delay to search for a proper crossing place. There was good feed for the horses where they were, and plenty of water, so that I knew they would fare better by remaining than if they were taken on to the Sound; whilst it appeared to me more than probable that I should have no difficulty, whenever I wished to get them, to procure a guide to go for and conduct them safely across, at the proper crossing place.

For a great part of the way we walked up to our ankles in water. This made our progress slow, and rendered our last day's march a very cold and disagreeable one. Before reaching the Sound, we met a native, who at once recognised Wylie and greeted him most cordially. From him we learnt that we had been expected at the Sound some months ago, but had long been given up for lost, whilst Wylie had been mourned for and lamented as dead by his friends and his tribe. The rain still continued falling heavily as we ascended to the brow of the hill immediately overlooking the town of Albany—not a soul was to be seen—not an animal of any kind—the place looked deserted and uninhabited, so completely had the inclemency of the weather driven both man and beast to seek shelter from the storm.

For a moment I stood gazing at the town below me—that goal I had so long looked forward to, had so laboriously toiled to attain, was at last before me. A thousand confused images and reflections crowded through my mind, and the events of the past year were recalled in rapid succession. The contrast between the circumstances under which I had commenced and terminated my labours stood in strong relief before me. The gay and gallant cavalcade that accompanied me on my way at starting—the small but enterprising band that I then commanded, the goodly array of horses and drays, with all their well-ordered appointments and equipment were conjured up in all their circumstances of pride and pleasure; and I could not restrain a tear, as I called to mind the embarrassing difficulties and sad disasters that had broken up my party, and left myself and Wylie the two sole wanderers remaining at the close of an undertaking entered upon under such hopeful auspices.

Upon entering the town I proceeded direct to Mr. Sherrats', where I had lodged when in King George's Sound in 1840. By him and his family I was most hospitably received, and every attention shewn to me; and in the course of a short time, after taking a glass of hot brandy and water, performing my ablutions and putting on a clean suit of borrowed clothes, I was enabled once more to feel comparatively comfortable, and to receive the many kind friends who called upon me.

Finding that a vessel would shortly sail for Adelaide, I at once engaged my passage, and proceeded to make arrangements for leaving King George's Sound.

XVI. THE BURKE AND WILLS EXPEDITION

[The purpose of the Burke and Wills expedition, which set out from Melbourne in 1860, was to cross the continent from south to north. By making a dash from his depot on Cooper's Creek, Burke succeeded in reaching the mouth of the Flinders River, which flows into the Gulf of Carpentaria. But through a series of mishaps, tragedy marked the end of the expedition. The two leaders perished from thirst and starvation on the Barcoo, and one of the men who had accompanied them, Gray, also died, of exhaustion. The fourth of the party, King, saved his life through the kindness of a native tribe with which he took refuge. The three following narratives consist of Burke's last despatch, which was found amongst the papers found at Cooper's Creek; of King's narrative and of Wills's account of the dash from Cooper's Creek to the Gulf. The two first-mentioned documents are contained in the pamphlet on *The Burke and Wills Exploring Expedition*, published at Melbourne, 1861; the third is from Wills's Journal, published in the volume entitled *A Successful Exploration through the Interior of Australia*, compiled from Wills's papers by his father, and published at London, 1863.]

(A) *Burke's Last Despatch*

The following is the last despatch written by Mr. Burke. It was found amongst the papers deposited on Cooper's Creek:

Depot No. 2, Cooper's Creek, Camp 65.—The return party from Carpentaria, consisting of myself, Wills, and King (Gray dead), arrived here last night, and found that the depot party had only started on the same day. We proceed on to-morrow slowly down the creek towards Adelaide by Mount Hopeless, and shall endeavour to follow Gregory's track; but we are very weak. The two camels are done up, and we shall not be able to travel faster than four or five miles a day. Gray died on the road, from exhaustion and fatigue. We have all suffered much from hunger. The provisions left here will, I think, restore our strength. We have discovered a practicable route to Carpentaria, the chief portion of which lies on the 140th deg. of E. longitude. There is some good country between this and the Stony Desert. From there to the tropics the country is dry and stony. Between the tropics and Carpentaria a considerable porton is rangy, but it is well watered and richly grassed. We reached the shores of Carpentaria on February 11, 1861. Greatly disappointed at finding the party here gone.

(Signed) ROBERT O'HARA BURKE, Leader.

April 22, 1861.

P.S.—The camels cannot travel, and we cannot walk, or we should follow the other party. We shall move very slowly down the creek.

(B) *King's Narrative*

Mr. Burke, Mr. Wills, and I reached the depot at Cooper's Creek on April 21st, about half-past 7 in the evening, with two camels—all that remained of the six Mr. Burke took with him. All the provisions we then had consisted of a pound and a half of dried meat. We found the party had gone the same day, and looking about for any mark they might have left, found the tree with DIG, April 21. Mr. Wills said the party had left for the Darling. We dug, and found the plant of stores. Mr. Burke took the papers out of the bottle, and then asked each of us whether we were able to proceed up the creek in pursuit of the party. We said not; and he then said that he thought it his duty to ask us, but that he himself was unable to do so, but that he had decided upon trying to make Mount Hopeless, as he had been assured by the committee in Melbourne that there was a cattle station within 150 miles of Cooper's Creek. Mr. Wills was not inclined to follow this plan, but wished to go down our old track, but at last gave in to Mr. Burke's wishes. I also wished to go down by our old track. We remained four or five days to recruit, making preparations to go down the creek by stages of four to five miles a day, and Mr. Burke placed a paper in the plant, stating what were our plans. Travelling down the creek, we got some fish from the natives, and, some distance down, one of the camels (Landa) got bogged, and although we remained there that day and part of the next trying to dig him out, we found our strength insufficient to do so. The evening of the second day, we shot him as he lay, and, having cut off as much meat as we could, we lived on it while we stayed to dry the remainder. Throwing all the least necessary things away, we made one load for the remaining camel (Rajah), and each of us carried a swag of about 25 lb. We were then tracing

down the branches of the creek running S., but found that they
ran out into earthy plains. We had understood that the creek
along Gregory's track was continuous; and finding that all these
creeks ran out into plains, Mr. Burke returned, our camel being
completely knocked up. We then intended to give the camel a
spell for a few days, and to make a new attempt to push on forty
or fifty miles to the south, in the hope of striking the creek. During the time that the camel was being rested, Mr. Burke and Mr.
Wills went in search of the natives, to endeavour to find out how
the nardoo grew. Having found their camp, they obtained as
much nardoo cake and fish as they could eat, but could not explain that they wished to be shown how to find the seed themselves. They returned on the third day, bringing some fish and
nardoo cake with them. On the following day, the camel Rajah
seemed very ill, and I told Mr. Burke I thought he could not
linger out more than four days; and as on the same evening the
poor brute was on the point of dying, Mr. Burke ordered him to
be shot. I did so, and we cut him up with two broken knives and
a lancet. We cured the meat, and planted it; and Mr. Burke then
made another attempt to find the nardoo, taking me with him.
We went down the creek, expecting to find the natives at the
camp where they had been last seen, but found that they had left;
and not knowing whether they had gone up or down the creek,
we slept in their gunyahs that night, and on the following morning returned to Mr. Wills. The next day Mr. Burke and I started
up the creek, but could see nothing of them, and were three days
away, when we returned and remained three days in our camp
with Mr. Wills. We then made a plant of all the articles we could
not carry with us, leaving 5 lb. of rice and a quantity of meat, and
then followed up the creek to where there were some good native
huts. We remained at that place a few days, and finding that our
provisions were beginning to run short, Mr. Burke said that we
ought to do something, and that if we did not find the nardoo, we
should starve, and that he intended to save a little dried meat and
rice to carry us to Mount Hopeless. The three of us then came to
the conclusion that it would be better to make a second attempt
to reach Mount Hopeless, as we were then as strong as we were
likely to be, our daily allowance being then reduced. Mr. Burke
asked each of us whether we were willing to make another attempt to reach the South Australian settlements, and we decided
on going. We took with us what remained of the provisions we
had planted—two and a-half pounds of oatmeal, a small quantity
of flour, and the dried meat—this, with powder and shot, and

other small articles, made up cur swags to 30 lb. each, and Mr. Burke carried one billy of water, and I another. We had not gone far before we came on a flat, where I saw a plant growing which I took to be clover, and, on looking closer, saw the seed, and called out that I had found the nardoo. They were very glad when I found it. We travelled three days, and struck a water-course coming south from Cooper's Creek. We traced this, as it branched out and reformed on the plains, until we at last lost it in flat country. Sandhills were in front of us, for which we made, and travelled all day, but found no water. We were all greatly fatigued, as our rations now consisted of only one small johnny cake and three sticks of dried meat daily. We campted that evening about four o'clock, intending to push next day until two o'clock p.m., and then, should we not find water, to return. We travelled and found no water, and the three of us sat down and rested for an hour, and then turned back. We all felt satisfied that, had there been a few days' rain, we could have got through. We were then, according to Mr. Wills's calculation, forty-five miles from the creek. We travelled on the day we turned back very late, and the following evening reached the nearest water at the creek. We gathered some nardoo, and boiled the seeds, as we were unable to pound them. The following day we reached the main creek; and knowing where there was a fine water-hole and native gunyahs, we went there, intending to save what remained of our flour and dried meat, for the purpose of making another attempt to reach Mount Hopeless. On the following day, Mr. Wills and I went out to gather nardoo, of which we obtained a supply sufficient for three days; and finding a pounding-stone at the gunyahs, Mr. Burke and I pounded the seed, which was such slow work that we were compelled to use half flour and half nardoo. Mr. Burke and Mr. Wills then went down the creek for the remainder of the dried meat which we had planted, and we had now all our things with us, gathering nardoo, and living the best way we could. Mr. Burke requested Mr. Wills to go up the creek as far as the depot, and to place a note in the plant there, stating that we were then living on the creek, the former note having stated that we were on our road to South Australia. He also was to bury there the field-books of the journey to the Gulf. Before starting he got 3 lb. of flour and 4 lb. of pounded nardoo, and about a pound of meat, as he expected to be absent about eight days. During his absence, I gathered nardoo and pounded it, as Mr. Burke wished to lay in a supply in case of rain.

A few days after Mr. Wills left, some natives came down the

R. O'HARA BURKE.

ROBERT O'HARA BURKE.
From " Tracks of McKinlay."

creek to fish at some water-holes near our camp. They were very civil to us at first, and offered us some fish; on the second day they came again to fish, and Mr. Burke took down two bags, which they filled for him; on the third day they gave us one bag of fish, and afterwards all came to our camp. We used to keep our ammunition and other articles in one gunyah, and all three of us live together in another. One of the natives took an oilcloth out of this gunyah, and Mr. Burke seeing him run away with it, followed him with his revolver, and fired over his head, and upon this the native dropped the oilcloth. While he was away the other blacks invited me away to a waterhole to eat fish; but I declined to do so, as Mr. Burke was away, and a number of natives were about who would have taken all our things. When I refused, one took his boomerang and laid it over my shoulder, and then told me by signs that if I called out for Mr. Burke, as I was doing, that he would strike me. Upon this I got them all in front of the gunyah and fired a revolver over their heads, but they did not seem at all afraid, until I got out the gun, when they all ran away. Mr. Burke, hearing the report, came back, and we saw no more of them until late that night, when they came with some cooked fish, and called out "white fellow." Mr. Burke then went out with his revolver, and found a whole tribe coming down all painted, and with fish in small nets carried by two men. Mr. Burke went to meet them, and they wished to surround him, but he knocked as many of the nets of fish out of their hands as he could, and shouted out to me to fire. I did so, and they ran off. We collected five small nets of cooked fish. The reason he would not accept the fish from them was, that he was afraid of being too friendly lest they should be always at our camp. We then lived on fish until Mr. Wills returned. He told us that he had met the natives soon after leaving us, and that they were very kind to him, and had given him plenty to eat both on going up and returning. He seemed to consider that he should have very little difficulty in living with them, and as their camp was close to ours, he returned to them the same day, and found them very hospitable and friendly, keeping him with them two days. They then made signs to him to be off. He came to us and narrated what had happened, but went back to them the following day, when they gave him his breakfast, but made signs for him to go away. He pretended not to understand them, and would not go, upon which they made signs that they were going up the creek, and that he had better go down. They packed up, and left the camp, giving Mr. Wills a little nardoo to take to us.

During his absence, while Mr. Burke was cooking some fish, during a strong wind, the flames caught the gunyah, and burned so rapidly that we were unable, not only to put it out, but to save any of our things, excepting one revolver and a gun. Mr. Wills being returned, it was decided to go up the creek and live with the natives, if possible, as Mr. Wills thought we should have but little difficulty in obtaining provisions from them if we camped on the opposite side of the creek to them.   He said he knew where they were gone, so we packed up and started. Coming to the gunyahs, where we expected to have found them, we were disappointed, and seeing a nardoo field close by, halted, intending to make it our camp. For some time we were employed gathering nardoo, and laying up a supply. Mr. Wills and I used to collect and carry home a bag each day, and Mr. Burke generally pounded sufficient for our dinner during our absence, but Mr. Wills found himself getting very weak, and was shortly unable to go out to gather nardoo as before, nor even strong enough to pound it, so that in a few days he became almost helpless. I still continued gathering; and Mr. Burke now also began to feel very weak, and said he could be of very little use in pounding. I had now to gather and pound for all three of us. I continued to do this for a few days, but finding my strength rapidly failing, my legs being very weak and painful, I was unable to go out for several days, and we were compelled to consume six days' stock which we had laid by. Mr. Burke now proposed that I should gather as much as possible in three days, and that with this supply we should go in search of the natives—a plan which had been urged upon us by Mr. Wills as the only chance of saving him and ourselves as well, as he clearly saw that I was no longer able to collect sufficient for our wants. Having collected the seed, as proposed, and having pounded sufficient to last Mr. Wills for eight days, and two days for ourselves, we placed water and firewood within his reach, and started. Before leaving him, however, Mr. Burke asked him whether he still wished it, as under no other circumstances would he leave him; and Mr. Wills again said that he looked on it as our only chance. He then gave Mr. Burke a letter and his watch for his father, and we buried the remainder of the field-books near the gunyah. Mr. Wills said that, in case of my surviving Mr. Burke, he hoped that I would carry out his last wishes, in giving the watch and letter to his father.

In travelling the first day, Mr. Burke seemed very weak, and complained of great pain in his legs and back. On the second day he seemed to be better, and said that he thought he was getting stronger, but, on starting, did not go two miles before he said he could go no further. I persisted in his trying to go on, and managed to get him along several times, until I saw that he was almost knocked up, when he said he could not carry his swag, and threw all he had away. I also reduced mine, taking nothing but a gun and some powder and shot, and a small pouch and some matches. On starting again, we did not go far before Mr. Burke said we should halt for the night, but, as the place was close to a large sheet of water, and exposed to the wind, I prevailed on him to go a little further, to the next reach of water, where we camped. We searched about, and found a few small patches of nardoo, which I collected and pounded, and, with a crow which I shot, made a good evening's meal. From the time we halted Mr. Burke seemed to be getting worse, although he ate his supper. He said he felt convinced he could not last many hours, and gave me his watch, which he said belonged to the committee, and a pocketbook, to give to Sir William Stawell, and in which he wrote some notes. He then said to me, "I hope you will remain with me here till I am quite dead—it is a comfort to know that some one is by; but when I am dying, it is my wish that you should place the pistol in my right hand, and that you leave me unburied as I die." That night he spoke very little, and the following morning I found him speechless, or nearly so; and about eight o'clock he expired. I remained a few hours there, but as I saw there was no use in remaining longer, I went up the creek in search of the natives. I felt very lonely, and at night usually slept in deserted wurleys, belonging to the natives. Two days after leaving the spot where Mr. Burke died, I found some gunyahs, where the natives had deposited a bag of nardoo, sufficient to last me a fortnight, and three bundles containing various articles. I also shot a crow that evening, but was in great dread that the natives would come and deprive me of the nardoo.

I remained there two days, to recover my strength, and then returned to Mr. Wills. I took back three crows; but found him lying dead in his gunyah, and the natives had been there and had taken away some of his clothes. I buried the corpse with sand, and remained there some days; but finding that my stock of nardoo was running short, and being unable to gather it, I tracked the natives who had been to the camp by their footprints in the sand, and went some distance down the creek, shooting crows and hawks on the road. The natives, hearing the report of the gun, came to meet me, and took me with them to their camp, giving me nardoo and fish. They took the birds I had shot and cooked them for me, and afterwards showed me a gunyah, where I was to sleep with three of the single men. The following morning they commenced talking to me, and putting one finger on the ground, and covering it with sand, at the same time pointing up the creek, saying, "Whitefellow," which I understood to mean that one white man was dead. From this I knew that they were the tribe who had taken Mr. Wills's clothes. They then asked me where the third white man was, and I also made the sign of putting two fingers on the ground and covering them with sand, at the same time pointing up the creek. They appeared to feel great compassion for me when they understood that I was alone on the creek, and gave me plenty to eat. After being four days with them I saw that they were becoming tired of me, and they made signs that they were going up the creek, and that I had better go downwards; but I pretended not to understand them. The same day they shifted camp, and I followed them; and, on reaching their camp, I shot some crows, which pleased them so much that they made me a breakwind in the centre of their camp, and came and sat round me until such time as the crows were cooked, when they assisted me to eat them. The same day, one of the women, to whom I had given part of a crow, came and gave me a ball of nardoo, saying that she would give me more only she had such a sore arm that she was unable to pound. She showed me a sore on her arm, and the thought struck me that I would boil some water in the billy and wash her arm with a sponge. During the operation the whole tribe sat round, and were muttering one to another. Her husband sat down by her side, and she was crying all the time. After I had washed it, I touched it with some nitrate of silver, when she began to yell and ran off, crying out, "Mokow! mokow!" (Fire! Fire!) From this time, she and her husband used to give me a small quantity of nardoo both night and morning, and whenever the tribe were about going on a fishing excursion, he used to give me notice to go with them. They also used to assist me in making a gourley, or breakwind, whenever they shifted camp. I generally shot a crow, or a hawk, and gave it to them in return for these little services. Every four or five days the tribe would surround me, and ask whether I intended going up or down the creek; at last I made them understand that if they went up I should go up the creek, and if they went down I should also go down, and from this time they seemed to look upon me as one of themselves, and supplied me with fish and nardoo regularly. They were very anxious, however, to know where Mr. Burke lay; and one day when we were fishing in the waterholes close by I

took them to the spot. On seeing his remains the whole party wept
bitterly, and covered them with bushes. After this they were
much kinder to me than before; and I always told them that the
white men would be here before two moons; and in the evenings,
when they came with nardoo and fish, they used to talk about
the "whitefellows " coming, at the same time pointing to the
moon. I also told them they would receive many presents, and
they constantly asked me for tomahawks, called by them "Bo-
mayko." From this time to when the relief party arrived—a
period of about a month—they treated me with uniform kindness, and looked upon me as one of themselves. The day on which
I was released, one of the tribe who had been fishing came and
told me that the whitefellows were coming, and the whole of the
tribe who were then in camp sallied out in every direction to
meet the party, while the man who had brought the news
took me across the creek, where I shortly saw the party coming
down.

(C) *Wills's Account of the Dash to the Gulf of Carpentaria*

Sunday, 16th December, 1860.—The horse having been shod
and our reports finished, we started at 6.40 a.m. for Eyre's Creek,
the party consisting of Mr. Burke, myself, King, and Charley,
having with us six camels, one horse, and three months' provisions.
We followed down the creek to the point where the sandstone
ranges cross the creek, and were accompanied to that place by
Brahe, who would return to take charge of the depot. Down to
this point the banks of the creek are very rugged and stony, but
there is a tolerable supply of grass and salt bush in the vicinity.
A large tribe of blacks came pestering us to go to their camp and
have a dance, which we declined. They were very troublesome,
and nothing but the threat to shoot them will keep them away.
They are, however, easily frightened; and, although fine-looking
men, decidedly not of a warlike disposition. They show the greatest
inclination to take whatever they can, but will run no unnecessary
risk in so doing. They seldom carry any weapon, except a shield
and a large kind of boomerang, which I believe they use for
killing rats, etc. Sometimes, but very seldom, they have a large
spear; reed spears seem to be quite unknown to them. They are
undoubtedly a finer and better-looking race of men than the
blacks on the Murray and Darling, and more peaceful; but in
other respects I believe they will not compare favourably with

them, for from the little we have seen of them, they appear to be mean-spirited and contemptible in every respect.

Monday, 17th December, 1860.—We continued to follow down the creek. Found its course very crooked, and the channel frequently dry for a considerable distance, and then forming into magnificent waterholes, abounding in water-fowl of all kinds. The country on each side is more open than on the upper part of the creek. The soil on the plains is of a light earthy nature, supporting abundance of salt bush and grass. Most of the plains are lightly timbered, and the ground is finer and not cracked up as at the head of the creek. Left Camp 67 at ten minutes to six A.M., having breakfasted before leaving. We followed the creek along from point to point, at first in a direction west-north-west for about twelve miles, then about north-west. At about noon we passed the last water, a short distance beyond which the creek runs out on a polygonum flat; but the timber was so large and dense that it deceived us into the belief that there was a continuation of the channel. On crossing the polygonum ground to where we expected to find the creek we became aware of our mistake. Not thinking it advisable to chance the existence of water ahead, we camped at the end of a large shallow sheet of water in the sandy bed of the creek.

The hole was about 150 links broad, and   * feet deep in most places. In many places the temperature of the water was almost incredibly high, which induced me to try it at several points. The mean of two on the shady side of the creek gave $97\frac{4}{10}$ degrees. As may be imagined this water tasted disagreeably warm, but we soon cooled some in water bags, and thinking that it would be interesting to know what we might call cool, I placed the thermometer in a pannikin containing some that appeared delightfully so, almost cold in fact; its temperature was, to our astonishment, 78 degrees. At half-past six, when a strong wind was blowing from south, and temperature of air had fallen to 80 degrees, the lowest temperature of water in the hose, that had been exposed to the full effect of evaporation for several hours, was 72 degrees. This water for drinking appeared positively cold, and is too low a temperature to be pleasant under the circumstances. A remarkable southerly squall came on between five and six P.M., with every appearance of rain. The sky however soon cleared, but the wind continued to blow in a squally and irregular manner from the same quarter at evening.

Wednesday, 19th December, 1860.—Started at a quarter-past

* Blank in original.

eight A.M., leaving what seemed to be the end of Cooper's Creek. We took a course a little to the north of west, intending to try and obtain water in some of the creeks that Sturt mentioned that he had crossed, and at the same time to see whether they were connected with Cooper's Creek, as appeared most probable from the direction in which we found the latter running, and from the manner in which it had been breaking up into small channels, flowing across the plains in a north and north-north-west direction. We left on our right the flooded flats on which this branch of the creek runs out and soon came to a series of sand ridges, the directions of which were between north half-west and north-north-west. The country is well grassed and supports plenty of salt bush. Many of the valleys are liable to be inundated by the overflow of the main creek. They have watercourses and polygonum flats bordered with box trees, but we met with no holes fit to hold a supply of water. At about ten miles we crossed a large earthy flat lightly timbered with box and gum. The ground was very bad for travelling on, being much cracked up and intersected by innumerable channels, which continually carried off the water of a large creek. Some of the valleys beyond this were very pretty, the ground being sound and covered with fresh plants, which made them look beautifully green. At fifteen miles we halted, where two large plains joined. Our attention had been attracted by some red-breasted cockatoos, pigeons, a crow, and several other birds, whose presence made us feel sure that there was water not far off; but our hopes were soon destroyed by finding a claypan just drying up. It contained just sufficient liquid to make the clay boggy. At ten minutes to seven P.M., we moved on, steering straight for Eyre's Creek, north-west by north, intending to make a good night's journey and avoid the heat of the day; but at a mile and a half we came to a creek which looked so well that we followed it for a short distance, and finding two or three waterholes of good milky water we camped for the night. This enabled me to secure an observation of the eclipse of Jupiter's (I) satellite, as well as some latitude observations. The night was so calm that I used the water as an horizon; but I find it much more satisfactory to take the mercury for several reasons.

Thursday, 20th December.—We did not leave this camp until half-past eight, having delayed to refill the water-bags with the milky water, which all of us found to be a great treat again. It is certainly more pleasant to drink than the clear water, and at the same time more satisfying. Our course from here, north-west by north, took us through some pretty country, lightly timbered and well grassed. We could see the line of creek timber winding through the valley on our left. At a distance of five miles there was a bush fire on its banks, and beyond it the creek made a considerable bend to the south-west. At two miles farther we came in sight of a large lagoon bearing north by west, and at three miles more we camped on what would seem the same creek as last night, near where it enters the lagoon. The latter is of great extent and contains a large quantity of water, which swarms with wild-fowl of every description. It is very shallow, but is surrounded by the most pleasing woodland scenery, and everything in the vicinity looks fresh and green. The creek near its junction with the lagoon contains some good waterholes five to six feet deep. They are found in a sandy alluvium which is very boggy when wet. There was a large camp of not less than forty or fifty blacks near where we stopped. They brought us presents of fish, for which we gave them some beads and matches. These fish we found to be the most valuable addition to our rations. They were of the same kind as we had found elsewhere, but finer, being from nine to ten inches long, and two to three inches deep, and in such good condition that they might have been fried in their own fat. It is a remarkable fact, that these were the first blacks who have offered us any fish since we reached Cooper's Creek.

Friday, 21st December.—We left Camp 70 at half-past five A.M., and tried to induce one or two of the blacks to go with us, but it was of no use. Keeping our former course were were pulled up at three miles by a fine lagoon, and then by the creek that flows into it; the latter being full of water, we were obliged to trace it a mile up before we could cross. I observed on its banks two wild plants of the gourd or melon tribe, one much resembling a stunted cucumber : the other, both in leaf and appearance of fruit was very similar to a small model of a water melon. The latter plant I also found at Camp 68. On tasting the pulp of the newly-found fruit, which was about the size of a large pea, I found it to be so acrid that it was with difficulty that I removed the taste from my mouth. At eight or nine miles from where we crossed the creek we passed another large lagoon, leaving it two miles on our left, and shortly afterwards we saw one nearly as far on our right. This last we should have availed ourselves of, but that we expected to find water in a creek which we could see, by the timber lining its banks, flowed from the lagoon on our left and crossed our course a few miles ahead. We reached it at a distance of four or five miles farther, and found a splendid waterhole at which we camped. The creek at the point flows in a northerly direction

BURKE AND WILLS'S ROUTE TO THE GULF OF CARPENTARIA,
1861.

From " Robert O'Hara Burke and the Australian Exploring
Expedition of 1860."

through a large lightly timbered flat, on which it partially runs out. The ground is, however, sound and well clothed with grass and salsolaceous plants. Up to this point the country through which we have passed has been of the finest description for pastoral purposes. The grass and saltbush are everywhere abundant, and water is plentiful with every appearance of permanence. We met with porcupine grass, and only two sand ridges before reaching Camp 71.

Saturday, 22nd December.—At five minutes to five A.M. we left one of the most delightful camps we have had in the journey, and proceeded on the same course as before, north-west by north, across some high ridges of loose sand, many of which were partially clothed with porcupine grass. We found the ground much worse to travel over than any we have yet met with, as the ridges were exceedingly abrupt and steep on their eastern side, and although sloping gradually towards the west, were so honeycombed in some places by the burrows of rats, that the camels were continually in danger of falling. At a distance of about six miles, we descended from these ridges to undulating country of open box forest, where everything was green and fresh. There is an abundance of grass and salt bushes, and lots of birds of all descriptions. Several flocks of pigeons passed over our heads, making for a point a little to our right, where there is no doubt plenty of water, but we did not go off our course to look for it. Beyond the box forest, which keeps away to the right, we again entered the sand ridges, and at a distance of six miles, passed close to a dry salt lagoon, the ridges in the vicinity of which are less regular in their form and direction, and contain nodules of limestone. The ground in the flats and claypans near has that encrusted surface that cracks under the pressure of the foot, and is a sure indication of saline deposits. At a distance of eight miles from the lagoon, we camped at the foot of a sand ridge, jutting out on the stony desert. I was rather disappointed, but not altogether surprised, to find the latter nothing more nor less than the stony rises that we had before met with, only on a larger scale and not quite as undulating. During the afternoon several crows came to feed on the plain. They came from an east-north-east direction, no doubt from a portion of the creek that flows through the forest that we left on our right. In the morning, as we were loading, a duck passed over, but it was too dark to see which way it went.

Sunday, 23rd December.—At five A.M. we struck out across the desert in a west-north-west direction. At four and a half miles we crossed a sand ridge, and then returned to our north-west by north course. We found the ground not nearly as bad for travelling on as that between Bulloo and Cooper's Creek. In fact I do not know whether it arose from our exaggerated anticipation of horrors or not, but we thought it far from bad travelling ground, and as to pasture it is only the actually stony ground that is bare, and many a sheep run is in fact worse grazing ground than that. At fifteen miles we crossed another sand ridge, for several miles round which there is plenty of grass and fine salt bush. After crossing this ridge we descended to an earthy plain, where the ground was rather heavy, being in some places like pieces of slaked lime, and intersected by small watercourses; flocks of pigeons rose from amongst the salt bushes and polygonum; but all the creeks were dry, although marked by lines of box timber. Several gunyahs of the blacks were situated near a waterhole that had apparently contained water very lately, and heaps of grass were lying about the plains, from which they had beaten the seeds. We pushed on, hoping to find the creeks assuming an improved appearance, but they did not, and at one o'clock we halted, intending to travel through part of the night. About sunset, three flocks of pigeons passed over us, all going in the same direction, due north by compass, and passing over a ridge of sand in that direction. Not to have taken notice of such an occurrence would have been little short of a sin, so we determined to go eight or ten miles in that direction. Starting at seven o'clock P.M., we, at six miles, crossed the ridge over which the birds had flown, and came on a flat, subject to innundation. The ground was at first hard and even like the bottom of a claypan, but at a mile or so we came on cracked earthy ground, intersected by numberless small channels running in all directions. At nine miles we reached the bed of a creek running from east to west: it was only bordered by polygonum bushes, but as there was no timber visible on the plains, we thought it safer to halt until daylight, for fear we should miss the water. At daylight, when we had saddled, a small quantity of timber could be seen at the point of a sand ridge about a mile and a half or two miles to the west of us, and on going there we found a fine creek, with a splendid sheet of water more than a mile long, and averaging nearly three chains broad: it is, however, only two or three feet deep in most parts.

Monday, 24th December, 1860.—We took a day of rest on Gray's Creek to celebrate Christmas. This was doubly pleasant, as we had never, in our most sanguine moments, anticipated finding such a delightful oasis in the desert. Our camp was really an agreeable place, for we had all the advantages of food and water, attending a position of a large creek or river, and were at the same time free from the annoyance of the numberless ants, flies, and mosquitoes that are invariably met with amongst timber or heavy scrub.

Tuesday, 25th December, 1860.—We left Gray's Creek at half-past four A.M. and proceeded to cross the earthy rotten plains in the direction of Eyre's Creek. At a distance of about nine miles we reached some lines of trees and bushes which were visible from the top of the sand ridge at Gray's Creek. We found them growing on the banks of several small creeks which trend to the N. and N.N.W.; at a mile and a half further we crossed a small creek N.N.E., and joining the ones above mentioned. This creek contained abundance of water in small detached holes from fifty to a hundred links long, well shaded by steep banks and over-hanging bushes. The water had a suspiciously transparent colour and a slight trace of brackishness, but the latter was scarcely perceptible. Near where the creek joined the holes is a sandhill and a dense mass of fine timber. The smoke of a fire indicated the presence of blacks, who soon made their appearance and followed us for some distance, beckoning us away to the N.E. We how-ever continued our course N.W. by N., but at a distance of one mile and a half found that the creek did not come round as we expected, and that the fall of the water was in a direction nearly opposite to our course, or about west to east. We struck off north half west for a high sand ridge, from which we anticipated seeing whether it were worth while for us to follow the course of the creeks we had crossed. We were surprised to find all the water-courses on the plains trending rather to the south of east, and at a distance of three miles, after changing our course, and when we approached the sandhills towards which we had been steering, we were agreeably pulled up by a magnificent creek coming from the N.N.W., and running in the direction of the fire we had seen. We had now no choice but to change our course again, for we could not have crossed even if we had desired to do so. On follow-ing up the south bank of the creek we found it soon keeping a more northerly course than it had where we first struck it. This fact, together with its magnitude and general appearance, lessened the probability of its being Eyre's Creek, as seemed at first very likely from their relative positions and directions. The day being very hot and the camels tired from travelling over the earthy plains, which by-the-by are not nearly so bad as those at the head of Cooper's Creek, we camped at one P.M., having traced the creek up about five miles, not counting the bends. For the whole of this distance we found not a break or interruption of water, which appears to be very deep; the banks are from twenty to thirty feet above the water, and very steep; they are clothed near the water's edge with mint and other weeds, and on the top of each side there is a belt of box trees and various shrubs. The lower part of the creek is bounded towards the north by a high red sand ridge, and on the south side is an extensive plain, intersected by numerous water-courses, which drain off the water in flood-time. The greater portion of the plain is at present very bare, but the stalks of dry grass show that after rain or floods there will be a good crop on the harder and well-drained portion; but I believe the loose earthy portion supports no vegetation at any time. The inclination of the ground from the edge of the creek-bank towards the plain is in many places very considerable; this I should take to indicate that the flooding is or has been at one time both frequent and regular.

Wednesday, 26th December, 1860.—We started at five A.M., following up the creek from point to point of the bends. Its general course was at first north-by-west, but at about six miles, the sand ridge on the west closed in on it, and at this point it takes a turn to the N.N.E. for half a mile, and then comes around suddenly N.W. Up to this point it had been rather improving in appearance than otherwise, but in the bend to the N.W. the channel is very broad. Its bed, being limestone rock and indurated clay, is for a space of five or six chains quite dry; then commences another waterhole, the creek keeping a little more towards north. We crossed the creek here and struck across the plain in a due north course, for we could see the line of timber coming up to the sand ridges in that direction. For from seven to eight miles we did not touch the creek, and the eastern sand ridge seceded to a distance, in some places of nearly three miles, from our line, leaving an immense extent of grassy plain between it and the creek. The distinctly marked feature on the lower part of this creek is that whenever the main creek is on one side of a plain, there is always a fine billibong on the opposite side, each of them almost invariably sticking close to the respective sand ridges. Before coming to the next bend of the creek a view from the top of a sandhill showed me that the creek received a large tributary from the N.W. at about two miles above where we had crossed it. A fine line of timber, running up to the N.W., joined an extensive tract of box forest, and the branch we were following was lost to view in a similar forest towards the north. The sand ridge was so

abrupt when we came to the creek, that it was necessary to descend into its bed through one of the small ravines adjoining it.
We found it partially run out, the bed being sand and strewed
with nodules of lime, some of which were from one half to two
feet long: they had apparently been formed in the sand downs by
infiltration.

Sunday, 30th December, 1860.—Finding that the creek was
trending considerably towards the east without much likelihood
of altering its course, we struck off from it, taking a ten days'
supply of water, as there were ranges visible to the north, which
had the appearance of being stony. A north-east by north course
was first taken for about seven miles in order to avoid them. The
whole of this distance was over alluvial earthy plains, the soil of
which was firm, but the vegetation scanty.

Saturday, 5th January, 1861.—On leaving Camp 84, we found
slight but distinct indications of rain in the groves, and a few
blades of grass and small weeds in the little depressions on the
plain : these indications were, however, so slight, that, but for
the fact of our having found surface-water in two holes near our
camp, we should hardly have noticed them. At a distance of about
two miles in a N.N.E. direction we came to a creek with a long
broad shallow waterhole. The well-worn paths, the recent tracks
of natives, and the heaps of shells, on the contents of which the
latter had feasted, showed at once that this creek must be connected with some creek of considerable importance. The camels
and horses being greatly in need of rest, we only moved up about
half a mile, and camped for the day.

Sunday, 6th January, 1861.—Started at twenty minutes to six
o'clock, intending to make an easy day's stage along the creek.
As we proceeded up in a northerly direction, we found the waterhole to diminish in size very much, and at about two and a half
miles the creek ran out in a lot of small watercourses. At the
upper end of the creek we found in its bed what appeared to be an
arrangement for catching fish: it consisted of a small oval mud
paddock about twelve feet by eight feet, the sides of which were
about nine inches above the bottom of the hole, and the top of the
fence covered with long grass, so arranged that the ends of the
blades overhung scantily by several inches the sides of the hole.
As there was no sign of timber to the north, we struck off to N.W.
by N. for a fine line that came up from S.W., and seemed to run
parallel with the creek we were about to leave. At a distance of
about three miles, we reached the bank of a fine creek containing
a sheet of water two chains broad, and at least fifteen feet deep in

I. D. *ff*

the middle. The banks are shelving, sandy, and lightly clothed with box trees and various shrubs. On starting to cross the plains towards this creek we were surprised at the bright green appearance of strips of land, which look in the distance like swamps. On approaching some of them, we found that there had been a considerable fall of rain in some places, which had raised a fine crop of grass and portulac wherever the soil was of a sandy and light nature; but the amount of moisture had been insufficient to affect the hard clayey ground which constitutes the main portion of the plain. The sight of two native companions feeding here, added greatly to the encouraging prospects; they are the only specimens of that bird that I remember to have seen on that side of the Darling.

7th January, 1861.—We started at half-past four A.M. without water, thinking that we might safely rely on this creek for one day's journey. We, however, found the line of timber soon begin to look small; at three miles the channel contained only a few pools of surface water. We continued across the plains on a due north course, frequently crossing small watercourses, which had been filled by the rain, but were fast drying up. Here and there, as we proceeded, dense lines of timber on our right showed that the creek came from the east of north; at a distance of thirteen miles we turned to the N.N.E. towards a fine line of timber. We found a creek of considerable dimensions, that had only two or three small waterholes, but as there was more than sufficient for us, and very little feed for the beasts anywhere else, we camped. I should have liked this camp to have been in a more prominent and easily recognizable position, as it happens to be almost exactly on the tropic of Capricorn. The tremendous gale of wind that we had in the evening and night prevented me from taking a latitude observation, whereas I had some good ones at the last camp and at Camp 87. My reckoning cannot be far out. I found, on taking out my instruments, that one of the spare thermometers was broken, and the glass of my aneroid barometer cracked; the latter I believe not otherwise injured. This was done by the camel having taken it into his head to roll while the pack was on his back.

Tuesday, 8th January, 1861.—Started at a quarter past five A.M. with a load of water, determined to be independent of all creeks and watercourses. At a mile and a half, found surface water in a small creek, and at a mile farther, water in two or three places on the open plains. The country we crossed for the first ten miles consists of fine open plains of arm argillaceous soils, too stiff and hard to be affected by the small quantity of rain that has fallen as yet. They are subject to inundations from the overflow of a number of small creeks, which intersect them in a direction E.N.E. to W.S.W. Nearly all the creeks are lined with box trees and shrubs in a tolerably healthy state; of the remains of dead trees there is only a fair proportion to the living ones. After traversing a plain of greater extent than the rest, we, at ten miles, reached the creek, proportionately large and important looking. The channel, however, at the point where we struck it, was deep, level, and dry; but I believe there is water in it not far off, for there were some red-breasted cockatoos in the trees, and native parrots on each side. On the north side there is a part bearing off to the N.N.W. The mirage on the plain to the south of the creek was stronger than I have before seen it. There appear to be sheets of water within a few yards of one, and it looks sufficiently smooth and glassy to be used for an artificial horizon. To the westward of the plains, some fine sandhills were visible, nearly in the direction in which the creek flowed. To the north of the creek the country undergoes a great change. At first there is a little earthy land subject to innundation. The soil then becomes more sandy, with stony pans in which water collects after rain; the whole country is slightly undulating, lightly timbered, and splendidly grassed. A number of small disconnected creeks are scattered about, many of which contained water protected from the sun and wind by luxuriant growth of fine grasses and small bushes. We passed one or two little rises of sand and pebbles, on which were growing some trees quite new to me; but for the seed pods I should have taken them for a species of Casuarina, although the leaf-stalks have not the jointed peculiarities of those plants. The trunks and branches are like the she oak, the leaves like those of a pine; they droop like a willow, and the seed is small, flat, in a large flat pod, about six inches by three-quarters of an inch. As we proceeded, the country improved at every step. Flocks of pigeons rose and flew off to the eastward, and fresh plants met our view on every rise; everything green and luxuriant. The horse licked his lips, and tried all he could to break his nose-string in order to get at the food. We camped at the foot of a sandy rise, where there was a large stony pan with plenty of water, and where the feed was equal in quality, and superior as to variety, to any that I have seen in Australia, excepting perhaps on some soils of volcanic origin.

Wednesday, 9th January, 1861.—Started at five minutes past five, without water, trusting to get a supply of water from the rain that fell during the thunderstorm. Traversed six miles of undulating plains covered with vegetation richer than ever. Several ducks rose from the little creeks as we passed, and flocks of pigeons were flying in all directions. The richness of the vegetation is evidently not suddenly arising from chance thunderstorms, for the trees and bushes on the open plain are everywhere healthy and fresh looking; very few dead ones are to be seen; besides which, the quantity of dead and rotten grass which at present almost overpowers in some places the young blades shows that this is not the first crop of the kind. The grasses are numerous and many of them unknown to me, but they only constitute a moderate portion of the herbage. Several kinds of spurious vetches and portulac, as well as salsolaceae, add to the luxuriance of the vegetation. At seven miles we found ourselves in an open forest country, where the feed was good, but not equal to what we had passed, neither had it been visited by yesterday's rain. We soon emerged again on open plains, but the soil being of a more clayish nature, they were not nearly so much advanced in vegetation as the others. We found surface water in several places, and at one spot disturbed a fine bustard which was feeding in the long grass; we did not see him until he flew up. I should have mentioned that one flew over our camp last evening in a northerly direction; this speaks well for the country and climate. At noon we came to a large creek the course of which was from E.N.E. to W.S.W.; the sight of the white gum trees in the distance had raised hopes, which were not at all damped on a close inspection of the channel. At the point where we struck it there was certainly no great quantity of water; the bed was broad and sandy, but its whole appearance was that of an important watercourse, and the large gums which line its banks, together with the improved appearance of the soil, and the abundance of feed in the vicinity, satisfied us as to the permanency of the water and the value of the discovery. Although it was so early in the day, and we were anxious to make a good march, yet we camped here, as it seemed to be almost a sin to leave such good quarters. The bed of the creek is loose sand, through which the water freely permeates; it is, however, sufficiently coarse not to be boggy, and animals can approach the water without any difficulty.

Thursday, 10th January, 1861.—At twenty minutes past five A.M., we left our camp with a full supply of water, determined to risk no reverses, and to make a good march. I should mention that last evening we had been nearly deafened by the noise of the cicadariae, and but for our large fires should have been kept awake all night by the mosquitoes. A walk of two miles across a well-

WILLIAM JOHN WILLS.

WILLIAM JOHN WILLS.
From " Tracks of McKinlay."

grassed plain brought us to a belt of timber, and we soon afterwards found ourselves pulled up by a large creek in which the water was broad and deep; we had to follow up the bank of the creek in a N.E. direction for nearly a mile before we could cross, when to our joy we found that it was flowing; not a muddy stream from the effects of recent floods, but a small rivulet of pure water as clear as crystal. The bed of the river at this place is deep and rather narrow; the water flows over sand and pebbles, winding its way between clumps of melalema and gum saplings. After leaving the river, we kept our old course due north, crossing, at a distance of one mile, three creeks with gum trees on their banks. The soil of the flats through which they flow is a red loam of fair quality and well grassed. Beyond the third creek is a large plain, parts of which are very stony, and this is bounded towards the east by a low stony rise, partly composed of decayed and honeycombed quartz rock in situ, and partly of waterworn pebbles and other alluvial deposits. At about two miles across this plain, we reached the first of a series of small creeks with deep waterholes: these creeks and holes have the characteristics peculiar to watercourses which are found in flats formed from the alluvial deposits of schistose rocks. The banks are on a level with the surrounding ground, and are irregularly marked by small trees, or only by tufts of long grass which overhang the channel and frequently hide it from one's view, even when within a few yards. At about five miles from where we crossed the river, we came to the main creek in these flats, Patten's Creek; it flows along at the foot of a stony range, and we had to trace it up nearly a mile in a N.N.E. direction before we could cross it; as it happened, we might almost as well have followed its course up the flat, for at a little more than two miles we came to it again. We re-crossed it at a stony place just below a very large waterhole, and then continued our course over extensive plains, not so well grassed as those we had passed before, and very stony in some places. At eight miles from Patten's Creek we came to another, running from S.W. to S.E. There was plenty of water in it, but it was evidently the re-result of recent local rains. On the banks was an abundance of good feed but very little timber.

Friday, 11th January, 1861.—We started at five A.M., and in the excitement of exploring fine well-watered country, forgot all about the eclipse of the sun until the reduced temperature and peculiarly gloomy appearance of the sky drew our attention to the matter; it was then too late to remedy the deficiency, so we made a good day's journey, the moderation of the midday heat, which was only about 86°, greatly assisting us. The country traversed has the most verdant and cheerful aspect; abundance of feed and water everywhere. All the creeks seen to-day have a course more or less to the east by south. The land improves in appearance at every mile. A quantity of rain has fallen here and to the south, and some of the flats are suitable for cultivation, if the regularity of the seasons will admit.

Saturday, 12th January, 1861.—We started at five A.M., and, keeping as nearly as possible a due north course, traversed for about eight miles a splendid flat, through which flow several fine well-watered creeks, lined with white gum trees. We then entered a series of slaty, low, sandstone ranges, amongst which were some well-grassed flats, and plenty of water in the main gullies. The more stony portions are, however, covered with porcupine grass, and here and there with mallee; large ant-hills are very numerous; they vary in height from two and a half to four feet. There was a continuous rise perceptible all the way in crossing the ranges, and from the highest portion, which we reached at a distance of about seven miles, we had a pretty good view of the country towards the north. As far as we could see in the distance, and bearing due north, was a large range, having somewhat the outline of a granite mountain. The east end of this range just comes up to the magnetic north; on the left of this, and bearing N.N.W., is a single conical peak, the top of which only is visible. Further to the west there were some broken ranges, apparently sandstone; to the E. of N. the tops of very distant and apparently higher ranges were seen, the outline of which was so indistinct that I can form no idea as to their character; the intermediate country below us appeared alternations of fine valleys and stony ranges, such as we had just been crossing. From here a descent of two miles brought us to a creek having a northern course, but on tracing it down for about a mile, we found it to turn to the south-east and join another from the north. We crossed over to the latter on a north-by-west course, and camped on the west bank. It has a broad sandy channel; the waterholes are large, but not deep; the banks are bordered with fine white gums, and are in some places very scrubby. There is abundance of rich green feed everywhere in the vicinity. We found here numerous indications of blacks having been here, but saw nothing of them. It seems remarkable that where their tracks are so plentiful, we should have seen none since we left King's Creek. I observed that the natives here climb trees as those on the Murray do, in search of some animal corresponding in habits to the opossum, which they get out of the hollow branches in a similar manner. I have not yet been able to ascertain what the animal is.

Sunday, 13th January, 1861.—We did not leave camp this morning until half-past seven, having delayed for the purpose of getting the camels' shoes on—a matter in which we were eminently unsuccessful. We took our breakfast before starting, for almost the first time since leaving the depot. Having crossed the creek, our course was due north as before, until, at about six miles, we came in sight of the range ahead, when we took a north-half-east direction for the purpose of clearing the eastern front of it. We found the ground more sandy than what we had before crossed, and a great deal of it even more richly grassed. Camp 93 is situate at the junction of three sandy creeks, in which there is abundance of water. The sand is loose, and the water permeates freely, so that the latter may be obtained delightfully cool and clear by sinking anywhere in the beds of the creeks.

Saturday, 19th January, 1861.—Started from Camp 98 at 5.30 A.M., and passing to the N.W. of Mount Forbes, across a fine and well-grassed plain, kept at first a north-by-east direction. At a distance of three miles, the plain became everywhere stony, being scattered over with quartz pebbles; and a little further on we came to low quartz ranges, the higher portions of which are covered with porcupine grass, but the valleys are well clothed with a variety of coarse and rank herbage. At about five miles we crossed a creek with a sandy bed, which has been named Green's Creek; there were blacks not far above where we crossed, but we did not disturb them. After crossing the creek, we took a due north course over very rugged quartz ranges of an auriferous character. Pieces of iron ore, very rich, were scattered in great numbers over some of the hills. On our being about to cross one of the branch creeks in the low range, we surprised some blacks,—a man who, with a young fellow apparently his son, was upon a tree, cutting out something; and a lubra with a piccaninny. The two former did not see me until I was nearly close to them, and then they were dreadfully frightened; jumping down from the trees, they started off, shouting what sounded to us very like, "Joe, Joe." Thus disturbed, the lubra, who was at some distance from them, just then caught sight of the camels and the remainder of the party as they came over the hill into the creek, and this tended to hasten their flight over the stones and porcupine grass. Crossing the range at the head of this creek, we came on a gully running north, down which we proceeded, and soon found it open out into a creek, at two or three points at which we found water. On this creek we found the first specimen of an eucalyptus, which has a very different appearance from the members of the gum-tree race. It grows as high as a good-sized gum tree, but with the branches less spreading; in shape it much resembles the elm; the foliage is dark, like that of the light wood; the trunk and branches are covered with a grey bark resembling in outward appearance that of the box tree. Finding that the creek was trending too much to the eastward, we struck off to the north again, and at a short distance came on a fine creek running about S.S.E. As it was now nearly time to camp, we travelled it up for about one and a half mile, and came to a fine waterhole in a rocky basin, at which there were lots of birds.

Sunday, 27th January, 1861.—Started from Camp 105 at five minutes past two in the morning. We followed along the bends of the creek by moonlight, and found the creek wind about very much, taking on the whole a N.E. course. At about five miles it changed somewhat its features; from a broad and sandy channel, winding about through gum-tree flats, it assumes the unpropitious appearance of a straight, narrow creek, running in a N.N.E. direction between high, perpendicular, earthy banks. After running between three or four miles in this manner, it took a turn to the west, at which point there is a fine waterhole, and then assumed its original character. Below this we found water at several places, but it all seemed to be either from surface drainage or from springs in the sand. The land in the vicinity of the creek appears to have received plenty of rain, the vegetation everywhere green and fresh; but there is no appearance of the creek having flowed in this part of the channel for a considerable period. Palm trees are numerous, and some bear an abundance of small, round dates (nuts) just ripening. These palms give a most picturesque and pleasant appearance to the creek.

Wednesday, 30th January, 1861.—Started at half-past seven A.M., after several unsuccessful attempts at getting Golah out of the bed of the creek. It was determined to try bringing him down until we could find a place for him to get out at; but after going in this way two or three miles it was found necessary to leave him behind, as it was almost impossible to get him through some of the waterholes, and had separated King from the party, which became a matter for very serious consideration when we found blacks hiding in the box trees close to us.

Sunday, February, 1861.—Finding the ground in such a state from the heavy falls of rain, that camels could scarcely be got along, it was decided to leave them at Camp 119, and for Mr.

Burke and I to proceed towards the sea on foot. After breakfast we accordingly started, taking with us the horse and three days' provisions. Our first difficulty was in crossing Billy's Creek, which we had to do where it enters the river, a few hundred yards below the camp. In getting the horse in here, he got bogged in a quick-sand bank so deeply as to be unable to stir, and we only succeeded in extricating him by undermining him on the creek's side, and then lugging him into the water. Having got all the things in safety, we continued down the river bank, which bent about from east to west, but kept a general north course. A great deal of the land was so soft and rotten that the horse, with only a saddle and about twenty-five pounds on his back, could scarcely walk over it. At a distance of about five miles we again had him bogged in crossing a small creek, after which he seemed so weak that we had great doubts about getting him on. We, however, found some better ground close to the water's edge, where the sandstone rock crops out, and we stuck to it as far as possible. Finding that the river was bending about so much that we were making very little progress in a northerly direction, we struck off due north and soon came on some table land, where the soil is shallow and gravelly, and clothed with box and swamp gums. Patches of the land were very boggy, but the main portion was sound enough; beyond this we came on an open plain, covered with water up to one's ankles. The soil here was a stiff clay, and the surface very uneven, so that between the tufts of grass one was frequently knee deep in water. The bottom, however, was sound and no fear of bogging. After floundering through this for several miles, we came to a path formed by the blacks, and there were distinct signs of a recent migra-tion in a southerly direction. By making use of this path we got on much better, for the ground was well trodden and hard. At rather more than a mile, the path entered a forest through which flowed a nice watercourse, and we had not gone far before we found places where the blacks had been camping. The forest was intersected by little pebbly rises, on which they had made their fires, and in the sandy ground adjoining some of the former had been digging yams, which seemed to be so numerous that they could afford to leave lots of them about, probably having only selected the very best. We were not so particular, but ate many of those that they had rejected, and found them very good. About half a mile further, we came close on a black fellow, who was coiling up by a camp fire, whilst his gin and piccaninny were yabbering alongside. We stopped for a short time to take out some of the pistols that were on the horse, and that they might see us before we were so near as to frighten them. Just after we stopped the black got up to stretch his limbs, and after a few seconds looked in our direction. It was very amusing to see the way in which he stared, standing for some time as if he thought he must be dreaming, and then, having signalled to the others, they dropped on their haunches, and shuffled off in the quietest manner possible. Near their fire was a fine hut, the best I have ever seen, built on the same principle as those at Cooper's Creek, but much larger and more complete: I should say a dozen blacks might comfortably coil in it together. It is situated at the end of the forest towards the north, and looks out on an extensive marsh, which is at times flooded by the sea water. Hundreds of wild geese, plover and pelicans were enjoying themselves in the watercourses in the marsh, all the water on which was too brackish to be drinkable, except some holes that are filled by the stream that flows through the forest. The neighbourhood of this encampment is one of the prettiest we have seen during the journey. Proceeding on our course across the marsh, we came to a channel through which the sea water enters. Here we passed three blacks, who, as is universally their custom, pointed out to us, unasked, the best part down. This assisted us greatly, for the ground we were taking was very boggy. We moved slowly down about three miles and then camped for the night; the horse Billy being completely baked. Next morning we started at daybreak, leaving the horse short hobbled.

XVII. STUART'S JOURNEY TO THE CENTRE OF AUSTRALIA

[THE following narrative of John McDouall Stuart's journey to the centre of Australia is taken from his Journals, edited by William Hardman, and published at London, 1864. The statement in the text, that the explorer named the hill near to the exact centre of the continent " Central Mount Stuart," after himself, is printed as it appears in Hardman's edition. But the original manuscript, in the Mitchell Library, Sydney, shows that what Stuart wrote was that he named the hill " Central Mount Sturt, after my excellent and esteemed commander of the expedition in 1844 and 1845, Captain Sturt." He placed a paper in a bottle on the top of a cone erected on the hill. That paper is now in the museum at Adelaide, and it shows that "Central Mount Sturt " was the name originally given. But Stuart was alive when Hardman published his Journals, and apparently approved of the alteration, which was made on the suggestion of the Governor of South Australia, Sir Henry Anthony MacDonnell.]

Journal of Mr. Stuart's Fourth Expedition—Fixing the Centre of the Continent, from March to September, 1860.

Friday, 2nd March, 1860, Chambers Creek.—Left the creek for the north-west, with thirteen horses and two men. The grey horse being too weak to travel was left behind. Camped at Hamilton Springs.

Saturday, 3rd March, Mount Hamilton.—Camped at the Beresford Springs, where it was evident that the natives, whose camp is a little way from this, had had a fight. There were the remains of a body of a very tall native lying on his back. The skull was broken in three or four places, the flesh nearly all devoured by the crows and native dogs, and both feet and hands were gone. There were three worleys on the rising ground, with waddies, boomerangs, spears, and a number of broken dishes scattered round them. The natives seemed to have run away and left them, or to have been driven away by a hostile tribe. Between two of the worleys we observed a handful of hair, apparently torn from the skull of the dead man, and a handful of emu feathers placed close together, the feathers to the north-west, the hair to the south-east. They were between two pieces of charred wood, which had been extinguished before the feathers and hair were placed there.

Sunday, 22nd April, Small Gum Creek under Mount Stuart, Centre of Australia.—To-day I find from my observations of the sun, 111° 00′ 30″, that I am now camped in the centre of Australia. I have marked a tree and planted the British flag there. There is a high mount about two miles and a half to the north-north-east. I wish it had been in the centre; but on it to-morrow I will raise a cone of stones, and plant the flag there, and name it "Central Mount Stuart." We have been in search of permanent water to-day, but cannot find any. I hope from the top of Central Mount Stuart to find something good to the north-west. Examined a large creek; can find no surface water, but got some by scratching in the sand. It is a large creek divided into many channels, but they are all filled with sand; splendid grass all round this camp.

Monday, 23rd April, Centre.—Took Kekwick and the flag, and went to the top of the mount, but found it to be much higher and more difficult of ascent than I anticipated. After a deal of labour, slips, and knocks, we at last arrived on the top. The view to the north is over a large plain of gums, mulga, and spinifex, with watercourses running through it. The large gum creek that we crossed winds round this hill in a north-east direction; at about ten miles it is joined by another. After joining they take a course more north, and I lost sight of them in the far-distant plain. To the north-north-east is the termination of the hills; to the north-east, east and south-east are broken ranges, and to the north-north-west the ranges of the west side of the plain terminate. To the north-west are broken ranges; and to the west is a very high peak, between which and this place to the south-west are a number of isolated hills. Built a large cone of stones, in the centre of which I placed a pole with the British flag nailed to it. Near the top of the cone I placed a small bottle, in which there is a slip of paper, with our signatures to it, stating by whom it was raised. We then gave three hearty cheers for the flag, the emblem of civil and religious liberty, and may it be a sign to the natives that the dawn of liberty, civilization, and Christianity is about to break upon them. We can see no water from the top. Descended, but did not reach the camp till after dark. This water still continues, which makes me think there must certainly be more higher up. I have named the range "John Range," after my

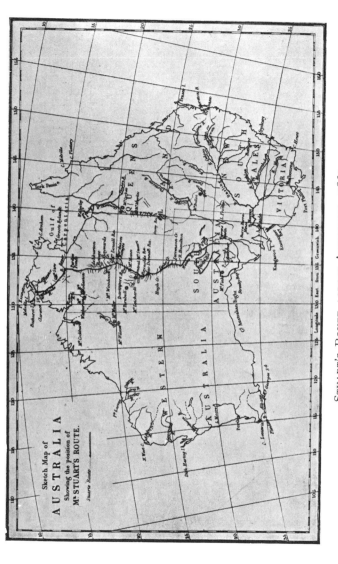

Sketch Map of
AUSTRALIA
Showing the position of
MᶜSTUART'S ROUTE.

Stuart's Route. ⸺

Stuart's Route across Australia, 1862.

From "Journals of John McDouall Stuart during 1858–9, 1860–1–2."

friend and well-wisher, John Chambers, Esq., brother to James Chambers, Esq., one of the promoters of this expedition.

Tuesday, 24th April, Central Mount Stuart.—Sent Kekwick in search of water, and to examine a hill that has the appearance of having a cone of stones upon it; meanwhile I made up my plan, and Ben mended the saddle-bags, which were in a sad mess from coming through the scrub. Kekwick returned in the afternoon, having found water higher up the creek. He has also found a new rose of a beautiful description, having thorns on its branches, and a seed-vessel resembling a gherkin. It has a sweet, strong perfume; the leaves are white, but as the flower is withered, I am unable to describe it. The native orange-tree abounds here. Mount Stuart is composed of hard red sandstone, covered with spinifex, and a little scrub on the top. The white ant abounds in the scrubs, and we even found some of their habitations near the top of Mount Stuart.

Wednesday, 25th April, Central Mount Stuart.—There is a remarkable hill about two miles to the west, having another small hill at the north end in the shape of a bottle; this I have named "Mount Esther," at the request of the maker of the flag. Started at 9 o'clock, on a course a little north of west, to the high peak that I saw from the top of Mount Stuart, which bears 272°. My reason for going west is that I do not like the appearance of the country to the north for finding water; it seems to be sandy. From the peak I expect to find another stratum to take me up to the north-north-west. Around the mount and on the west side, the country is well grassed, and red sandy soil; no stones. To the north and south of our line are several isolated hills, composed principally of granite. At ten miles there is a quartz reef on the north side of the south hills.

Wednesday, 27th June, Hayward Creek.—This morning we see signal fires all around us. It was my intention last night to have gone this morning to Kekwick Ponds to water the horses, then to give them the day to rest and proceed to-morrow back again to the large creek, and go on to the distant hills that I was steering for on the 25th inst., but, after considering the matter over the whole night, I have most reluctantly come to the determination to abandon the attempt to make the Gulf of Carpentaria. Situated as I now am, it would be most imprudent. In the first place my party is far too small to cope with such wily, determined natives as those we have just encountered. If they had been Europeans they could not better have arranged and carried out their plan of attack. They had evidently observed us passing in the morning, had examined our tracks to see which way we had gone, and knew we could get no water down the creek, but must retrace our steps to obtain it above them; they therefore lay in wait for our return. Their charge was in double column, open order, and we had to take steady aim to make an impression. With such as these for enemies in our rear, and, most probably, far worse in advance, it would be destruction to all my party for me to attempt to go on. All the information of the interior that I have already obtained would be lost. Moreover, we have only half rations for six months, four of which are gone, and I have been economizing as much as I possibly could in case of our having to be out a longer time, so that my men now complain of great weakness, and are unable to perform what they have to do. Again, only two showers of rain have fallen since March, and I am afraid of the waters drying up to the south, and there is no appearance of rain at present. The days are now become very hot again, and the feed for the horses as dry as if it were the middle of summer. The poor animals are very much reduced in condition, so much so that I am afraid of their being longer than one night without water. Finally, my health is so bad that I am hardly able to sit in the saddle. After taking all those things into consideration, I think it would be madness and folly to attempt more. If my own life were the only sacrifice, I would willingly risk it to accomplish my purpose; but it seems that I am destined to be disappointed; man proposes, but the Almighty disposes, and his will must be obeyed. Seeing the signal fires around, and dreading lest our black friends at Kekwick Ponds might have been playing a double part with us in spite of their Masonic signs, I gave them a wide berth, and steered for Bishop Creek. Arrived there in the afternoon, and found that the creek had not been visited by natives since we left. These natives do not deposit their dead bodies in the ground, but place them in the trees, and, judging from the number of these corpses which we have passed between this and the large creek, where they made their attack upon us, they must be very numerous. These natives have quite a different cast of features from those in the south; they have neither the broad flat nose and large mouth, nor the projecting eyebrows, but have more of the Malay; they are tall, muscular, well-made men, and I think they must have seen or encountered white men before.

XVIII. STUART'S JOURNEY ACROSS THE CONTINENT

Friday, 18th July, 1862, Priscilla Creek.—Started at 8.15, course north-west. Passed over grassy plains and stony rise; when at three miles, seeing the termination of a range in a bluff point, changed my course to 310°. Proceeded, still crossing stony hills, consisting of ironstone, slate, and a hard white rock, which is broken into rectangular fragments; also over broad valleys, which are covered with grass that when green must have stood very high, but is now so dry that it breaks off before the horses. My horse being first, collects so much on his front legs that I have been obliged to stop, pull him back, and allow it to fall, so that he may step over it, go on, get another load, and do the same. At six miles and a half, after crossing a plain, crossed a deep bamboo creek; this I have named "Ellen Creek." Proceeded over two other stony rises and valleys of the same description, and came upon extensive plains, well grassed, and of beautiful alluvial soil; crossing them towards the bluff point at fifteen miles, came upon the Adelaide between me and the bluff, which is about a mile further on; the river is about eighty yards wide, and so still that I could not see which way the current was. I suppose its being high tide was the cause of this. The banks are thickly lined with bamboo, very tall and stout, very steep, and twelve feet down to the water's edge; the water appeared to be of great depth, and entirely free from snags or fallen timber. The range on the opposite side of the river, for which I was directing my course, being the highest I have seen in this new country, I have named it after His Excellency the Governor-in-Chief of South Australia, "Daly Range," and its highest peak to the north "Mount Daly." Before reaching the river, at thirteen miles, we passed a high conspicuous tent hill, at right angle, north-east to our line; this I have named "Mount Goyder," after the Surveyor-General of South Australia. Followed the river on a north course for about a mile, when I was stopped by a deep side creek of thick bamboo, with water; turned to the east, rounded the bamboo, but found myself in a boggy marsh, which I could not cross. This marsh is covered with fine grass, in black alluvial soil, in which is growing a new kind of lily, with a large broad heart-shaped leaf a foot or more across; the blossoms are six inches high, resemble a tulip in shape, and are of a deep brilliant rose colour; the seeds are contained in a vessel resembling the rose of a watering-pot, with the end of each egg-shaped seed showing from the holes, and the colour of this is a bright yellow. The marsh is studded with a great number of melaleuca-trees, tall and straight. As I could not cross, I had to round it, which took me a little more than an hour; when I got upon some low undulating rises, not far from Mount Goyder, composed of conglomerate ironstone and ironstone gravel, which seem to produce the springs which supply the marsh. Camped on the side of the marsh, to give the horses the benefit of the green grass, for some of them are still troubled with worms, and are very poor and miserable, and I have no medicine to give them, and there is not a blade of grass on the banks of the river—all has been burnt within the last four days. Native smoke in every direction.

Saturday, 19th July, Lily Marsh, Adelaide River.—Started at 9.10, course 20° east of north. At three miles crossed some stony rises and broad alluvial grassy valleys; at four miles met the river, had to go half a mile to the south-east to round it. Again changed to my first course; at seven miles and a half crossed a creek with water. The country to this is good, with occasionally a little ironstone and gravel, timber of stringy-bark, and a little low gum scrub. Having crossed this creek, we ascended a sandy table-land with an open forest of stringy-bark (good timber), palms, gums, other trees and bushes; it has been lately burnt, but the roots of the grass abound. This continued for about three miles. There is a small stony range of hills to the west, which at the end of the three miles dropped into a grassy plain of a beautiful black alluvial soil, covered with lines and groves of the cabbage palm trees, which give it a very picturesque appearance; its dip is towards the river; in two miles crossed it, and again ascended low table-land of the very same description as the other. At fourteen miles struck another creek with water, and camped. The country gone over to-day, though not all of the very best description, has plains in it of the very finest kind—even the sandy table-land bears an abundant crop of grass. The trees are so thick that I can get no view of the surrounding country; the tall beautiful palm grows in this creek. Native smoke about, but we have not seen any natives. There are large masses of volcanic rock on the sides of this creek. At about a mile to the eastward is a large body of springs that supply water to this creek, which I have named "Anna Creek." Camped at ten minutes to three o'clock.

Sunday, 20th July, Anna Creek. The mosquitoes at this camp have been most annoying; scarcely one of us has been able to close his eyes in sleep during the whole night: I never found them so bad anywhere—night and day they are at us. The grass in, and on the banks of, this creek is six feet high; to the westward there are long reaches of water, and the creek very thickly timbered with mela-leuca, gum, stringy-bark, and palms.

Monday, 21st July, Anna Creek and Springs.—Again passed a miserable night with the mosquitoes. Started at eight o'clock; course, north-north-west. At three miles came upon another ex-tensive fresh-water marsh, too boggy to cross. There is rising ground to the north-west and north; the river seems to run be-tween. I can see clumps of bamboos and trees, by which I sup-pose it runs at about a mile to the north-north-west. The ground for the last three miles is of a sandy nature, and light-brown colour, with ironstone gravel on the surface, volcanic rock occa-sionally cropping out. The borders of the marsh are of the richest description of black alluvial soil, and when the grass has sprung after it has been burnt, it has the appearance of a rich and very thick crop of green wheat. I am now compelled to alter my course to 30° south of east, to get across a water creek coming into the marsh, running deep, broad and boggy, and so thick with trees, bushes, and strong vines interwoven throughout it, that it would take a day to cut a passage through. At three miles we crossed the stream, and proceeded again on the north-north-west course, but at a mile and a half were stopped by another creek of the same description. Changed to east, and at half a mile was able to cross it also, and again went on my original bearing. Continued on it for three miles, when we were again stopped by another running stream, but this one I was able to cross without going far out of my course. Proceeded on the north-north-west course, passing over elevated ground of the same description as the first three miles. At seventeen miles came upon a thick clump of trees, with beautiful palms growing amongst them; examined it and found it to have been a spring, but now dry. Proceeded on another mile, and was again stopped by what seemed to be a continuation of the large marsh; we now appeared to have got right into the middle of it. It was to be seen to the south-west, north-west, and south-east of us. Camped on a point of rising ground running into it. The timber on the rises between the creeks is stringy-bark, small gums, and in places a nasty scrub, very sharp, which tore a number of our saddle-bags: it is a very good thing the patches of it are not broad. The grass, where it has not been burned, is very thick and high—up to my shoulder when on horseback. About a mile from here, to the west, I can see what appears to be the water of the river, running through clumps of trees and bamboos, beyond which, in the distance, are courses of low rising ground, in places broken also with clumps of trees; the course of the river seems to be north-north-west. On the east side of the marsh is also rising ground; the marsh in that direction seems to run five or six miles before it meets the rising ground, and appears after that to come round to the north.

Tuesday, 22nd July, Fresh-water Marsh.—As the marsh seems to run so much to the east, and not knowing how much further I shall have to go to get across the numerous creeks that appear to come into it, I shall remain here to-day and endeavour to find a road through it to the river, and follow up the banks if I can. I have a deal of work to do to the plan, and our bags require mending. After collecting the horses, Thring tried to cross the marsh to the river, and succeeded in reaching its banks, finding firm ground all the way; the breadth of the river here being about a hundred yards, very deep, and running with some velocity, the water quite fresh. He having returned with this information, I sent him, King, and Frew, mounted on the strongest horses, to follow the banks of the river till noon, to see if there is any obstruction to prevent my travelling by its banks. In two hours they returned with the sad tidings that the banks were broken down by watercourses, deep, broad, and boggy; this is a great disappointment, for it will take me a day or two longer than I expected in reaching the sea-coast, in consequence of having to go a long way round to clear the marsh and creeks. The edge of the marsh was still of the same rich character, and covered with luxuriant grass. The rise we are camped on is also the same, with ironstone gravel on the surface; this seems to have been a favourite camping place for a large number of natives. There is a great quantity of fish bones, mussel, and turtle shells, at a little distance from the camp, close to where there was some water. There are three poles fixed in the ground, forming an equilaterial triangle, on the top of which was a framework of the same figure, over which were placed bars of wood; its height from the ground eight feet. This has apparently been used by them for smoke-drying a dead blackfellow. We have seen no natives since leaving the Roper, although their smoke is still about us. On and about the marsh are large flocks of geese, ibis, and numerous other aquatic birds; they are so wild that they will not allow us to come within shot of them. Mr. Kekwick has been successful in shooting a goose; it has a peculiar-shaped head, having a large horny lump on the top resembling a topknot, and only a very small web at the root of his toes. The river opposite this, about a yard from the bank, is nine feet deep.

Wednesday, 23rd July, Fresh-water Marsh.—Started at 7.40, course 22° east of south, one mile, to round the marsh; thence one mile south-east; thence east for six miles, when we struck a large creek, deep and long reaches; thence three-quarters of a mile south before we could cross it. This I have named "Thring Creek," in token of my approbation of his conduct throughout the journey; thence east, one mile and a half; thence north for nine miles, when I again struck the large marsh. Thring Creek has been running nearly parallel with the north course until it empties itself into the marsh. The country gone over to-day, after leaving the side of the marsh, as well as the banks of the creek, and also some small plains, is of the same rich description of soil covered with grass; the other parts are slightly elevated, the soil light with a little sand on the surface of a brown colour; timber, mixture of stringy-bark and gums, with many others; also, a low thick scrub, which has lately been burnt in many places, the few patches that have escaped abounding in grass. I have come twelve miles to the eastward to try to round the marsh, but have not been able to do so; the plains that were seen from the river by those who came up it in boats is the marsh; it is covered with luxuriant grass, which gives it the appearance of extensive grassy plains. I have camped at where the Thring spreads itself over a portion of the marsh. There is rising ground to the north-west, on the opposite side, which I suppose to be a continuation of the elevated ground I passed before crossing the creek, and the same that I saw bearing north from the last camp. I suppose it runs in towards the river.

Thursday, 24th July, Thring Creek, Entering the Marsh.— Started at 7.40, course north. I have taken this course in order to make the sea-coast, which I suppose to be distant about eight miles and a half, as soon as possible; by this I hope to avoid the marsh. I shall travel along the beach to the north of the Adelaide. I did not inform any of the party, except Thring and Auld, that I was so near to the sea, as I wished to give them a surprise on reaching it. Proceeded through a light soil, slightly elevated, with a little ironstone on the surface, the volcanic rock cropping out occasionally; also some flats of black alluvial soil. The timber much smaller and more like scrub, showing that we are nearing the sea. At eight miles and a half came upon a broad valley of black alluvial soil, covered with long grass; from this I can hear the wash of the sea. On the o her side of the valley, which is rather more than a quarter of a mile wide, is growing a line of thick bushes, very dense, showing that to be the boundary of the beach. Crossed the valley, and entered the scrub, which was a complete network of vines. Stopped the horses to clear a way, whilst I advanced a few yards on to the beach, and was gratified and delighted to behold the water of the Indian Ocean in Van Diemen Gulf, before the party with the horses knew anything of its proximity. Thring, who rode in advance of me, called out "The Sea!" which so took them all by surprise, and they were so astonished, that he had to repeat the call before they fully understood what was meant. Then they immediately gave three long and hearty cheers. The beach is covered with a soft blue mud. It being ebb tide, I could see some distance; found it would be impossible for me to take the horses along it; I therefore kept them where I had halted them, and allowed half the party to come on to the beach and gratify themselves by a sight of the sea, while the other half remained to watch the horses until their return. I dipped my feet, and washed my face and hands in the sea, as I promised the late Governor Sir Richard McDonnell I would do if I reached it. The mud has nearly covered all the shells; we got a few, however. I could see no sea-weed. There is a point of land some distance off, bearing 70°. After all the party had had some time on the beach, at which they were much pleased and gratified, they collected a few shells; I returned to the valley, where I had my initials (J.M.D.S.) cut on a large tree, as I did not intend to put up my flag until I arrived at the mouth of the Adelaide. Proceeded along the valley; at one mile and a half, coming upon a small creek, with running water, and the valley being covered with beautiful green grass, I have camped to give the horses the benefit of it. Thus have I, through the instrumentality of Divine Providence, been led to accomplish the great object of the expedition, and take the whole party safely as witnesses to the fact, and through one of the finest countries man could wish to behold—good to the coast and with a stream of running water within half a mile of the sea. From Newcastle Water to the sea-beach, the main body of the horses have been only one night without water, and then got it within the next day. If this country is settled, it will be one of the finest Colonies under the Crown, suitable for the growth of any and everything—what a splendid country for producing cotton! Judging from the number of the pathways from the water to the beach, across the valley, the natives must be very numerous; we have not seen any, although we have passed many of their recent tracks and encampment:. The cabbage and fan palm trees have been very plentiful during to-day's journey down to this valley. This creek I named "Charles Creek," after the eldest son of John Chambers, Esq. : it is one by which some large bodies of springs discharge their surplus water into Van Diemen Gulf; its banks are of soft mud, and boggy.

Friday, 25th July, Charles Creek, Van Diemen Gulf.—I have sent Thring to the south-west to see if he can get round the marsh. If it is firm ground I shall endeavour to make the mouth of the river by that way. After a long search he has returned and informs me that it is impracticable, being too boggy for the horses. As the great object of the expedition is now attained, and the mouth of the river already well known, I do not think it advisable to waste the strength of my horses in forcing them through, neither do I see what object I should gain by doing so; they have still a very long and fatiguing journey in recrossing the continent to Adelaide, and my health is so bad that I am unable to bear a long day's ride. I shall, therefore, cross this creek and see if I can get along by the sea-beach, or close to it. Started and had great difficulty in getting the horses over, although we cut a large quantity of grass, putting it on the banks and on logs of wood which were put into it. We had a number bogged, and I was nearly losing one of my best horses, and was obliged to have him pulled out with ropes; after the loss of some time we succeeded in getting them all over safely. At two miles came upon an open part of the beach, went on to it, and again found the mud quite impassable for horses. Stopped the party, as this travelling is too much for the horses, and taking Thring with me, rode two miles to see if the ground was any firmer in places; found it very soft where the salt water had covered it, in others not so bad. Judging from the number of shells banked up in different places, the sea must occasionally come over this. I saw at once that this would not do for the weak state in which my horses were, and I therefore returned to where I had left the party, resolving to recross the continent to the city of Adelaide. I now had an open place cleared, and selecting one of the tallest tress, stripped it of its lower branches, and on its highest branch fixed my flag, the Union Jack, with my name sewn in the centre of it. When this was completed, the party gave three cheers, and Mr. Kekwick then addressed me, congratulating me on having completed this great and important undertaking, to which I replied. Mr. Waterhouse also spoke a few words on the same subject, and concluded with three cheers for the Queen and three for the Prince of Wales. At one foot south from the foot of the tree is buried, about eight inches below the ground, an air-tight tin case, in which is a paper with the following notice:—

"South Australian Great Northern Exploring Expedition.

"The exploring party, under the command of John McDouall Stuart, arrived at this spot on the 25th day of July, 1862, having crossed the entire Continent of Australia from the Southern to the Indian Ocean, passing through the centre. They left the City of Adelaide on the 26th day of October, 1861, and the most northern station of the colony on 21st day of January, 1862. To commemorate this happy event, they have raised this flag bearing his name. All well. God save the Queen!"

(Here follow the signatures of myself and party.)

As this bay has not been named, I have taken this opportunity of naming it "Chambers Bay," in honour of Miss Chambers, who kindly presented me with the flag which I have planted this day, and I hope this may be the first sign of the dawn of approaching civilization. Exactly this day nine months the party left North Adelaide. Before leaving, between the hours of eleven and twelve o'clock, they had lunch at Mr. Chambers' house; John Bentham Neals, Esq., being present, proposed success to me, and wished I might plant the flag on the north-west coast. At the same hour of the day, nine months after, the flag was raised on the shores of Chambers Bay, Van Diemen Gulf. On the bark of the tree on which the flag is placed is cut—DIG ONE FOOT—S. We then bade farewell to the Indian Ocean, and returned to Charles Creek, where we had again great difficulty in getting the horses across, but it was at last accomplished without accident. We have passed numerous and recent tracks of natives to-day; they are still burning the country at some distance from the coast.